PRAISE FOR DANNY O. COULSON AND
NO HEROES

"The FBI has been and remains a highly disciplined and centralized agency. Nonetheless, a neglected part of its history is the contribution of its skilled and diverse agents. . . . By focusing on the personalities and resourcefulness of agents directly involved in counter-terror operations, Coulson repairs this gap in our understanding of the FBI's history."

—The Washington Post

"Riveting. . . . A gripping memoir of a remarkable man. . . . An extraordinary and fascinating insider's view of the [FBI], its politics, and its people."

—Abilene Reporter-News (TX)

"Coulson is an immensely likable braggart who tells great stories. . . . Presenting the right mix of gossip and crime fighting, this engrossing work should quickly move off the shelves."

—Publishers Weekly

"A heck of a book. . . . *NO HEROES* is good stuff, from battles with druglords to battles with FBI bureaucracy. His story, as a 'lead from the front' warrior . . . rings true."

—Ocala Star-Banner (FL)

"A memoir-cum-how-to-manual for the aspiring Dirty Harry of the family."

—Kirkus Reviews

"Takes readers to the front lines. . . . A fascinating insider's perspective on the bureau and a rare look at its culture, internal politics, and personalities."

—The Seattle Skanner

NO HEROES

Inside the FBI's Secret Counter-Terror Force

DANNY O. COULSON
& ELAINE SHANNON

POCKET BOOKS

NEW YORK LONDON TORONTO SYDNEY SINGAPORE

POCKET BOOKS, a division of Simon & Schuster, Inc.
1230 Avenue of the Americas, New York, NY 10020

Copyright © 1999 by Danny Coulson and Elaine Shannon
Afterword copyright © 2001 by Danny Coulson and Elaine Shannon

Originally published in hardcover in 1999 by Pocket Books

ISBN: 0-671-02062-5

First Pocket Books paperback printing April 2001

10 9 8 7 6 5 4 3 2 1

POCKET and colophon are registered trademarks of
Simon & Schuster, Inc.

Cover design and illustration by James Wang

Printed in the U.S.A.

This book is dedicated to Daniel O'Neal Coulson, whose earliest memories are of my going off to some new adventure, and to the rest of the Coulsons who indulged my frequent absence with understanding and support. To the First Fifty, the Plank Holders of the HRT, the greatest privilege I will ever have in my life is to have served with you in times of conflict. Servare Vitas.

—DANNY O. COULSON

For Dan Morgan and Andrew Shannon Morgan.

—ELAINE SHANNON

ACKNOWLEDGMENTS

The idea for this book came from a woman who had heard many FBI agents over the years tell stories about their adventures and believed that no book had ever captured the true spirit of those men and women. She enlisted the support of two dear friends, Ray and LeRoy Jahn, who encouraged me to write this book. The three ganged up on me with this argument: "You should write this book, if not for anything else, for your children. They really do not know who you are. Even if it's never published, you'll have a story for them." Thank you, Debbie Coulson.

We could never have finished this book without the help of Jim Adams, Tase Baily, Bill Baker, Leon Blakeney, Bill Buford, Joe Corless, Connie Hassel, Henry Hudson, John Hotis, Weldon Kennedy, Phil King, Ken Lovin, Wayne Manis, Bob McCartin, Horace Mewborne, Jr., Kerry Noble, Larry Potts, Bob Ricks, Buck Revell, Dee Rosario, Tom Sheer, John Simeone, Chris Todd and Amelia A. Gomez, Clint Van Zandt, William Webster, and many men and women who still serve in the FBI and the Department of Justice who offered their recollections.

My partner, Elaine Shannon, is not only a fantastic writer, she is a patient teacher. Without her efforts this book would be no more than a pile of papers in a box in my closet. Morris O. Coulson set me on my path and made sure I headed straight. Doc, Jeff, Jenn, and Jessie gave me faith in the future.

—DANNY O. COULSON

Time to write is the ultimate luxury. Thanks especially to my husband, Dan Morgan, and my son, Andrew Shannon Morgan, for giving me time and love. Thanks to Michael Duffy for reprieve from daily journalistic duties. Thanks to Wendy King for skillful research. Thanks to Todd Shuster, of the Zachary Shuster Agency, for indefatigable enthusiasm. Thanks to Jane Cavolina, our editor, for crisp, incisive advice.

——ELAINE SHANNON

CONTENTS

BOOK SIX
Texas ☆ 481

Afterword ☆ 597

Index ☆ 603

APRIL 19

We were finishing up breakfast with some old friends in Fort Worth when we heard the first news bulletin, something about a big explosion up in Oklahoma.

Jennifer and Jessie put down their forks and gaped at the television. Debbie gave the screen a quick glance, then smiled at me. "Well, I won't expect to see you for a while. Guess I'll be buying a house myself."

"No, it's not my territory," I said confidently, taking another swig of coffee. "We don't even know what it is. Could be a break in a gas main."

My pager went off, displaying a number I knew by heart. "It's SIOC," I said. The Strategic Information and Operations Center at the Hoover building in Washington.

Told you so, Debbie's calm green eyes said.

John O'Neill, the headquarters official in charge of domestic terrorism investigations, answered. His voice was flat. "I guess you heard, a bomb went off in Oklahoma City. Nine oh two A.M."

"Yes, it's all over the news."

"A lot of people have been killed and injured. We don't know what we have. Ricks needs help. Can you catch the next flight?"

"We're right in the middle of some thunderstorms," I said. "Nobody in Texas is getting on a plane. I'll drive."

"Fine. Tell your wife you won't be coming home soon."

"She knows." As far as Debbie was concerned, my middle initial stood for Outtahere.

I kissed my endlessly tolerant—and did I mention saintly?—spouse good-bye and turned to the girls. "Hey, guys, I have to go to work. See ya around the square."

I hopped in the car and floored it for Pop's place, where I'd been bunking since my orders came through to take command of the Dallas field office. For a Texas boy, it was a transfer from heaven, but the devil took his cut—nearly a year away from Debbie and the kids. They had stayed back in Washington to finish out the school year. This week, Easter break, was supposed to be a reunion, conjugal visit, and house-hunting junket, and I was gone again. Not that Deb needed me. Buy a house? Debbie Coulson had been born in the wrong century. She could have wrangled a team aross the Oregon Trail, cleared a few acres with an ax and handsaw and built a place herself, and she'd still look better than Michelle Pfeiffer. Everyone called her the Woman with Only One Fault—lousy taste in men.

The all-news station said the nine-story Murrah Federal Building must have been hit by a massive truck bomb, because it looked like the Marine barracks in Beirut, with its whole front gone and daylight showing clear through. *Is this the start of something bigger?* I wondered. The only gun I had on me was a little Heckler & Koch P-7. Fine for off duty, but I had no idea what I was heading into. I threw some jeans and a few shirts into a duffel bag, called the office, and asked Biff Temple to bring me my Browning Hi-Power and half a dozen magazines. The Browning has a higher capacity than the P-7 and has been my favorite weapon since my days on the Hostage Rescue Team.

Biff met me on the road, just off I-35 heading north out of Dallas. The storm was in full roar when he pulled up, jumped into the front seat of my Ford Explorer and gave me my trusty Browning. "Thought you might need this too," he said, grinning, pulling a steno pad from under his jacket. I took notes obsessively, as was well known to every agent in my command. Enough of them had been sent back to their desks to fetch paper and pen with the fatherly admonition "How the hell can you remember what we're doing here if you don't write a god-damn thing down? You think I asked you here to see what kind of tie you're wearing?"

"What do you hear?" I asked.

"Nothing much new. Looks like a bunch of us will be following you up." The Dallas ERT—Evidence Response Team, a unit specially trained by the FBI lab to collect and catalog forensic evidence at a crime scene—had been notified to pack up and pull out, he said, and so had our SWAT team.

I laughed. "Hell, every one in the bu will be working this before it's over. Gotta get going. See you tomorrow."

Texas gully washers not only get you very wet, but they make a great show. You tend to think of storm clouds as black or gray, but these had streaks of green and blue, and they were hurling lightning bolts like neon javelins.

Only I was not in the mood for a show today. Patience is not a virtue I have ever possessed. This could turn out to be the greatest mass murder in U.S. history, and here I was, creeping like a snail through a monsoon. Gusts rocked the Explorer as I bored into the storm. The wipers could not even begin to keep up with the blasts of water and hailstones pummeling the windshield. As I slogged up I-35, I thought about putting the red light on the roof but decided against it. I was driving practically blind and dared not go more than forty miles an hour, twenty in some stretches.

My cell phone rang. It was CBS correspondent Rita Braver. Somehow she had guessed I'd be heading for Oklahoma City, and she charmed the Dallas FBI switchboard into linking her to my car.

"Everybody in Washington is saying it's Middle Eastern. Do you think that's right?"

"No, it's not. It's a bubba job," I said, using our politically incorrect shorthand for redneck bomb-throwers.

"Why? It looks like all the other truck bombings coming out of the Middle East and—"

"It's bubbas," I said stubbornly. "It's April nineteenth."

April 19. My mind flashed back to that moment, two years before almost to the hour, when I was sitting in the SIOC, watching the television in anguished silence as the first thin thread of smoke coiled out of the Branch Davidian compound outside of Waco.

I went back further, to the morning of April 19, 1985, when I led the Hostage Rescue Team into the Ozarks to surround a racist paramilitary training camp. Not many people outside the hate movement remembered that episode, which had a happier ending—the men we were after laid down their arms and nobody got hurt.

"Bubbas? Is that going to be the theory of the case?" Rita persisted.

"No, there is no theory of the case," I retorted. "We don't develop a theory and look for the evidence that fits.

Reporters do that. You can broadcast your theory and if it doesn't pan out, you can make up another one. We can't do that. We'll gather the evidence, and the evidence will tell us who did it. Right now, I think it's bubbas. But I could be wrong."

A crisis is a wave of energy. When you go to a crisis, you can feel the energy on the back of your neck. You smell it, the way you smell lightning before a storm. If you don't know how to deal with it, it will kill you.

I felt the wave the minute I walked into the old red-brick building. The energy in that command post came from the event, not from the weather that blasted and howled at the building. I don't know how many crisis command posts I've walked into in my life, but this one was just like all the rest. It was a good ten degrees warmer than outside because of body heat. A couple of hundred people were swarming around, dashing this way and that, or seated at folding tables, with phones to their ears, scribbling on legal pads or steno notebooks. Technicians knelt on the floor, running more phone lines and computer cables or fixing partitions.

A lead coordination center was already up and running, with representatives from all of the federal agencies, the state police, and the Oklahoma City Police Department. They were sending out leads to field offices all over the country.

I spotted Bob Ricks, the special agent in charge of the Oklahoma City field office, down at the far end of the space, in a long, skinny room dominated by a conference table. This was the executive area, where most of the decisions would be made, and where we would gather for briefings. Bob was on the phone to HQ, asking to have more agents flown in from anywhere—FBI, ATF, Customs, Secret Service. He could use just about every trained investigator the federal government employed.

I pulled up a chair alongside him. "What can I do to help you?"

Bob shook his head. "I'm busy putting out fires right now. Take a look at what we've done so far and make any changes you see are needed. As soon as things slow down a little, we can talk."

I was eager to get out to the bomb site, but the first thing that had to be done was to harness all that raw energy vibrating through the room. In a crisis of this magnitude, everybody within a thousand miles wants to run in to help the survivors and to bring to justice the monsters who wreaked such death and sorrow. When you're in the middle of that well-meaning throng, you can't help but be swept up in the rush of adrenaline. The energy will begin to drive the commanders and ultimately the investigation. You can ride the rush just so far. It will drive you relentlessly for hours, but sooner or later, it will dump you right on your ass. When fatigue takes over, you begin to lose your capacity for rational thought. We rely upon this phenomenon in hostage situations, to wear out hostage takers. Sometimes we forget that we're riding the same roller coaster.

"Bob, this is going to take a long time," I said. "This time tomorrow all of these people will fall into exhaustion, and we won't get anything done. We need to send half these people home to get rest. Suggest we work eight-to-eight shifts. We need to keep going around the clock."

Ricks nodded. "I'd made a note to do that. Can you get with the supervisors?"

"Gotcha," I said. "Another thing. Somebody's got to coordinate the bomb site. There are bound to be a lot of problems there."

There was a crater full of rubble that had to be pored over, inch by square inch. In the dimming light and pandemonium of the rescue effort, it would be easy for the most conscientious ERT people to overlook, contaminate, or mislabel a few tiny bits of trash that might hold traces of explosive residue, shards of a timing device, or some other forensic evidence.

"I'm completely overwhelmed at this point with the investigation," Ricks said. "You take the building, and I'll handle the rest for now."

I wasn't halfway across the room before Bob called out, "Danny, we just heard from the lab that we're not to collect any evidence until the lab guys get here." The lab was flying its most experienced bomb technicians in from Washington, but they had been delayed by the weather.

"That sounds like a lot of bullshit to me," I said with my usual tact. "Do they know the rain will wash their evidence right down the storm drains if we don't get started? I'm on my way over to the site. I'll take a look and call the lab about their stupid idea."

I grabbed a waterproof parka from the Explorer and walked four blocks to the site.

As I rounded the corner, the energy wave almost knocked me back like the blast from an oven. There was a sound like a million bees humming. Only it was human voices, thousands of them, sobs and shouts blending together to make a loud murmur.

The TV footage had not done justice to the awful gaping hole. On the screen, the images suggested the building's face had blown off. Up close, the wound was much uglier, as if a giant scoop had reached deep into the building's guts and raked the floors down. The day-care center on the front side of the second floor had taken the worst of it. Debris was all over the streets and sidewalks for hundreds of yards. Days later we were to find an ear three blocks from the blast site.

My God, I thought, *those firefighters and rescue personnel are brave.* The building could come crashing down any second in a final death shudder. The Oklahoma City Fire Department, the emergency medical technicians, rescuers from all over, teemed about the wreckage, seemingly oblivious to the danger. Every few minutes, a gurney came out of the rubble with a body bag on its way to the triage center.

The rain had slacked up to a light drizzle, but from the look of the sky, that wouldn't hold. I jogged back over to the CP, called HQ, and asked for Tom Thurman, who ran the lab's explosive unit.

"Tom, I understand your concern about having your own guys do the scene," I said, "but we're getting ready for another thunderstorm. It's gonna come down like a cow pissing on a flat rock. We've got to pick up the evidence in the street. We won't go into the building or start sifting until your guys get here."

"Go ahead and get the stuff off the street," Thurman said. "We'll start a more detailed search tomorrow."

I made sure that the FBI ERT personnel partnered up with evidence recovery specialists from the Bureau of Alcohol, Tobacco and Firearms. We definitely did not need the problems we had encountered during the World Trade Center investigation, when teams from the two agencies fought like strange cats. In one instance an ATF agent had changed the label on an evidence bag in order to claim credit for the find. We gave the ATF managers places in the command post so that they didn't set up their own operation. "We can't have them or our guys running their own pass patterns," I said. We needed to work together on every level. No secrets.

I looked up Genetta Clark, the field office photographer. Some years before, she had done a photo surveillance for me on a drug case, snapping Mexican traffickers from a broken-down barn several hundred yards from their stash house. She was hunched down in the muck for days with a lens the length of a rifle barrel.

When she showed up at the command post, Genetta turned on her heels and gave me a big smile, a quick hug and that I-know-you're-going-to-make-me-miserable look again. "Okay, what do you need?"

"Pictures from every angle of that building: ground shots, aerials, front and back. Can you do it?"

"You know I can. I'm the best. Can I use your name to get a plane?"

"Sure. You were going to use my name anyway. Just get me tons of very good photos."

"You got it."

I made another call, to the guy I wanted at my side whenever I got into a fight. He was Jim Adams, the ASAC, Assistant Special Agent in Charge, of the Dallas FBI office. "Are you ready to come up and play? I need some help managing the bomb site."

"How soon do you want me there?"

"It's too late to leave tonight, but I need you here very early in the morning. Get some sleep and get up at the crack of dawn and get here. This is going to be a real mess before it's over."

"See you tomorrow, early." This was typical of Jimmy.

No hesitation, no questions. He would rather tackle a huge problem than do anything else. We had met back in the early eighties at the FBI Academy, just after I had been named commander of the Hostage Rescue Team. A crisis-management instructor with the Special Operations and Research Unit, Jim had helped me set up the team.

Jim's only fault that I knew of was that he liked to ride Harley-Davidson motorcycles, when anybody knows that the Suzuki Intruder, which I am proud to own, is infinitely superior. Now that is a motorcycle, fourteen hundred cubic centimeters of raw power, a huge rear tire with a kicked out front. Well, everyone can't be perfect. Nothing gave Adams more pleasure than to amble into one of Dallas's finest restaurants dressed in leather chaps, a leather vest with an American eagle on the back, and a do rag on his head. Patrons stepped aside as this six-foot, 235-pound outlaw biker stepped up to the bar and ordered iced tea.

Outside our cubicle, agents were hard at work following what would prove to be our best lead. Richard Nichols, a maintenance man at the Regency Towers across the way from the Murrah building, his wife, Bertha, and their nephew Chad were getting out of their 1990 red Ford Fiesta when the bomb went off. A 250-pound piece of steel came smashing down on the hood of their car, miraculously missing all three. It was the rear axle of the truck that had contained the bomb.

Sergeant Melvin Sumpter of the Oklahoma County Sheriff's Office pointed out the axle to Jim Norman, who had been designated FBI case agent because he was a bomb technician and domestic-terrorism specialist for the Oklahoma City office. Norman located the vehicle identification number etched into the axle and handed it off to James Elliott of the Oklahoma City ERT unit. Elliott called the National Insurance Crime Bureau, which maintains a database of VINs of all U.S.-registered cars and trucks. The truck, he learned, was a twenty-footer that belonged to Ryder Rental Inc. Ryder's database showed the truck had been rented two days before from Elliott's Body Shop in Junction City, Kansas. The renter's name was Robert Kling.

By midafternoon, FBI agents were in Junction City, interviewing shop owner Eldon Elliott, cashier Vicki Beemer, and mechanic Tom Kessinger. As Elliott recalled, Kling was in his twenties, with small, piercing eyes, a long, thin face, pale skin, and a military-style brush cut.

The name "Robert Kling" was clearly phony. He had given his address as 428 Malt Drive, Redfield, South Dakota, and his destination as 428 Maple Drive, Omaha, Nebraska. It took Jim Elliott no more than a couple of phone calls to determine that no such addresses existed.

Another clue—a taunt, perhaps—was the date of birth on Kling's driver's license: April 19.

Investigations are like anything else in life. Some days you're the windshield, and some days you're the bug. I knew we'd have a lot of downs in this case, but it was a great feeling to start off this way, with a solid identification of the man in possession of the truck at the time of the bombing.

With all this good news coming in, I decided to take my own advice and pack it in around midnight. I drove over to my hotel room and called Pop, who had been overseeing a construction site when I left. I needed to let him know why I hadn't been sitting on the couch, patting my foot anxiously until he rolled in from Massey's saloon.

"You guys okay up there?"

"Sure."

"Any chance that building may fall down on you?"

"We don't think so. The rains aren't helping, things are shifting around, but if it looks bad, we'll get out."

"Well, when you catch the sons of bitches, you oughta string 'em up."

"You know we'll catch them. We always do, and somebody'll string them up."

We said our good-byes.

I took a quick, boiling shower and crashed.

Why had I set the alarm for five o'clock in the morning? What city was I in? I sat up on the edge of the bed, trying to shake the cobwebs out of my head. Then it all came back in a rush. It wasn't a bad dream.

I took another scalding shower, threw on a pullover, Royal Robins pants with pockets all over, and a light black windbreaker, stuck my Browning Hi-Power into my belt, and hoisted my briefcase, just like any other business executive going to a routine day at the office. On the way through the lobby, I grabbed a styrofoam cup of coffee for the road.

Ricks was at the CP when I arrived. We started looking at the leads that had come in and the ones we were sending out. The storm front had finally moved on. Within an hour and a half, Dave Williams, a lab bomb specialist who had handled the World Trade Center case and hundreds of less famous bombings, flew in, and Jim Adams drove into the parking lot.

Williams, Adams, and I walked over to the bomb site. Williams didn't say much, just stood and studied what was left of the Murrah building for a long time. Then he turned and walked over to a parking lot next to the Journal Record building. Burned-out, twisted wrecks of cars, vans, and trucks were everywhere, as if a napalm bomb had landed in the middle of them. Teams of agents were putting debris from the cars into small sifting boxes, then running magnets over the siftings to catch even the smallest metal fragments.

I noticed a huge piece of asphalt covering a large section of the lot.

"Dave, where did that come from?" I asked. Dave pointed up at the top of the Journal Record building. "See that part of the structure where it looks like a roof has been pulled off? See how it's slanted on an angle this way?"

Jim and I nodded.

"When this thing went off, it created a vacuum that sucked all of the air out of this entire area," he explained. "As the force dissipated, the vacuum was filled by the air rushing back in and it sucked that part of the roof off of the building and pitched it back toward the blast site. It fell here on the parking lot."

Adams and I just looked at each other. How did he do that?

Dave spit a plug of tobacco on the ground. "Let's go inside," he said.

We headed down a ramp into the Murrah building's parking entrance. A fine powdery gray dust—pulverized concrete—hung on the air and covered our boots and pants. The dust made haloes around the emergency lighting installed by the rescue personnel. The whole place seemed to be teetering on a few frail pillars. National Guardsmen and firefighters were erecting scaffolding to keep huge pieces of concrete from falling. Even before they were finished, firefighters were crawling into the rubble to look for victims.

Williams squinted at the cracks and stress marks in the floors and pillars.

"I need to go up in the building," he said finally. "Want to come along?"

We followed him to the interior stairway and climbed floor by floor to the roof. At very few times am I quiet, especially if I'm with a friend. At this moment, I just did not feel like talking.

Halfway up, I walked over to the edge of the floor and looked down into the void. Cranes were lifting huge sections of floor and other debris from the pile. Rescue workers were crawling all over the pile, some disappearing down holes in the rubble. Every now and then another gurney with a body bag was pushed out of the debris by rescuers or National Guardsmen. I didn't see any stretchers bearing survivors.

Something like a movie formed in my head. *People are arriving for work. Some are having a cup of coffee at their desks. Some are dropping off their children at the daycare center. The building quakes, and then there's a deafening roar, and then silence. Their whole world has just disappeared in a giant blinding flash. The people on the upper level tumble with the floors into the basement. The whole damned building comes down on top of the people on lower levels. On top of the children.*

I scanned the circle of destruction, the twisted frames of cars on the street and in the lots, the smashed shops and carryouts across the street, the warped roof on the Journal Record building. Finally I broke the silence.

"Dave, what the hell are we looking at? What could have caused all this?"

He walked over to my side and stared down at the scene

below us. "From what I can see, it appears to be a low-speed explosion. Fourteen thousand to fifteen thousand feet per second. It looks like a fertilizer-and-fuel-oil bomb. See how the floors have fallen in on each other? A low-speed explosion lifts the structure until it breaks away from its supports and then the floors fall down crushing everything. There's a lot of heaving and pushing. TNT, C-4, and dynamite are high speed. They blast everything. You don't see this kind of damage from a high-speed bomb."

How he figured this was beyond me. I just shook my head for about the ninetieth time. "How big was it, do you think?"

"Probably about four thousand pounds. I can't tell you the exact composition. We haven't examined the debris for traces yet, but it looks like we're dealing with fertilizer and fuel oil." Fertilizer and fuel oil. The main charge in the truck bomb at the World Trade Center had been urea nitrate, a compound derived from urea, a common fertilizer. Many bombs set by the Irish Republican Army were a mix of ammonium nitrate fertilizer and fuel oil.

I pulled out my notebook and wrote down, "Williams—14,000–15,000 FPS. Fertilizer. 4,000 (composition)."

Later that morning Williams and I sent HQ a preliminary estimate of the size and possible main charge, to be passed to offices covering leads.

While Dave went off to check on the progress of the evidence recovery, Adams and I found the Dallas command post, a motor home stuffed with electronics and parked a block away, beside the YMCA. We stole a cup of coffee from Mike Holly, our telecommunications ace, and knocked some dust off.

Adams set his cup down. "You know, there was a lot of damage to the Y. We ought to take a look."

Broken glass, metal debris, and wallboard were scattered all over the floor. Doors were knocked off their hinges. Fine concrete dust covered everything. We made our way in the dim light toward the front of the building, where the Y day-care center had been. Out front there was a tot lot, directly across from the Murrah building, at a ninety-degree angle. We pulled open a jammed door and stepped inside.

This was the moment I came closest to losing it. There were kids' drawings on the walls, toys scattered on the floor, baby beds, bookshelves, and midget chairs. How many times had I picked Jessie up from a place just like this? I had always thought the closest thing to heaven I would ever see was that roomful of wide-eyed, curious toddlers taking in the wonders of their new world.

This beautiful scene had turned into a hell at 9:02 A.M. on April 19, 1995. The blast from the bomb had torn into the front of the YMCA, blowing the windows into thousands of shards of flying glass that tore through the building. The floor was covered with bits of window glass. Blocks, mats, and paint pots glittered as if encrusted in a blanket of sleet. Crayon drawings and finger paintings were slashed, toys shredded, bookcases turned over. Debris had peppered the baby beds like buckshot.

The blast wave coming through this room must have felt like a locomotive. A Gerber baby-food jar filled halfway with applesauce was embedded in a cork bulletin board. Other baby-food containers had smashed like eggshells against the wall. Every parent knows how tough those things are. I had fed Doc, my eldest son, from jars like these hundreds of times. My hands would get slick, wiping his face after he had spewed out the hated green beans or carrots, and I would drop them on the floor. I had never managed to break one.

Adams and I crunched across the glass-covered linoleum in silence, with none of our usual wisecracking banter. I'm sure he was thinking about his two children, just as I was picturing Doc, Jeff, Jennifer, and Jessie when they were finger-painting age. *What kind of a human being could do this?*

As we walked back toward the door, Jim stopped and pointed down toward a wall. Not two feet from the floor was a tiny bloody handprint, and then a second, and then a third that trailed off into a blood streak that ran to the floor.

And these were the lucky ones. They were so small their heads were below the level of the windows. Most suffered only cuts, bruises, and of course the emotional scars they would have forever. These lucky children went through hell. The ones across the street in the Murrah building were consumed by it.

I took a deep breath and headed for the door. *Stay cool,* I said to myself. *You're no good to anybody with your adrenaline pumping like blood out of a slashed artery.*

I shoved my emotions back into their box and locked down the lid. I'd built that box more than twenty-nine years before, back when I started looking for trouble. Walking back to the command center, I thought about my thirty years in the FBI. I'd taken a lot of pride in locking up more than eight hundred armed and dangerous suspects, in bringing all my people home from every operation, in never having had to kill anyone. I thought I'd seen and done it all. Well, I hadn't. I had never run up against people who would declare war on little children. Anyone parking a truck outside the Murrah building could not help but see the day-care center on its second floor and the tot lot outside the Y. At nine o'clock, many children would just have been dropped off and would have been standing at the windows, waving to their parents. The people who had done this were pure evil. Catching them was the closest thing I'd ever felt to a calling from God Almighty.

I still don't understand evil, I reflected. *I probably never will.*

But I had gotten to know it well. It had become as familiar to me as Debbie's voice, our children's laughter, or the gun I had strapped on nearly every day since July 25, 1966, when I signed on the dotted line and packed up for the FBI Academy. I couldn't know then what I know now, but I've always known this: to survive, you have to look the monster in the eye and outthink it. When you're dealing with haters, with their mad energy, paranoia, and piano-wire tangles of ideas, you have to climb inside their heads and figure out their next moves. If you don't, they shoot you. Or you shoot them, which is not much better. Kill a terrorist, make a martyr. Hand his fellow fanatics a rallying cry for the next time.

And make no mistake about it, there will be a next time. When I was a law student, in love with my history and law books, I marveled at how, whenever a standard-bearer fell during the making of this nation, there was always someone else to step forward to catch the falling flag of liberty. Now I know it's as hard to kill a bad idea as a good one.

BOOK ONE

A NEW KIND
OF KILLER

We have black people who are our deadly ene-
mies. A black pig, a white pig, a yellow pig, a pink
pig—a dead pig is the best pig of all. We encour-
age people to kill them because the police consti-
tute an army.

—ELDRIDGE CLEAVER,
 Black Panther minister of information,
 November 1, 1970

BOOK ONE

1

By the time I got to law school, though, I had a sense
of the dark side and something drove me to find out
more. I tried to explain my idea to Pop in the spring of
'64, when we went out for a twilight ride on Uncle Will's

Back around 1964, when I was in my first year at
Southern Methodist University Law School, I got this
idea that I could make a difference. Maybe it was my take
on sixties idealism or maybe it was four generations of
cowboys and stockmen peering down at me. Or maybe it
was all those Saturday matinees at the Fort Worth picture
show, gazing up at the silvery profiles of Randolph Scott,
Henry Fonda, and John Wayne. Mom and Pop thought
the law would set me on the path of fame and fortune,
but I knew I couldn't settle into a slick Dallas law firm,
prop a pair of $500 boots on a desk the size of a pool table
and help chiselers carve up ranch land into housing
developments or handle divorces for spoiled rich people.
The world was made up of good guys and bad guys. I was
going to be one of the good guys.

Exactly how I was going to get into the saving-the-
world business was not entirely clear to me at the time.
I'd solve that problem when I came to it. In the meantime, I figured I'd prepare for the task ahead by poking
around in the dark corners of the human condition. I had
almost no idea what I was looking for. I'd grown up in a
modest, tidy, little house in a neat, little neighborhood. I
hadn't had much in the way of toys and things, but I'd had
something kids don't have now. Freedom. Weekend
mornings, I took off on my bike, looking for a few pals to
play sandlot ball or go fishing. My mother waved good-
bye and called after me, "Be home for supper." What parent today, rich or poor, would let their kids roam around
town till twilight?

By the time I got to law school, though, I had a sense of the dark side, and something drove me to find out more. I tried to explain my idea to Pop in the spring of '64, when we were out for a twilight ride on Uncle Will's place outside Hamilton, Texas. Pop was lounging in his saddle, smoking a cigarette with one leg draped over the horn, listening to the crickets and gazing at the setting sun. Young hotshot that I was, I couldn't bear to let him enjoy the peace of the moment.

"You won't believe where I went last week, Pop," I said cheerfully. "The American Nazi Party had a rally in Dallas. Some guy talked about all the problems in the country and blamed the Jews, blacks, and every minority. I guess you and I are okay. He didn't mention the Irish or the Scots."

Pop sat up so fast he nearly spooked his horse, and mine too. It was as if a bolt of lightning had shot from his head right through his body and into his saddle. That old paint wheeled a couple of times before Pop got him under control. *Morris is real pissed,* I said to myself with satisfaction. *A lot of people have learned the hard way, don't piss off Morris.*

"Why would you go see those crazy sons of bitches?" he glowered.

"I don't support what they believe in," I replied earnestly. "I wanted to hear what they had to say. It's important to understand them, and I don't know much about them. Hell, they almost took over the world."

"Yes, I know," Dad said, spitting out his words. "They almost killed me doing it. There's not a lot you have to know about those assholes. They are *evil.*"

"Pop, I know they're evil, but you have to understand what's evil so you can deal with it. Knowing what's evil helps you to understand what's good and how to protect it."

"I reckon you're about half a bubble off plumb," Pop said with resignation. Morris O'Neal Coulson had seen more than he wanted of Nazis when he followed General George Patton across Europe, lugging a Browning automatic rifle that was probably bigger than he was. But he let the matter drop. I guess he thought I was going through a phase.

As I looked toward graduation in 1966, I announced that I intended to become a Navy fighter pilot, the nearest thing the twentieth century could produce in the way of a knight in shining armor. In my dreams, I rammed the dawn sky at Mach one, dived like an osprey, and deftly hitched the tailhook of my Skyhawk onto the slender cable strung across the deck of the aircraft carrier that I called home.

I was exactly the kind of young man the Navy wanted, the local recruiter assured me. I was destined for the elite Judge Advocate General Corps. The Navy had enough pilots. It needed lawyers to whip its young salts into line.

While brooding over this dispiriting news, I wandered into an antique-gun store, where I met the man who changed my life—FBI special agent Charley Brown. Charley and I struck up a conversation. He was investigating a theft of some valuable old firearms from New Mexico. That sounded like fun to me. As he went on about all the bank robbers and kidnappers he had run to ground, it occurred to me that the FBI was a ticket to good-guy land. I would get a badge, a gun, $185 a week basic pay, plus all the soaring triumphs and mortal terror that I'd hoped to enjoy as an air warrior.

The only hitch was, I had to ease the Bureau

recruiters' minds about Mama's uncles. One day Kyle Clark, the ASAC—assistant special agent in charge—of the Dallas office called to inquire, "Do you associate with any of your grandfather Donald's half brothers?"

"No," I said, "I think I only saw them one time and I don't even know their names."

"Good thing. One of them served time at Leavenworth on stolen-car charges."

"Oh, no," I groaned. "No one in the family really knows them. Is that going to hurt my chances?"

"Dunno, son," Clark said.

I stewed for a while until Clark called with good news. "Well, you're in. They decided to take you in spite of your relatives." And also in spite of the fact that I looked more like the typical tunnel rat than the six-foot-three, blond poster boys beloved by J. Edgar Hoover.

I was so enamored with the vision of myself as a gangbuster that I very nearly skipped the Texas bar exam and drove to Mexico. Only none of my classmates would go with me. Also, Pop got on my back about taking the damn test because you never know, you might need that credential. So I took it and I passed.

Mama sat there in stunned silence when I started packing up for the FBI Academy. Frances Mavinee Donald Coulson was the daughter of farmers and the wife of a cowboy. She didn't want her only son to grow up to be a cowboy, and as far as she was concerned, an FBI agent was just a cowboy in a suit. Besides, she couldn't imagine why anybody would ever want to leave Texas. She actually stopped speaking to me. Except for rare, brief moments of reconciliation, she didn't relent until she was on her deathbed twenty years later.

Pop made a halfhearted effort to back her up. "I can't

believe you spent seven years in college to be a college cop," he grumbled. But the twinkle in his eyes gave him away. That song about seeing Paree was right on the money. Pop didn't talk about the war much. He had been assigned to a field hospital for a while, and I expect the memories were too awful to dredge up. He liked to boast about the time he paid for his leave in Paris by selling surplus cargo parachutes to the ladies of the night, who dyed them black and made silk dresses. The war taught Pop a lot of things, among them, that Texas wasn't the hub of the universe. Mama never forgave him either.

In 1967, after a rookie stint in New London, Connecticut, I was assigned to the big New York field office. I was pumped. The Big Apple had it all—Mafia dons, Wall Street con men, dope kingpins, Tammany Hall grafters and grifters, Most Wanted poster boys.

Only the FBI wouldn't let me chase them. Instead, I landed on an internal-security squad whose sole task was keeping tabs on a bunch of elderly Bronx residents who belonged to a club with Communist ties. Squad supervisor John Dooley solemnly informed me that the director wanted to know where every Red in New York was at every moment so that when we went to war with the Soviet Union, we could round up these old folks and intern them. Upon reviewing the case files, I discovered that fully a third of these people had long been employed as FBI informants. I almost laughed out loud, only as far as I could tell, Dooley, who stood five feet ten inches tall, weighed well over two hundred pounds, and sported the great shock of white hair favored by Hoover-era managers, didn't have much of a sense of humor.

The squad's old-timers hunched over their desks from

nine to five, verifying their targets' residences and vacation plans by making pretext phone calls, posing as magazine salesmen or travel agents. I was twenty-six, a lousy liar, and restless, so I decided to conduct my investigations in person. My first task was to verify the address of a club member whom I'll call Sadie Grotz. I caught the subway to the Bronx. As I was wandering around her apartment building looking for the super, a neatly dressed woman in her mid-seventies decided I looked lost and offered to help me. "Do you know Sadie Grotz?" I ventured.

"Of course, I know Sadie Grotz," she said. "I'm Sadie Grotz. What can I do for you?"

Flustered, I blurted out, "I'm with the FBI."

She gave me a big smile and stuck out her hand. "Well, I'm really glad to meet somebody from the FBI. I always believed that after all my years with the Communist Party that somebody from the FBI would come and talk to me."

She invited me in to her apartment and fixed me a cup of tea and cookies. She said she was loyal to the United States and looked upon her membership in the local Communist Party as a social club where she saw friends from her trade union days, back in the 1920s and 1930s. We had a nice discussion.

When I reported to Dooley that I had just had tea and cookies with Sadie Grotz, the Red Menace, he turned beet red and started trembling. I thought he was having a heart attack.

"Your contact with Mrs. Grotz can have very serious consequences for your career," he sputtered. "It may cost you your job. You have to have Bureau permission to talk to a member of the Communist Party. Don't tell anyone what you've done. Go home and pray that Mrs. Grotz doesn't call the office and ask to see you again."

Mama, you were right, I thought ruefully. *I work for a bunch of crazy people.* However, I'd inherited Mama's stubborn genes and Pop's too, so I pestered Dooley with questions and wisecracks until he banished me to the motorcycle surveillance team.

I'd never spent much time on a motorcycle before, but after a few sessions with an instructor who thought he was Chuck Yeager on rubber, I discovered that my 500cc BMW was almost as good as a jet fighter and used a lot less gas. I jumped curbs, screamed down sidewalks, slid sideways down alleys, and tore through parks. Once, while chasing a bank robber, I jumped a traffic light, zipped between lanes of traffic, pulled slightly to the front of his Cadillac, and dropped the motorcycle underneath his left front tire. I lunged for his door, yanked him out of the car, and was advising him of his rights while he was still peering down at his fender, looking for the crushed body of the fool who had fallen under his headlights.

Then I moved to the fugitive squad, the office's dirtiest, least desirable job. I couldn't believe my luck. Only the fittest—the quickest, strongest, nastiest, shrewdest, most corrupt—survived the mean streets of Harlem, Brooklyn, and the South Bronx, and I got paid to catch them. Night after night, I tested myself physically and intellectually against men capable of *anything*.

I rationalized that the high I felt came from doing the Lord's work, dragging killers and bloodsuckers out of the neighborhoods, making life a little easier for the shop owners, the old people, and the kids. But, God help me, I loved it. I lived for that high when we actually put our hands on someone who thought he was invisible.

The only part that bothered me was seeing the kids. When the night was done, I went back to the apartment at Eighteenth and C where I lived with Carol, an Eastern Airlines flight attendant instructor I had recently married. I stashed my reeking hiking boots in the kitchen near the front door, stood under the shower till the hot ran out, and fell into nice cool sheets. Those kids with their hungry eyes, peeping out into the hallways as we hustled by with some sweating, cursing guy in tow, they were trapped in the stench and the noise.

None of the curious little boys who edged up to get a better look at the FBI guy lived with their fathers. Their hungry looks reminded me how much I had missed Pop when he was off in the war. I had been two years old when he left, and I knew him only by the V-mails that Mom read me.

But the emptiness had been filled by other strong, honest men. Mom and I lived in Wichita Falls with her parents, Raymond and Lunette Donald. My dad's parents, Bernard and Iola Coulson, lived across town. Grandpa Bernard dispensed justice with a stern, sure hand. Whenever I got into a fistfight with my cousins Jimmy and Gayle, Bernard stormed out into the yard, grabbed all of us under his arms, and hung us on the picket fence by our belts. His horses, attracted by the ruckus, drifted up from the back lot and nibbled our jeans as we wriggled, trying to free ourselves. You don't hang on a fence very long before your legs go to sleep, and you start screaming to be released. At that, Bernard stalked out and stood before us, boots anchored in the parched grass.

"You boys learned your lesson yet?"

"Yes." "Yes!" "We're sorry." "We won't do it again!"

"Do *what* again?"

"Whatever it was that got us hung on the fence!"

"You boys still don't get it. Family don't fight family!"

He left us hanging out there a while more, until we thought about it, and finally let us down.

We didn't stop fighting altogether, but we made sure we didn't fight around Bernard. We knew that Bernard loved us, but if we broke his commandments, his wrath descended upon us as if it were God's own. The great family story was about the night my uncle Kenneth came home about two A.M. When he straggled down to breakfast and pulled his chair up next to Morris, who was a teenager at the time, Bernard informed him that he was not to stay out that late while he lived in his home. Kenneth protested that he had turned twenty and was, indeed, going to get married the very next day.

"That's the rules," Bernard decreed. "And that's it."

"I'm a man now," Kenneth said. "I can come and go as I want, and I can take you now."

"Kenneth, I wouldn't mess with Bernard," Iola warned as she fussed over the biscuits.

"Mama, I'm a man now, and I'm going to come and go as I please," Kenneth said.

A look of disgust passed over Bernard's face. He slowly unfurled himself from his ladder-back chair and stood to his full five-foot-eight-inch height.

"Okay, let's go out back and settle this." As soon as they got into the backyard, Bernard decked Kenneth. Then he walked back inside, not even breathing hard, and finished his coffee. Kenneth lay sprawled on the grass for a while, collected himself, and staggered back to the breakfast table. They all sat in silence. Morris bit his lip and suppressed a wicked grin.

Finally Iola spoke. "Kenneth, you should know by now not to mess around with Bernard."

Kenneth looked up. "I'll be in on time tonight."

Bernard smiled and kept on sipping Iola's coffee. I never did understand how this fit in with the command-ment "Family don't fight family." But it was effective.

If Bernard personified rules, Pop was all about hard work. Even today in his seventies, he works as if he were forty. Sometimes I think he rests between blinks of his blue eyes. When he was seven, Pop sacked fruit at the local market, and he encouraged me to do likewise. At nine years old, I ran a traveling shoeshine business from my Radio Flyer wagon.

When I turned fourteen, Pop put me to work on the loading dock of a Fort Worth warehouse he was running. That turned out to be the best preparation I ever had for the FBI. An agent has to communicate easily with people from all walks of life, from the president of a bank that had been robbed to the bank robber's girlfriend. Unlike many of my classmates, whose youthful experiences had been confined to people of their own age and social class, I had gotten to know all kinds of people: merchants, truckers, railroad men, salesmen, day laborers. The color of your skin and your station in life mean nothing when you and your partner are racing to unload a boxcar before the Texas sun heats the air inside to 150 degrees. All you really care about is that you're both sweating a lot, and it'll take the two or three of you to get that car emptied. You talk about really important things, like how hot it is, what you're going to do after work, where you'll go for the weekend, and how little Morris pays you.

Just after my eighteenth birthday, Pop helped me get another cushy job, breaking and training horses, with a lit-tle rodeoing on the side. The cowboy business lost its romance after about twelve hours of rolling around in fresh manure, but it reinforced Pop's lessons in honesty and persistence. My bosses didn't give a damn about pedigree or education. All that mattered was what kind of a hand you were and whether you were a straight shooter and willing to put in a hard day's work.

Every time I saw the kids in the projects, I wondered how they would have fared if they had had men like Bernard and Morris in their lives. As things stood, a lot of them, when they got older, would find jail an improvement and death no loss at all.

2

I didn't think I'd ever get accustomed to the smell of the city. The instructors at the FBI Academy had failed to mention that when your partner said, "I'll hit the front. You watch the rear," he was not looking out for your safety. Staking out the alley side of an apartment in the South Bronx meant standing ankle-deep in garbage, breathing air foul with urine, feeling rats scramble across your boots. If you were out there long enough, somebody was bound to heave a bag of beer bottles, cigarette butts, and dirty diapers off a fire escape and onto your head.

Whenever we could, Carol and I headed for the country, to a little cabin in the hills outside Rocksbury, New York. The place was too tame and too green to pass for Wichita Falls. It needed some mesquite scrub, a good dust storm, and a pounding from baseball-size hailstones.

Still, I could shake off the city for a few hours and let my mind drift back to those bright Saturday mornings when I perched on the front of Bernard's saddle, hollering and hanging on to the horn for dear life as we raced across a meadow that smelled of sunflowers and cow manure.

I was in Rocksbury on the morning that changed the course of my life. It was Saturday, May 22, 1971. I rose just past dawn, slipped on a sweatshirt, shorts, and running shoes, tiptoed outside, took a deep breath, and let the air wash over me. A fine mist rose from the forest floor. Below me lay the valley, neatly checkered with rows of clapboard houses with broad porches, big yards, and old shade trees. I loped down the path wondering how many rabbits I'd flush, and wound up in Bud's general store, which boasted the hottest coffee in New York, found an empty stool, and spotted the New York *Daily News* on the counter. The headline was a punch in the gut. Two New York police officers shot dead. Waverly Jones, thirty-three, and Joseph Piagentini, twenty-eight, had been ambushed after answering a call to the Colonial Park houses at 159th Street and Harlem River Drive. Both men had been shot from behind. Jones, who was black, had taken four rounds and had died of a bullet to the brain. Piagentini, who was white, had been shot a dozen times.

Shot in the back, no chance to fight back—it was my worst nightmare. Jones had three children, Piagentini, two. I raced through the article, feeling the anger well up inside of me. I imagined what it must have been like for their wives to answer a knock at the door and find a grim-faced officer standing there.

It could have been me. I've walked in and out of that project dozens of times, and every other project in the city. I shoved the thought aside. *Nah. I'm bulletproof. Cops and agents die because they make mistakes.*

The Academy instructors assured us that with our experienced supervisors, superior training, and keen minds, we were not going to make any mistakes. This was a crock, but it served its purpose. They knew that we had to lock down into complete denial in order to go out and do our jobs. They made sure nobody graduated without the invisible box where we were to stash all our feelings. In our line of work, anger, fear, hate, even love, are distractions, luxuries to be saved for days off, if we get them, and our families, if they can wait long enough.

I sure would like a crack at these guys. I finished my coffee, put the paper aside and walked to a pay phone a quarter mile down the road. "FBI, can I help you?" the switchboard operator answered. "This is Coulson. Anybody looking for me?"

"Oh, yes, I have a message to connect you to Mr. Renaghan. Hold on."

Tommy Renaghan, my partner Bill Baker's roommate, was on an organized crime squad. I wondered what he wanted with me. All I knew about organized crime was that the agents who worked it knew every good Italian restaurant in the city.

"Doc, you still playing in the mountains?" Tommy said.

"Yeah. I just saw the paper about the cops, what gives?"

"We're in it. The president ordered the Hoov to investigate and find out who did it. We have a Bureau special. It's called NEWKILL. They want some fugitive guys. They picked you and Baker. I'm in too. They put you and me as partners. You need to get back down here first thing Monday. We're going to get real busy."

Normally, we didn't do murder cases. Murder was, and is, a local crime, to be prosecuted in state court. But then, there was federal jurisdiction, and there was Hoover jurisdiction. I jogged back to the cabin, told Carol the news, and brooded until Sunday night, when we threw our things in the back of the car and headed south to the city.

3

The next morning, I took an early bus to the office on Sixty-ninth Street, rode the elevator to the sixth floor, and made my way to a bull pen consisting of several rows of spare desks shoved into what had been an unoccupied corner of the field office. I stuck my head into a cubicle backed by windows overlooking Third Avenue.

"Hello dere," Joe Corless said, grinning. "How was your vacation?"

"Looks like my vacation is over," I said, beaming.

Joe Corless, the bank-robbery-squad supervisor tapped to run the special, was the coolest guy in the office. Thin, balding, and dressed off the rack, he was not the kind of guy you picked out in a crowd. But he was one of the few middle managers who could announce, "Follow me," and expect to hear any footsteps besides his own.

I hadn't been an agent very long before I figured out that the term *FBI leadership* was one of those oxymorons, like *military intelligence* and *journalistic ethics*. While all senior FBI people liked being associated with the mystique of the mythical Inspector Erskine, most of them had no idea what to do with an actual bad guy. The FBI of Hoover's day was a time warp, where petty infractions like wearing colored shirts killed careers, while mediocrity in solving real crimes was not only tolerated but rewarded.

It took the leader of a gang of bank robbers to explain FBI culture to me. This guy was a tough customer who ruled his gang with an iron hand. After we had arrested most of his crew, he cut a deal and started helping us sort out his jobs from those of his competitors. One day, I showed him a photograph from a robbery we were trying to solve. "Yeah, that was us," he said agreeably.

"I think you drove the getaway car in this job," I ventured.

He jumped out of his seat so fast I thought he was going to rip out my Adam's apple. "Drive? Drive? Man, *I go in!* I don't drive, motherfucker. I can't believe you thought I would *drive!*"

"Aw, gee, I'm sorry, Lester," I stammered. I realized that while he and his pals all looked like bank robbers to me, everybody on the inside knew the difference between the real men, whose job was to go in, and the drivers and the lookouts, who liked being known as badass bank robbers but who didn't want to take the risks associated with the job.

That's when it hit me. *We're not that much different.* All of us have the title, special agent of the Federal Bureau of Investigation. But there are really two kinds of agents, and those of us on the inside know exactly who is which.

There are the men and women who go in. They love the thrill of the chase, sparring physically and intellectually with all types of adversaries—fugitives, spies, white-collar criminals, child molesters, gangsters, bank robbers, or drug dealers. They look for confrontational situations where they can test themselves. They enjoy the intense bonds of comradeship that form among partners on dangerous assignments. Their humor is cutting, disarming, and often outrageous. They like to make decisions and to be held accountable. Do they like being FBI agents? You bet they do. They treasure the image and the legend of the FBI. But they value the work and the friendships even more. These are the agents that you literally have to throw out the door when they reach retirement age, and we miss them desperately.

Then there are those who are in it for the glamour. They like to hang out with high-level officials and politicians. They'd rather go to a state dinner than catch a murderer. They live by four principles. One, avoid making decisions that have consequences. Two, plan every move to enhance your career. Three, if a dangerous arrest is about to go down, be sick, have other plans—do anything that will not put you in a position to be criticized. Fourth and most important, get good haircuts, and buy expensive suits and really expensive suspenders. Believe me, the suspenders thing works.

One of my supervisors not only cowered behind his desk whenever we went out, he spent his time reading our reports from the bottom of the page up, using a ruler. If he read backward, he reasoned, he could focus on checking spelling without being distracted by content. Headquarters doled out letters of censure to supervisors who forwarded reports containing spelling errors, and their pay was docked. If our reports made no sense, nobody suffered, except the victims of crime and the taxpayers.

This supervisor was definitely a driver. In fact, the vast majority of FBI leaders are drivers. Instead of pouring their energies into the real job of the FBI, they spend their time trying to beat out their peers. Once they start on the road to administrative advancement, they spend more time positioning themselves for the next promotion than they do on their current assignment. Since their superiors know and enjoy a good suck-up when they see one, they climb like mountain goats.

If any FBI agent reading this book has a question about how he or she is perceived by our fellow agents, I have a simple test. If you have to ask the question, then you are a driver or possibly even a lookout. If you go in, you don't have to ask.

Me? Not only do I go in, I don't even like to talk to drivers.

Joe Corless went in. He was always out on the streets with the troops, usually taking the most dangerous and thankless jobs like kicking in a door or confronting a wacko. He convinced us we could take down every bad guy in New York if we worked hard enough. And if we screwed up, he took the heat. As commander, he said, he was responsible for everything we did, right or wrong. There was not a street agent in New York who would not go through a brick wall for him.

When I stuck my head into his office, Joe put down his paperwork and brought me up to speed. Shortly before ten o'clock on Friday night, Waverly Jones and Joe Piagentini had driven into the Colonial Park complex to answer a call from a woman who said her husband had slashed her with a knife. The two officers settled things down and were walking back to their patrol car when they were blindsided.

There were witnesses, two teenage girls, a teenage boy, and a cabdriver, who described two black men who had been sitting on the hood of a light blue Mustang, then had fallen in behind the cops and opened fire. Jones had died instantly. Piagentini had pleaded for his life as the gunmen fired, over and over. Once the cops were down, their attackers took their service revolvers, shot Piagentini with his own gun, and ran into the darkness. The good news was that there were fingerprints on the blue Mustang.

"Just pray that they keep the guns and we can recover them," Corless said.

The case agent for NEWKILL was Bob McCartin, who belonged to the "racial squad." Bob was the Bureau's leading specialist on crimes committed in the name of black extremism. The previous October, he had tracked down Angela Davis, at the time a Top Ten list fugitive charged with the murder of a California judge.

"Obviously, the Piagentini and Jones murders amounted to a premeditated, well-planned execution," McCartin told us. "It doesn't look like an arrest that went south. Too many shots. Too vicious. Doesn't look like an organized crime hit either. Taking the cops' guns was stupid. No normal criminal would take that kind of risk. The guns must have some symbolic meaning. It's got to be a cause, something in the black nationalist, black terrorist community. But who?"

The hair stood up on the back of my neck, and not just because the crimes were so cruel and senseless. If the case was being classified as terrorism, then under our rules, it was the property of the Security Division and so was I. I was damned if I was going to work for Security again. It was nothing against McCartin personally. He was as solid an agent as they came. But Security was ruled by Hoover toadies in SOG, Seat of Government, as the director called FBI headquarters. During my brief, unhappy stint in the division I had been appalled to find how much time was being wasted collecting voluminous dossiers of gossip, rumor, and paranoid, ill-informed conjecture about radical activists who were no more national security risks than Pop.

As if he had read the scowl on my face, McCartin said with special emphasis, "This is a crime and we'll work it like a crime. This is not a security case. This is a criminal investigation that will focus on specific crimes. We intend to solve each crime they commit, and especially this one."

What McCartin meant was that we would start at the crime scene and follow the leads outward, wherever they took us. No politics. No SOG meddling. Just solid connect-the-dots investigative work.

Well, this gonzo biker was good to go. I nodded eagerly and eyed Tommy Renaghan and Bill Baker. "Ready to head uptown?" I said.

McCartin held up a hand as if to say, *Not so fast*.

"You guys shouldn't think we're here to solve just one murder case," he said grimly. "If we're correct, there may be more attempts to kill policemen. And you, as well."

4

McCartin began going over, point by point, a shooting that had occurred forty-eight hours before the murders of Jones and Piagentini.

On the night of May 19, NYPD officers Nicholas Binetti and Thomas Curry were sitting in their patrol car in front of the home of Manhattan district attorney Frank Hogan when a yellow Maverick sped by the house, heading south on a northbound lane of Riverside Drive. The two officers gave chase. At 116th the driver pulled alongside the patrol car, smiled broadly, and ducked. The passenger opened up with a .45-caliber machine gun. The officers were at St. Luke's Hospital and were expected to pull through, but they were in bad shape. Curry had been shot four times in the face and head. Binetti had taken a dozen rounds in his torso and limbs but had managed to whisper part of the license number of the Maverick before he passed out.

At about eight-thirty in the evening on May 21, the night Piagentini and Jones were assassinated, a young black man delivered a fat envelope to the lobby of *The New York Times* building and ran away. The envelope referred to "the shooting of two NYPD pigs on Malcolm's birthday." May 19 would have been the forty-sixth birthday of Malcolm X, the Nation of Islam leader assassinated by rivals in 1965.

The envelope contained a .45-caliber bullet, a note, and a license plate from the yellow Maverick wrapped in the edition of the *New York Post* that reported the shooting.

"Here are the license plates sort [*sic*] after by the fascist pig state," the note said. ". . . Just as the fascist marines and army that occupy Vietnam in the name of democracy and murder Vietnamese people in the name of American imperialism are confronted with the guns of the Vietnamese Liberation army, the domestic armed forces of racism and oppression will be confronted with the guns of the Black Liberation Army, who will mete out in the tradition of Malcolm and all true revolutionaries real justice."

"The Black Liberation Army is a new one on me," McCartin said. "But I'll lay odds it's some kind of splinter off the Black Panthers, likely people from the Cleaver faction."

The Panther Party, Bob explained, was in the throes of a bloody internal power struggle between the majority, headed by Huey Newton of Oakland, and a dissident faction led by Eldridge Cleaver. Newton had toned down his bellicose rhetoric since emerging from prison in 1970 and was appealing to mainstream liberals and civil rights activists by advocating antipoverty work, community organizing and a breakfast program for children.

The party's young firebrands shifted their allegiance to Cleaver, a hard-line Marxist who scoffed at Newton and insisted that nothing less than armed revolution would redress racial injustice. Cleaver had fled the country after assaulting a California policeman. He was now ensconced in a villa in Algiers, the self-styled Panther "ambassador" to Algeria's leftist regime. He was exhorting black radicals to go underground, set up cells and wage urban guerrilla warfare on American society. He boldly advocated the assassination of President Nixon and the murder of authority figures, especially policemen. "A black pig, a white pig, a yellow pig, a pink pig—a dead pig is the best pig of all," he told one journalist. "We encourage people to kill them because the police constitute an army."

In March of 1971, Newton and Cleaver expelled each other from the Panther Party. The New York and New Jersey chapters of the Panther Party swore allegiance to Cleaver, while the Oakland and Los Angeles chapters stuck with Newton. Factional warfare broke out. Dead bodies started piling up on both sides.

The notion that the BLA was a Panther spin-off was a theory. There was only one way to find out. Ask people. Baker, Renaghan, and I drove up to the Colonial project and started pounding the halls.

We hung out around the basketball courts, talking to everyone that showed up to play a game of shirts and skins. We walked the many pathways leading to the project at different times of the day trying to find someone who had seen something. But nobody knew anything of value.

Meanwhile a second set of communiqués signed by the "Black Liberation Army" were delivered to The New York Times and WLIB on May 24. These messages took credit for the assassinations of "the two Gestapo pigs," meaning Piagentini and Jones. The author of both communiqués appeared to be the same—but who?

A week or so into the case, McCartin ushered us into the office library where he had set up a projector and a tripod-mounted screen.

"Let's talk about motive," he said. "Take a look at this. It's a movie called The Battle of Algiers. It's about the Algerian revolution against the French colonial government in the 1950s."

According to an NYPD undercover team who had spent two years inside the New York Panther chapter, the film was required viewing.

As flickering black-and-white images filled the screen, I watched, riveted, as young Muslim rebels dodged French gendarmes by ducking and weaving through the tangled walkways of the city's ancient Arab quarter. *So that's what the Casbah looks like,* I said to myself, settling comfortably into my bu-chair.

The exotic spectacle suddenly became very real to me when a woman in a gauzy robe and veil drew a pistol from a basket and slipped it to a young man. He confronted a policeman, stuck the gun to his head, and pulled the trigger.

The film offered all sorts of practical lessons in guerrilla warfare—how to use bolts to enhance a pipe bomb's blast, how to compartmentalize information. A drive-by machine-gunning in the European quarter of Algiers looked exactly like the Binetti-Curry shooting. Most of the time, the guerillas killed policemen with a stealthy approach from the rear, the close-range shot to the back of the head, the fast fade into the crowd—that was exactly the tactic that had been reenacted in the murders of Piagentini and Jones.

"It could happen to any street cop, detective, or agent," McCartin said. "We don't really know what these people look like. We could walk past them covering a lead and be shot down just the same way."

"You're right," I said. "But look at the film and what we know about the murders. In both situations, cops were attacked from the back, by cowards who didn't even have the guts to ambush from the front. They don't want to risk a gunfight with a cop at all. So we should make it a point never to walk side by side. One agent should get out of the car and take the lead. The second, the driver, should get out of the car, look around, then follow twenty to twenty-five paces behind his partner. They can't get both of us in the first volley. And then they'll have to deal with a live guy who's ready for a fight."

Baker nodded slowly. "At least it'll give us a chance. These guys may decide to pass if they think they can only get one.

"Besides," he added, his gray eyes narrowing, "if I'm with Doc, they'll want to shoot him personally, and I'll have a chance to get away."

"Thanks, asshole," I replied. "I haven't seen you covering any leads on the street yet. You think they'll come into the office and shoot you?"

Baker smiled serenely. "Doc, I've saved you so many times, I've lost count."

Like most partners, we fought like two strange bulldogs. We were best friends and about as different as any two people could be. Bill Baker, the son of an airline pilot, had spent his youth on Long Island, where he worked as a lifeguard in order to make an intense study of the beaches, especially their female visitors. He had graduated from the University of Virginia and had joined the U.S. Air Force to become a fighter pilot. After hotdogging in the clouds one time too many, he was transferred to the Air Force Office of Special Investigations, which handled counterespionage cases. When his enlistment was up, he joined the FBI.

Baker had about as much use for Hoover-era Bureau politics as I did, so he landed on the fugitive squad too, but he looked like Cary Grant doing it.

"You know, Baker, with those fancy clothes that you

wear, no one would want to put bullet holes in you," I sniped. "They'd just stick you up, take your suit, and haul ass. Then we could start looking for a terrorist that dressed like a G-man."

McCartin ignored our squabbling. "Thirty feet apart," he said. "Unconventional. I like it. I'll take it to Corless, make sure everybody else hears about it. But there's something else here we need to understand. Look at the way the terrorists deliberately targeted the police. And the French police took the bait, played right into their hands. They overreacted. You know what happened ultimately, don't you? The French lost."

I could understand why. As much as I hated to watch policemen being murdered, the scenes from the government's dirty war were horrific. Suspected guerrillas were hung upside down, beaten and tortured. French paratroopers swarmed the Casbah, trashing businesses and cafés, rounding up whole families, ripping toddlers from their mothers' arms. At the sight of a weeping father lifting the legless body of his dead son from the rubble of a building bombed by French police officers, my eyes misted up and I said to myself, *If I lived in Algeria, I'd be a terrorist too*.

"The BLA and likely the people in New York City expect that there will be hell to pay for the murder of policemen," McCartin said. "They'll expect us to come in like the Marines and kick down doors and drag people away for interrogation. That *will* not happen. We can't be bullies. We *will* not start a riot. Cops and agents are in these neighborhoods every day. We don't want to get any of them ambushed because we've overreacted. We've talked with the New York City police officials and we've agreed that we will be very careful about our responses.

"So," he concluded, "be professional. Be deferential to everyone you talk with. Someone, sooner or later, will tell us what we need to know."

I looked at Baker. He nodded. We could not allow ourselves to play into the paranoia of extremists. We would wear our usual suits and ties, or windbreakers and jeans. There would be no camouflage, no riot helmets. The people we were chasing were armed like Charlie Company, but McCartin and the police brass agreed not to heavy up with automatic weapons such as M16s. We would carry revolvers and shotguns, which were universally recognized as traditional defensive police sidearms.

That was fine by me. The last thing I wanted was a machine gun. The Kent State massacre was still fresh in everyone's mind. The mere sight of a military weapon could inflame a city crowd. I had no desire to find myself dodging bricks and bottles thrown by passersby. Besides, in the city, an ordinary twelve-gauge shotgun was a far more formidable weapon than an automatic rifle. At fifteen yards, a shotgun would blast a huge hole in a man's chest, while a submachine gun would inflict a mortal wound only if three to four rounds struck vital areas. No rational person would want to face a shotgun.

Don't assume you're looking for rational people, I reminded myself, thinking back to *The Battle of Algiers,* with its monstrous scenes of paratroopers torturing Arab dissidents and murdering their children.

If that's what they believe America is like, then we've got a problem.

5

Headquarters Identification Division, which handled fingerprint matching, identified the latent prints on the first BLA communiqué as belonging to Richard Moore and Eddie Josephs, members of the New York Panther chapter and fugitives from the Panther Thirteen trial.

This was a huge breakthrough, the first forensic evidence we had that put a face and name to the Black Liberation Army.

Not long after this, the NYPD arrested Moore and Josephs as they were trying to stick up the Triple O Social Club in the Bronx. Their .45-caliber submachine gun was the same weapon that had been fired at Binetti and Curry.

For one sweet moment, we thought we had cracked the whole case. Baker even offered to buy drinks at our favorite watering hole, the Sun Luck Restaurant at Sixty-eighth and Lexington. If Moore and his crew shot Binetti and Curry, it stood to reason that they also shot Piagentini and Jones.

But they didn't. The .45-caliber rounds that had killed Piagentini and Jones didn't come from any of the guns seized at the Triple O. None of the witnesses from Colonial Park picked out Moore or his pals from the lineup.

"Look, we always hope for luck, but we shouldn't expect we'd get this lucky," Corless said. "We have a larger group than we'd hoped. We'll just have to keep digging and hope they keep acting stupid."

It was a long, hot, tedious summer. I wore out a good set of hiking boots and Baker scuffed up his Italian loafers

47

tramping through the neighborhoods. Hundreds of leads wound up dead ends.

One morning, Baker, McCartin, Renaghan, and I, suffering from simultaneous caffeine-withdrawal syndrome, headed for the Grill, our favorite uptown coffee shop. Hoover thought drinking coffee in the office was a waste of time, and of course, 99 percent of the agents drank coffee, so everybody had to leave the office and drive to a coffee shop far enough away that the office brass wouldn't catch us, all of which took a lot more time and money than drinking coffee at our desks.

"We have to get smart about this case," McCartin said. "We can't keep randomly interviewing everyone in New York City. So what do we know? Well, we know these guys are serious about killing cops. Also, they don't hold down jobs. They have to stay on the run or risk getting caught. But they have to live. So how do they support themselves?"

"They need money, and probably lots of it," Baker said. "Nothing in the files would indicate they're getting funding from any group we know of."

"Hell, the Panthers have a hard time paying their own rent," McCartin said, nodding. "They can't be giving the BLA very much if any money."

"Remember, Willie Sutton robbed banks because that's where the money is," I said. "These guys don't mind shooting it up with cops. They wouldn't hesitate robbing banks."

McCartin nodded. "It's a place to start. We'll talk to Joe when we get back. We'll need some help from the bank-robbery guys."

The bank-robbery squad printed up stacks of surveillance photos from unsolved bank robberies. We carried them around in our pockets, like baseball cards, and showed them to every witness and snitch we met. The worst that could happen was that we would solve some bank robberies, and who knew? We might just get lucky.

6

On August 28, 1971, San Francisco police officer George Kowalski, patrolling in his radio car at Folsom and Sixteenth in San Francisco, was ambushed by two black men firing a machine gun from their 1965 Oldsmobile. Kowalski chased the Olds until it crashed. The cops arrested the driver, nineteen-year-old Anthony Bottom, and the triggerman, Albert Washington. Bottom was a middle-class college dropout who had hung around the Oakland Panthers. Washington had recently escaped from a prison for the criminally insane. Bottom was carrying the .38 Smith & Wesson police special taken from the body of Waverly Jones. As ballistics tests quickly showed, Washington's .45-caliber pistol, which he had fired at Kowalski, was the gun that had killed Jones.

Bottom boasted to his cellmate that he and Washington and a few others had killed two cops back in Harlem. The cellmate, a longtime police informant, promptly ratted Bottom out.

The witnesses to the Piagentini and Jones murders picked Tony Bottom out of the lineup as the man who had shot Waverly Jones.

But the teenage girls insisted that Washington was not the second man, the one who had shot Joe Piagentini. Moreover, Washington's prints didn't match the prints from the blue Mustang.

Tracking back through recent bank-robbery reports, we found that Albert Washington and two New York Panthers had been arrested for an armed robbery in Harlem. Washington had been bailed out of the Tombs by a man named Gabriel Torres. We put out a nationwide alert to our field offices on the names Washington, Bottom, and Torres.

Salt Lake City field came up with a hit on Washington. He had been arrested the previous January for running a red light and carrying a concealed weapon. With him had been one Francisco Torres, who belonged to a Puerto Rican militant group called the Young Lords.

A check of surveillance pictures from unsolved bank robberies in San Francisco bore fruit. Tony Bottom and Francisco Torres could be seen robbing Fidelity Savings and Loan on July 21. Francisco Torres also showed up at the September 17 robbery at the Bank of America in Bernal Heights.

NYPD detectives arrested the Torres brothers, then flipped Gabriel's wife and Francisco's girlfriend by threatening to bust them as accessories. They said that Gabriel and Francisco had been meeting for months with Bottom, Washington, and a man who called himself "Jonas" or "Herman." The talk had been all about guerrilla warfare,

revolution, and "community self-defense," a code for
killing cops.

As the women told the story, on the night of May 21,
the five men had arrived at the Torres apartment shortly
after 11 P.M., turned on the television, and waited eagerly
for news of the assassinations. Bottom was exultant, brag-
ging, "We offed two pigs, we offed two pigs." He
explained that he had shot a black cop, meaning Waverly
Jones, and "Jonas" had killed a white cop, meaning Joe
Piagentini.

A records check found that the Olds driven by
Bottoms and Washington had been bought on August 5
by a man named Samuel Lee Pennegar, who had listed
bogus addresses on the car registration and his California
driver's license application.

The Torres women recognized the photo on
Pennegar's driver's license as "Jonas." One recalled that
"Jonas's" girlfriend in San Francisco had recently had a
baby boy.

That detail was just the opening we needed. The
baby's birth certificate recorded the father as Herman
Bell. Bell, twenty-three, was born in Benton, Mississippi,
raised in New York, had briefly attended junior college in
Oakland, then took up with the Panthers. The Oakland
police had his prints from a 1969 arrest. Ident—the
Identification Division at FBI HQ—reported that Bell's
prints matched the latent prints lifted from the blue
Mustang.

Bell's name, photo, and description and the warning
"Armed and Dangerous" were plastered in every police
station and sheriff's department in the United States.

But there was a bigger mystery to be solved. Was there
a connection between the Piagentini-Jones murders and

the Binetti-Curry shootings? Were we dealing with a few crazies or a real army, with a disciplined, hierarchical structure, like the guerrilla force in *The Battle of Algiers*? Had we bumped into two of many cells of an extremist underground in the United States? How big was it? Where was it? Where would it strike next?

7

It was time for strong measures. I located a snitch I call Johnny Dee. Johnny, man about town, knew just about everybody in Queens. He had a gift of gab and came off as a harmless kid.

"You spending any time with the Panthers?" I asked him.

He shook his head. "Ver-ry little. Those guys are crazy. You could get in a world of shit just being close to them. I don't even like going to the office, never know when the cops will come busting in or something. With all the heat, you could get shot just hanging out at their crib."

"You hear anything on the street?"

"Yeah, some say they doing banks. Gettin' bread for the revolution."

"You got any names for me?"

"Maybe, you got anything for me?"

"COD, Johnny. COD. Give me what you have, and if it proves out, I'll have some money for you."

"Danny, goin' to need a down payment. I'm short."

I reached into my pocket and pulled out my one and only ten-dollar bill—my money for lunch for a week. Bigtime FBI. We were trying to solve a homicide, and I was laying out my lunch money. The FBI did not pay up-front money. FBI agents did. But it came out of their own pockets. I folded the ten and passed it to him.

"Let's hear it."

"Word is that a guy named John and some other dudes are doing banks in Queens. They got a broad with them. Name is Joanne. Chesimard. I seen her a couple of times."

I pulled out a surveillance photo from the robbery of a Bankers Trust branch in Jackson Heights, Queens, on August 23.

"That's the bitch," Dee said, nodding. "Wearing a wig, but that's the bitch."

"Do you know where they crib? Can you get close to them?"

"Hell, no, and I don't want to. I haven't seen her or the other dudes for a long time. Word is they move around and don't trust anyone. They think everyone is a snitch. That's all I know."

"If this checks out, I'll have some more bread for you," I promised, making a mental note to hit up Corless for his lunch money.

After we dropped Johnny off I radioed Jim Murphy, the case agent on the Bankers Trust heist.

Two blocks away, you could tell that this man had to be named Murphy. We called him Jim, or Murph, but if you were in any kind of trouble, you would call him "sir." He was a beefy six-footer, with a round face and confident smile. Before he landed at the FBI, he had been with an

NYPD tactical squad, a post reserved for New York's finest, biggest, and toughest.

To our delight, we learned that while on the NYPD, Murphy had dressed as a woman and walked the streets of crime-ridden neighborhoods as a decoy. We offered him a week's pay to wear his frock to work. Pity the poor muggers who didn't realize that this lonely old lady was a slightly pissed off Patrolman Murphy.

Murphy entered Corless's office wearing a quizzical look. "My man says a guy named John and some other Panthers are doing banks here, and Joanne Chesimard is in the robberies," I said. "He made her photo. Says she's wearing a wig."

"John has to be John Leo Thomas," McCartin said. "He's in charge of Panther newspaper sales. Joanne Chesimard—I think she's very young, has sold papers for Thomas. We need to look at Fred Hilton, Avon White, Frank Fields, Andrew Jackson, and a guy named Myers, can't remember his first name. They were all selling newspapers for John Leo. Just a bunch of punks."

Corless looked up from his desk. "These punks may be your BLA."

"Maybe," McCartin said.

He went over to the Security Division to pull files on all those names and about ten others that had come up. *Finally,* I thought, *here's a chance for the security boys to justify their existence. We really need some good info, especially some pictures.*

McCartin found some decent snapshots, but otherwise the files were disappointing. The security division's informant coverage had been directed almost exclusively at Panther leaders. The only suspected BLA member who had any standing in the Black Panther Party was

John Leo Thomas. The rest were kids. As we were to find over and over again, leaders of extremist groups were rarely involved in crime. High-profile movement types talked the talk, but they had all the power, money, sex, and status they needed. They weren't about to risk it all for hard time at Leavenworth or Attica. The people who became terrorists and assassins—Lee Harvey Oswald, James Earl Ray, and later, Tim McVeigh and Terry Nichols—were on the margins of radical movements of the left or right. They had nothing much going on in their lives and were looking for somebody to blame and something to do. These were the ones who soaked up the rhetoric, took it literally, and because they had nothing to lose, acted on it. They didn't show up on the screens of law enforcement, the press, or even the movement hierarchy until they did something terrible.

A search of NYPD files came up with a few hits on some of the names. Andrew Jackson, twenty-five, had been indicted in the murder of Huey Newton aide Samuel Napier, along with Richard Moore, Eddie Josephs, and four other New York Panthers. He was wanted for questioning in the Binetti-Curry case. Twymon Ford Myers, twenty, had a long juvenile record and was notorious in the neighborhoods for violence. Informants said Joanne Chesimard, twenty-four, specialized in helping Panthers accused of crimes escape to Algeria.

Murphy was grinning like a kid on his first visit to F.A.O. Schwarz. He had been batting zero in the Bankers Trust job. Suddenly he had an armful of promising suspects. I was afraid he was going to hug me and crush me to death.

Murphy put together a photo spread to show bank

employees and customers present during the Bankers Trust job. Several witnesses present identified the tall, gangly guy next to Joanne Chesimard as Andrew Jackson and the short, chunky guy as Frank Fields. We swore out federal fugitive warrants for the whole bunch.

Some of them took off for Georgia. We were elated when a telephone call from the Atlanta field office relayed word that Andrew Jackson and two other young New York Panthers had been caught sticking up a grocery store on November 7 and were now cooling their heels in the De Kalb County jail. In their apartment, the police had found piles of fake ID cards and a bomb made of a pound of TNT, a stick of dynamite, and a bottle of nitroglycerin. Twymon Myers and Freddie Hilton might be in Atlanta too. The Atlanta police thought they were behind the recent, unprovoked murder of a cop.

Our joy was quashed on December 12 when the three fashioned a crowbar from a pipe and jimmied their way out of jail.

On the morning of December 20, we got an urgent call from the NYPD. At about 9:35 A.M. NYPD patrolmen Stephen Wiedler and Raymond Chair had almost been killed in Maspeth, Queens, while chasing three men and a woman in a stolen car. One of the men leaned out and hurled a fragmentation grenade under the police car. The cops managed to roll out of the doors seconds before the gasoline tank exploded. A man had called United Press International and claimed credit in the name of the "Attica Brigade of the Afro Liberation Army."

A bystander identified one of the men as Andrew Jackson and the woman as Joanne Chesimard. We linked up to the NYPD comm system and sent out a thirteen-state alert.

"What about running an informant into the group?" I suggested.

"No way," McCartin said. "Remember how the Algerian guerrillas initiated recruits? They sent them out to kill a cop. That was the test to see whether they were police snitches. Anybody we try to run into the BLA is likely to be called upon to commit murder. Our best shot is to turn a captured member."

"Who do you think we could flip?" said Renaghan.

"Frank Fields is supposed to be a real weakling," McCartin said. "He's fat and soft. Word is that he'll flip if we catch him." We all nodded wisely.

We sent out a teletype advising offices all over the country of the latest attack on police officers and to be on the lookout for John Leo Thomas and any of the dozen or so young militants associated with him.

On New Year's Eve, agents in the Tampa field office got a tip that Thomas and his bunch were in a cheap motel. They drove out to the place and came face-to-face with Fields, who opened fire on the agents, missed, turned, and fled. Agent Ed Tickle took aim with his model 870 shotgun and returned fire. Ordinarily a buckshot round fired from more than sixty yards would have been ineffective. This was not Frank's lucky day. One pellet struck his head and killed him.

"So this was your weak link?" Baker scoffed to McCartin. "Don't any of these guys just give up?" It was a statement, not a question. We were in for a long, tough ride before we put these guys away.

8

Whenever the telephone rang in the middle of the night, my hand grabbed the receiver before the second ring and my heart pounded like a jackhammer. Most of these O-dark-thirty calls meant that somebody on my squad had a bad guy cornered and we had to go roust him out. I picked up the band-instrument case that held my shot-gun, threw on my clothes, and waited on the corner to be picked up and handed a photo and a brief outline of the investigation.

On a raid, my job was to be the first man through the door. It wasn't because I was the best or the bravest but because HQ decreed that the point went to the shotgun, the most intimidating weapon in our arsenal at the time. The shotgun could only be carried by a firearms instruc-tor. Having practiced target-shooting since I was eight, I had made perfect scores on the FBI range and so quali-fied as an instructor. When a door had to be breached, I got the shotgun and I took the point.

Of course, my fellow agents claimed that I went first because I was the squad's shortest agent, and the body armor covered more of the important parts of my torso. My partners used what we called a key—most people would call it a ram—to knock a door down. Then they threw me through the entrance and came in closely behind me. My job was to push the shotgun in the face of what we hoped would be a sleeping fugitive and scare him so badly that he couldn't react. We had learned that with surprise, speed, and violence of action, we could overwhelm even the most dangerous suspect without firing a shot. We considered it unprofessional—Hollywood, Dirty Harry bullshit—to get suckered into unnecessary gunplay. Deadly force was to us what the ejection seat was to a jet jockey, a bad last resort.

It was not that we were a bunch of candy-ass pacifists. All of us were perfectly capable of doing whatever it took to save lives. When a crazed bisexual named John Wojtowicz and his buddy Sal Natuarale took nine Chase Manhattan Bank employees hostage in the Flatbush branch, my squad was called in. Negotiations failed. Wojtowicz wanted a pile of money and an airplane to take his lover, Ernie Aron, to Denmark for a sex-change operation. Jim Murphy volunteered to chauffeur the gunmen and hostages to JFK International, dodging potholes with Natuarale's shotgun propped on his ear. As he pulled up on the tarmac, Murphy yanked the shotgun barrel up, pulled a revolver hidden under the seat, and shot Natuarale dead. At the same instant, two other agents reached through the car window, grabbed Wojtowicz's rifle, and dragged him out of the van. If you saw *Dog Day Afternoon*, you know the whole weird story.

In Murphy's place, I would have done exactly the same, but when it was just me and a bad guy, I fell back on my wits and the black belt I'd earned while in law school. Once, when a bank robber named Jimmy Tyrone Williams drew a shotgun on me, I became so enraged that he dared point a gun at me—me!—that I swung my own shotgun like a pugil stick, slammed its butt into his stomach, grabbed his throat, kneed him in the groin, and pinned him to the floor until my backup arrived. "Can you believe it, this son of a bitch almost made me shoot him," I ranted at Baker as Jimmy struggled to get some air back into his lungs. The cops who were cuffing him gave me an are-you-nuts look, but Baker understood exactly what I meant. Under the FBI deadly force policy, I should have killed him because he was clearly an imminent threat, but as I saw it, if I did, Jimmy won. I would be no better than him, and I most assuredly was. Jimmy was stoned on heroin. I was clearheaded and fit.

As far as I'm concerned, busting into a darkened, booby-trapped apartment in the dead of night isn't a bad deal. What's unbearably hard is not knowing what door to hit.

That's why the call I got from McCartin in the early-morning hours of January 28, 1972, plunged me into despair.

"You better get to the office," Bob said. "There's been another shooting. Two cops, salt-and-pepper team, on Avenue B and East Eleventh. Ambushed from the rear."

"Shit," I said numbly. "Both dead?"

"Yeah," McCartin said. "Both of them shot in the head, multiple entry wounds. Rookies. Ex-marines, served in Vietnam together."

"And they had to come home to America to get killed."

Shortly before eleven o'clock the night before, foot patrolmen Gregory Foster, twenty-one, and Rocco Laurie, twenty-two, had been winding up their shift in the East Village when they dropped into a greasy spoon called the Shrimp Boat to inquire about a double-parked car. As they left, three young black men walked up behind them and opened fire. As the cops fell onto the snowy sidewalk, the gunmen moved in and shot out Foster's eyes. They shot Laurie in the groin six times. They scooped up the cops' service revolvers as trophies, and one of them did an end-zone victory dance, firing his gun in the air. Then they all vanished into a side street.

Foster, who was black, had grown up in the Bronx and Queens, had two small children, and was attending law school. Laurie, who was white, came from Staten Island, where he was famed as a star high-school athlete. He and his wife had just bought a little starter home.

Two more young wives had been awakened in the middle of the night by a police chaplain and two officers with red-rimmed eyes. My stomach knotted up, and I let the box open a little.

"You know, catching bad guys has been just a job until now," I said. "It's been fun and exciting, but now it's personal."

"Yeah," McCartin said, nodding. "I never felt one way or another about anyone I ever arrested. This bunch is different. They kill and I think they like it. Can you imagine the asshole who danced around after he killed those kids? Too bad there wasn't a stakeout squad in the area to blow these sons of bitches away."

In a deli near the murder scene, the NYPD found a satchel that contained black militant literature, disassembled guns, and newspaper clippings about the Piagentini-Jones case. Fingerprints lifted from the bag's contents were traced to Andrew Jackson and Twymon Ford Myers.

United Press International received a claim of responsibility signed the "George Jackson Squad of the Black Liberation Army." "This is the start of our spring offensive," it said. "There is more to come." The writer took credit for two other unpublicized attacks on city policemen that week, the stabbing of a patrolman sitting in a radio car, and the nonfatal shooting of an officer at a routine traffic stop.

There were witnesses, bystanders who had gotten a pretty good look at the killers' faces. They picked out photos of Andrew Jackson and three other New York Panthers—Ronald Carter, Ronald Anderson, and Henry "Sha Sha" Brown.

We looked everywhere we could think of and dug a lot of dry holes. Not one of our suspects seemed to be anywhere in the city. Toward midnight on February 15, the phone dragged me out of total-zero sleep again. A message from the St. Louis field office had clattered out of our noisy old teletype machine. The night supervisor read it to me.

St. Louis patrolmen Larry Tinney, twenty-two, and Richard K. Archambault, twenty-three, had stopped a maroon Oldsmobile sedan for a routine license-plate check when the four men inside started firing. Archambault fell to the pavement with three rounds in his stomach and legs but managed to return fire. So did Tinney.

A team of undercover narcotics cops who happened to be in the neighborhood rushed Archambault to a hospital in time to save his life. Some of the cops took off after the sedan, its occupants blasting away with everything they had until their car slammed into a chain-link fence. Sha Sha Brown and Thomas "Blood" McCreary were captured. Twymon Myers made it over the fence and vanished. Ronald Carter's body was found in the backseat, shot, apparently accidentally, by one of his pals.

Ballistics determined that Carter had been killed by Rocco Laurie's .38 police special. The car had been purchased not long before by a couple who fit the description of Joanne Chesimard and Andrew Jackson.

Twymon Myers, Andrew Jackson, and Joanne Chesimard. Every time something bad happened, those three seemed to be in the thick of it. All the evidence and the informant reports suggested they were the driving forces of the East Coast BLA. I went to bed and woke up in the morning thinking about them. I spent more time in the crummy apartments, shooting galleries, and stash houses than I did in my own home, a fact that was frequently pointed out to me by my wife. It didn't help that when I was home, my head was still out there in the streets. I tried to explain that this was more than just a case for all of us. It had become our passion. We were dealing with a new kind of killer. Most police killings involved confrontations in which police were attempting to arrest someone. These involved vicious, calculated attacks on unsuspecting people who happened to wear blue.

9

One spring day, Baker woke me up at about three o'clock in the morning with the news that one of his sources said that Twymon Myers was holed up in an apartment building in the Bronx. Would I pick Baker up in ten minutes?

We went screeching up to the Bronx and met at the Forty-second precinct. McCartin, Tommy, Murph, John Ford, and some NYPD detectives joined us. We worked out a quick plan to hit the apartment. Just as I was about to slide on the turtle shell the point man always wore, Baker grabbed it away from me.

"Oh, no, your wife is about to have a baby," he said. "I gotta go through first."

"You've never gone first in your career," I scoffed. Before I could grab it back, he already had the vest strapped on and was checking out my shotgun.

"Don't argue with me," he commanded. "I'm handling this one. You come second."

I rolled my eyes. "Okay, Baker, see that little thing inside of that little round thing? That's the trigger. If Twymon tries to shoot you, pull it. Can you remember that?"

We hit the door, looked left, looked right, cleared the closets, the bathroom, the hot-water-heater compartment, under the beds. Nobody home. Another dry hole. Baker yanked off the vest and handed it back to me. It occurred to me that he would love some small sign of appreciation for his gesture. Let's see, how could I show him that I cared?

"You *knew* it would be empty, you son of a bitch," I announced loudly, so everybody else could hear. "You set up the whole thing. You *knew* this was a dry run. Now I gotta go through first the next time. If you think this counts for going in first, you're crazy."

One more rule of the game is, never say anything good to your partner. Never say thanks for taking a risk for you. Just be willing to die for him, because he will for you if it comes to it.

Baker gave me that thousand-watt smile that kept him surrounded by beautiful women and waved me toward the car. "Since I just saved your life, you buy breakfast," he said. "These entries make me hungry."

For all the excitement in my life, nothing made my

heart beat faster than the first time I saw my son. Daniel O'Neal Coulson arrived right in the middle of Hoover's funeral on May 4, 1972, screaming bloody murder. He had a fat little bulldog mug, and for a while I thought he might be the reincarnation of the Hoov. He had the temperament as well as the face.

In my line of work, I never knew when I would get home, or when I would be leaving. I said a lot of good-byes. I tried to find as much time for him as I could. I put him in an infant seat, held it like a basket of bread, and walked the streets of Manhattan. We did Chinatown together. He sat on the table, sucking on his bottle, and I ate dim sum.

Doc made his first trip to Texas to see Morris and Mavinee before he was two. He spent most of his time visiting Pop's haunts, including Massey's bar. When we were about to head North, Pop wouldn't come out to the car to say good-bye. Didn't want the boy to see him cry. Two decades later, Pop and I would pin my son's police badge on him when he became an officer in Beaverton, Oregon. Morris and Danny both cried a little at that one.

For the first time in my life, I started thinking about my own mortality. I hoped I would be around to take care of my son, to teach him about life and to provide for his financial security.

My concession to fatherhood was to double- and triple-check our plans to make sure everything went down smoothly. I was still young and bulletproof, and anyway, danger wasn't a choice. It was my job. It was what I did. No, it was more than that. It was what I was.

In fact, I decided to plunge deeper into it. About the time Doc was born, I volunteered for one of our new Special Weapons and Tactics teams that would handle the most dangerous arrests and hostage rescues.

I led the SWAT team that handled arrests in violent crime cases. We deployed at least once a week and sometimes every couple of days.

My work rubbed off on Doc. One day when he was about three, he walked into the living room where I was watching college football. He had a water gun stuck into his shorts.

"What do you have there, Doc?" I said.

He looked at me with those Morris Coulson blue snapping eyes and said, "Don't touch, berry danerous," and turned and waddled out of the room. This was my first clue that families, not individuals, join the FBI.

For all the joy my son brought me, I had this gnawing in my stomach every time I thought about Twymon, Andrew, Joanne, and the rest of the BLA bunch. Not a day passed that we didn't chase some tip, however wispy.

10

On September 29, 1972, the Manufacturers Hanover Trust at 1355 Oakpoint Avenue was robbed, and witnesses said one of the subjects looked like a female with a fake beard. I figured it had to be Joanne Chesimard.

NYPD detective Bill Herman came up with an informant who identified another of the robbers as Johnny

Rivers, a common criminal. Witnesses at the bank picked Rivers out of a photo line-up.

At 5:00 A.M. the next day, Erroll Myers, Herman and I climbed into a dark brown delivery van that looked like a United Parcel Service truck and drove to the neighborhood where Rivers was cribbing. Other detectives waited in unmarked cars and on foot, in doorways.

At 6:30 A.M., the radio sputtered. "Be alive down there," said a cop who was hiding in a niche near the entrance to the apartment building. "Here's your boy, and he's heading your way. He's in a real hurry, probably needs to cop a fix."

I could feel the adrenaline rushing through my body. All my senses sharpened. It was time. Myers swung the door open. Herman and I jumped Rivers, slammed him down to the ground, and turned him onto his chest, pushing his face into the pavement. Rivers was known as a badass shooter, and we didn't want him to go into his act. I think he was actually relieved that Herman finally said, "Police." He must have thought he was being mugged.

Herman lifted Rivers as if he were a puppet and tossed him into the van. He had choreographed the ambush so smoothly that no one on the street knew what had happened. We could go after Rivers's pals before the word got out that he was missing.

Later we joined Herman and Rivers in an interview room at the Seventy-ninth Precinct. Herman had a big smile on his face. Rivers looked glum. "He's all yours," Herman said cheerfully.

"Are you the FBI?" Rivers asked warily.

Myers flipped out his credentials and nodded.

"I'll talk to you, but I don't like that cop," Rivers

whined. "He's big, ugly, and nasty and says I'm gonna go away for the rest of my life in a federal pen."

I glanced at Myers and saw him tighten his lips to suppress a smile. Herman was one hell of a Bad Cop. We took the cue and did our Good Cop routine. With exaggerated courtesy, we read Rivers his rights and showed him the standard FBI Advice of Rights Form.

"I know my rights," he grumbled. "I done this before. I need to help myself now."

Johnny said Twymon Myers, Joanne Chesimard, Freddie Hilton, and Avon White were involved in the robbery. He led us to their apartment, but it was empty, except for a little makeup, fake beards, and glue.

11

"I need some help," I announced. "We're going to see Twymon's mother, and she's going to tell us where he is."

"Fat chance," McCartin sighed. "But it's worth a try."

It was after dark when we pulled up about a block from her apartment building in Harlem. "Don't tell me," McCartin moaned. "She lives on the fifth floor."

"You got it. All fugitives live on the fifth floor, or their mothers do."

"I'm getting too old for this."

"After you. Age before beauty."

I waited until Bob got about fifteen feet ahead and followed, looking left and right as we went.

At the fourth floor, Bob reached down and unsnapped the top of the holster that held his Smith & Wesson .357 magnum revolver. I carried an identical gun on my hip. Our six-shooters were going to come in real handy if we got into a fight with, say, Jesse James. The BLA was another story. We knew from bank surveillance photos, witnesses, and informants that just about everybody in the BLA packed a Browning Hi-Power and scads of extra magazines. Twymon Myers was known to be adept with this formidable weapon. He had shot his way out of many a scrape by loading his Hi-Power with twelve-round magazines and blasting away like Rambo.

We had all jammed extra rounds into our pockets, but I knew we could never reload a revolver fast enough to outshoot a Browning Hi-Power. The firearms instructors at the FBI Academy—we called them "the range guys"—had to approve all official weapons. A notoriously hidebound bunch, they had summarily rejected our plea for high-capacity pistols to bring us to parity, at least, with the people we were hunting. I was crestfallen, because I yearned to own a Smith & Wesson Model 59, which had just come on the market and was about the slickest thing around. The 59 was a nine-millimeter, constructed like the Browning, but with sixteen rounds in each magazine. The range guys pronounced the S & W gun unreliable and suggested we carry two revolvers instead. In other words, they wanted us to defend ourselves with two guns that held less ammunition than one Browning magazine and took three times as long to reload. This was another good reason to avoid firefights altogether.

By the time I stepped onto the fifth-floor landing,

McCartin was listening at the door, standing to the side to keep his body protected by the wall. You absolutely never stand in front of a door that you're about to knock on. Doors offer no protection, not even from handguns, and certainly not from a magazine full of nine-millimeter hornets screaming through the wood and into your mush brain. I slid opposite from Bob and listened. We heard the murmur of a TV, but no live male voices. I knocked.

"Who is it?"

"Mrs. Myers, it's the FBI. We'd like to talk to you."

I expected to hear, "Go away, I'm not talking to the FBI." The door opened and there stood a beaten-down black woman.

"Come in. I don't know where Twymon is, so why are you here?"

"Mrs. Myers, we have a warrant for Twymon's arrest and we want to talk to you," McCartin said softly.

"Twymon don't come around here, he would never come here because he knows you're looking for him."

But she didn't slam the door on our noses. McCartin kept her talking. "Ma'am, your son is in very serious trouble. We'd like to get this resolved so that no one gets hurt, him or us."

I interjected every so often, but mostly I watched her eyes, trying to figure out what was going on in her head. Why did she let us in? She was not going to tell us anything. Maybe she was just curious to see what the FBI guys looked like. Maybe she just wanted to know who was hunting her son down, and what to expect when he was caught.

Most of the time, I was a hard-ass, but my heart went out to this lady. She must have had high hopes for her son when he was an infant. She must have dreamed a mother's dream about his future. She could never have imagined that one day he would be sought as a murderer. Here we were asking her to help us find him and possibly get into a shooting match with him.

"Will you at least take our names and if you talk to him or get a message to him, have him call so we can arrange a peaceful surrender," McCartin pressed. "If we or some cop stumbles onto him, you know there'll be trouble and someone will get hurt."

She just nodded her head. We thanked her and left, descending the stairs as cautiously as we had climbed them.

"She'll never call, you know," McCartin said. "And he'll never surrender."

"Got that. I just hope we can trap the SOB before some cop or agent stumbles onto him."

12

In early 1973, BLA suspects staged four ambushes on pairs of NYPD officers. Fortunately, all eight cops survived these unprovoked attacks. One shooter was identified as Andrew Jackson.

Police Commissioner Patrick Murphy, under pressure from the policemen's union, ordered a thousand extra tours of duty, assigned unmarked police cars to trail marked police cars through rough parts of town and put all NYPD detectives on overtime.

Shortly after midnight on May 2, New Jersey state

troopers Werner Foerster and James Harper, patrolling the Jersey Turnpike, stopped a 1965 Pontiac LeMans for a routine traffic check. The three people in the car opened fire, killing Foerster and wounding Harper. Police units responding to Harper's distress calls discovered the body of former Panther deputy information minister James F. Coston, and Joanne Chesimard, alive, bloodied and defiant. A third ex-Panther named Clark Edward Squire fled on foot but was caught. Coston and Squire had been escorting Chesimard to a new hideout in Philadelphia when the troopers stumbled onto them. Harper and Foerster had no idea what they were up against when they pulled over that old Pontiac.

I was visiting my folks in Texas when Renaghan called to fill me in. It was a short, sad conversation. We had wanted so desperately to round up the BLA before another police officer stumbled into them. We had failed. Another officer's wife had answered a knock at her door and had seen a police chaplain standing there.

Joanne Chesimard was charged in New Jersey with Foerster's murder, the attempted murder of Harper, and the grenade attack on NYPD patrolmen Wiedler and Chair in December 1971. The Panthers had been very successful in beating the rap in local courts, so as insurance we filed federal cases against her for the Bankers Trust and Manufacturers Hanover robberies.

Baker, Murphy, and I arranged for the U.S. Marshals to bring her to federal court in Brooklyn, to arraign her on the federal charges. She glared at us with ice-pick eyes. When Baker took her hand to press it on the inkpad, she spat in his face. It's not easy to fingerprint someone who's cooperating. It's almost impossible to print someone who resists. Baker and Murphy had to force her hands down onto the table and her fingers onto the cards. She struggled every step of the way, cursing and screaming. If we had been the Nazis that she imagined, we would have knocked her lights out. There was no way we intended to let ourselves fall into the trap of overreaction, as she clearly hoped.

13

In early June, one of Jim Murphy's informants alerted him that Twymon Myers and Freddie Hilton were about to meet at an apartment in Brooklyn. To thwart surveillance, Fred was to show up first and wait out on the stoop to see if things were cool. If they were, he'd signal Twymon.

In search of an observation post, Murphy went to the apartment building across the street, knocked on the door of a fifth-floor apartment, and explained his mission to the elderly tenant.

"I don't take to no cop killers," the old man said warily, "you can use this place."

Murphy, Baker, McCartin, Renaghan, and I holed up in the apartment with radios to alert the surveillance units on the street. I stationed myself by a window with a .308-caliber Remington sniper rifle. I would use it to give cover if Twymon and Freddie tried their spray-and-pray tactics on our guys.

A crew of NYPD detectives showed up in construction clothes and hard hats and started repairing potholes. John O'Neil, a veteran detective from Herman's robbery squad, added a note of gritty realism by springing for a couple of six-packs of beer, which he passed around at lunchtime.

All of a sudden Freddie Hilton showed up on the street. A skinny twenty-year-old, he looked like a high school kid. I leaned close to the windowsill as he stopped to watch the "crew" work. O'Neil turned his back on Hilton and drained a beer can. *There's no way Fred made him for a cop*, I chuckled.

I nestled my rifle stock into my shoulder, peering at Hilton through the scope. With its magnification, I could see a shape on his left side, at belt level. *A nine-millimeter Browning Hi-Power, I bet, and he's gotta have extra magazines.*

"Murph, put it out that he has a pistol in his waistband, left side, butt forward," I said, keeping my eyes fixed on Hilton.

A police siren wailed in the distance. As it drew closer, I could see Freddie turning his head right, then left, then scanning the upper floors of the buildings around him. I stepped back several feet inside the darkened room so that he couldn't see me. He put his hand on his gun. I clicked off the safety of my rifle. *Please, God, don't let him try to take out that sector car.*

"Oh, shit, here it comes, down to our left," Baker said. The crosshairs of my scope were aligned on Hilton's chest. I didn't have time to get back on target if I looked toward the car and he started shooting. He turned his back and slid sideways into the building's doorway, half-crouching, his back jammed against the side. If those patrolmen stopped in front of the doorway, Hilton could cut them down before they could draw their revolvers.

Baker let out his breath. "They're going past." The car cruised past Hilton and pulled over about sixty feet down the street. Hilton peered out, then stepped down onto the sidewalk and watched as the officers leapt from their car and ran into the next building. Hilton walked toward the empty police car, evidently intending to see if another officer remained inside. Then shots rang out from the roof of the building the policemen had entered. Hilton jumped and stared skyward.

Freddie, be cool. This isn't about you. Be cool, I chanted to myself, keeping my crosshairs on his chest. No need for a head shot here. The .308 would knock him down if I struck him anywhere in the upper torso. I couldn't afford to go for the head and miss. Freddie was still looking up at the roof when two of the "repair crew" jumped him from the rear.

As I saw him go down under about four hundred pounds of detective, I lowered my rifle and unscrewed my face. "This could have gotten real shitty," I grumbled to Murphy and Baker. "What the hell brought those guys down here?"

Only after Freddie was handcuffed and speeding away in the back of a police car did we find out what had caused the other Murphy, the one the law was named for, to raise his ugly head. Two NYPD plain-clothes detectives, one black and one white, had taken positions on the roof of a building across the street from us. If Hilton had tried to escape the dragnet by jumping from roof to roof, these men would have headed him off. Just as Hilton appeared on the street below, an elderly woman flung open the door at the top of the stairwell, spotted the two detectives, one of whom was toting a shotgun, and asked what they were doing. "Police business, ma'am," one explained. Still suspicious, she went back to her apartment, dialed 911, and reported them. The dispatcher fired off a radio call to the sector: "Report of burglary in progress, subjects armed."

The patrolmen who answered that call drew their guns, dashed up the stairwell, saw the detectives, and in the confusion, shot one of them in the foot. The last I heard the detective had a hell of a lawsuit against the department.

After his fingerprints and mug shot were taken at the precinct, we put Hilton into the back of an FBI car, sandwiched between McCartin and me, for the ride to federal magistrate's court in Manhattan. Murphy drove.

Hilton stared straight ahead, but as we bumped along, he gradually relaxed. Finally, he drew a breath and spoke. "Who are you guys, anyway?"

"Coulson."

"McCartin."

"Murphy."

"Oh, I heard of you guys," he said cockily. "We know who's chasing us, you know."

"Fred," I said, "if you know our names, why didn't you call us and arrange to come and surrender? Our number's in the book, you know."

His eyes sparkled maliciously. "You guys just don't get it, do you? We're at war. The people are at war with this fascist government. I'm a soldier on my side, and you're soldiers on your side, and we won't ever surrender."

I twisted around and looked square at him. "No,

Freddie, we're not at war," I said. "If we were at war, you'd have a great big hole in your chest from my rifle. I had you in my sights for about ten minutes. We were watching you from the time you walked up the block."

No one said a word for the rest of the ride into the city.

14

That afternoon Jim Murphy walked into the squad area.

"I think I know where Andrew Jackson is," he said. "My guy thinks he spotted Denise Oliver, who's with Andrew, and thinks he's seen Andrew too. It's a fifth-floor walk-up at One Hundred and Fifty-eighth and Amsterdam."

"Can we set up to take him on the street?" I asked. Going into an apartment was risky.

"Not a chance," Murphy replied. "He's scared to death. He never comes outside at all, afraid of all the heat."

"I wonder how you run a revolution if you never go outside," McCartin said slowly. "Hey, maybe that means the revolution is petering out."

Shortly before six o'clock the next morning, we dropped Joe at the building and waited around the corner as he picked the lock. In moments, the radio crackled. "I'm in." Joe had definitely missed his calling.

Erroll Myers and I grabbed our shotguns, blew through the door, and trotted lightly up the stairwell, followed by Murphy and Renaghan with the ram. Corless and Henry Schutts, the new Special Agent in Charge, recently arrived from headquarters, brought up the rear. Baker and two other agents took the stairs to the roof to cut off any escape.

Erroll and I stood on either side of the door, while Tommy and Jim swung the big ram and bashed the door open. I ran into the living room, then the kitchen. Once I cleared them with a glance, I rushed to catch up with Erroll, who had barged into the bedroom and now had his shotgun inches from Andrew Jackson's nose. Holding my shotgun steady with my right hand, I pulled back the sheets with my left hand, revealing a naked Denise Oliver. She let out a plaster-cracking shriek. I yanked her out of the bed and slung her by the arm toward Corless. He flung her backward. Schutts found himself holding an attractive nude woman who was screaming her head off.

Jackson's pistol lay on the nightstand, but he didn't go for it. Instead, he stuck his hands up in surrender, yelling, "Don't shoot, don't shoot." As Jackson was handcuffed, Schutts covered the lady with a sheet, at which point she calmed down.

I turned to Corless. "How come you gave the naked girl to the boss?"

"Looked like a job for the SAC." Corless grinned. "We need to get him used to this type of stuff."

"You guys owe me big time," Jackson announced as we drove to court. "I kept Twymon from shooting you."

"Oh, yeah?" I said. "Let's hear it."

After the Manufacturers Hanover robbery, he said,

Baker and McCartin came to the building where Twymon and he happened to be hiding in an abandoned apartment. Andrew and Twymon watched through the peephole as the FBI agents quizzed the super. How did they make McCartin and Baker for agents? Easy, Andrew snorted. Short haircuts and Baker's white shirt.

Twymon leveled his Browning Hi-Power, whispering, "This is our chance to kill an FBI agent."

"Fool, we gotta go," Jackson hissed. "There's cops swarming all over the place." But Myers was excited, jumping around like a kid on chocolate until Jackson, the bigger of the pair, wrapped his arms around him and held him until he settled down.

"Well, Andrew, thank you," I said. "Just remember you're alive to talk about it. Guess that makes us even."

He nodded and stared out the window.

Back at the office, McCartin was quiet for a long time. "That was creepy," he said at last. "You think Andrew was bullshitting?"

Murphy looked up from his paperwork. "Probably not. Twymon is a crazy son of a bitch."

"Hell, Bob, he would have shot you in a minute," I offered. "He probably wouldn't shoot Baker, though. Wouldn't want to put holes in that nice suit."

"Okay, I'm done," McCartin said, stacking his paper. "Let's get a drink."

McCartin seldom drank. He usually went straight home. This was about as close as he ever came to showing that anything fazed him. We headed for a neighborhood saloon Baker and I knew to be friendly and drank a beer or three. McCartin talked about his five kids. Baker ragged me less than normal. I think we were all feeling a little less bulletproof than we usually did.

I jammed those ideas back in the box. Thinking about dying was for poets, not folks in my line of work. If I gave in to it, I wouldn't last any longer than a batter who thought about swinging and missing.

The next day, I roared into work early, ready for more. *Pretty damn good,* I bragged to myself. *Guess they'll be teaching this one at Quantico.* The Jackson arrest went down just about perfect. It proved the value of our SWAT philosophy—scare the shit out of them, and they'll give up.

Little did I know. Years later, Corless disclosed to me that HQ actually reprimanded him for the way we arrested Jackson. Corless hadn't calculated the weight of the agents who hit Jackson's apartment and didn't do an engineering study of whether the landing would support the agents' bodies and gear. No matter that we had caught one of the most dangerous terrorists in the United States without spilling a drop of his blood or anyone else's. No matter that we had not violated any of Jackson's rights.

When Corless eventually recounted this bizarre turn of events, for once in my life I couldn't manage a smartass remark. "Why didn't you tell us?" I stammered.

"I didn't want you to think all the people we worked for were idiots."

"We thought that anyway."

"Well, I still didn't want to say it."

15

On August 25, 1973, the New Orleans police arrested about a dozen young black men who had perpetrated a series of bank robberies in the name of the BLA. While wrapping up the case, a New Orleans police officer took a hard look at a mug shot of Herman Bell, who was now on the FBI's Ten Most Wanted list. He recalled that he'd seen a man who looked a lot like Bell talking to a waitress at a local bar. He and his partners alerted the NYPD and the FBI, then trailed the waitress home, spotted Herman Bell emerging from the house, and arrested him.

The waitress, it turned out, was Bell's San Francisco girlfriend. After Bottom and Washington were arrested in San Francisco, Bell had taken his woman and their baby son to New Orleans, where she took a job and he proselytized young men to rob banks for the revolution.

One of his followers, Rubin Boris Scott, turned state's evidence and led the cops to a farm in the Mississippi Delta, near where Bell was born. Scott said he had seen Bell burying a gun there. Sure enough, the earth yielded up Joe Piagentini's service revolver, the one that had been taken from him as he lay dying in Harlem.

Assistant District Attorney Robert K. Tanenbaum of Manhattan took it from there. Herman Bell, Anthony Bottom, and Albert Washington were sent to prison for life for the first-degree murders of NYPD officers Joseph Piagentini and Waverly Jones.

The BLA West was finished, but the more numerous BLA East was still on the streets, and we didn't have a good handle on it.

That's when we were blessed with the second break. On September 17, 1973, a team of NYPD detectives hit a BLA crib in the Bronx and rousted out Avon White.

We desperately needed an insider, and because Avon was wanted for bank robbery but not murder, we could offer him a deal. Avon looked to be ripe for the picking. He was built like a defensive lineman, but he was only twenty-three years old, and he looked a little scared.

"Now's the time you've gotta start looking out for yourself because you're facing some heavy, heavy time here," McCartin told him in a fatherly way. "We've got you cold on bank robbery. There's some people who are going to go down real hard and go to jail for the rest of their lives. Avon, you need to choose."

"You're not walking," I added, "but we'll talk to the U.S. attorney. We want your cooperation. However much you help us will determine how much we help you."

Avon hesitated. *He looks interested. He's thinking, which for him is not easy.*

"I don't want to be in jail with any of these guys," he said warily.

Sold. I flicked my eyes at McCartin. He gave me the same look back.

"We can assure you you'll be in a separate facility," McCartin said.

Avon pondered this information. "Okay," he said finally.

McCartin and I pulled out a folder of bank-robbery and gang photos and started showing them to Avon, one by one. His job, we explained, was to pick out snapshots of himself and his buddies.

A few minutes into this process, a sly grin spread across his face and all 235 pounds of Avon shook like a bowl of Jell-O. "You guys think you're so smart," he guffawed. "You been talking to a person for months who spends every night with Twymon. You think the person is cooperating, but you're wrong."

McCartin and I looked at each other quizzically. Scores of people were being interviewed, some of them five or six times a week. Who'd been snookering us?

"Can't you figure it out, big-time FBI?"

"Okay, Avon. You got us," I said. "Who is it?"

"Phyllis Pollard. She's his old lady."

"Oh, shit. I can't believe it."

Phyllis was a known BLA associate. We talked to her regularly, and so did Detective Cliff Fenton.

Avon was enjoying his coup. "You got any more bank robbery pictures?"

Bob reached into the folder, grabbed a stack, and dropped them on the table. Avon flicked through them quickly and pulled one out.

"See this dude right behind the counter with a revolver? That dude is Phyllis."

"Naw, that's a guy."

"That's Phyllis. She ugly."

"Hey, one more question," McCartin pressed. "Tell us about the code." We had found evidence of coded messages in searches and on several people we had arrested. We sent scores of documents down to the FBI lab's cryptographers, but they were unable to break the code.

Now Avon was really full of himself. He leaned forward in his chair, took my pen, and wrote the words CURAD WHITE. Underneath each letter, he wrote a number from one to ten.

C U R A D   W H I T E
1 2 3 4 5   6 7 8 9 10

Thus, the address—251 West Fifty-seventh—would become UDCDH.

I laughed too. "How in the hell did you come up with that code?"

"We were all sitting out on a stoop one evening. We'd been trying to come up with a number code we could all remember. I looked down next to the garbage can and saw a Band-Aid box laying on the ground. It said Curad White. It had ten letters and none repeated. That's our code and we've used it ever since."

McCartin sat back in his chair as a big grin spread across his face. "Avon, you want a job when this is over? They could use a guy like you in the lab in Washington."

"I don't think so, man. Working for you guys could ruin my reputation."

Then he came out with a tale that would pop up in my nightmares for a long time to come.

A few months earlier, Avon said, Twymon Myers was walking up Jessop Street in the Bronx, heading for an apartment that served as a BLA safe house, when he saw a dark sedan pass him and pull to a stop. He made the vehicle for an unmarked government car. He figured the pair of young white men in the car were FBI agents.

"He thought about wasting both of them," Avon told us. Twymon had his Browning Hi-Power under his coat and extra magazines in his pocket. He would come up behind the agents, shoot them in the head, and run off. With his cap low on his brow, he was sure he wouldn't be recognized.

But then the agents did something that confused him. The redheaded one got out of the car and headed for the building, but the short, dark one stayed by the car for a few seconds and let his partner walk well ahead of him.

"Twymon thought he could get one of them," White explained. "But he was afraid that the other one would turn and shoot him. They were too far apart to kill both of them. He didn't want to get killed by the other fed. So he just crossed the street and kept on walking."

I got a prickly feeling on the back of my neck. Erroll Myers was a tall redhead. The short, dark agent Avon was talking about had to be me. Erroll and I had been up on Jessop Street, covering leads in the time frame Avon described. We knew about the apartment that was Twymon's destination. We had spent days in the neighborhood, interviewing everybody we could find about the BLA.

I was right about the lesson of The Battle of Algiers. *Walking thirty feet apart was the smart thing to do, if I do say so myself.*

I took notes as Avon spilled his guts. When he was done for the day, I thanked him nicely and handed him back to the jailer. Once he was out of earshot, I turned to McCartin. "Do you know who he was talking about?"

"Sure, it was you and Erroll. Had to be."

I breathed a deep sigh. "Do you know how many times we've all dodged a bullet from Twymon?"

"We'll never know how many times we've lucked out in this case. And probably in a few others too."

I allowed myself to contemplate that prospect for a few seconds, then shoved it into the box. Thinking about near-death experiences gives me an awful headache.

"I'm going to call the FBI lab and tell them what a bunch of dumb asses they are," I said.

Then we drove over to Cliff Fenton's office to break the news about Phyllis Pollard. "Shit," Fenton said. "You sure she's with Twymon?"

"Avon swears to it. Thinks it's a big joke."

Fenton had some news for us too. "We just got a tip from a source we don't know much about. He says he can give us the building and apartment number where Twymon is staying. Guess what. We've been covering leads two buildings away."

Cliff left a message for Phyllis with a friend. When she called, Cliff arranged to meet her at a coffee shop. There, Cliff quietly walked her out to a car where a couple of our agents arrested her on federal bank-robbery charges. This was for her own good, to keep her out of harm's way while we went after her boyfriend.

Then we prepared an arrest plan. Corless had been promoted to HQ, so we went to our new supervisor, Bill Jones, "We have to assume he's heavily armed," I said. "He has a Browning Hi-Power, a Swedish K submachine gun, probably some conventional grenades, and maybe a thermite grenade."

"Holy shit," said Jones, a former Marine artillery officer who was not easily impressed. "Have you guys ever seen what a thermite grenade can do? We used them in Vietnam to destroy artillery tubes. You want to call in an air strike on this guy?"

Jones was joking, of course, but he was dead serious about not going into Myers's apartment after him.

"We'll just wait for Twymon to come to us," he said.

I was relieved. I hadn't been looking forward to taking the point against a thermite grenade, which burns with a white-hot flame that melts metal and is practically impossible to extinguish. If it went off in a building, it would burn the whole place down, starting with yours truly.

We decided to blanket the neighborhood with black plainclothes cops and agents. We white guys would be in vans and cars all around the perimeter. Sooner or later, Twymon would have to move, especially if Phyllis didn't come home to the crib. He might come out to make some calls or split to a new location. If he figured out that we had her, he might be crazy enough to come down to the FBI office and try to break her out.

McCartin and I grabbed our trusty Hagstrom's map of the Bronx and sped north. Bob drove. Using a ballpoint pen, I made x's on the map to show where we needed coverage. Every time I radioed out a location where officers or agents should go, someone would respond that he would take that position. Bill Herman, John Clark, Jack Flynn, and all of the rest of the cops who had helped us find Johnny Rivers showed up. After all the months of work, no one wanted to miss this one. There would be scores of cops and agents all around the neighborhood, and every one of them knew what Twymon Myers looked like. We'd all been gazing at his picture every day for months.

As night fell, Bob eased our car onto the street near the apartment. I sat in the front seat with a shotgun in my lap and the map on the seat. Black detectives and agents strolled leisurely past us, as if they hadn't a care in the world. If they shared the fear I was feeling, none of them showed it. A six-foot-seven-inch giant wearing a BIG APPLE cap and bulky jacket sauntered by. "Pig motherfucker," he snarled, and spat on our fender. It was Jim McIntosh, FBI agent, a former college basketball star who was known around the office as Apples or Mac.

As you get ready to make an arrest, strange things happen to your senses. The first thing that I notice is a metallic taste in my mouth, as if I have a bunch of pennies and nickels on my tongue. My senses go into hyperdrive. My hearing and sight seem keener. My peripheral vision wraps around until I feel as if I have eyes in the back of my head. My palms get sweaty. As my body went through all those changes, I said a quick prayer. Most of my prayers are quick. *God, don't let anybody get hurt, and help me to do the right thing. I don't want to let anyone down.*

We knew that Twymon used the phone in a candy store on the east corner. We had positioned some agents and detectives one floor under his apartment. I hoped they would see him as he left the apartment and catch him in the confines of a hallway with no place to go and no innocent bystanders in the way. Other agent-cop teams were in the adjoining buildings.

I checked my new Smith & Wesson 59. No, the FBI Academy range guys, certified geniuses though they were, hadn't approved our request for high-capacity semiautomatics, but I had no intention of going up against a guy like Twymon Myers without an edge, so I had saved my money and surreptitiously bought myself a 59. So did several of my partners. We all knew HQ would butcher our careers if we were caught using unauthorized weapons. On the other hand, it wouldn't be any comfort to our widows and mothers to know that when we went down, it was in strict compliance with FBI rules and regulations.

Bob gripped the wheel, ready to give chase in the car or on foot. The radio crackled. It was a guy under Twymon's apartment. "We have somebody coming down the stairs. Can't make out if it's him or not. Too dark. We're going to let him go. If it's not him, we'll spook Twymon in his apartment. He's coming out. Someone check the candy store."

I had removed the bulb in the interior dome light in our car so that I could open the door without giving away our position. Bob started the car and I opened my door just a crack. I wanted to be able to get out quick if the shit hit the fan.

From across the street came another radioed message. "Possible subject coming down the steps, heading east toward the candy store, right description. Can't tell for sure. Heads up at the candy store and get ready."

The team closest to the store got a clear look at the man's face. It was Twymon all right, dressed in a heavy wool coat. Just as he crossed the threshold, NYPD detective Col Holland grabbed him by the shoulder. Twymon spun away, pulled his Browning, and opened fire. One shot struck Holland in the ankle.

Twymon ran to the curb, took cover behind a parked car, and started spraying the area. As he rose up slightly, FBI agent John Ford fired at him from across the street with one of those unauthorized, unreliable Smith & Wesson Model 59 pistols. A round struck Twymon in the cheek and knocked him to the ground. But he quickly righted himself and kept blazing away.

Bob and I sprinted down the sidewalk toward the candy store. I could hear rounds buzzing by my head and pinging on the car beside me. As I rounded the corner, I spotted McIntosh crouching behind a gumball machine, struggling to reload his old-fashioned five-shot Smith & Wesson revolver. He had obeyed the range guys and was now fresh out of options.

Bullets from cop and FBI guns sparked on the pavement and pelted the car that Twymon was using as a shield. McCartin fired two rounds from his .357 Magnum. Bob wasn't afraid of the range guys, he just trusted that big old Magnum, and now I could understand why. It sounded like a cannon compared to the pop-pop-pop of the thirty-eights and nine-millimeters everyone else was firing.

Bob's first round hit Twymon in the knee. He lurched forward. The second shot hit him in the chest.

Dear God, he's still moving! This guy's not human. His hands dropped toward his waist. *He's going for a grenade.*

I rushed him. This wasn't a heroic act. I was within fifteen feet of him. A retreat wouldn't put me or the others out of range of the white hell of a thermite grenade. The only thing to do was to get to him, grab his hands before he pulled the pin, and kick whatever he was going to throw at us down the sewer.

I dropped my shotgun, seized his shoulders as he slid to the ground, flipped him on his back, pulled his hands away from his body and pinned his right hand with my left knee. Then I grabbed his left hand with my right and locked my left hand onto his throat, flattening him into the pavement. Bob was beside me, reaching into Twymon's pockets for the grenade. Twymon looked into my eyes and I looked into his. Then his eyes went dim and rolled back into his head.

I held him down until an ambulance rolled up and Henry Schutts tapped me on the shoulder. "Danny, go with him to the hospital. Call me when you get the condition of the officers." My heart was pounding out of my chest. I handed Henry my shotgun. Bob and I grabbed Twymon and put him on a gurney. There were three other stretchers, for officers Col Holland, John Clark, and a bystander, all with leg or foot wounds. I said another quick prayer of thanks for the discipline of the officers and agents on the street. From the second I started my rush, none of our men had fired a single round.

It was red light and sirens all the way to the hospital. In the movies you would expect the ambulance carrying a brutal killer to go by way of Chicago, but Twymon got the same emergency ride as the cops and the citizen he had tried to murder. At Harlem Hospital ER, two doctors and a team of nurses attended to him as quickly as our wounded.

"He's dead," an ER doctor told me. "There's nothing we can do. We'll just have to take him downstairs. It gets pretty busy around here. We have live people to take care of."

An attendant and I pushed the body to the morgue in the basement. An aide undressed the corpse, labeled it with a toe tag, and lifted it into one of those gruesome morgue drawers.

I pushed it closed.

I caught the elevator back upstairs to check on our wounded, who were doing well. Then I noticed that I had blood on my hands. I stood at the sink and washed and washed. My hands and arms got clean, finally, but Twymon's blood stuck to my cuff.

I sat in a chair by the door and, for the first time that night, thought about what had happened. My mind traveled to the talk we had with Mrs. Myers. *That poor old woman, she'll cry for him if nobody else will.*

I wondered what was going on in Twymon's head when he looked into my eyes. Did he see himself dying gloriously for the revolution? I knew what was in my mind. I'd been filled with rage. He had shot two of my friends. I'd wanted him to die. I had thought of him as a psychotic criminal. Now all I could think of was how stupid all this bloodshed was.

As I sat in the chair, some attendants walked by with

yet another gurney. On it was a man with a long butcher knife sticking out from his chest. He was moaning softly. They parked him in the small room across from me. I just shook my head. *There sure are a lot of people who want to kill somebody tonight.* I heard a loud moan and a scream. The patient with the knife in his chest burst through the door, hollering and pushing nurses and attendants around like children.

I jumped up to try to help. Then I thought better of it. For just about the only time in my life, I walked away from a fight. I just stood there and watched as two orderlies muscled him back down onto a stretcher. Subduing a man in shock was beyond me at the moment.

I hitched a ride with another agent—I don't even remember who—and went back to the office. When I arrived at the squad area, Bill Jones was meeting with McCartin, agent Bob Fox, and Chief Harold Schrieber of the NYPD.

Jones greeted me warmly as I came through the door. "Doc, we were just talking," he said pleasantly. "Someone has to tell Phyllis what happened to her man. We don't want her to hear it on the news."

"Fine with me. Send someone to tell her."

"We are. It's you."

"Goddammit," I sputtered. "Why me? You get paid the big bucks. You do it."

"I get paid the big bucks to tell you to do it," Jones said as affably as before. "Besides, you know her."

"Okay, okay. Foxie, drive me down. I'm about tapped out."

I arrived at the Thirteenth precinct and walked into the detective bureau. An officer looked up from his desk. "Hi, Doc. What happened up there?"

"He's dead. Where's Phyllis?"

"Through that door."

I pushed the door open and peered into a dark room. Two metal folding chairs were in the very center. Phyllis sat on one and a small portable TV with rabbit ears sat three feet away. A black-and-white cowboy movie was flickering on the screen.

I carried a folding chair to her side and sat down next to her. She stared at the TV as if in a trance. Before I could speak, she cut me off.

"You had to kill him, didn't you?" she said in a flat voice, her eyes never leaving the screen.

"Yes."

"I knew you would. He never would be taken alive. He practiced constantly what he would do when you came. I knew he'd die."

"I'm sorry for you. We'll see you in a couple of days about the bank robbery. We have to wrap that up."

"I know, I'm just tired."

"Me too."

I got home about three o'clock in the morning. I unlocked the front door and walked up to my son's room. He was just a toddler, a bundle of energy who stayed still only when he slept. A night-light allowed me to see him. He was sleeping peacefully in his baby bed. He had those funny little pajamas with feet.

I just stood there and watched him sleeping for a few minutes. I wondered what baby dreams he was dreaming. *One mother's son chose a path to death tonight,* I thought. *This child will not.*

"He's dead. Where's Phyllis?"

"Through that door."

I pushed the door open and peered into a dark room. Two metal folding chairs were in the very center. Phyllis sat on one and a portable TV with rabbit ears sat three feet away. A black-and-white cowboy movie was flickering on the screen.

I carried a folding chair to her side and sat down next to her. She stared at the TV as if it in a trance. Before I could speak, she cut me off.

"You had to kill him, didn't you?" she said in a flat voice, her eyes never leaving the screen.

"Yes."

I knew you could kill. Oliver would be taken alive. He practiced control... Dr. ... he would do when you came. I knew he'd die?

"I'm sorry for you. We'll see you in a couple of days about the bank robbery. We have to wrap that up."

"I know. I'm just tired."

Me too.

I got home about three o'clock in the morning. I unlocked the front door and walked up to my son's room. He was just a bundle of energy who stayed still only when he slept. A night-light allowed me to see him. He was sleeping peacefully in his baby bed. He had those funny little pajamas with feet.

I just stood there and watched him sleeping for a few minutes. I wondered what baby dreams he was dreaming.

One mother's son chose a path to death tonight, I thought.

This child will not.

BOOK TWO

TO SAVE LIVES

It's a whole lot better to go up the river with seven studs than a hundred shitheads.

—COLONEL CHARLIE BECKWITH,
founder of Delta Force

1

One morning in early 1982, I got a call from John Byron Hotis, special assistant to Director William Webster.

"Doc, can you come up and see me? Judge Webster has given me the ticket on the proposal for the new tactical unit. I need to pick your brain."

I stopped what I was doing and caught the elevator for the seventh floor.

Yes, to everyone's surprise, most of all my own, I was now a lawyer at HQ. Joe Corless had talked me into transferring to Washington back in 1975, when Clarence Kelley was the director. "Sooner or later, you're going to get sick of working for other people," he told me. "You'll want to make your own decisions."

I took his point. Also it was a day job, and I'd have weekends free for making Lego castles with Little Doc. At times I had gone months without seeing him awake. Anyone who mentioned the FBI to my wife was not in for a cheerful response.

My first HQ job was working for Hotis, then the head of the Office of Congressional Affairs. I was the liaison to the congressional committees headed by Senator Frank Church and Representative Otis Pike; in the wake of Watergate, these committees launched wide-ranging investigations into illegal activities by the White House, the intelligence community, and the FBI. It was my happy task to give the committees security-division documents revealing that its COINTELPRO domestic intelligence program had illegally maintained at least a half million surveillance files on mostly law-abiding citizens. Also, I was in charge of handing over papers from Hoover's personal files that disclosed, among other things, the extent of the bugging and wiretapping of Dr. Martin Luther King, Jr. My reward for a job well done was another masochist's dream job, liaison to the House assassinations committee as it reexamined the investigations of the murders of President John F. Kennedy, his brother Robert, and King.

My experience on the Hill taught me, as no abstraction could, how immensely destructive the Bureau could be when it sacrificed law to what its leaders falsely imagined to be order. I spent countless hours with House Civil Rights Subcommittee chairman Don Edwards, a liberal California Democrat who was the Bureau's most dogged critic. We were poles apart ideologically, but I came to appreciate Edwards's libertarian instincts. Anybody who read the Hoover files, including me, came away with a healthy distrust of giving the FBI too much power. For the rest of my career, every time I had to make a tough call on a Bureau operation, I mentally ran the options through the Edwards gut test: What will Don Edwards say when he hears about this? Obviously, you can't run the FBI to please every politician, but you should always know what your critics are going to say. If you can't stand the heat, don't turn on the gas. At times I despaired that I had totally lost touch with the reasons I had joined the FBI. But I came away from the Hill a little wiser, a lot humbler and more tolerant, and less naive about politics than I had been when my world revolved around the culture of the field office.

Through it all, Hotis and I became fast friends. We debated arcane points of constitutional law while pumping iron in the HQ gym. John weighed in at about 165 and wore those wimpy half-glasses. Unless you saw him in the weight room, you'd never know that he was an ex-Marine who had arms like legs and was a charter member of the Three Club, the people who could bench-press over three hundred pounds.

Webster, a former federal appeals court judge and good-government Republican who took the Bureau's helm in February 1978, transferred me to the inspection staff and then, in 1981, made me Bureau disciplinarian. In my string of no-win paper-pushing HQ desk assignments, this was hands down the most thankless, but I consoled myself that Webster saw me as part of the solution, not part of the problem, and trusted me to do the job right.

Hotis, meanwhile, soared to a seventh-floor office that commanded a panoramic view of all of Pennsylvania Avenue and the Mall beyond—a tangible sign of his status as Webster's most valued adviser. Webster had met Hotis during his confirmation hearings and decided he was just the bright young man to help him drag the FBI into the late twentieth century. John had a law degree from Duke, a master's in law from Harvard, and a doctorate from Yale. His office was a jumble of books, articles, magazines, and unframed photos, and you were just as likely to find a volume of poetry as a law text. In place of the self-congratulatory plaques with which most HQ officials decorated their walls, John had real art that he bought himself. Also, Webster was impressed by Hotis's work with Attorney General Edward Levi and the congressional oversight committees in drafting guidelines to rein in the Security Division.

Talking to John got to be just as good as talking to the director. So when John called me to chat about a new concept for an FBI counterterror tactical team, I was in his office at warp speed. This was an idea that had crossed my mind only every day for the past ten years.

I could remember exactly when and where it planted itself in my brain: early on the morning of September 5, 1972. Bill Baker and I were humping around Manhattan, chasing leads in the NEWKILL case. The news came over the FBI car radio that at 4:30 A.M. European time, eight Palestinian commandos who called themselves Black September had burst into Olympic Village in Munich, killed two Israeli athletes and taken nine others hostage. The terrorists said all would be executed unless Israel freed two hundred Arab prisoners.

2

All day and into the night, Baker and I stayed glued to the radio and to the television after we finally got home.

Tomorrow it could be London, Athens, or Manhattan. Sooner or later everybody who was anybody showed up in the Big Apple. I muttered to Baker, "If it were going down here, you know who'd get the ticket."

"Yep," he replied bleakly. "Us, and we aren't ready for it." Since our SWAT teams weren't up and running yet, the regular violent-crime squads tackled whatever came along, from cop killers to aircraft hijackers, if they weren't too sophisticated. We logged so much time locking up crackpots we should have hung out a shingle that said "Nuts-R-Us."

Most of them were so inept that we didn't bother with a complicated arrest plan. It went something like this. *We'll hit the front door. You guys cover the back.* If they fought, we just knocked them upside their heads and grabbed their guns and their crummy little bombs. We took the BLA and the Weather Underground seriously, but we knew they had no intention of dying for their cause. Sometimes they did anyway, but it was purely accidental. All their talk about going out in a blaze of glory was just talk.

Black September, on the other hand, meant it and knew how to do it and take a lot of people along. Munich was our welcome-to-the-NFL moment.

Eighteen hours into the standoff—about ten o'clock at night, Munich time—a deal was struck, for a Lufthansa 727 and safe passage to Cairo. There was a news blackout for some hours and then, on the morning of September 6, came the announcement that all the athletes were dead.

The whole sorry story filtered out over the next day or two. The airplane had been a lure to dislodge the terrorists from their barricaded corner of the Olympic Village. West German Chancellor Willy Brandt had secretly issued orders not to let the plane leave the ground. The problem for the police commanders then became containing the fury of the terrorists once they realized they'd been lied to. More than five hundred German police and soldiers were deployed to the Munich airport, only to be kept milling in the rear while the commanders cast desperately about for a solution.

As the helicopters bearing the terrorists and their

captives were about to touch down on the airport tar-mac, five members of the Munich police sniper team were sent out to the front line and ordered to shoot the Palestinians on sight. As the terrorists disembarked from the choppers, the snipers opened fire, killing one man and wounding two others.

The guerrilla leader scrambled to cover and unleashed a barrage of machine gun fire that knocked out the control-tower radio system and jury-rigged floodlights. His comrades executed the hostages with machine guns and grenades. For the next hour and a half, with the bulk of the German troops still standing down, the snipers, now firing blind, traded potshots with the terrorists, until five Palestinians, including the leader, were dead. At that point, the remaining three surrendered.

The more I heard, the more outraged I became. What were the West German authorities thinking? To expect five sharpshooters to pick off eight terrorists in the dark, without night-vision scopes or backup, was just loony. After the first shots rang out and the terrorists declined to die on cue, it was no longer a rescue opera-tion, just a gunfight.

I ached for those poor snipers, having served as an FBI sniper myself on many stakeouts. I never actually had to fire a shot, but one thing you learn from staring at the world through crosshairs is that you're no James Bond. No matter how good you are, you can only shoot at one bad guy at a time. Those snipers had to know that the instant they squeezed off the first rounds, all hell would break loose, the terrorists would boil up like hor-nets, and it would be a miracle if anybody walked out alive. That the snipers managed to pick off five terrorists in pitch darkness attested to their superior marksmanship, but in law enforcement, unlike war, success is never measured by the number of adversaries killed. All that counts is lives saved, and the Germans scored zero.

The terrorists, on the other hand, had staged a publicity coup unparalleled in the history of criminality. The images of those hooded commandos, broadcast around the world, were indelible and would cast a long shadow on the international Olympics. Who could ever again play in the games or attend them or even watch them on television without remembering Munich and feeling a twinge of dread that it might happen again? And, of course, it probably would, now that Black September had shown how easy it was to bring the great powers to their knees.

As we Monday-morning-quarterbacked the events of Munich in our SWAT training and while sitting around the office, we came to some humbling realizations about our own situation.

"I can't see Nixon and Kissinger letting a bunch of twenty-year-old street guys humiliate them like that," McCartin remarked at one of our bull sessions.

"Yeah," Baker said. "There'd be a lot of saber rattling. Scabbard rattling, anyway. There would have been a hell of a siege. And we would've put more men into the fight. But we wouldn't have done any better."

"Hell, no," I said. "We can certainly take a shot and make it count, but no way we could've knocked out all eight at one time. When you get past the show, if it happened here, we would've failed too."

I hope somebody above my pay grade is thinking about this. But they weren't. The movers and shakers in Washington seemed totally preoccupied with Watergate and Vietnam. The great issues of the day concerned me too, but not as much as catching crooks and staying alive. If a gang of extremists grabbed a busload of people at, say, the Statue of Liberty or Yankee Stadium, the guys looking down the business ends of a bunch of black-market AK-47s would be me and my buddies.

I collected every newspaper and magazine article I could locate about international terrorism. I peppered the firearms instructors and, later, our SWAT instructors with questions and ideas about how we might improve our tactics. Even after I was transferred and left active SWAT duty, I kept up on developments in the tactical-operations field by combing Bureau monographs and after-action reports on what are now called "high-threat tactical operations." I had to assume that if the balloon went up, the Bureau would throw every warm body with tactical experience into the thick of things.

Other agents who had earned their bones on SWAT teams or violent-crime squads, or both, were thinking along the same lines. At in-service SWAT sessions, I'd hear the same words, over and over: "We're not ready for the big one." None of us doubted that we could win any gunfight we got into. But we'd almost surely lose the hostages. We were pretty much clueless until the Israelis showed us how it was done, at a hellhole called Entebbe.

On June 27, 1976, eight pro-Palestinian guerrillas hijacked an Air France airliner to the airport at Entebbe, Uganda, where they were granted protection by the left-ist dictator Idi Amin. The hijackers announced they would execute the 105 passengers and crew unless Israel released fifty-three jailed Palestinians. In the middle of the night of July 3, 1976, as the terrorists were on the verge of making good their threat, a hundred Israeli commandos landed their blacked-out C-130s on the tarmac, collected the hostages, killed seven terrorists and twenty-two Ugandan soldiers, and destroyed Amin's MiG fighter fleet for good measure. Four Israelis lost their lives—three hostages shot in the cross fire and Colonel Jonathan "Yoni" Netanyahu, the strike-force leader and brother of future prime minister Benjamin Netanyahu.

Among the wounded at Entebbe was a West German observer named Ulrich Wegener. After its humiliation at Munich, the Bonn government had assigned Wegener to create a counterterror force called the GSG-9 (Grenzschutz-Gruppe-9, or Border Protection Group 9). Wegener was training with Israeli counterterror specialists when the Entebbe raid was launched.

The GSG-9 team soon faced its own test. In October of 1977, a Lufthansa flight was hijacked by two Palestinian men and two women and forced to fly six thousand miles over four days, ending up in Mogadishu, Somalia. After murdering the pilot, the leader, a ranting sadist who called himself Captain Mahmoud, packed the cabin walls with plastic explosives, sprinkled the eighty-two passengers with liquor, and announced the plane would be blown up within minutes if Germany did not pay him $15 million and liberate the jailed Baader-Meinhof gang.

German state minister Hans Jurgen Wischnewski flew to Mogadishu and tricked the terrorists into believing that the demands had been met. The lie gave Wegener and his team time to land their darkened 727 at the far end of the airstrip and haul ladders to the aircraft's doors. Wischnewski sent an "urgent" radio message that lured the gang into the cockpit. At that instant, the commandos fired stun grenades into the cabin and raced down the aisle, cutting down the terrorists as they emerged from the cockpit door. Three Palestinians were killed, the fourth injured. None of the passengers or commandos were seriously hurt. The operation was over in ten minutes.

Free-world governments were beginning to catch on. France's GIGN (Groupement d'Intervention de la Gendarmerie Nationale) distinguished itself by rescuing thirty children from Somali terrorists in 1976. The British government's counterterror force, the Twenty-second regiment of the Special Air Service, demonstrated its prowess in May of 1980, when six men from Iran's Arab-speaking province of Khuzestan seized the Iranian embassy on Prince's Gate and took twenty-one hostages, including three Britons. Six days into the siege, the men tossed an Iranian diplomat's corpse out the front door and announced a hostage would die every half hour unless Tehran freed ninety-one Khuzestani political prisoners. Within minutes, twenty SAS commandos breached the embassy's roof and windows with explosives, leapt through the holes, and shot the Khuzestanis as they opened fire on the hostages. One Iranian hostage died. The rest escaped injury, as did the commandos. SAS leader Michael Rose, who would later serve as the United Nations commander in Bosnia, was awarded the Queen's Gallantry Medal for his group's performance.

The first U.S. counterterror team, First Special Forces Operational Detachment-Delta, was established in 1978, in the wake of a hostage crisis that gripped the nation's capital. In March of 1977, a handful of members of the Hanafi Muslim sect simultaneously assaulted three Washington buildings—B'nai B'rith headquarters, a mosque on Embassy Row, and the city hall—killing a radio reporter, wounding Washington's future mayor Marion Barry, and taking some 150 hostages. The D.C. police and the FBI Washington field SWAT team were stymied. Luckily for everyone, the ambassadors of Egypt, Iran, and Pakistan read the Koran and prayed with the Hanafi leader until he surrendered, thirty-nine hours into the standoff.

The incident forced President Carter and his senior advisers to face the fact that the next time might not be negotiable. Carter authorized the supersecret unit known as Delta Force. Delta's father was Colonel Charles "Charging Charlie" Beckwith, a Green Beret and Vietnam vet who had trained in unconventional warfare with the Twenty-second SAS. He modeled Delta on the SAS, and the two teams frequently trained together at the SAS base in Hereford, England, or the Delta compound at Fort Bragg, North Carolina.

To this day, the Army doesn't admit there is such a thing as Delta, but its cover was blown by the Desert One catastrophe of April of 1980. Delta commandos had landed in the Iranian desert, aiming to rescue the fifty-three Americans held hostage by Iranian radicals since the previous November. One of the Navy helicopters sent to ferry them to Teheran collided with an Air Force C-130 transport and caused a fuel truck to blow up, killing eight Air Force airmen and Marine helicopter pilots. This heartbreaking accident was not of Delta's making. If a bus hauling the Denver Broncos to the Super Bowl crashed, we wouldn't say the team lost the game. I thought it grossly unfair that the affair tarnished Delta's public image. Inside the international brotherhood of tactical guys, the commando team retained its luster, attracting the best and brightest people in the

Army. Delta was, and is, known for its superb planning process, its scientific approach to assaults, and its extraordinary marksmanship and physical training. It is equal or superior to any other counterterror force in the world.

The U.S. Navy formed its own counterterrorist unit, SEAL Team Six, in August 1980. SEAL Team Six probably had the most difficult counterterrorist mandate of any unit in the world: rescuing hostages on ships, ocean liners, and boats on the high seas, as well as neutralizing terrorists on oil platforms and other targets at sea. Richard Marcinko, its first commander, was a Vietnam vet known for doing the hardest jobs in the most outrageous manner. He competed ferociously with Beckwith. I once asked him if his mandate extended to a puddle of water on a landing strip where a hijacked airplane was parked. "Yup," he said, nodding. "That's enough water to call in the SEALs."

3

The creation of Delta and SEAL Team Six didn't mean the rest of us could rest easy. Our homegrown yahoos didn't dress as sharp as Abu Nidal's boys, but they could kill you just as dead, especially now that every bicycle thief and gang-banger in America didn't leave home without a Colt AR-15 assault rifle or at least a nine-millimeter pistol with a fourteen-round magazine.

Our SWAT teams still weren't up to the threat, and they knew it. While Delta and SEAL Team Six were developing surgical shooting skills for dynamic—meaning fast-moving—hostage rescues, FBI SWAT guys were still making it up as they went along. Readiness was a joke. SWAT teams practiced together once or twice a month, like military reservists, but concentrated primarily on their regular caseloads. Their guns and gear were ancient, for which they blamed the Academy's firearms training unit, which had run the SWAT training program since its inception. The range guys were the best marksmanship instructors in the world. No one knew more about how to get a bullet from point A to point B. But they didn't have a clue about what we were up against in the real world. The range guys still insisted that the FBI's official sidearm had to be the trusty old revolver, with the same capacity as the ones packed by Wyatt Earp. Many agents had taken to carrying unauthorized semiautomatics, as my buddies and I had done since 1972. Still, it was a hell of a thing to have to choose between your safety and your career. It was not until 1990 that ordinary field agents were given permission to switch to high-capacity guns.

Another dispute arose concerning our combat shooting stance. The range guys were still teaching the agents to shoot from the hip, holding their pistols with one hand, exactly as it had been done when the Bureau took down John Dillinger. Younger marksmen were interested in exploring a new shooting technique developed by competition shooters and adopted by a number of big-city police departments. In the so-called Weaver method, the shooter held his gun at eye level with two hands and sighted down the barrel. This technique was

more accurate and faster than hip-shooting, which
meant it was safer for officers and bystanders alike, but
the more senior range guys wouldn't hear of it. Nor were
they interested in the cutting-edge gear sported by some
police SWAT teams. Frustrated Bureau SWAT guys took
to scrounging and bartering with military bases and
National Guard units for lighter body armor, load-
bearing vests, better communications equipment, and
even extra ammunition.

The SWAT teams' urgent pleas for more advanced
weapons, technology, and tactics reached the ears of Jim
McKenzie, the assistant director who was in charge of
the FBI Academy and the SWAT training program.
McKenzie, one of the youngest FBI executives ever to
make ADIC, realized the SWAT program had to be reinvented and had the guts to make it happen.

In late 1978, McKenzie wrested control of SWAT
from the range and handed it over to Conrad (Connie)
Hassel, a chain-smoking ex-Marine who had seen action
in Korea and Vietnam, had a master's degree in crimi-
nology and ran a small shop—a sort of SWAT think
tank—called the Terrorist Research and Management
Staff. Working out of a windowless room in the
Academy's basement, sandwiched between the gun-
cleaning room and Hoover's old fallout shelter, Hassel
and his staff started studying things like hostage negotiations, crisis management, and the personalities and
causes that drove terrorist groups around the world.

McKenzie renamed Hassel's outfit the Special
Operations and Research Unit (SOARU), and brought in
behavioral scientists and psychologists. To modernize
SWAT tactics, McKenzie and Hassel drafted a clique of
young firearms instructors recently transferred to

Quantico from various field offices. They scared the hell out of the older range guys. Naturally, the SWAT teams loved them.

Installed at SOARU, they were nicknamed "the wild bunch." The range guys had a hundred reasons why you couldn't do something, but the wild bunch had a hundred ways to do it and would usually show up to help. Jim Adams and Tase Bailey, former Marine officers with Vietnam combat experience, knew close quarter battle and air operations. Bob "the Rock" Taubert taught the surgical use of submachine guns. Ed Kelso and Bowen Johnson, the explosives experts, were inventors and improvisers who could usually be found at their desks, making grenade simulators into flash-bang diversionary devices or door-breachers. Roger Nisley, whose height and piercing eyes reflected his Cherokee Indian heritage, was a fine shot, a black belt, and a strategic thinker who approached every problem the way Bobby Fischer eyed a chessboard, seeing ten or twenty moves ahead. Don Bassett specialized in crisis management. He could turn a field phone, a manual typewriter, and a couple of orange crates into a forward command post.

John Simeone, a gregarious former St. Louis cop who could talk his way into anywhere, went out in search of military counterterror techniques and equipment that could be adapted for law enforcement. Before long, he had a Rolodex of contacts inside Delta, the SEALs, the SAS, GSG-9, the Israeli military, and GIGN. Simeone cleverly parlayed SOARU's relative poverty into an asset. The FBI was no threat, so commandos who had never talked tradecraft with rival outfits—the Army and Navy, for instance, and the French, Germans, and Brits—traveled to the FBI Academy and traded toys and war stories.

Charlie Beckwith took a shine to Simeone—characters attract, I guess—and invited the SOARU agents to join Delta in exercises. That was a rare treat, because the Delta's inner sanctum—Fort Bragg's former brig, off-limits to all but a favored elite—was cluttered with wonderful state-of-the-art stuff. The FBI agents were eager students of Delta's innovations in gathering and using tactical intelligence, breaching—explosive entry techniques—and instinctive shooting, in which an operator entered a room, engaged his target as quickly and effectively as possible, yet spared any hostages.

But Hassel, Simeone, and the other agents taught the commandos one important fact of life. If they got involved in a crisis on U.S. soil, they could forget about secrecy. Everybody was going to know who they were, what they did, and also how, where, and with what. For agents who spent much of their adult lives in prosecutors' offices and courtrooms, this was obvious. But to Delta and the SEALs, who seldom left the military cloister, it was strange and shocking news. They had somehow gotten it into their heads that they could pull a who-was-that-masked-man act, as the SAS did at Prince's Gate. For example, while war-gaming hostage-taking scenarios in preparation for the 1980 Olympics at Lake Placid, New York, a Delta officer said breezily, "You give us FBI credentials for cover. We'll take this thing down and drift away."

"You can't do that," Simeone replied. "There are all kinds of laws involved. You can't disguise yourselves as FBI agents. We're responsible for our actions."

"The CIA would let us do it," the officer persisted.

"That's in a foreign arena," Simeone said. "This is domestic. And you can't just drift away. There would almost certainly be a federal grand jury. There would probably be a congressional investigation. And maybe a New York grand jury." Even if the terrorists were foreigners, even if they replicated the horrors of Munich, there would still be an inquiry into whether government authorities were justified in using deadly force. Those who engaged the terrorists would likely be cleared, but they would still have to submit to the process.

"You mean, if I shoot these people, you'll take me into *court*?" Beckwith shouted incredulously.

"That's right," Simeone replied. And not only that, all Delta's weapons would be seized and submitted to ballistics tests to determine which gun had fired what shots. Beckwith's men found this an unbelievable heresy. Their guns were custom-made to fit their hands, and anyway they didn't want strangers touching their stuff. "We'll *never* give up our weapons," stormed a Delta colonel.

"If you don't give them to us, we'll subpoena everything in your gun vault," Simeone replied evenly. "If we don't, the defense lawyers will."

Then, Simeone went on, there was the question of civil liability. Everybody from individual commandos up through the chain of command to the Secretary of Defense himself could be sued in civil court by a suspect's family, or by the suspect himself, if he survived, or by any hostage or bystander hit by a ricochet. The FBI and the U.S. Attorney General were constantly being sued. Most of the suits were eventually dismissed, but agents were accustomed to months, even years, of legal wrangling. And God help any soldier who forgot where he was and hosed down a room with his M-16. He could be indicted for manslaughter or even murder.

A murder rap? Beckwith got cold feet. He decided

Delta's operations were best kept overseas and in the black.

It took a little longer for the message to reach higher-ranking officials in Washington. The top managers at both the Pentagon and FBI HQ hadn't spent much time thinking the idea through and persisted in the belief that the military teams would resolve any important confrontations with terrorists.

A moment of truth came in the spring of 1981, during a SOARU-sponsored hostage-rescue exercise code-named Masquerade. After observing Delta and the Washington Field Office's SWAT team play out a hostage-rescue scenario, senior officials from FBI HQ, Justice, and the Pentagon took part in a tabletop exercise that simulated the pressure-cooker atmosphere of a crisis command post.

At one point, General James Vaught, head of the Pentagon's task force on terrorism, spouted the military's conventional wisdom: "Just give us a cup of coffee, and we'll go in there and do what we have to do, and then we'll get into our helicopters and fly off into the sunset."

Into the sunset? John Otto, the FBI's executive assistant director, threw his hands over his head. Someone from SOARU spoke up. Oh, no, Delta couldn't just go home. There would be all sorts of things to do after the smoke cleared—evidence to be gathered, forensics tests, firearms examinations. The operators would need to give grand jury testimony, of course, and . . .

Testimony? Now the grunts of dismay came from the Pentagon VIPs. No way. Training Delta operators was a long, expensive business. If they were forced to appear, even in a grand jury, their covers would be blown. They could no longer work undercover to collect intelligence and conduct surveillances overseas.

There was a lot of flapping around until the State Department representative remarked dryly, "You don't have to worry. The President will never authorize the use of the military in the United States." The Posse Comitatus Act, passed during the Reconstruction period, prohibited the use of the military for civilian law enforcement unless the President issued a written waiver. Ronald Reagan or any other President was highly unlikely to do so, except under the most extraordinary circumstances. "Americans will never accept it," said the man from State.

"Well, who's gonna do it if the military doesn't?" Otto asked.

"The FBI," the State Department man replied.

"But the FBI doesn't have the capability," Otto protested.

"I suggest," the diplomat said, "you get ready to do it."

Otto returned to HQ and gave Director Webster the news. Which, from Webster's point of view, was not good. One of the worst blotches on the Bureau's reputation was the disastrous 1973 siege at Wounded Knee, South Dakota. In that instance the American Indian Movement had occupied Wounded Knee as a protest against the U.S. Bureau of Indian Affairs. The Nixon administration panicked and overreacted, deploying dozens of FBI agents and U.S. marshals to surround the Indian encampment. During the seventy-one-day siege, inexperienced, poorly supervised agents and deputy marshals swathed in camouflage gear engaged in pointless firefights with the Indians, killing two protesters and wounding two others. A deputy marshal and an FBI agent were badly hurt as well. Webster was appalled that acting director L. Patrick Gray had let the Bureau get sucked into this bloody, foolish paramilitary venture. He swore that no such thing would happen on his watch.

Besides, keeping a counterterror team in constant readiness was expensive. It cost tens of thousands of dollars to train an FBI agent, and then there was his or her salary. Military salaries were lower. Young commandos were a lot cheaper, to be perfectly crass about it.

On the other hand, Webster didn't relish the thought of FBI SWAT operators standing around helplessly, as had happened at the Hanafi Muslim siege. What if the big one popped at, say, the Los Angeles Olympics in 1984? Was Webster going to tell President Reagan the FBI didn't do terrorists? No, he certainly wasn't.

So, if the FBI was going to get the ticket, we had better be ready for it. Webster sent word to McKenzie to put SOARU to work on something like a civilian equivalent of Delta.

The wild bunch probably had a beer or three over that one. Webster couldn't know it, but McKenzie, Hassel, and the other SOARU men had been working on that very idea for quite a while, only they hadn't figured out how to sell it to HQ. They had intensified their efforts some months before, when they realized that people in Washington had no idea how far behind the curve the SWAT program had fallen. Also, Roger Nisley had noticed a Justice Department bulletin declaring that the FBI had the capability to rescue hostages from hijacked airplanes. This, of course, was ridiculous. An aircraft rescue required intricate maneuvers, timed to the split second, that could only be accomplished by a tactical team with full-time, intensively-trained, well-equipped agent-operators possessing exceptional physical and marksmanship skills. Part-timers, however brave and heavily armed, couldn't come close. Nisley read the bulletin aloud in the SOARU bullpen. There were hoots of derision until somebody piped up, "Hey, guys, this is no laughing matter."

McKenzie listened quietly as the SOARU agents made their pitch. "It'll never fly," he said, shrugging, and strolled back to his office.

But at about five the next morning, everybody in the unit got a telephone call from McKenzie. "I couldn't sleep," he said. "You guys are onto something. Write me a proposal."

They produced a white paper and drove to Washington to present it to a gathering of the Bureau's top executives—who nearly threw them out of the Hoover building. The FBI culture glorified bright generalists who could be thrown into a case and solve it. It had a strong aversion to anything that smacked of an elite unit. "You guys have heard too many caps go off," John Otto snapped.

And that was that—until Webster got interested and assigned John Hotis to bird-dog the project. McKenzie and Simeone arranged a series of briefings and demonstrations for Webster and Hotis, culminating with a tour of the Delta compound at Fort Bragg. Delta and SEAL Team Six staged a rescue and takedown exercise, a spectacular sound-and-light show whose message was, these are the best run-jump-and-shoot guys in the business. Then came the "junk on the bunk" drill, in which Webster was to meet the commandos one by one, chat about their specialties, and look at their equipment.

As they made their way through Delta quarters,

Webster whispered to Simeone, "What do they have that we don't have?"

"Lots of things," Simeone whispered back. Delta had night-vision equipment, breaching and diversionary devices, communications gear, body armor, advanced weaponry, electronics of all sorts—the list went on and on.

Webster nodded sagely and took a closer look at the array of guns and gizmos. But there seemed to be something missing. He turned a puzzled face to Major General Richard Scholtes, commander of the Joint Special Operations Command, who oversaw Delta, SEAL Team Six, and other DOD counterterror activities.

"I don't see any handcuffs," Webster said.

"We don't have handcuffs," Scholtes responded crisply. "It's not my job to arrest people."

Oh? Oh! Webster's eyebrows curved like his beloved St. Louis arch as the realization dawned that since the military resolved situations with bullets, there might be no one left to be taken to jail. Scholtes's remark had conjured up a nightmare scenario that could make Kent State look like a picnic.

Webster brooded all the way back to Washington. The no-handcuffs story would become part of Quantico lore. As the story was told and retold, Scholtes was inevitably described as a gung-ho war-fighter with a bloodthirsty glint. This was not fair to Scholtes, who understood the legal, political, and security hazards of engaging terrorists on American soil and emphatically did not want the mission. He told me, years later, that he had deliberately calculated his remark in hopes of provoking Webster into moving ahead with an FBI counterterror team. Webster had been deliberating the idea thoughtfully and slowly, like the judge he had been. So, Scholtes said, he thought he'd try to nudge Webster off the dime.

Scholtes knew his man. He made a lasting impression on the director. When Webster got back to Washington, he told Hotis he would likely move the plan, if his remaining reservations were put to rest.

At that point, Hotis brought me in.

"You know, Quantico has done a good job with this project," he said. "They've convinced me that our SWAT teams can't handle a serious situation like Prince's Gate, and we all know the Army doesn't want to do a job inside the United States. Frankly I don't want them to do jobs in this country."

"Well, what's the problem?" I said, shrugging. "Write the memo and recommend to the Judge that he approve the concept."

Hotis leaned back in his chair and took off his sissy glasses.

"Webster is very concerned that we not create a commando unit. He says he doesn't want a bunch of colonels sitting around Quantico sharpening their bayonets. He wants them to think and act like FBI agents. The problem is, how do we insure that they don't become commandos, that they remain FBI agents?"

"It's pretty straightforward," I said. "You pick the right leader, give them a mission statement, and monitor what they do and how they train."

Hotis nodded. "That's my position too."

If I had been a little faster on the uptake that day, it would have occurred to me that he knew very well how I felt about FBI agents who forgot who they were. He must have heard my rant about the Pine Ridge investigation a hundred times. The episode was a big reason I opted out of the field and went to HQ.

It happened back in June 1975. My New York field SWAT team, along with dozens of other agents from New York and elsewhere, was deployed to the Pine Ridge Indian Reservation in South Dakota to track down the assassins of FBI agents Jack Coler and Ron Williams, who had been ambushed and shot in the head, execution style, while investigating the murder of an Indian-rights activist named Jeanette Bisonette.

When I drove up to our motel in Rapid City, I was horrified to see three range guys dressed in camouflage utilities, their pants bloused into their boots. One actually had on a tiger stripes, a jungle cammy pattern worn in Vietnam. And a black beret! I didn't know what was worse, these guys' arrogance or their ignorance. If they had done the least amount of reading, they would have known that the people of Pine Ridge were paranoid about the U.S. government, with good reason. The reservation was the site of the infamous massacre of 1890, in which the U.S. Army Cavalry had slaughtered three hundred Indians, mostly women and children, encamped beside Wounded Knee Creek. Then there was our needlessly bloody confrontation with AIM at Wounded Knee in 1973.

If we were to have any hope of solving the Coler-Williams case, we'd have to have the cooperation of the local people, which would be tough enough without the insult of FBI agents decked out like *Soldier of Fortune* centerfolds. Just about everybody in Pine Ridge had a gun or two and had been hunting game since childhood. Stirring up antigovernment passions was a good way to get somebody shot. I assembled the New York agents and announced that our dress of the day was blue jeans. Weapons were to be covered by a shirt or jacket, and shoulder weapons would stay in the cars until there was some indication they were needed. No matter what those idiots from the range did, we would remember that we were not the Army and would not look like the Army.

After that, the murder investigation went well enough. Eventually our prime suspect, AIM activist Leonard Peltier, would be convicted of the murders and sentenced to two life terms. But I made myself a promise. *Next time I go on a mission, I'm going to run it. And everybody who works for me is going to look and act like a professional. The people we meet are going to remember us kindly and tell their boys, "Now, that was a man."*

Something about Hotis's smile suggested he remembered my screed. But he just said, "I have to work this out and then convince him that we should do it. I'm even struggling with the name for the team."

I shook my head. "Do you think the name makes that much difference?"

"Of course it does. The name should remind them of why we need a team. As far as I'm concerned, there is only one reason to go forward with this project, and that's to keep people alive in hostage situations. What do you think about calling it the Hostage Rescue Team? HRT?"

"Well, it certainly has a high-sounding ring to it, kind of like apple pie, motherhood, and Chevrolet. Not much doubt about what their job is. Webster would like that, I'm sure."

Hotis nodded his head happily. He liked it when I

agreed with him. "Some people have suggested Super SWAT."

"That sounds pretty stupid."

"Well, it's not as bad as Killer Bees. That came up at the executive conference."

"Are you serious?"

"No, it was just a joke, but some people just don't like the idea at all and ridicule it every chance they get."

I got up out of my chair. "Got to run. Paperwork, you know. When are you going to straighten up this mess? Looks like a bomb hit this place."

As I grabbed the knob, Hotis finally got around to the real reason for the meeting. "Doc, are you interested in this?"

"You're damned right I am. But Quantico will push one of their own to run it. No one will want a lawyer in charge. No one likes lawyers. I'm not sure I like them either."

"You might be surprised," Hotis said coolly. "If this gets approved, throw your hat in the ring."

"Don't worry, I'll give it a chance. Anything would be better than working in this building."

Before long, a communication went out to the field announcing that FBI HQ was creating a new position, Assistant Special Agent in Charge to command the HRT. I filled out an application, walked down the hall, and paused to steel myself outside the office of my supervisor, the executive assistant director in charge of administration—the great and powerful Oliver B. "Buck" Revell.

4

Whenever I walked into Big Buck's office, I was always
afraid that if I screwed up, he would just pick me up and
toss me out into the hall, or out his window onto
Pennsylvania Avenue. This fear was totally illogical. The
seventh-floor windows were plate glass, several inches
thick, and could neither be opened nor penetrated by
my 160-pound frame.

The Buckster was on the large size of huge—six foot
four and somewhere between 215 and 275 pounds,
depending on whether you asked him or his wife,
Sharon. He had an ego so big the joke around the
Bureau was, "We gave Buck a zip code but he wanted an
area code." The other thing to know about Buck was that
he had the temperament of a mother grizzly. If he was
on your side, you could sit back and enjoy watching him
crush everything in your path. If, on the other hand, you
got crossways with Buck, it was ugly.

When I was on the Hill, I sometimes arranged for
Buck to brief congressional staff members on our proposed legislation. Hill staffers tend to be young and
cocky, and some are downright obnoxious. Buck never
understood why they were so deferential to him. Simple.
Before I ushered him through the door, I called ahead to
say he had a terrible temper and if they pissed him off,
he would reach across the table and squeeze their heads
like grapes. He thought I had smoothed the way for him
and was properly appreciative.

Like everybody else, occasionally I caught the full
measure of Revell's wrath. There was the time I disci-

plined an agent who had gotten into a fistfight with a construction flagman on George Washington Parkway. Phil King, a former Navy diver, was inching along in a line of cars merging into one lane when the flagman became enraged for some reason and started beating King's car with his flagpole.

When King got out of the car, the flagman threatened to whack him with the flag. King punched him and knocked him to the ground. Someone called the police. The officer decided not to cite either man. The whole thing came to absolute zero, except that King dutifully reported the incident to his supervisor, who referred it to the Office of Professional Responsibility. OPR investigated and sent a short recital of facts to my disciplinary unit. We decided to recommend that Revell give King an "oral admonishment."

I pitched the completed report into my out box and waited for the bomb to go off. When the telephone rang, I picked up the receiver and stretched out my arm full length to protect my eardrums.

"Coulson! This is Buck! Get up here. I just got your package on the guy who thinks he's a boxer. I cannot believe your recommendation!"

As I walked out the door, my assistant Doug Ball looked up from his desk and gave me a mortician's grin. "I'll notify your next of kin."

"I'm not afraid of Buck," I lied.

Buck's secretary gave me a warm smile. "Boy, are you in trouble."

"Thanks."

Buck was seated behind his Buick-size mahogany desk in a high-backed leather chair. Files were piled around the edges of his desk and papers were spread all over the top. He lit a match to the bowl of his pipe. The swirling smoke made his head look like Mount Saint Helens.

As Buck began to rant, I sat stoically, nodding my head when it seemed appropriate.

"I can't believe that you recommended an oral admonishment for this guy. He acted like a jerk. We can't have our guys going around and getting in fights over traffic disputes. I thought you were a lawyer. Where did you go to law school?"

"SMU."

"That's the problem. Is that school accredited? He must really think he's a tough guy. I can't believe you didn't recommend suspension or at least a letter of censure!"

As Buck talked, he sucked on the pipe until it was a raging furnace. Every few minutes, he took the pipe from his mouth and waggled it at me for emphasis, sending a great black cloud of smoke billowing over his head.

"You just give me one good reason why I shouldn't give him fifteen days on the bench."

"Well, Buck, he won the damned fight. We need people who know how to win fights."

Revell exhaled with a mighty whoosh, blowing fiery embers into the air. Sparks and ashes floated onto his jacket, singeing it, and onto some important documents. He started slapping his flounder-sized hands on his desk, beating out small fires that were erupting from his papers.

"Won the fight!" he thundered, still smacking the smoldering papers. "Won the fight! I'll show him a fight. You call him right now and tell him the next time he gets into a fight, I will personally take him behind the barn and show him a real fight. Do you understand?"

"Yes, sir. Is there anything else?"

"No. You just be sure that you call him personally. Now get out of here."

I backed smoothly out of his office, like the butler in a Fred Astaire movie. "You always cause trouble in here," the secretary said. "Should I call the fire department?"

"No, I don't think a fireman would want to go in there for a while. See ya."

Phil King was extremely grateful. He promised to be a good boy. He had no desire to meet the Buckster behind the barn.

Fortunately, Buck's rages blew over like storms at sea. We were trading jokes the next day. I admired his intellect and especially his guts. We lived in a city of butt coverers and handwringers who lived by the motto "Don't make a decision unless someone else can take the blame." Buck didn't second-guess himself. What Buck liked about me, as far as I could tell, was my habit of telling him what I thought. He didn't always like what I had to say, but at least he knew I was giving him an honest opinion.

Officially, the career board, an assembly of midlevel FBI officials, was in charge of reviewing applications for the job of HRT commander. Their recommendation would go to the director, who would discuss it with the executive conference. The Buckster's vote outweighed everybody else's. If I wanted the job, I had to have Buck's blessing, so he was my first stop.

Fortunately, he was in a good mood. "Are you sure you want to do this?" he said, puffing gently on his pipe. "You're going to be assigned to a field office soon, and before long you'll be going out as an inspector. This could really take you out of the career path, you know."

"Buck, I don't care about that stuff," I pleaded. "I think this is a great job. I really would appreciate your support."

"Do you think we need a lawyer commanding a team like this?"

"Hell, Buck, I know a lot more about tactics than I do about lawyering. Just look at my application. I spent the first ten years of my career in the FBI involved in tactical operations. I've arrested five hundred fugitives. I've run a five-man SWAT team. We were involved in dozens of tactical entries in New York. I wasn't born in the legal counsel division, you know."

Buck gazed at me like Buddha. A few weeks later, his secretary summoned me to his office. I hustled down the corridor. Buck was not known for patience. When I walked in, she smiled and motioned with her head toward the inner sanctum. Was she smiling because she knew I had screwed up something and was about to get killed?

Was Buck going to set his desk on fire again?

Buck got up from his desk, grabbed my hand in his big bear paw, and pumped it. "Congratulations. Webster just approved your promotion to the HRT."

I beamed back and stammered my thanks. This was my all-time dream job, more than fighter pilot, more than SAC. I couldn't believe I'd actually snagged it. I wanted to hug somebody, but there was nobody in the room but Buck, and he was too big and mean.

Anyhow, his face was serious. "You know this is going to be a very hard job," he said. "We've got to keep this thing in proper perspective. You're *not* to re-create Delta. You have to remember this is an FBI deal."

"Listen, we're on the same sheet of music," I said.

"I'm not a military guy. I'm an FBI agent and I look at things a little differently. We have a lot to learn from Delta and SEAL Team Six, but we have our way of doing things."

In the days that followed, I discovered the full irony of my situation. My work on the Hill and in the discipline unit, which I had considered a detour, made me exactly the kind of person Webster wanted for the HRT.

Everything he had tried to do to reform and restore the FBI would be lost if we slid back into the abuses of the Hoover era. At the same time, he realized a counterterror team would have to push the envelope, legally as well as physically. So, while several members of the career board had favored several well-known tactical specialists, Webster insisted on a lawyer as the team's first commander. In his eyes, the fact that I had been steeped in the dark side of the Bureau's history was an asset. Our many conversations about protecting the constitutional and civil rights of citizens had convinced him I knew the stakes of failure. If the HRT went over the line, it would ruin us all, including him.

Of course, Webster didn't say any of these things when he called me into his office. He was a gentleman and assumed me to be a gentleman also, with all the awareness, judgment, and restraint the word implied.

We sat at a coffee table, him stiffly upright in a straight-backed chair, me facing him. "This is a very difficult job," he began. "We've never done anything like this before. I want you to know one thing. I expect the FBI to have the best counterterrorist team in the world. We're the best and we should have the best, and I expect you to do it."

"I will do it, sir."

"If you need something, if things aren't happening, you come see me. Good luck."

"Thank you, sir."

And that was it. I left. I was stoked. I was standing at the bottom of the biggest mountain of my life. Now I just had to figure out how to climb to the top.

5

Webster promised to give me the FBI's best people. Now the trick was to find them. I found it hard to clarify what that meant until I spent an evening in a restaurant near the Pentagon with Charlie Beckwith. I was rambling on about how I wanted individuals who would show initiative, yet who knew that no one member, even the commander, was as important as the team, men and women who thought no job was too big, yet no task too small. One minute, they might be taking on the biggest, baddest gang of cutthroats on the face of the earth. The next, they might be sweeping out a holding area. I wanted risk takers but not risk seekers. I knew that most of the applicants would be former military people. That was fine. Most of them were disciplined, experienced, and fit. But I didn't want any tortured souls lugging around unfinished business from Vietnam.

Beckwith grinned his wolfish grin and sliced the air with a massive hand. "Danny, it's a whole lot better to go up the river with seven studs than a hundred shit-heads."

I stared. That was *exactly* what I was trying to say. No shitheads! As usual, this wise old Georgian had cut right to it. The Delta Force no-shitheads rule became one of my life principles. Better a few good agents than many unsuitable ones.

The question was, how to make sure we spotted every last one of those who did not belong on this team. Most shitheads were up-front about it. If you had any doubt, you only had to watch how they treated secretaries, clerks, and anybody else they didn't think they had to suck up to. Still, I had come across people who seemed pleasant and competent until you put them in a stressful situation, at which point they turned into raving, snarling, obstructive, obsessive egomaniacs. The middle of a hostage situation was not the time to find yourself saddled with a head case.

I called Dr. David Soskis, a Philadelphia psychiatrist who had advised the disciplinary unit on cases from time to time. I needed a new kind of psychological test.

"What's the first attribute you're looking for?" Soskis asked.

"A sense of humor. I want people who take their job very seriously but not themselves. Guys who can use humor to break tension."

"Good. Humor is a sign of intelligence."

"That's what I'm looking for. People with a lot of ideas that can keep people alive."

"There are the standard psychological tests," Soskis said. "And psychological interview techniques. The behavioral scientists at Quantico can help you develop those."

What about the shithead factor? I explained Beckwith's principle. Soskis agreed with me that it was brilliant. Not scientific, but brilliant.

"You'll have to learn to deal with the concept of subliminal judgments," he said. "Do you know what that means?"

"Nope. I don't have a clue."

He explained that I would develop either negative or positive impressions of certain candidates. "I think you should trust your judgment," he said. "There's almost always a good reason for the feeling that you don't trust somebody, even if you can't put it into words. You won't be able to articulate your judgment, or explain how you reached it, but you should trust it, because that judgment will likely be a valid one."

Cut away the twenty-dollar words, and this was the same advice Beckwith had given me. "You can do your psychological testing, but how you feel inside your gut, go with that," Charlie had said. I hoped my gut was up to the job.

My first meeting at Quantico with Connie Hassel and the wild bunch was tense. I knew that they had hoped that one of their number, possibly John Simeone, would be the first HRT commander. Here I was, an interloper from HQ, reaping the fruits of all their hard work. Not only that, they were not even going to be in the HRT. They were too senior to be mere operators, and HQ had vetoed their proposal for a management structure that included them. The only managers would be me and my deputy. They had to disperse to SWAT teams or other field management jobs, or else remain at Quantico as trainers.

They were a classy bunch. Whatever resentment they

felt didn't show. They put their backs into the task of selecting the fifty operators. I asked Simeone to join me as my deputy and chief executive officer. He had trained with every counterterrorist team in the free world. I would learn much from him.

The SOARU guys devised an excellent plan for testing candidates for physical strength, psychological health, intelligence, endurance, and marksmanship. It was a tough course but not impossible. The Bureau was loaded with weight lifters, marathon runners, sharpshooters, and swimmers. "John, we need to make one thing clear," I said. "We're not looking for iron men. A HRT operator is supposed to be a good special agent. A good agent works twelve to fourteen hours a day. It's possible to do that and be in very good physical condition, but I don't want anybody who blows through his cases so he can get in his ten miles a day."

"I agree," Simeone said. "They need to be FBI agents first."

The first group of candidates—fifty men and one woman—arrived on a Sunday evening. Simeone, the rest of the trainers, and I wore dark suits, white shirts, and conservative ties as we greeted them at the Academy. We wanted to instill in them the idea that this was an FBI team, not a military unit.

We ushered them into a classroom where, written in bold letters on the blackboard at the front, was the HRT motto: "To Save Lives."

"That's your only mission," I said, pointing to the board. "To preserve human life. However it turns out, take pride in this. You've already gone through one of the most difficult selection courses in law enforcement. You've been found suitable to be an FBI agent."

The candidates were issued T-shirts, shorts, and navy blue cargo pants—no equipment that had a military look. Everyone got a wristband to be worn twenty-four hours a day. This was a test to see if they followed instructions.

After the first event—a four-mile run—the candidates shinnied up twenty-foot ropes hanging outside the gym. They would climb these ropes again and again. Then it was on to the gym to max out on push-ups and pull-ups.

We focused heavily on upper-body and hand strength because commanders at Delta, SEAL Team Six, and the European services had all told us that it was an operator's most important physical attribute. Often the most difficult part of a counterterrorist operation was not the fight itself but getting to the scene in the first place. That could involve climbing, jumping, swimming, running, crawling, walking, or fast-roping out of helicopters. All these required extraordinary upper-body strength.

Push-ups and pull-ups had to be executed according to protocols demonstrated by Al Beccaccio, unit chief of the physical training unit. Push-ups were done with hands shoulder-width apart, back straight, chest lowered to touch the fist of the instructor, who was counting out the repetitions. Pull-ups started from a dead hang, with no swinging to build momentum. Any deviation and the repetition did not count.

I watched each candidate's face to see how attentive he or she was to Beccaccio's instructions. I wanted men and women who followed orders exactly. During a mission, attention to detail might be the difference between success or failure, life or death. I looked for tenacity. I was more interested in a man or woman who struggled and used every last ounce of energy to do fifteen pull-ups, someone who would only stop after being totally exhausted, than in an individual who jumped on the pull-up bar, cracked off twenty-five, and jumped down, hardly out of breath.

Marksmanship was another make-or-break test. Quite a few candidates arrived at the Academy with their own weapons, tricked out with sophisticated sights, grips, and other attachments that they hoped would give them an edge. To level the field, we confiscated all personal guns and issued everyone standard .357 magnum revolvers.

Proficiency on the FBI's linear, static ranges was meaningless. HRT members would have to shoot while running and think while shooting. Eventually, they would practice rescue scenarios with live ammunition, shooting hostile targets placed just inches from their comrades, who would pose as hostages. Don Bassett set up a special range with an obstacle course that forced agents to run, dodge, and shoot under stress.

Aquaphobia—fear of water—was an automatic disqualifier, since we might have to stage a rescue on a hijacked boat in the middle of the night or swim to a land objective. The candidates were blindfolded, asked to step off a fifteen-foot diving platform, fall to the water, and without coming up for air, locate a brick at the bottom of the pool. An instructor on the platform called out, "Hold your nose and grab what's most valuable to you." Most agents grabbed their crotches. The exception was a man who held his nose with one hand and his toupee with the other. "Guess we all have our own priorities," I muttered.

Every candidate researched a topic and prepared a

term paper. A good part of our mission would involve research on equipment and techniques that would refine our lifesaving skills. To test powers of observation, we rousted the candidates out at three o'clock in the morning and took them to a classroom, where they were shown a videotape of an actual terrorist incident, then told to write an FD-302, an FBI report. Some of them recorded nearly every detail. Others appeared to have slept through the entire event.

Two of the toughest physical events were the obstacle courses and the U.S. Marine Corps confidence course. The confidence course consisted of two five-story structures. The stairway to heaven was a giant ladder, its two vertical posts crisscrossed with rungs made of sawed-off telephone poles. You had to stand on a rung, reach above your head, grab the next rung, swing your legs up, then do it all over again. Supported with guy wires, it shook, rattled, and rolled terrifyingly with every move you made.

"What the hell are we doing up here?" I muttered to Simeone after we had hoisted ourselves up to the top rung.

"You said you wouldn't make the agents do anything you wouldn't do," he replied.

"I did? Why didn't you stop me?"

"It sounded good at the time."

"Next time, stop me."

But he didn't. We moved on to the platform climb, which consisted of four poles to which were affixed horizontal platforms, sort of like a five-story, open-sided bookcase. You could shinny up the poles from platform to platform or you could reach up, grab the edge of the platform, and flip yourself up.

I took a six-pack of beer and laced the plastic holders through my belt. When Simeone and I got to the top, I popped a couple.

"I'm too old for this job," Simeone groaned.

I handed him a lukewarm Budweiser. "But not to drink beer."

"I'm never too old or too tired to drink a beer."

"You know, if we fall off of this son of a bitch, we won't have to worry about getting older."

The confidence course was voluntary, but most of the candidates ran it. Those who elected to watch didn't make the team.

One candidate stood out—Benjamin Clarey, a powerfully built black man. Ben was constantly cracking jokes, laughing, and doing everything he could to break the tension. He was probably trying to deal with his own stress, but he also helped alleviate the stress felt by his teammates. *God, please let him get through this course,* I prayed. *He's exactly the type of man I'm looking for.*

The FBI had its own obstacle course behind our gym, which was almost identical to the Marine version, except that some sinister son of a bitch without regard for us vertically challenged guys had raised every obstacle two to six inches higher than the ones the Marines used. The course started out with a leap high in the air to a parallel bar and a flip over the bar. Then came a series of obstacles, ending up with another climb of that damn twenty-foot rope.

As I watched the candidates straining and puffing, I didn't have the heart to tell them that my ten-year-old son had run the course as if he had been tossing himself around the monkey bars at the playground. I took Little Doc to the Academy most weekends after his soccer and baseball games. He fooled around with the equipment while I got ready for Monday.

The candidates ran the athletic events first as individuals, then in five-person teams. We told them they would be judged on the achievement of their teams. Yet some either did not believe us or failed to understand the team concept.

On one team, four of the men worked together to push and haul one another over the obstacles. The fifth left his mates behind and sprinted out front, finishing in near-record time. This individual was one of our best athletes, but he washed out because we wanted people who would do anything to see the team succeed, even if it meant finishing in a slower time.

Most agents thought the easiest part of selection was a track event in which they sprinted two hundred yards, then did push-ups, pull-ups, and squat thrusts, then repeated the sequence. They didn't know we were deliberately trying to exhaust them to see whether the stronger agents would help the weaker ones.

Don Glasser, a former SEAL who had won the Navy's fleet heavyweight boxing championship and would later claim the National Toughest Cop Alive trophy, did his sprint, knocked off his pull-ups and push-ups, then ran back, hoisted a struggling teammate to the pull-up bar, and lifted him up and down.

No one who failed the body carry could be an HRT operator. The ability to pick up a hostage, comrade, or suspect and dash to safety was fundamental. Roger Nisley and Tase Bailey showed the candidates the basic techniques of a fireman's carry, then told them to sprint sixty yards, pick up a buddy, and sprint back to the starting line. One picked up his partner, sprinted the length of the gym, and dumped him on the ground so hard that he would have been injured if Nisley hadn't jumped in to break his fall. The candidate walked away, with no apology and no show of concern for his fellow agent. He had one of the fastest times, but his callousness cost him a place on the team.

Soskis and the behavioral-science staff ferreted out a few more candidates who were short in the empathy department. One man seemed to be sleepwalking through his interview. There was no excitement, no energy, and no intensity. His mood lightened only when Soskis asked him to talk about a firefight in Vietnam. Suddenly, he became animated, almost euphoric, as he described a fierce battle in which several of his buddies had been killed, as well as a large number of Viet Cong. We rejected him.

Another guy's psychological tests worried Soskis, but he couldn't explain why in plain English. Referring to this troublesome fellow by number—we used numbers, not names, as a "blind" to reduce the risk of evaluator bias—Soskis kept spouting shrink jargon like "He seems to be high in certain dimensions that we find troubling," and "He seems to be low in other areas in which we would like to have more consistency."

"I have no idea what you're talking about," I sputtered in frustration.

"Okay, let's find out who he is," Simeone said. He pulled the guy's folder and read off the name.

"Oh, him," I said. "He's an asshole." This candidate was arrogant and had continually failed to follow instructions.

"That's it." Soskis grinned. "That's what I was trying to say. He's an asshole."

Chalk up one for the Beckwith no-shitheads rule.

"Is that why I'm paying you all this money, for you to figure out which guys are assholes?" I needled. "I didn't come in on a load of watermelons. I know an asshole when I see one."

Soskis gave me the serene professional smile I found maddening. "I was just trying to broaden your depth of understanding of the psychology of the mind. I had hoped that I would not have to stoop to the language that you seem to be most comfortable with. If you are more comfortable with *asshole,* then asshole it will be."

The most feared and despised psychological stress test turned out to be the mock news conference. Each of the candidates had to prepare a canned press release describing a counterterror action, then stand for questions from "reporters," in reality FBI Academy instructors. The questions were unrelenting and outrageous, designed to bait the agents into losing their cool. What's more, they came from several parts of the room at once. I wanted to see who could brief a skeptical press, or, for that matter, HQ or Justice Department officials. Very few could. Almost no one would look at the tapes of his performance afterward. Men who had led SWAT operations against the meanest, craziest people in America got the sweats when asked to meet the press. And our "journalists" were actually rather tame, with their short hair and Bureau suits. I wondered what would happen when these candidates encountered a bona fide baggy-khaki-wearing, shaggy-haired journalist who already had a notebook full of quotes from deputy sheriffs, police sergeants, and assistant DAs who not only had no allegiance to the FBI but who probably hated our collective guts.

That summer, we put 150 candidates through the selection course. In the end, we picked fifty extraordinary people.

Jeff Wehmeyer, who headed the Washington Field Office SWAT team, was probably the best all-round candidate. I made him the third-ranking supervisor, chief operating officer, to line him up for the deputy's job when Simeone departed to a classified counterterrorism mission at the Defense Department. Jeff helped John and me with planning, training manuals, and mountains of paperwork when we were getting organized. I knew from many days and nights of talking with him that he shared my view that deadly force should be an absolute last resort. As a Marine corporal in Vietnam, Jeff had been in more than his share of firefights, and he hoped never to see another one. The only thing that gave me pause was Wehmeyer's hair. No matter how much time and money I spent at the barber, my spiky brown-black hair looked as if I had chopped it with a K-bar knife. Most of the others on the team also had pretty bad hair. But Jeff's short, straight, blond hair looked as neat after he had fast-roped out of a helicopter as when he went to a wedding. We told him he should have been a Secret Service agent. Ever notice how they have perfect hair, even when riding on the running boards of the presidential limousine? We say they wear hundred-mile-an-hour hair epoxy.

Horace Mewborn was our tactical intelligence officer. No one had ever seen the emergency that could make Horace raise his voice. He had maybe winced, maybe, when friendly fire blew off a chunk of his arm near the Cambodian border. To look at him, you would never guess that he had been a Green Beret. With his silver hair, aquiline features, and wry wit, Horace could have passed for a judge in some small Southern town. It amused him to brief us in a Carolina accent so thick that some of the guys would raise their hands and ask for a translator. "Have you ever thought of going to school for English as a second language?" I asked him. Horace had an astounding memory and, better yet, the good judgment to tell us what we needed to know, without cluttering his intel briefings with colorful but irrelevant details.

Don Glasser had the body of Paul Bunyan, but what appealed to me was his inventive mind. He had a knack for figuring out the safest place to try to grab a bunch of bad guys. In Seattle, he once finessed a tricky arrest. He had tracked a bank robber to a hotel. Many law enforcement people would simply have knocked down the guy's door, but Glasser knew that the robber was trigger-happy and somebody would get shot, almost certainly the robber and maybe an agent. So he asked around the hotel and found out that the man had asked to use a private office to type a letter. He went into the office, rolled a standard FBI "warning and waiver of rights" interview form into the typewriter carriage, and typed the robber's name at the top of the form. When the robber sat down at the desk, he spotted his name and became absorbed in reading the FBI form. Glasser exploded through the door and had a shotgun pointed at the robber's head before he could go for his gun.

Larry Bonney ranked near the top on both the physical proficiency tests and intelligence and was also the FBI's only ordained minister. After a few years as a young agent, he had answered God's call, resigned, and become a preacher. But he'd missed the FBI and re-upped. When he got word that the HRT was being formed and heard the motto, "To Save Lives," he felt God was calling him again. Bonney had an unconventional way of looking at things and an instinct for an adversary's weakest point. I made him the leader of one of the assault teams, specializing in stronghold and aircraft assaults. Bonney always led us in prayer before a mission. It was surreal to see this minister praying with an MP5 submachine gun slung around his neck.

For physical courage, nobody topped Marty Brown, who took the entire selection course, including all the runs and climbs, the swims and the shooting, with a broken leg. When he arrived, he presented me with a doctor's note saying that the break was not severe enough to keep him off the course. Every time he jumped, he landed on his good leg and winced as his injured leg touched down. A few years later, Marty would shoot a gun out of the hand of a terrorist who was about to kill one of his partners.

Phil King, the Navy diver whose fight with the flagman had nearly caused Buck Revell to torch his desk, was assigned to the maritime team and became the unit's dive instructor. He was also our most enthusiastic practical joker. Once, during a later selection course, Phil stood, stopwatch in hand, a short distance from the finish line of the four-mile run. As the candidates ran by him, he'd look at the watch and yell, "C'mon, step it up, you're almost halfway there and you're about a minute behind your time." Some sped up, and you could see on their faces that they meant to gut it out to the very end. When they rounded the bend, they saw the finish line and burst past it with looks of sheer ecstasy. Others developed the phantom-turned-ankle syndrome. There were probably more turned ankles within twenty yards of Phil King than anyplace else on the earth on that particular day. Phil's joke became a regular part of the course. It gave us some insights into character we might otherwise have missed.

The snipers had the hardest, coldest, loneliest job, so I figured they deserved the best leader. That was Steve Wiley. Wiley, who stood about six foot one and weighed maybe 170 pounds, was so thin we asked him to wear a long-sleeve shirt when we went out for a hamburger.

Wiley was patient, stoical, and sensitive, which made him the ideal sniper-observer. While the operators were waiting in the rear in a fairly comfortable holding area, the snipers were out front, exposed to the elements, often in the worst possible weather. Their job was to observe our targets' habits and radio data back to base. Our behavioral scientists would chart the hostage takers' sleep cycles and estimate when they were in their deepest slumber, usually around three o'clock in the morning. That was when we would move in.

I took special pride in signing on Tommy Norris, a former Navy SEAL who had won the Congressional Medal of Honor in Vietnam. Ratso Norris had lost an eye and part of his skull to a North Vietnamese AK-47 round. After years of plastic surgery and physical therapy, he had passed the FBI entrance tests easily, but the drivers in personnel worried that we would set a precedent if we took a one-eyed applicant. The case had landed on my desk in the legal counsel office.

"Yeah, that might set a precedent," I said. "We'll probably have to take another Congressional Medal of Honor winner with one eye if he applies. But I'll take the risk." Not only did Norris turn out to be a great field agent, he passed the HRT competition easily. I assigned him to run an assault team.

The most valiant candidate didn't make the team. Every instructor and probably every candidate rooted for Mary Ann Sullivan because she never asked for special treatment and demonstrated over and over again that she wouldn't quit. Raised in a military family with six brothers, Sullivan was a strong swimmer, runner, and sharpshooter. She sailed through the psychological evaluations and the research projects. She was unflappable in the press conference.

But like almost all women, she didn't have the requisite upper-body strength. She did well in the early stages of the obstacle course, jumping up to high bars and flinging herself over a variety of obstacles. About halfway through the course loomed an obstacle with two horizontal parallel pipes eight feet off the ground and three feet apart. By the time she got to this obstacle, she didn't have the spring in her legs to leap to the first pipe. She jumped and missed and jumped again. Finally she shinnied up the vertical wooden post to the pipe, pulled herself up and over, and dropped.

"That took a hell of a lot of guts," Simeone whispered. "I don't think I would have shinnied up that pole. She'll be picking splinters for a week."

She continued on through the course, beaten up, scratched up, and splintered up but still full of courage. "We need her in this unit," I told Simeone. "I'll think of something."

By the time she reached the twenty-foot rope climb, she had no strength left. Her competitors did everything they could to cheer her on, yelling, "Come on,

Mary Ann. You can do it." She pulled herself up a few feet, then dropped back, then pulled up again, until she fell to the ground, totally spent. She picked herself up, shook her head, smiled, shrugged, and said, "I'm sorry, guys."

She never did complete the obstacle course as an individual. But she went through the rest of selection anyway. When she reached the end and faced that rope, her teammates boosted her up the first few feet and she finished the climb on her own. Everyone gave out a cheer when she touched the top. Even the SOARU evaluators could not help but cheer.

At the end of the week, Mary Ann had bruises on her bruises and scrapes on her scrapes. I am sure that she was as tired, worn-out, and beat-up as she would ever be in her life. As I bid the candidates farewell on the last day of selection, she came up to me and shook my hand, looked me in the eye, and said, "Thanks for letting me have the opportunity. I really enjoyed it." Well, I'm not really sure that she enjoyed it, but I knew that she had given it her all.

I thought about selecting Mary Ann based on her other scores and her courage but decided that it would be inappropriate and unfair. Operators scaled buildings, cliffs, and the sides of ships with ninety-pound packs and fast-roped out of helicopters without safety straps. Anyone who couldn't hold on to a rope could be killed and could endanger the lives of others.

I created a new position for her, a support-staff agent, handling logistics, equipment, supplies, intelligence, and training. She applied for the job and won it hands down. She proved to be particularly good at surveillance. Who would believe that the attractive young lady with long blond hair and blue eyes was an FBI counterterrorist specialist?

The operators made no bones about their admiration of her physical beauty, but I never had to call anybody down for sexual harassment. It was hard to imagine anyone victimizing Mary Ann Sullivan.

After a few years, Mary Ann married an agent named Bob Carlson. He went through selection and became an HRT operator. These two had one of the best marriages I ever saw, which just shows how tough both of them were. On one HRT family excursion, a canoe trip down the Shenandoah River, Bob regaled us with the story of how Mary Ann had helped him overcome his allergy to domestic work. She was constantly badgering him to help out around the house. Finally, in frustration, she challenged, "Tell me one thing productive you've done around here in the last six months."

"I got you pregnant," Carlson said, beaming, thinking he had just made the ultimate comeback.

"No, you did *not*," she shot back, her blue eyes snapping fire.

Carlson gasped, and then they both broke up. Bob loved Mary Ann's slashing, fearless wit, as we all did. She was never down, never out, never at a loss. She could think on her feet in a dicey situation. Bob started helping with the cleaning. They went on to have five kids. Given their genetic history, I wouldn't want to get crossways with any of them.

6

There is a quantum leap from traditional SWAT team tactics to the tradecraft practiced by Delta, the SAS, and other counterterror units. When SWAT officers enter a building, they move slowly and stealthily, taking cover wherever they can find it, using shields if possible and mirrors to look around corners, into closets, and under beds.

Counterterror units rush entrances with a blinding, deafening clamor, then engage their adversaries in close-quarter battle, an art developed by the SAS and refined at Delta. To the uninitiated, it looks like total confusion. It is, however, the most thoroughly planned and rehearsed of all tactical options, and by far the most dangerous to the rescuers. Explosives are used as diversions and for breaching—breaking through a door or wall. The operators rush into the crisis area tossing stun grenades to disorient and blind hostages and bad guys. It is not that much different from the "surprise and scare the shit out of them" tactics we used on the bank robbery squad in New York, just more technical and sophisticated.

When the Delta commander invited us to Bragg for exercises in February of 1983, I jumped at the chance. I was not too anxious to have nine-millimeter bullets slamming into a target inches from my face. Still, what better place to start than at the feet of the masters?

John Simeone, Jeff Wehmeyer, a couple of operators, and I reported to the Delta shooting house, a multiroom concrete structure. Its walls were wood-lined with steel

147

backing. The steel stopped the bullets, and the wood trapped them so that they did not bounce back into the room. Except for some holes in the walls, the interior looked like that of any office building. It was sleeker than the shooting house we had built on the FBI range, an ugly but functional structure made of plywood backed by twelve-foot-high stacks of sand-filled tires. The purpose was the same: to simulate actual hostage-rescue combat situations in which operators would fire to the left, the right, in front of, and behind themselves.

Inside the house, Delta operators took turns as hostages or, occasionally, admitted guest hostages. Vice President George Bush, visiting Bragg, seemed perfectly at ease with the notion of playing a hostage in a live-fire situation and, the Delta guys told me, was rather disappointed when the Secret Service insisted on caging him in a bulletproof glass enclosure.

I didn't rate a glass box. A Delta operator ushered me to the side of the room and told me to stand next to a life-size silhouette of a hooded terrorist with a machine gun. Simeone and Wehmeyer were placed next to cardboard terrorists in other corners.

"Sir, I'd advise you not to move," the operator said, sliding toward the rear door.

"Right," I responded. Did this crazy son of a bitch think I would move? Move, hell, I was doing good just to stand there and not fall over.

The lights dimmed so that I could barely see. Then came a roar and a blast of hot air, as if someone had opened a smelter oven a foot from my face. I wanted to close my eyes but forced them to stay open. I had to see this.

I glanced at the door just in time to spot four Delta

operators clad in black assault suits, their faces covered with balaclavas, climb through a neat, oblong hole that had been blown in the door by a shaped explosive charge. A flash-bang grenade detonated to my right, rendering me temporarily blind and deaf. So much for keeping my eyes open. By the time I regained my senses, the target next to me had four neat, closely spaced holes in the forehead. I found to my great relief that I still had the same number of holes in my body that I'd come into the room with. The assault had been so fast and the diversion devices so effective that neither I nor any other FBI agent, no matter how well trained, would have been able to respond.

In the weeks we spent with Delta, our operators started out with a simple scenario, taking out several targets in one room. Then they graduated to two-man, three-man, four-man, and five-man room-clearing techniques, in which the danger of friendly fire injuries was geometrically greater. Standard law enforcement training scenarios never positioned an operator down range from the shooter. In close-quarter battle, operators shoot across the room, engaging targets two or three feet from one another. No shot is off-limits and everything is down range.

As the training became more intense, some of the operators were assigned to become "injured" and drop out. Their partners stepped in to take over their responsibilities and were forbidden to help fallen comrades until the assault had been completed. It went against the grain, but if a terrorist could foil a hostage rescue by inflicting an injury, then almost any rescue could be thwarted.

Delta training scenarios emphasized extreme precision in neutralizing threats and saving hostages. To that end, Delta instructors did everything they could to put stresses on our agents and present unexpected kinds of shoot/don't shoot decisions. Sometimes we'd enter a room expecting to engage hostile targets and find only hostages. Other times we'd find a hostage next to every hostile target so that a series of perfect shots was required.

These drills really made us appreciate our new weapon—the Heckler & Koch MP5 submachine gun. It was the weapon of choice for Delta, the SAS, and other European counterterror teams, but most of the HRT trainees had never wielded one before they came on the team. Once they did, they fell in love. The MP5 was extremely accurate. At twenty-five yards, you make a pattern in a target no bigger than a half dollar. It was easy to operate and completely reliable. Cold, rain, snow, mud, sleet—the MP5 did its job. It was compact, with a telescoping stock so it could be fired like a conventional shoulder weapon or, with the stock collapsed, used for close-quarter combat.

More than anything else, Delta taught us the importance of planning and rehearsal. We spent as much time and effort on rescue scenarios as a theater company planning a Broadway opening. First, the assault commander and leaders of individual subunits would come up with a tabletop plan. Tactical planners blocked out the room on paper, designating certain quadrants as fields of fire, others as fields of movement.

Then full-dress rehearsals would begin, first in slow motion, then at full speed. A scenario that looked like a free-for-all had, in fact, been painstakingly choreographed. Each operator was assigned a position and an area of responsibility. He knew exactly where he was supposed to go, the path he would take to get there, and where all his partners were to go. Each operator knew his own movement and shooting patterns and those of everyone else on the team as well.

Rehearsal areas were mocked up to resemble as closely as possible the real crisis site. When time was short, the house to be assaulted would be laid out on the ground with engineer's tape. In some protracted operations, counterterrorist teams actually constructed an exact replica of part of a building or borrowed a twin of an airplane that had been hijacked.

The commander himself did not draw up plans but rather critiqued schemes proposed by the team leaders. This was an added safeguard to make sure that the commander's ego did not become overly invested in any particular scheme. Also, Delta team leaders played a relentless game of "what-if." Nobody wanted fear of the commander to bias the operators' critiques.

During one of the training scenarios, I was informed early on that the "terrorists"—played by Delta operators—would take "hostages" in a building in the Delta compound, then demand a bus to take them to an aircraft. The HRT would be expected to execute one of two options, either ambush the bus near the range, several miles down the road, or mount a rescue on the plane.

"How about we ambush the bus right after the hostage-taking?" I asked the Delta commander.

"Oh my God," he said, roaring with laughter. "You'll scare the shit out of these guys. They'll never guess you'll do it inside the compound. They're going to be relaxed, thinking you won't hit them till they get to the range. Great idea."

"The only problem is, I don't have a sniper team yet," I said.

"Well, hell, I've got snipers," he replied, still chuckling. "You can use my snipers."

The Delta snipers absolutely loved the idea of ambushing their buddies when they least expected it. Even better, the exercise was going to be filmed for training purposes.

As the exercise began, the nine Delta "terrorists" swaggered out to the "news cameras" and issued all sorts of demands and outrageous comments. They were strutting around defiantly, evidently enjoying playing bad guys, when—*bam!*—a flash-bang landed in the middle of them. Delta snipers began firing from the buildings. HRT operators, who had hidden in a warehouse behind some construction equipment, moved in to assault. The Delta operators put up a furious fight. It is a tribute to their training, experience, and reactions that in spite of the surprise, they were still able to open fire.

We rescued the hostages. We did everything else almost perfectly. We were innovative. We were imaginative. We were aggressive. Still, we lost a couple of people.

We consoled ourselves with the thought we would never face terrorists as well trained, equipped, or courageous as Delta operators. "Go home tonight and pray to God that no Delta personnel ever decide to go bad," I told Don Brigham, one of our "dead."

Still, we all knew that for all the fun we had trumping Delta's finest, it would have been much better if the negotiators had walked them out to surrender and taken all our men home that night. If this had been a real-life hostage-taking, I would have been preparing for two funerals.

*   *   *

Later that summer, Simeone and I traveled to Hereford, England, to learn tactical planning from the SAS. Stiff after the long flight and the train ride from London, we left the base for a run through the village. Jogging in the cool, damp air, past neat cottages and ancient shops, was glorious, but we became totally lost. Every time we stopped and asked someone for directions back to the SAS base, we ended up in a schoolyard or in front of a pub. It took us about an hour and a half to find the main gate.

Our SAS hosts got a big kick out of our confusion. "It's the nature of the people in Hereford to protect us," explained an officer. "They believe that if you have business with the SAS, you damn well ought to know how to get there, and if you have to ask directions, you're probably a terrorist or stupid, and in any event they aren't about to help you."

Prank-the-Yank seemed to be the local game. The next morning, I rose at dawn and was shaving at the sink with not a stitch on when the door swung open and a little old lady walked in carrying a tray with a steaming mug of tea. "Good morning, sir," she said sweetly as I grabbed for a towel. "I hope you like tea. Would you like cream with it?"

"She's worked for the officers' mess for longer than any of us can remember," an SAS man told me at breakfast. "She walks into anyone's room at any time. She seems to take great pleasure in embarrassing us."

Of all the teams that we dealt with, the SAS was probably the least technically sophisticated. Americans are totally preoccupied with the impact of bullets upon human tissue and constantly strive to increase the effectiveness of handgun rounds with hollow points, soft points, post points, or other innovations. The Brits had little interest in this sort of research. Standard British-issue hardball ammunition was good enough, as far as they were concerned.

Nor did the SAS share the FBI's emphasis on defensive tactics training and unarmed combat. Most of the people in SOARU and HRT had studied martial arts. When I asked an SAS sergeant major if I could observe some of their defensive tactics classes, he looked at me and smiled. "For defensive tactics we rely on two things—nine-millimeter pistols and beer bottles."

The SAS had it over everybody else when it came to planning. They plotted out every operation to the minute details. They broke down every training scenario, devising options for any eventuality. Even if they decided to make a stronghold assault, they also planned open-air, sniper, and mobile assaults, in the event that the terrorists decided to leave their lair and take their hostages with them.

Early one morning I was awakened by a knock at my door. "Get your kit together," called an SAS officer. "We leave in half an hour."

Simeone and I scrambled to dress, then stood outside, watching the operators who lived off base arrive. Our guys would roar up in Ford Explorers and Toyota Land Cruisers. The Brits emerged out of the cold, dark night on their bicycles, occasionally jingling the bells on their handlebars to warn pedestrians to get out of the way.

A C-130 took us to Edinburgh, where the SAS commander reported to the chief constable. He was in direct contact with the Prime Minister's cabinet in London.

Nothing would happen without the consent of the constable and the cabinet members responsible for decision-making. Once the cabinet members decided negotiations had failed, they would order the chief constable to execute a document turning over command to the SAS for tactical resolution.

After the handoff was made, John and I were tail-end Charlies with an assault group. We rode in closed vans to a dike next to a pump station where the terrorists were holed up. We disembarked our vans and crept up the dike just short of its crest. When the assault order was given, the SAS operators sprang up over the rise, rushed down the hill, breached the doors and windows, and in a matter of seconds "killed" all the terrorists and rescued all the hostages. Then the SAS handed the site back to the chief constable.

What a difference from the way we do things. The whole British government from the prime minister and cabinet down to the operators took counterterrorist training seriously and participated in exercises. Everyone understood his responsibilities and those of all the other players. There was absolutely no confusion about command and control. The lines were neat and crisply defined. By contrast, I had not met anyone in the U.S. Department of Justice or at the White House who had a clue about how a counterterror operation worked, what the capabilities of the various agencies were, and who was to do what. Clearly, I thought, we would have to educate not only ourselves, but everyone else in a position to decide when and if the HRT was to be deployed.

7

Our coming-out party was a nuclear terrorism scenario staged near the Los Alamos National Weapons Laboratory in New Mexico and sponsored by the Department of Energy. The premise: terrorists had seized a nuclear warhead and kidnapped a scientist who knew how to detonate it. We were to rescue the scientist. A military weapons team was to render the device safe. SWAT teams from the Midwest field offices would go after bad guys who were not at the location where the hostage was being held. To add a little spice, the bad guys would be played by our own trainers from SOARU.

The whole exercise would be observed closely by representatives from FBI headquarters, where some executives still did not like the idea of HRT and would use any excuse to dismantle it. The audience would also include terrorism experts from the White House, Justice, and the Pentagon.

This was our first chance to prove ourselves. If we blew it, it would probably be our last. We came very close—two inches, to be exact. As the Air Force C-130 carrying our equipment rolled to a stop at a military base outside Albuquerque, an HRT operator drove our Ryder rental truck onto the tarmac and toward the front of the plane. That was a flat violation of airport rules. And then—

Omigod. Oh, jeez. Stop, you dumb son of a bitch! He was heading the truck under the wing. The top of the truck was roughly even with the wing's underside. I didn't have time to do anything but gulp in a ton of air.

156

My brain fast-forwarded to a horrific vision. The truck is ripping the wing off the aircraft. Airplane fuel is pouring onto the runway. A lake of it is right under the plane's belly. One spark ignites the vapor-filled wing tank, and the crates of ammunition and explosives packed in the C-130 erupt. I remembered Beckwith telling me how helpless he had felt at Desert One, when the chopper careened into the C-130, and there was a gasoline explosion and a blue fireball. *Balllooee,* as he put it. Beckwith always got tears in his eyes when he talked about leaving those charred bodies in the sand.

Hey! God's with us, or somebody has pumped some extra air into the C-130 tires. The truck had missed the wing by a couple of inches. I let out my breath with a whoosh.

I could see the uh-oh look on the truck driver's face. He climbed down, walked over to me, and made some inane comment like "Rather be lucky than good."

"Yeah, I'd rather be smart than stupid," I replied. "You almost fucked up this whole thing. Okay. It's over. Let's get unloaded, and don't drive that damned truck anywhere near the plane again."

I turned on my heel, got into my four-wheel drive, and headed for the DOE training facility, a Spartan two-room affair, where the rest of the men were milling. The team leaders approached me, their faces grave. There was big, big trouble. The dinner DOE had delivered was white bread and bologna sandwiches, pickles, and apples. They didn't mind sleeping twenty-five to a room or working in the searing days and freezing nights of the New Mexico desert, but they were damned if they were going to eat cold bologna.

I started laughing. They glowered. Even Phil King

had no sense of humor about bologna. "Okay," I said. "You guys pool your money. Assign one person to go into town, buy the food you want. There's a stove down at the end of the room. You cook it, you eat it, and you clean up after yourselves. That's the end of it."

I didn't blame them. They wouldn't see many hot meals for a while, especially Wiley's sniper-observer team. After dinner we got a call from the main command post. Our targets were holed up in a cabin out in the desert.

We deployed our snipers. They pulled on gillie suits—English gamekeeper's canvas coveralls, sewn with artificial and real local foliage—then belly-crawled to positions ringing the cabin. Once in place, they lay prone and almost motionless for twelve-hour shifts, photographing the cabin with long-distance lenses and radioing information on the bad guys' patrols. They used a laser range finder—a device that measures the exact distance to a target from the sniper's position—and some basic trigonometry to calculate the length of an antenna on the cabin's roof. This data enabled Defense Department communications specialists to assess the frequency and type of radio. The snipers trained night-vision gear on the cabin and guided two operators to its outer wall, radioing them whenever they spotted a terrorist patrol. The operators took readings with a radiation measuring device to determine whether the stolen warhead was inside. Then they snuck back to the rear, again with the help of the snipers.

Back at the command center, we enlarged the snapshots to calculate the cabin's exact measurements. We laid out the floor plan with plywood and built a life-size wooden facade of the cabin. We knew exactly how high off the ground the windows were, and how long our ladders had to be so that our operators could practice breaching the windows and doors. When the operators went through the red doors and windows, it would be for the fiftieth time, not the first.

After four hours of watching and rehearsing, we were told the negotiations had failed and the terrorists were threatening to execute the scientist. It was now three o'clock in the morning. "Okay, Charlie, let's do it," I told Charlie Prouty, the assault commander.

Prouty and the operators crept close to the cabin via gullies and ravines that hid their movements. The breachers fixed a shaped charge to the door. At a signal, they detonated it, cutting a neat rectangle, while another operator tossed a flash-bang grenade through a window. Bob Taubert, who was playing the leader of the terrorists, squeezed off two rounds from his shotgun before we "killed" him and the rest of the bad guys.

I learned a lot that night. The good news was, our adversaries didn't have the time or the presence of mind to kill the hostage, and as our own trainers, they had a better idea of what to expect than anyone else we would ever face. Taubert told us they had been totally preoccupied with fending off the assault. His assessment validated our overall strategy, which was to try to get the terrorists to focus on the rescue team and ignore the hostage. If this was achieved, all we had to do was win the gunfight, and we knew we could do that.

The exercise proved to Judge Webster that we were ready for prime time. Acting on his assurances, President Reagan issued an executive order designating the FBI as the lead agency to deal with any terrorist act at the summer Olympics to be held in Los Angeles in 1984. The announcement didn't sit well with Los Angeles police chief Daryl Gates, who was openly antagonistic to the FBI. In August of 1983, a despondent Spaniard had pushed his way into the Spanish consulate in Los Angeles, taken four hostages, and demanded to have his family flown to Puerto Rico. The FBI field office assumed jurisdiction, but no sooner had an FBI negotiator started a dialogue with the hostage taker than LAPD officers used a pretext to get him off the phone. He returned to find that an LAPD detective had taken over the negotiations. Before long he talked the man out of the consulate. This sorry episode fueled resentments between L.A. field and the LAPD for years afterward.

When he heard that the FBI was coming, Gates promptly announced that his SWAT team was more than capable of doing the job. He added that his guys could have pulled off the rescue of the hostages in Iran if they had been at Desert One instead of Delta Force.

That last bit was over the top, but we got the picture. We were on a collision course. If the big one blew at Los Angeles, a turf fight could lead to tragedy.

We couldn't reason with Gates. No mere mortal could do that. There was only one thing to do. We had to work it out with Jeff Rogers, the LAPD SWAT team leader. As it happened, he was one of John Simeone's ten thousand best friends. Simeone and I flew out to Los Angeles and met Rogers at the LAPD watering hole. We faced off over tall mugs of draft.

"You know," I began, "we have to figure out a better way of doing business. Our bosses are going to put the two of us into a trick bag." A trick bag is a situation in which no matter what you do, you come out a loser.

"Yeah, I know." Rogers nodded. "There's too much fighting among the brass."

"It's what the FBI brass does best, that's for sure," I said. "But if things turn to shit, and we have an incident, they'll tell you and me to handle it. Then what?"

Jeff nodded. "Then the monkey will be on our backs."

"Right," I said. "Look, if you get the ticket, the HRT will hold your ladders." The ladder thing was commando talk for "support you."

"If we get the ticket, I expect you to hold ours," I said.

"Agreed."

I turned on my most engaging smile, the one I used with congressmen and those armadillo-hide HQ secretaries. "And," I added, "if you try to take the job from us, I promise to shoot you between the tits."

Rogers threw his head back and laughed. "You know *we* wouldn't do that."

"Like hell you wouldn't."

By the time we had drained our mugs, we were, if not friends, at least allies. It turned out that we had a lot in common. LAPD SWAT had trained with the SAS and Delta, as we had, and they had MP5 submachine guns, explosive breaching equipment, and high-end electronics. Over the next mug or two or three, we made a list of joint training exercises.

The most elaborate war game was Rogers's idea: a hostage-taking scenario in the top two floors of a twenty-five-story high-rise in central L.A. There would be live hostages and live fire. The terrorists would be played by cops from the suburbs. Toward the end, they'd put their clothing on mannequins so our snipers could "kill" them.

Our job was to take the twenty-fourth floor. To reach it, we would crawl through a system of service tunnels and ascend the service stairs. Rogers's team was to take the twenty-fifth floor, a tougher job because in the scenario, terrorists had blocked off the stairwell. The only way to get there was to string extension ladders across from the top of the building next door.

"We haven't ever done this before," Rogers said dubiously. "Have you?"

"Sure," I said breezily. "It's not bad once you get used to it. Just don't look down. Hell, I hate heights, but it really is easy."

We went out to Pepperdine University and found two multi-story buildings close enough together that we could slide extension ladders from one to the other. We practiced until Jeff was comfortable, or at least resigned.

"I envy you," I said. "It's an exciting approach."

"Do you want it?"

"Nope. You're the city guys. We mostly run around in the woods."

On the night of the exercise, when we received the signal to move to "phase line green," the last place of cover and concealment prior to hitting the building, I felt my adrenaline pumping. Gates and his command staff were watching, as well as Revell and Wayne Gilbert from HQ and White House officials.

Word came that negotiations had failed. The terrorists had announced they were ready to start executing hostages. We had to move.

To get to the building without being detected, we loaded the operators into Ryder trucks, closed the doors, and drove to the rear of an adjoining building. Fifty operators clambered into the basement, and we wriggled on our stomachs into a subterranean passage that linked the two high-rises.

About a hundred feet in, one of our most competent operators suffered claustrophobia. I had never known this guy to be afraid of anything, but the ride in the pitch-black truck and the dank tunnel got to him. His team leader slid back next to me and whispered that we had a problem. Our man was sweating profusely and saying he was sorry that he was letting the team down.

All of his teammates rallied around him. "You can make it. You're gonna do it."

"Come on back here with me," I said. I was near the end of the line with the technical agents who were reeling out phone line. Radios were unreliable twenty feet under the earth, and I had to be able to communicate with the command post so that Rogers and I could coordinate our assaults.

Phil King, who was on the point, sent word back that he had reached the end of the tunnel, had climbed the ladder that led to the trapdoor into the building's basement, and had peeked through an opening with his night-vision scope. And there was a problem. A bad guy armed with a submachine gun was patrolling the basement.

"It's going to be impossible to arrest him without alerting the others," King said. "He has a radio. I can hear him talking to somebody." One word from him, and the bad guys would make good on their threat to kill hostages if there was a rescue attempt.

I advised the command post, then radioed King, "Make a demand of surrender. If he doesn't comply immediately, neutralize the target." The terrorist ignored King—which was to be expected, since he was a mannequin. Using the infrared aiming device affixed to his MP5, King popped the dummy's head open with a nine-millimeter round.

We clambered up the ladder, crossed the basement, and climbed twenty-four stories up the service stairs, taking cover in a stairwell leading to our objective. I could feel every ounce of the weight of my weapon, body armor, and comm gear. I sure as hell would rather have come across a ladder.

Rogers, on the other hand, was probably wishing for our nice solid tunnel. He had assured the LAPD brass that his men would be tethered to a safety line as they inched across that ladder twenty-five stories above the ground. Actually, the only line they had came out of Rogers's mouth. He decided it would take too much time to hook and unhook each man, so he didn't do it. Rogers's guys were good, though. They negotiated the ladder, crept down the stairwell from the roof to the twenty-fifth-floor landing, and waited as their breacher fixed a shaped charge to the door. At the same time, Jaime Atherton, our breacher, stuck a charge to the twenty-fourth-floor door.

"Ready," I told the command post.

The controllers notified the officers role-playing terrorists to join the hostages and prop their guns against the bad-guy mannequins. Then they gave me the go-ahead.

"We're up," I radioed Rogers. He began the countdown. "I have control. Stand by. Five. Four. Three. Two. One. Execute. Execute. Execute."

On the count of two, HRT and LAPD snipers firing from the neighboring building shot mannequins nearest the windows. On the command "execute," the breaching explosives detonated. Operators tossed stun grenades inside, then rushed through the doors and machine-gunned mannequins inches from hostages.

From outside, all that could be seen was the strobe-light effect of stun grenades popping, the eerie glow of flashlights mounted on submachine guns, and periodically the flicker of a submachine gun as another mannequin was neutralized. Clearing the floors was complicated by the darkness and the number of rooms and closets. Before it was over, we had gone through two dozen stun grenades and hundreds of rounds of ammunition. The hostages had been instructed to jump up, resist, and impede us to make the scenario more realistic, but none did. Later, they said they were so disoriented and frightened by the demeanor of the rescuers, the stun grenades, and the live fire that they flattened themselves to the floor and kept their heads down.

I had to hand it to Gates. He didn't exaggerate his team's abilities by much. "If my family is ever held hostage and HRT isn't around, I sure hope you get the ticket," I told Rogers.

As we were mopping up, we stripped off our Nomex fire-retardant jumpsuits and our body armor before we melted in the southern-California heat. We looked around for something cold to drink and spotted a huge liquor store across the street from our crisis site.

Don Glasser was the first through the door. Standing six foot three and 230 pounds in his running shorts, nylon mesh tank top, and high-top assault boots, he looked like a gladiator from *Blade Runner*. His cocked and locked Browning Hi-Power automatic bulged out of an SAS holster rig that extended from waist to midthigh. I swung open the door just in time to hear one of the patrons say, "Look at that crazy mothafucker with that big gun on. There's some real shit going on here tonight."

As things turned out, no real shit happened at the

L.A. Olympics. Our intelligence division reported that word had gotten out in the extremist community that Los Angeles was a hard target. In case anybody missed the point, Rogers distributed T-shirts that depicted a cowering bunch of terrorists and the legend "We Dare Ya. LAPD SWAT."

I reminded myself not to let our triumph over the mannequins go to our heads. If we had been playing for keeps, some of our people would have gotten dinged up or killed. I might have bought the farm myself. The more war games I played, the more I became convinced of this truth. "No guts, no glory" may work fine for athletes, but when real bullets are flying, it's just a shopworn cliché.

8

Not long after the Olympics, I was in the gym pumping iron when Larry Bonney eased himself onto the next bench and bored into me with those eyes that had caused so many sinners to tremble and repent. *How does he do that?* I marveled, waiting to hear what he expected me to do. Bonney was a lighthearted guy, but when he decided to be serious, everyone knew it. I knew it because he was frowning, and he had picked a time to work out when no one else was around. I dropped my dumbbells on the floor and sat up.

"Doc, we need jobs," he said. "We didn't come on this team just to train."

"I know." I nodded. I had been pondering the problem myself, and so had Bonney's fellow team leaders. Some bored joker had stuck up a sign that parodied the SAS slogan "Who dares, wins." Only our slogan said sarcastically, "Who demonstrates, wins."

Exercises are indispensable, but until you go out in the real world, you don't really know what it takes to stay alive on the street. The people who kept their wits about them—and who were the least likely to overreact—tended to be those who had spent a lot of time in rough neighborhoods. A few HRT agents had logged plenty of street duty, as I had, on robbery and fugitive squads in New York or Los Angeles or Miami. But since violent crime was not a priority for the Bureau in those days, many of the younger men had been assigned to white-collar crime squads or foreign counterintelligence. Few had the arrest experience of a John Simeone or a Charlie Prouty. They were fine athletes and they performed adroitly during exercises, but those were scrimmages, not games. They needed to do grunt work out in the field and make a couple of hundred arrests of nasty, unpredictable felons.

Moreover, as the commander, I needed to watch them do it. People could change when reality reared its ugly head and the bullets flying around were lead, not wax. I had to see what everybody on the team was made of, and soon, before we were plunged into a Black September scenario. I didn't want to have to play the Super Bowl the first time out of the locker room.

Which is why, in September of 1984, I offered HRT's services to Wayne Manis, our man in Coeur d'Alene.

Manis, an Arkansan I had gotten to know during SWAT training, had spent the last sixteen years on the East Coast, chasing the Ku Klux Klan around Alabama and working undercover against La Cosa Nostra. He had recently moved to the two-man office covering the Idaho panhandle, where he hoped to have weekends free to fish and hunt.

Instead, he was back in the seven-days-a-week grind. It seemed that a lot of people in the paranoid anti-government fringe liked to lose themselves in the wilds of the Pacific Northwest. No sooner had Manis settled on a house than he found himself the case agent in charge of investigating a crew of white supremacists who had embarked on a bloody rampage. They were believed to be behind the firebombings of a porn movie house in Seattle and a synagogue in Boise. There were also indications that they had committed the June 18, 1984, assassination of Denver radio talk-show host Alan Berg, who had been ambushed and shot thirteen times with a MAC-10 submachine gun. They were apparently raising funds by counterfeiting and sticking up banks and armored cars.

The case was named BRINKROB for their most spectacular heist, the July 19, 1984, holdup of a Brink's truck in Ukiah, California, which had netted them a $3.8-million war chest. A pistol dropped at the Ukiah scene had been traced to one Andrew Barnhill, twenty-seven, who lived in Laclede, Idaho. Manis and his partner, Joe Venkus, searched Barnhill's house and found documents suggesting the existence of a racist underground group. At the same time, agents posted around the region were reviewing arrest records, conducting interviews, and analyzing calls that had originated at pay phones near a motel where the Ukiah robbers were believed to have cribbed. By the time I called Manis, he had a theory of the conspiracy and a list of twenty or so suspects, all with ties to the extremist fringe, most with previous arrests.

"They call themselves The Order, or sometimes Bruders Schweigen, Silent Brotherhood," Manis said. "They hate blacks, Jews, and homosexuals. And us. They call the federal government the Zionist Occupation Government, and they think they have a religious commitment to take it down."

"Something like the Klan?" I asked.

"A lot worse. The Klan is just a bunch of bullies, drunks, and rednecks who pick on poor people. Attacking the government has never been a part of their MO. These guys are heavily armed, and smart, and they think they're in a holy war. They think they're angels of God, taking on Satan's children."

What? I thought I had run across every nutty idea in the world. "This is a new one on me," I marveled.

"Me too, and it scares the hell out of me," Manis said.

The leader of The Order was Robert Mathews, thirty-one, born in Texas and reared in Phoenix. Active in rabid racist and anti-communist causes since his teens, Mathews had found his way to the Aryan Nations compound in Hayden Lake, a few miles northeast of Coeur d'Alene. He worked in the cement plant in Metaline Falls, an Idaho hamlet just south of the Canadian border.

The bright, twisted mind behind Aryan Nations was Richard Girnt Butler, a sixty-six-year-old former Lockheed engineer who aimed to carve a white separatist state out of the Pacific Northwest backcountry.

Every year, Butler threw a big bash called the Aryan World Congress, which attracted an array of former Klansmen, survivalists, skinheads, conspiracy theorists, and religious fanatics of various stripes. Butler wore a vaguely Gestapo-like uniform and punctuated his speeches with the Nazi salute, but his appeal was much more complex than garden-variety neo-Nazism. He postured as a Christian soldier, spiritual leader of the Church of Jesus Christ Christian. The church's creed declared Jews to be "the natural enemy of our Aryan (White) Race . . . a destroying virus that attacks our racial body to destroy our Aryan culture and the purity of our race."

Underlying this motto was an elaborate ideology of hate called Christian Identity, a brew of Nordic and Celtic mythology, Nazism, apocalyptic fundamentalism, and hoary conspiracy theories involving Jewish financiers. When he arrived in Coeur d'Alene and found out about Butler, Manis hit the religion section at the local library and studied up on the Christian Identity movement. The idea, first known as British Israelism, had cropped up in the 1870s, among a handful of religious radicals who interpreted ancient texts to mean that the legendary "lost tribes of Israel" had wandered out of the Middle East and settled in England and northern Europe. When the belief immigrated to the United States in the thirties, it mingled with racism, anti-Semitism, and xenophobia, and mutated into a dogma that held that the New Jerusalem prophesied in the Book of the Revelation was actually the United States. White Aryans, it said, were God's chosen people, the only true descendants of Adam, and, come Judgment Day, the inheritors of the earth.

Identity belief divided up into two strains, one meaner than the next. The more benign form was called the "one seedline" theory. It acknowledged that all humans were descended from Adam but claimed that only northern European peoples were the elect of God; present-day Jews were actually members of a minor Black Sea ethnic group who had no real claim to the name Israel.

Butler espoused the more vicious form of Identity, the "two seedline" theory. This dogma asserted that Jews and people of color were not human at all. Jews were demonic beings, "serpent's seed," descended from an entirely mythical coupling of Eve and Satan in the Garden of Eden. The only true human was Abel, the son of Adam and Eve and father of the white race. As Cain, the son of Eve and Satan, killed Abel, so the dogma went, Cain's descendants, the Jews, would conspire against the righteous white descendants of Abel. People with brown and black skins were dismissed as soulless, subhuman "mud people," pre-Adamic creatures put on earth to serve white men, like horses and cattle.

Identity believes the American government to be the Great Satan. Identity believers referred to the U.S. government as ZOG, for Zionist Occupation Government, because they thought Satan had infiltrated it through the Jews. Gun laws, income taxes, affirmative action—these were all the devil's doing, his way of weakening and subjugating white citizens. In fact, Identity taught that Satan controlled all world governments, all major institutions, including the media, the entertainment industry, and of course, the United Nations, and all major religions, including mainstream religious leaders from the Pope to Billy Graham to Jerry Falwell.

As far as I was concerned, Identity was terrifying because it transformed hate into a religious duty and sanctified murder itself as an act of faith. As every student of history knows, the bloodiest wars have been waged in the name of God. The insidious thing about Identity was that it exploited the fears of badly educated, rootless, patriotic, God-fearing Americans who would never have thought of saluting a picture of Hitler nor dressing up in sheets and pointy hats. Identity offered poor whites a romantic vision of themselves as Christian soldiers battling the soldiers of darkness. If you got past the rhetoric—not that many Identity worshipers did—there was no difference between Hitler's concept of the master race and Identity's view of God's chosen people. The final solution of the Nazis and Identity's notion of Christ's final triumph ended up in the same place: genocide.

Manis doubted that Robert Mathews himself was an Identity purist. He also dabbled in Norse lore, neo-Nazism, and plain old secular race hatred. He had spent time with Robert Miles, a Michigan Klansman once convicted for blowing up school buses. Miles had concocted a unique white-power religion that held that God's chosen people were descendants of angels and Nordic giants and could be recognized by their freckles. However, a number of the people around him, including Mathews's mistress, Zillah Craig, were hard-core Identity worshipers. Mathews no doubt encouraged and used their religious fervor to drive them to ever more daring terrorist acts.

The event that had set Mathews's campaign of violence in motion occurred just five weeks before Butler's Aryan World Congress of July of 1983. On June 3, a sixty-three-year-old North Dakota farmer named Gordon Kahl died in a gunfight with law enforcement officers and FBI agents in a northeast Arkansas hamlet named Walnut Ridge.

Gordon Kahl was an unlikely martyr. Except for his World War II service as a combat flier, he had spent his life on the family farm. In the late seventies, he had become a radical activist. He hooked up with Posse Comitatus, a Christian Identity group that believed that the federal government was illegitimate and so was the income tax system. Kahl stopped paying taxes; he was convicted of tax evasion, and sentenced to probation. He refused to acknowledge the judgment or to meet with a probation officer. A federal warrant was issued for his arrest. On February 13, 1983, as Kahl was leaving a Posse Comitatus meeting in Medina, North Dakota, a group of lawmen approached him to serve the warrant. Kahl opened fire with a Ruger Mini-14 assault rifle, killing two deputy U.S. marshals and wounding three other officers. Then he fled, leading lawmen on a four-month cross-country chase.

The image of a white-bearded grandfather barreling across the heartland in an old Nash Rambler struck some people in the funny bone. Kahl's likeness popped up on T-shirts that said, "Go, Gordie, Go," and, "Gordon Kahl is my tax consultant."

The story ended as tragically as it had begun. Kahl was run to ground in Walnut Ridge, where he had taken refuge in a bunkerlike dwelling dug into a hillside by a survivalist couple named Leonard and Norma Ginter. As FBI agents, U.S. marshals, state troopers, and local authorities surrounded the place, Sheriff Gene Matthews of Lawrence County, Arkansas, rashly burst through the door. Kahl shot Matthews square in the chest. The sheriff crawled to safety but bled to death outside. Matthews had managed to fire one round that pierced Kahl's brain, killing him instantly. Not realizing that Kahl was dead, the besieging law enforcement officers shouted threats and warnings until somebody had the brilliant idea of pouring fuel down the chimney. The place went up in flames. Not much remained of Kahl's body, which was finally identified with dental X rays.

All of us in law enforcement would mourn this day, not only for the needless death of Gene Matthews, but also because it elevated Gordon Kahl to the far right's pantheon of dead saints. Extremists all over the country gave credence to the rumor that the FBI had summarily executed Kahl, then incinerated his corpse and murdered Matthews to cover up the truth.

By the time Butler convened his Aryan World Congress, the air was thick with talk of vengeance. Louis Beam, a former Texas Klansman who called himself the Aryan Nation's "ambassador at large," sounded the call to arms: "I'm here to tell you that if we can't have this country, as far as I'm concerned, no one gets it."

Robert Mathews left the Congress with a new light in his eyes. Some weeks later, at a convention of the National Alliance, a white supremacist organization based in Arlington, Virginia, he made his debut as a firebrand orator, calling upon his audience to attack "the filthy, lying Jews and their parasitic usury system."

When he returned to Idaho, Mathews summoned eight men to his farm: Aryan Nations members Dan Bauer, Denver Parmenter, Randy Duey, and Bruce Carroll Pierce; Denver Klansman David Lane; Richard Kemp and Bill Soderquist from the National Alliance;

and Mathews's neighbor and closest friend, Ken Loff. Richard Butler was all talk. It was time for red-blooded white men to take action. They had to go underground and become urban guerrillas.

Mathews placed Loff's baby daughter in the center of their circle and had each man swear an oath. "I have a sacred duty," it went, "to do whatever is necessary to deliver our people from the Jew and bring total victory to the Aryan race. We hereby invoke the blood covenant and declare that we are in a full state of war and will not lay down our weapons until we have driven the enemy into the sea and reclaimed the land which was promised to our fathers of old, and through our blood and his will, becomes the land of our children to be." In the months that followed, Mathews and his eight disciples recruited others.

"Have you read *The Turner Diaries?*" Manis said.

No, I confessed.

"It's Mathews's Bible." Manis laughed. "Get ready to read some real trash, but if you don't understand the book, you'll never understand what we're dealing with and how they hate the government, especially the FBI."

The book's author was William Pierce, a former American Nazi Party member who founded the National Alliance. Pierce, a physicist with a formidable intellect, was the philosopher king of the extremist movement. He disdained Christian Identity and other religious movements as so much superstition, but he shared Butler's vision of a "white living space." Pierce called for the destruction of the U.S. government, "the malignant monster . . . the single most dangerous and destructive enemy our race has ever known."

"Enjoy," Mary Ann Sullivan said, dumping a half

dozen copies of Pierce's masterwork onto my desk. I am sure that the proprietors of the right-wing bookstore thought she was just another blond Aryan looking for the true message.

I cracked the cover and began to read.

"Today it finally began! After all these years of talking—and nothing but talking—we have finally taken our first action. We are at war with the System, and it is no longer a war of words."

The plot, a sort of futuristic *Spartacus* for bigots, is about a small band of white guerrillas who mounted an insurrection against a tyrannical left-wing Jewish government. "We have allowed a diabolically clever, alien minority to put chains on our souls and minds," mourns Earl Turner, the book's protagonist. "Why didn't we roast them over bonfires at every street corner in America? Why didn't we make final end to this obnoxious and eternally pushy clan, this pestilence from the East . . . ?"

After the government dispatches roving bands of blacks to brutalize white people who defy the "Cohen Act" outlawing private ownership of firearms, Turner and his comrades form an underground resistance movement they call The Order. They blow up FBI headquarters and the U.S. Capitol, seize the nation's nuclear arsenal, and rain warheads on New York City, Tel Aviv, and Moscow. The Soviet Union retaliates. Nuclear holocaust ensues. Western civilization as we know it is finished. The "wise and benevolent" white men of The Order end up ruling the world, or what's left of it, which isn't much.

I had to fight the urge to take a shower every few pages, but I persisted to the thrilling conclusion. Pierce's pumped-up fantasy of resourceful Aryan warriors was to the fringe right as *The Battle of Algiers* was to the militant left: entertaining and also practical, with step-by-step instructions in making truck bombs and advice on how to maintain underground cells.

Inside Mathews's band, we now know, there was a lot of grandiose talk about assassinating prominent people, including former Secretary of State Henry Kissinger, banker David Rockefeller, producer Norman Lear, international financier Baron Elie de Rothschild, and Morris Dees, leader of the Southern Poverty Law Center, which crusades against the hate movement. After a while, Mathews's rookie terrorists settled on talk-show host Alan Berg, an easier target. The likely motive: Berg had recently insulted two influential Identity proselytizers—Jack Mohr, a retired army colonel who headed the Citizens Emergency Defense System, and the Reverend Pete Peters, pastor of the Laporte, Colorado, Church of Christ and leader of an Identity recruitment organization called Scriptures for America.

Manis and the agents working with him probably knew more about the violent fringe right than nearly anybody else in government or academia, but they didn't have nearly enough hard evidence to swear out warrants for Mathews and his crew, much less prosecute them. Tracking the movements of two dozen or so people over the last year was a monumental task. When it came to covering their tracks, they weren't the KGB or the Weather Underground, but they weren't total buffoons either.

It was clear to me, as it had been to Manis, that The Order was the most important domestic terrorism threat in the nation. Headquarters had assigned a dozen or so more agents from the Western states to help with legwork, but nothing like the number who would have been deployed if a bunch of crazed bigots had been shooting up media celebrities and banks within range of the *Washington Post* or *The New York Times*.

"I know you need help," I said. "Would you like for us to come out?"

"I hadn't thought of calling you guys yet," Manis said. "It's not an HRT mission right now. Of course, these guys are heavily armed. This thing could turn dirty any minute. They're listening in on our radios, and they won't hesitate to shoot at law enforcement."

What could be worse? What could be better? Studying at the feet of Professor Manis would be a great postgraduate course in domestic terrorism for my guys. Not to mention me. Besides, chasing fugitives was just about the most fun thing anyone could ever do. I was itching to tackle these screwballs myself.

"Listen, Wayne, HQ is typecasting us as commandos, and that's not good," I pressed. "We're agents first. We can follow leads for you. We're real good at surveillance. We've got cold-weather capability, and I know damn well you'll be freezing your rear off before this is over. We've got digital voice privacy in all our cars, the only mobile voice privacy system in the whole country. We can go into an area and set up a secure radio system for you, and our guys can work with yours.

"And," I added, "if there's trouble, if somebody wants to have a shoot-out, you have the best shots and tactical agents in the country working for you."

"Well, if you put it that way, we sure can use the investigative help." Manis laughed. "We've got more leads than we know what to do with."

All I had to do was convince Buck Revell.

9

Buck said no. Not only no, but hell no. "I'm not sending you guys out to cover leads in Idaho!" he growled. "What if something happens back here in Washington? You'll be two thousand miles away and I can't get you back for a day."

I badgered. I pleaded. "Our guys need to work. If you don't use us, we'll become just like Delta. Not enough work. Every counterterrorism leader in the world has to struggle to find jobs for their people, especially at first." Finally, we cut a deal. Buck was pretty reasonable if you let him beat you up for a while. He said Wehmeyer, Mewborn, and Bonney could take a few operators to Idaho. Most of the team and I would stay home to protect the nation's capital from tourists crazed by the humidity and lack of public bathrooms.

"Good hunting," I said forlornly as I saw Horace and Jeff off. It was worse than all the times I had stood on Pop's loading dock, thinking about the pile of cartons I had to stack, watching the other kids head for the pool.

Horace slapped me on the shoulder. "We'll save a couple for you, Doc."

Once the guys arrived in Idaho, things moved fast. Manis found that Order member Gary Lee Yarborough had rented a storage locker in Sandpoint, up the road from Hayden Lake. Yarborough was an ex-con, a red-headed Yosemite Sam look-alike who had fallen in with Mathews while working security at the Aryan Nations compound. Manis thought the locker might hold some of the loot from the Ukiah job. The search had to be

covert, meaning, for intelligence gathering only, because
there wasn't enough evidence to start arresting people.
Manis swore out a sealed search warrant. HRT communications specialist Dennis Hughes, who happened to be
a very good lockpick, did the honors, black-bagging the
storage shed while Mewborn and HRT operator Mike
Fain stood security. They found no money, but there
were interesting papers and a pile of weapons, including
a silencer, which was illegal. They put everything back
just the way they had found it and left.

A few days later, Yarborough got spooked by an FBI
surveillance team and moved out of Sandpoint to a cabin
in the woods. Only one dirt road led into the place, so it
was impossible to approach the house without being
spotted. On October 18, Manis told three agents to borrow a U.S. Forest Service truck, dress up like rangers,
and drive down the dirt road in leisurely fashion. When
they eased to a stop near the cabin, Yarborough opened
fire on them.

They made a strategic retreat and called in reinforcements. Armed with a search warrant, Wehmeyer, his
assault team, and some SWAT teams raided Yarborough's
place that night. They found a mother lode of evidence—
Order documents in codes devised by Mathews, names,
addresses, snapshots and license numbers of local law
enforcement officers, explosives and all sorts of weapons,
including two MAC-10 submachine guns that had been
modified to shoot full automatic. The FBI lab ballistics
section quickly determined that one of them was the Alan
Berg murder weapon. Incredibly, Yarborough had pre-
served the best possible evidence short of a confession.

Yarborough faded into the woods, got to a phone, and
called Order members Robert and Sharon Merki, who

were living in Boise. Robert, a middle-aged aviation engineer, had joined the Identity movement and signed on with Mathews after he was laid off by Boeing. Now he was counterfeiting money with a printer in his garage. The Merkis alerted Mathews and other Order members who were staying in motels and houses in Boise.

The whole bunch lit out, heading north. As we were later to learn, they rendezvoused briefly in Bluecreek, Washington, where Order paramilitary expert Randall Rader had set up a training camp. Then they dispersed.

The trail went cold for a spell. The HRT detail returned to Quantico. But we still had a hole card.

On November 25, Mathews and Yarborough drove to Portland International Airport to pick up Order member Tom Martinez, who was flying in from Philadelphia. What Mathews did not know was that his old friend Martinez was now working for the FBI as an informant. Martinez had gotten arrested in Philadelphia while attempting to buy a fifty-cent lottery ticket with a phony fifty-dollar bill handcrafted by Robert Merki. Martinez was a former Klansman and National Alliance member, but he did not share Mathews's enthusiasm for urban warfare. It took him about ten minutes to decide to save his skin by offering to work for the FBI.

Around Thanksgiving, Mathews called Martinez from a pay phone and asked him to fly out to Portland. Agents handling Martinez in Philadelphia alerted Ted Gardner, SAC of the Portland Field Office. Gardner and his squads put together an arrest plan.

Driving out of the airport, Mathews pulled an evasive maneuver and shook the surveillance team. Agents had to canvass all the motels in the area to locate Mathews's car at the Capri motel. The next morning, when Mathews emerged from his room, an agent ordered him to halt. Mathews ignored the order. He walked slowly at first, then lit out running and ducked behind a concrete wall. When agent Art Hensel rounded the corner, Mathews fired twice, catching Hensel in the leg and foot. Before he could finish Hensel, Kenneth Lovin, a former firearms instructor and graduate of my old unit, the New York bank robbery squad, used his shotgun to blast the pistol out of Mathews's hand. Mathews sprinted several blocks, flagged down some workers, told them he had hurt his hand working on his car, and hitched a ride to the emergency room. Only he never checked in. He begged another ride heading east toward Mount Hood, where Order members Richard Scutari and Frank Silva and their wives were using a vacation cottage as a safe house.

The day was not a total loss. We had Gary Yarborough in jail. He had heard the commotion and climbed out of his back window into the arms of agents, one of whom happened to be black. Also, the car Mathews left behind yielded up weapons, some of the Ukiah proceeds, and a stack of documents, including the address of the Mount Hood safe house.

By the time the agents got there, Mathews and his pals were gone. Gardner and his team of agents grabbed an Order associate who had been hanging about at the Capri motel and doubled him. On December 3, the associate tipped the Portland office that Robert Mathews and most of his band were on Whidbey Island.

Whidbey Island, located in the middle of Puget Sound, is the Pacific coast's answer to Martha's Vineyard, a vacation resort dotted with modest cabins and A-frames, reachable mainly by ferry from Everett, Washington. The Merki family knew it well and had rented a place on the island after the gang had scattered out of Boise. Over the next few weeks, other Order members descended on the island. Mathews himself arrived in the back of Frank Silva's car.

Mathews holed up with Richard Scutari and his wife and daughter in a two-story cedar chalet on a high bluff overlooking Puget Sound. It was about an eighth of a mile from the main road. The clearing was surrounded on three sides by a dense stand of towering Douglas fir and spruce. On the fourth side was a cliff that plunged a hundred feet to the sound. Other Mathews followers— Silva, Randy Duey, Bruce Carroll Pierce, Randy Evans, Mike Norris, and Mark Jones—found lodging nearby.

Mathews whiled away the hours drafting a "Declaration of War" to be sent to the newspapers to reveal the Order's existence. "Throughout this land, our children are being coerced into accepting nonwhites for their idols, their companions and worst of all their mates," he wrote. "All about us, the land is dying. Our cities swarm with dusky hordes. The water is rancid and the air is rank. Our farms are being seized by usurious leeches and our people are being forced off the land. The Capitalists and the Communists pick gleefully at our bones, while the vile hook nosed masters of usury orchestrate our destruction. What is to become of our children in a land such as this? . . . The Aryan yeomanry is awakening. A long forgotten wind is starting to blow. Do you hear the approaching thunder? It is that of the awakened Saxon. War is upon the land. The tyrant's blood will flow."

Word that Mathews had been located reached me as I was walking into the office from the gym, my hair still wet, getting ready to tackle the never-ending paperwork. Mary Rollins, my secretary, motioned me over to her desk and held out the receiver. On the other end of the line was Wayne Gilbert, the deputy assistant director of the Criminal Investigations Division.

"Doc, Buck wants you guys to saddle up and get out to the West Coast with an advance team," he said.

I covered the receiver with my hand. "Mary. Get Jeff and Verne in here." "Verne" was Horace Mewborn's nickname. His genteel North Carolina accent was nothing like the moronic redneck drawl invented by actor Jim Varney for his "Verne and Ernest" commercials, but Horace/Verne could take a joke, which was more than you could say for at least half the FBI and the entire Justice Department.

"What's the deal, Wayne?"

"Mathews and other members of The Order have been tracked to Whidbey Island. They're located in two or three houses. Buck wants you to go out and give Seattle Division a hand. But you can only take one section. He still wants someone in Washington in case there's another incident."

"Wayne, one section is a little light if this turns out to be a standoff," I protested. "I'd like to take the entire team."

"Buck says no. You know how he feels about all of you guys being gone at the same time. Call Portland and Seattle and get the details."

Wehmeyer and an advance team left within the hour. I followed with the blue section—twenty-five operators and snipers—later that afternoon. The SWAT teams from Portland, Seattle, and Butte would meet us on the island.

Flying three thousand miles from Andrews Air Force Base to Whidbey Naval Air Station took our C-130 about nine hours. When the back loading-ramp dropped, I walked down into the cool night air where Jeff stood with agent Mike Burns, the Seattle SWAT team leader.

Jeff didn't look happy. "You won't like it. We'll talk in the car."

Al Whitaker, the SAC in Seattle and the on-scene commander, had refused to let our sniper-observers do their jobs. As Jeff was preparing to send them into the woods around the cabin, Whitaker stopped him, protesting that Mathews might spot them. Jeff tried to convince Whitaker that his fears were unfounded. If you didn't know they were there, you wouldn't see those snipers in their tricked-up gillie suits until you fell on top of them. Whitaker remained skeptical. He had never seen us in action and had no idea what we could do.

Jeff tried another tack. He proposed to send Don Glasser and Bob Core into the woods dressed as wood-cutters, a common occupation on the island. Whitaker rejected that idea as well. The result of all this, Jeff told me, was that we had a big intelligence gap. We had no idea how many people and guns were with Mathews, so we couldn't make a sensible plan of action.

I located Whitaker and tried to work things out. He was nervous about authorizing any move that might lead to an FBI bloodbath. I told him I appreciated his concern, but after all, this was the very type of situation the team had been created to handle. Normally, Revell would have overridden Whitaker, and that would've been the end of it, but Buck was out of the country.

Finally, Whitaker said, "Okay, go, but be careful."

"Don't worry," I replied. "I'll be on-scene with the

team that goes for Mathews. The SWAT teams will take the other locations. Things will go okay."

Whitaker looked dubious but nodded brusquely. We moved in on December 7. We were on the ground at four o'clock in the morning so we could have the place surrounded by dawn. The plan was for Bonney's assault team to wade through waist-deep freezing water, hit the beach, and scale the bluff. Wehmeyer and I would take the other twenty men through the woods to circle the front of the cabin. Glasser led the column. I brought up the rear.

The night air was the wet cold that gets into your bones. We were all wearing camouflage utilities and Gore-Tex parkas, but my fingers still ached as I gripped my MP5. I had never seen trees so tall, and they were so close together that they shut out the sky altogether. It was like being inside a coal mine at midnight. The ground was soft with ferns and the humus of decaying plants. We had night-vision goggles, but even so, each of us put a hand on the shoulder of the man in front to keep from stumbling and making noise. I was thankful for our secure radios. Mathews had just shot one FBI agent. I didn't want to be compromised and get into a running gunfight with him in these woods.

We arrived at our positions well before dawn and waited for Bonney to report that he had made the climb and had the back door closed. In a matter of minutes, he radioed. "Charlie Leader to Alpha One."

"Alpha One," I answered. "Go ahead."

"Alpha One, be advised that we are in position. The black side is secure."

We had Mathews trapped.

Each of us found a tree that he could hide behind. I

selected my personal tree, put my back to it, and actually caught about three minutes of sleep. I was awakened by my radio. "Doc, have you really checked out your tree?" It was Jeff. I had picked one that wasn't quite wide enough to hide me. The rest of the team had selected what looked like giant redwoods.

"Oh, shit. Catch this." I tossed my MP5 over to Jeff and jumped over a fallen tree to join him behind his comfortably wide trunk.

"You need to be more careful about your cover," he said, smiling. "Look at this place. I haven't seen vegetation this thick since I left Vietnam."

I rubbed my temples. We had no idea how many people were in the house or how many weapons they had. "We should have deployed snipers." I brooded. "Hell, we could have put the entire HRT in here and not have been compromised."

As the light came up, we could see two cars parked down by a shed, only feet from the cabin. "We need to try to disable those cars," I whispered to Jeff. "We don't want someone jumping into one and tearing off down the road."

Jeff radioed Rick Warford, one of our sniper team leaders. "Alpha Two to Sierra Two. Can you slip down and disable the two cars?"

"Can do. Stand by."

Warford, a hulk who would strap a hundred pounds of free weights to his waist and do pull-ups and dips, slipped out of most of his gear and armed only with his Hi-Power, crawled across the clearing and slid into the shed. My radio crackled. It was another sniper. "Look at that crazy Warford. He's sawing the tires off of the car." Rick had found a tree saw in the shed and was using it to slice all eight tires in two. "I wanted to be sure the tires were real flat," he explained.

At dawn I instructed the negotiator from the Seattle Field Office to announce our presence and to demand surrender. He had brought what had to be the puniest megaphone in the world. Hell, I couldn't hear the damned thing and I was twenty feet from it.

Negotiations did not go well. The negotiator talked over his pipsqueak horn throughout the day. Robert Merki and Randy Duey, who had been arrested down the road by the SWAT teams, were brought in. They called out to Mathews to give himself up, but he didn't reply. Finally, we persuaded Mathews to accept a telephone so we could talk in normal voices. Merki got on the phone with Mathews and begged him to save himself to fight another day. Mathews refused.

Around eleven o'clock that night, Ian Stewart, the stepson of Robert Merki, walked out of the cabin with a bag full of money—about $40,000, as it turned out—and a letter from Mathews that amounted to a suicide note. "I have been a good soldier, a fearless warrior," it said. "I will die with honor and join my brothers in Valhalla."

Mathews was polite to the negotiator during their telephone conversations, but nothing could induce him to walk out. Jeff, Horace, and I discussed the possibility of enticing him to the front window on a pretext of passing him something, then having two or three large operators jerk him out the window. I reluctantly shelved the idea as too risky to the operators.

We brought in portable lights and a generator borrowed from the fire department to light up the yard. I talked to Mathews myself, reporting that the lights were for his protection in case he surrendered. By explaining, I hoped to avoid aggravating his paranoia.

"Who are you?" he asked.

"Danny Coulson. I'm the HRT commander. Let's talk about this, things are not as bad as you think."

I thought he was listening. For the rest of the brief conversation, he was deferential to me. He kept calling me "sir." "Yes, sir." "No, sir." I had a feeling that I was making a connection. I wondered if I should continue the conversation. I felt that if I had a chance, I might just be able to talk him out. But the policy of the FBI at the time absolutely forbade the commander to enter into the negotiations. The thinking was that the negotiator could play for time by meeting every demand with the comment, "Well, I'll have to check with the boss." Obviously, the boss had no excuse for delays. So I turned the phone back over to the negotiator.

As the night dragged on, fatigue became a factor for the HRT and SWAT operators, who had been working without a break for more than twenty-four hours. Wayne Gilbert and Al Whitaker decided on a shift change. Fresh SWAT operators who had just arrived from Los Angeles and San Francisco would take the perimeter. Gilbert and I agreed that the HRT was no longer needed and should return to Washington. Mathews wasn't going anywhere, and if he tried, almost a hundred SWAT operators would welcome him with open arms. We went back to the Naval Air Station and awaited our C-130. We would leave sometime during the morning.

During the night, Mathews stopped answering the negotiation phone. Around mid-morning, while we were at the airport loading our gear, Whitaker ordered the Seattle and Butte SWAT teams to shoot tear gas—more than 250 rounds—into the second floor of the cabin where Mathews crouched. At about two o'clock in the afternoon, when nothing had been heard from Mathews in some time, it appeared he might be dead or incapacitated. The Seattle SWAT team threw flash-bangs into the ground floor and stormed inside. Manis and the Butte SWAT team stood just outside, poised to rush the steps to take the second floor. This was a serious miscalculation. Mathews had a gas mask and was unfazed by the massive gassing. Hearing the SWAT operators on the level below him, he fired his machine gun through the floor in a methodical zigzag pattern. Manis told me later that he had heard slugs buzzing an inch or two above his forehead. It was a miracle that neither he nor anybody else was hurt. The SWAT teams beat a hasty retreat.

Late in the afternoon, Whitaker and the SWAT leaders got to worrying that Mathews would try to make a break for the woods out of his back door, where our portable lights didn't reach. In the gloom, he would be practically impossible to spot until it was too late. A helicopter with a dazzling spotlight was brought in to light up the backyard between the house and the edge of the forest. Mathews fired through the ceiling at the chopper, forcing it to pull back. Then he started firing into the woods where the Portland and Los Angeles SWAT teams were positioned, driving them off the perimeter.

Our takeoff had been delayed. We were still at the Whidbey Naval Air Station while all this was going on. Whitaker called me there and asked me to come back. My men and I jumped in our cars and trucks and drove back to the staging area. Whitaker told me the story of the long, disastrous day and asked me to be prepared to take back the perimeter.

I walked back up the road and called my team leaders together. "Jock up. We may be going back on line."

I got my kit bag out of the car and put on my gear, then slammed a magazine into my MP5. Mewborn and I were talking about how to get Mathews out of the cabin when we heard gunfire, then popping sounds. Then the sky lit up.

"The cabin's on fire," someone shouted.

We got out of the car and stared in stark amazement. Bit by bit, we pieced together what had happened. Somebody in the command center had had the idea of shooting a lighting flare into the cabin to backlight it so that the SWAT teams could see exactly where Mathews was. The flare had set the wooden cabin on fire. Rather than surrender, Mathews had elected to stay inside and burn to death.

Fred Kingston, one of our assault team leaders, looked at me grimly. "We may be very glad we were up here when that thing went off."

"You got that right," I said. I gazed at the light in the sky and thought of the new martyr to hate we'd made. *See you in hell, Robert Mathews. You won this one. The next one's mine.*

BOOK THREE

THE COVENANT, SWORD AND ARM OF THE LORD

It's finally happened—It's on us now!
The world is seeing it—The war has begun!
The sun is darkened—Moon's turned to blood;
City streets overflow—with crimson flood!
Kings of the earth—Captains of this world,
Out to make war, with God's Christ and his Lord.
Fowls of heaven, Eat the enemies' flesh.
Who can make war with the beast? We can!

> —Battle hymn, *Covenant, Sword and*
> *Arm of the Lord*

1

On March 28, 1985, Horace Mewborn and I were making our rounds of the HQ terrorism section, checking
out the latest trends in terror and anarchy, when
Horace answered a page and pulled me aside with his
Chuck Yeager we're-losing-an-engine-or-two-so-you-
might-want-to-buckle-up drawl. Dan Kelly, the assistant
special agent in charge in Little Rock, was calling with some
sort of bubba problem.

We commandeered a windowless cubicle in the
dreary beige and gray suite, poured a couple of cups of
fine, if muddy, FBI coffee, and tried to kill the taste with
white stuff while we waited for the call to be patched
through.

The phone rang. "You got a job for me, Dan?"

"Yeah, I think so," Kelly said. "The U.S. attorney
wants us to serve a couple of warrants on the CSA."

"What the hell is the CSA?"

"It's the Covenant, Sword and Arm of the Lord. A
white hate group. A guy named Jim Ellison runs it.
He's in a heavily fortified compound down in the
Ozarks, near Mountain Home, Arkansas. Could be a
hundred people in there. We know they have rockets,
machine guns, assault rifles. We think they have hand
grenades and Claymore mines, and maybe anti-tank
rockets."

Kelly marched through his brief in a Bureau mono-
tone, but I could feel the tension in his voice. The CSA,
he said, had assembled a paramilitary force renowned
throughout the extremist underground. Racist Rambos

from all over the United States, including some Order men, had trained there. Ellison had stockpiled literally tons of weapons, and his people knew how to use them. Men and some women drilled daily in the Endtime Overcomer Survival Training School, which contained a mock village called Silhouette City. This was a live-fire course much like the FBI's Hogan's Alley, where agents honed their quick-reaction skills by shooting at cardboard and plywood "bad guys" who lurked half-hidden around every corner. Only the targets in the CSA shooting range were figures of policemen, with Stars of David painted over their hearts.

There was no way to sneak up on the compound. It had an elaborate early-warning system. Patrols hiked around the grounds every night. The only road in was dirt and gravel. An approaching car could be heard twenty miles away.

What Kelly was describing in his matter-of-fact way was the closest thing to a mission impossible we had ever encountered. It was what we call a blivet, shorthand for five pounds of manure in a one-pound bag.

I started laughing. "Jesus Christ, you gotta be kidding me. I think I'm busy. Call the fucking military. Sounds like a job for Delta."

Kelly laughed too. He knew the law against using the military as well as I did. "No, I think this is a job for you. Can you guys come down and take a look at it for us?"

"Sure. But you have to get Blasingame to get permission from Buck." Jim Blasingame was Kelly's boss, the SAC of the FBI division in Little Rock. Blasingame, an old pal from our days together on the inspection staff, was a step ahead of me. By the time I handed the phone to Horace and caught the elevator to the seventh floor,

Blasingame had talked to Revell, the only person with authority to deploy the HRT, and the deal was done.

If Kelly was right, we were about to meet the most heavily armed, best-trained, most-determined paramilitary force any U.S. law enforcement agency had faced in modern times.

2

When it was time for me to head South, I went home to break the news to Little Doc. Carol and I had not been making a go of the marriage and, following a period of separation, we had got divorced. She wanted space, so we never fought about custody. Doc stayed with me, and visited Carol from time to time.

"We have a job," I said. "It's in Arkansas. It's going to take a long time. You'll have to stay with your mother. I'll call you every night and let you know how things are going, but I won't see you for a long time."

"Okay." He nodded. He was great about it. He didn't ask a lot of questions about where I was going. He knew more about FBI work than most new agents. Many times my beeper would go off and I'd disappear for a few days. Horace or some other agent usually stayed with Little Doc. This time, Horace had to come with me.

I didn't like leaving him for long. Thirteen was a roller-coaster age even when I was around to crack the whip. I didn't dwell on the possibility that I might not get back. In my job, you can't think that way. But I knew I'd be in the thick of things, and there was always the chance of an airplane or helicopter crash. I signed a pile of blank checks and left them with his mother so that if I was incapacitated or killed, Doc would have the things he needed.

On impulse, I called a friend and asked her if she'd like to come over and keep me company while I packed. It wasn't a very romantic invitation, but then, there was nothing more between Debbie Conner and me than there was between me and Horace or Jeff. Debbie was a schoolteacher who had been our neighbor in Herndon when we first moved down from New York. We'd met Debbie when Doc, then four, marched out of our new house, knocked on her door, and demanded, "Do you have any children?"

"No, darlin'," she'd replied, "only the one in my tummy."

"Will you play with me?"

She had telephoned Doc's mom and played with our lonely kid for the better part of the afternoon.

Over the years, Debbie and I became pals. We lived in different suburbs now, but we never lost touch. I sought her out for the wise, straightforward advice that helped me through the first months of my tumultuous separation and my endless child-rearing quandaries. Recently, it had been my turn to offer a shoulder because Debbie and her husband, a Navy engineer, had split up, leaving her with three children under nine. Neither of us was ready to think about a new entanglement, but it was comfortable hanging out together, trading off taking the kids for pizza and G-rated movies and sharing a beer late in the evening.

Debbie's eyes widened when she walked through the door of our small house and saw the floor totally covered with submachine guns, ammunition belts, gas masks, bulletproof vests, camouflage clothing, rain gear, boots, knives, and all sorts of little gadgets. She knew vaguely that I was with the FBI, but somehow I had never gotten around to telling her about the HRT.

"What kind of job are you going to?" she gasped. "You look like you're going to war."

"Well, I don't sell shoes for a living." I grinned.

She smiled uncertainly, and there was a look in her eyes I didn't quite get. It was as if a curtain had fallen. Much later, she told me that she was remembering all the times her father, a Navy cryptographer named Bob Hyatt, had pulled out his plain brown suitcase, tossed in his uniforms, and disappeared for days on "jobs." He had been gone for three weeks during the Cuban missile crisis. *War has been declared,* she remembered thinking, *and they forgot to tell the rest of us.* While I was packing, she had her eye on Doc, who was making out as if this were all routine to him. She understood, as I didn't, that he wasn't as nonchalant as he looked.

At the time, Debbie kept all that to herself and busied herself with folding and stacking my cammies.

"Naw, Deb, here's how we do it," I said, demonstrating how to roll them up. She sighed, shook her head, and watched despairingly as I crumpled, shoved, and stomped, wine-maker style, until the pile of stuff fit in my duffel.

"Guess terrorists don't care if you have that clean, pressed, and starched look," she said, grimacing.

I arrived in Little Rock early the next morning and checked into the Legacy hotel, a turn-of-the-century landmark. I was admiring the elegant bathroom fittings, which would have lasted about ten minutes in a New York hotel before someone stole them, when there was a knock at the door. "Doc?"

It was Horace. He had been in Little Rock for more than a week with Jeff Wehmeyer, and four other HRT advance team members, laying the groundwork for the deployment of the full complement.

"Verne! Come in. Did you see all the brass in here?"

"Sure did. Don't be getting your screwdriver out and taking the stuff home with you."

I flopped on the bed. He pulled up an antique chair. We had a problem to solve. "Verne, what do we know about the ATF guy Buford?" Horace had warned me by telephone that Bill Buford, the head of the Little Rock office of the Bureau of Alcohol, Tobacco and Firearms, was indispensable. He'd been keeping tabs on Ellison for nearly six years and had personally produced a lot of the evidence on which the warrants were based.

But would Buford play? From what I'd heard, he had poured his heart and soul into the CSA investigation. He wouldn't necessarily welcome an incursion on his turf. Who would? The FBI had a terrible habit of hogging the glory. Every agent has heard the joke about the federal law enforcement K-9 competition. Bones are awarded to the DEA dog for finding drugs, to the Customs dog for sniffing out contraband, and to the ATF dog for locating explosives. At the last minute, the FBI dog charges onstage, does something unmention-able to the other dogs, steals their bones, and calls a press conference to take credit. I didn't want to swipe Buford's bone or meet a single reporter, but he had no way of knowing that.

"Doc, he's a good guy," Horace said as if reading my mind.

"Good guy" is about the best thing we ever say about a man or woman.

The U.S. attorney loved him, Horace continued. Everybody in the state government knew and respected him. "He's your kind of guy," Horace added. "He was a Green Beret in Vietnam, a medic, saw lots of action."

"Oh, hell," I sighed. "No wonder you like this guy. Another Special Forces brother. Were you guys in the same unit? Is he a cousin, or what?"

"Now, Doc, we never even crossed paths," Horace said patiently. "I tell you what. When you meet him, I guarantee you'll want to take him back to the team with you."

Now that was the *supreme* compliment.

"Okay, Green Beret brother," I said, looking straight in Horace's eyes. "One last question. Does he have any cowboy in him?"

"Well, not cowboy like you. He didn't spend his youth falling off horses and bulls. If you mean, is he a wild man?—absolutely not. He knows better than anyone how dangerous these guys are, and he wants to do this as a siege or mobile assault on Ellison. He knows more about this compound and the personalities of the subjects than anyone. We're lucky to have him on board. If things turn to shit, I'd want him on my side."

That was good enough for me. Risks were part of the job, but I didn't go out looking for danger, and I didn't want anybody around me who did.

I kicked off my boots—yes, cowboy boots—and struggled into a suit and tie. We headed for the FBI office in the federal building a few blocks away. Just after we passed through the security doors, I spotted a lanky, rawboned man with piercing eyes, high cheekbones, broad shoulders, thinning hair, and no waist. He reminded me of Sam Shepard.

"Bill, come here and meet Danny Coulson," Horace said.

Buford offered a strong hand and a quick smile.

"Bill, before we go in with all the bureaucrats, I need to know something," I said. "Can you partner up with me for the duration? I need you with me until we get this handled. I'll have my HQ call yours if you want to get it cleared."

"No, that won't be necessary. I'm with you guys until we finish. One way or another." That was it, no talk about who was in charge or who would get the credit.

Inside the field-office conference room, I saw a familiar face. It was Jack Knox, whom I had known back in New York, where he handled stolen-securities and stock-fraud cases. About six months earlier, Horace told me, Buford had approached Knox to help him with the CSA investigation. Buford had enough evidence to arrest Ellison for making automatic weapons and silencers, which were federal felonies, but gun violations didn't pull down much jail time in Arkansas. Buford knew that if he could prove Ellison and his pals were involved in terrorism, they could be charged under the racketeering law, which could expose them to heavy-duty prison time. Some of them might flip if they thought they were looking at ten or twenty years in the slammer. Only the Department of Justice wouldn't file a racketeering indictment without FBI participation. So Buford had asked Knox to work with him on the case.

That told me Buford knew his stuff. Knox was very, very good at complicated conspiracy cases. In New York, his squad was considered the most sophisticated and intellectual in the office. It was certainly the best dressed. Once I ran into Jack while he was leading my roommate Jay Vasquez, another stock squad member, into the office in handcuffs, with a couple of suspected stock swindlers tagging along behind. Vasquez looked just like the perps—gray flannel, rep tie, the full Gordon Gekko. Knox and Vasquez did frantic semaphores with their eyebrows until the dumb fugitive hunter figured out he should keep his mouth shut and not blow Jay's cover. I could never get over how Jack and Jay and the crew could make so many arrests and look so good doing it. I showed up at the office in a torn T-shirt, nursing cuts and bruises and dragging a suspect who looked as if he had been run over by a garbage truck.

So here we were, sixteen years later, working a case together, but he was still going to be neat as a pin and I was going to get cold, dirty, and nicked up. There really was order in the universe, I thought, at least as far as dictating who stayed clean and who got dirty.

3

Buford and Knox filled me in on what they knew about the CSA from local people and their informants. In the weeks and months to come, as the racketeering investigation progressed and some Ellison cronies made plea bargains, they would learn much more. The saga of the CSA as they eventually pieced it together went something like this:

The group had started out peacefully enough, as a deeply fundamentalist sect founded in the mid-1970s by Jim Ellison, an Illinois-born ironworker and itinerant preacher who had been expelled from the Lincoln Christian Church Seminary after a doctrinal dispute. With his wavy forelock, frayed denims, piercing blue eyes, and soaring flights of rhetoric, Ellison came on like a cross between John the Baptist and James Dean, a passionate rebel with a direct pipeline to the Almighty. Ellison preached that the Second Coming of Christ prophesied in the Book of the Revelation was imminent. He calculated that the Apocalypse, the final battle between Christ and the Antichrist, would unfold in the summer of 1978.

Ellison attracted a following of working-class teens and young adults struggling to extricate themselves from the drug scene. Also, he appealed to a handful of deeply fundamentalist couples, mostly young, poor, and rootless, who found establishment churches hollow and materialistic and who yearned to raise their children far from "Babylon," as they called the strip malls and honky-tonks of blue-collar America.

In 1977, Ellison and his flock, which numbered about 150 men, women, and children at its peak, decided to follow the path of Jesus and the prophets and plunge into the wilderness, the better to hear God's voice as the doomsday deadline approached. They took out a mortgage on a 244-acre plot of land on Bull Shoals Lake, a hundred-mile-long body of water nestled in the Ozark Mountains that formed the border between Arkansas and Missouri. They built houses, a church, a school, and various outbuildings, ran electric power lines and dug cesspools. They christened their commune Zarephath-

Horeb, two Old Testament names that signified a place for spiritual refining and communion with God. The men got jobs clearing timber for local landowners or cut and sold cedar. People around Mountain Home, the nearest village, nicknamed them the "cedar boys," regarded them as friendly hippies, and hired them to repair tools and cars.

Ellison preached that the ungodly, amounting to 90 percent of the world population, would perish in the Tribulation—fires, pestilence, earthquakes, and riots—which Revelation said would precede the Apocalypse. Only God's elect, safe in their refuges, would survive, but they'd have to be completely self-sufficient. To lay in enough supplies, Ellison convinced his people to sell everything they owned, down to wedding rings and family heirlooms. They ate as little as possible and labored hard to complete the compound. They didn't read newspapers, watch television, or listen to the radio. They rarely talked to people in Mountain Home. When the world didn't end on schedule, Ellison made a new calculation, postponing the cataclysm for a few months.

Waiting for Judgment Day must have been a rush for a while, but nobody can live day to day in a state of high drama. After the apocalyptic vigil had dragged on for a year or so, the bottled-up emotions in that backwoods compound must have been thick enough to choke on. I didn't need Soskis to explain to me how the sect's initial excitement might have soured into paranoia.

Just when the congregation was probably on the verge of hysteria from isolation, anxiety, and hunger, the mail brought some preaching tapes from one John Todd, a California-based lay preacher who was peddling a personalized version of the moldy international-Jewish-conspiracy hokum. Todd claimed that before he found Jesus, he had been the Grand Druid of the Council of Thirteen, a pagan cabal that was plotting with Satan worshipers, witches covens, and Jewish financiers to infiltrate all governments and institutions, blot out national boundaries, and rule the world as Satan's surrogates.

It was an intricate tale that knotted around itself like a tough old vine, but the part that got the congregation's attention was this. During the Tribulation, bad people weren't just going to kill one another. They would spill out of the cities and rampage around the countryside, looting, raping, and murdering. They would seek out Christian refuges to steal their stockpiles of food and rape their women. God wanted his chosen to protect themselves. Ellison and his people needed no further inducements. They got right to work, took extra jobs, and scraped together $52,000, which they used to buy weapons.

The final step in the transformation from sect to violent cult was the introduction of Christian Identity belief. Toward the end of 1979, Ellison went to Missouri to raise money for the commune by taking a metalworking job on a U.S. Department of Defense project constructing missile silos. One Sunday, he drove to Schell City, Missouri, and looked up the Church of Israel, which was run by Dan Gayman, a "two-seedline" Identity proselytizer prominent in the fringe right.

Ellison was electrified by Gayman's ranting and took a tape of some of his sermons back to the compound. The church elders were shocked at Gayman's anti-Semitic vitriol, but Ellison persuaded them that Identity explained some mysteries as no other doctrine could. They began with the premise that everything that happened on earth was God's will. Why had God caused blacks to be enslaved and oppressed? If the Jews were God's chosen people, why were they slaughtered in the Holocaust? If the victims were evil—counterfeit people, as Identity called them—then God's harsh judgment upon them began to make sense. Furthermore, why had God turned Ellison's feet toward Schell City, if not to bring the congregation into the Identity fold? It took about six months of talking and praying, but in the end, the elders succumbed.

Ellison cut his hair short, military style, gathered the elders in a sacred ceremony, and insisted they sign a "Declaration of Non-Surrender," in which they vowed to fight to the death for Jesus. They were now Christian soldiers of the Aryan elect, commissioned to set the Apocalypse in motion by launching the first strike against Satan. They had to kill for Christ to fulfill the prophecies of Revelation. Only when the world was cleansed of Jews, blacks, federal agents, homosexuals, and all other servants of Satan would Christ return to establish the New Jerusalem. Then they would reign in glory, holy proconsuls enthroned at His right hand.

In 1981, Ellison and his men served as the security force at a convocation of extremist groups hosted by the Illinois-based Christian Patriots Defense League. Resplendent in camouflage and weighted down with weapons, Ellison was filmed by an ABC television network crew. The spotlight proved addictive. He thought up a more macho name for the commune—the Covenant, Sword and Arm of the Lord. He designated CSA elder Kerry Noble, a former Baptist minister, as his public relations man and started granting interviews. He set up a printing operation to publish pamphlets full of anti-Semitic invective. In October 1982, he hosted his own extremist hatefest at the compound.

At the Aryan World Congress in July 1983, Ellison was moved by the rousing eulogies for Gordon Kahl. Like Robert Mathews, he found inspiration in *The Turner Diaries* and vowed to take the battle to the government. "The sword is out of the sheath, and it's ready to strike," he declared. "For every one of our people they killed, we ought to kill a hundred of theirs." While Mathews went off to form a *Turner*-like cell in the Pacific Northwest, Ellison declared himself the white resistance leader of the American heartland.

If Ellison had contented himself with mouthing off, we would have left him to stew in his own sorry juices. But he was spreading more than hate.

In fact, during 1983 and 1984, Ellison was concocting a series of half-baked plots, in league with his sidekick Richard Wayne Snell, a white-bearded Oklahoman who had no use for the spiritual side of commune life but who hung around because he liked shooting the machine guns.

Snell and Ellison firebombed a Jewish community center in Bloomington, Indiana, and a gay church in Springfield, Missouri. The places were empty at the time, so they didn't kill anybody. They tried to blow up the Red River natural-gas pipeline at Fulton, Arkansas, but the explosive fizzled. The first fatality occurred in November 1983, when Ellison dispatched Snell to rob a pawnshop in Texarkana to raise money for the terrorist campaign. Snell killed the pawnbroker, William Stumpp, in the mistaken belief that he was Jewish.

Snell got away, and on December 26, 1983, he and Ellison, accompanied by CSA members Kerry Noble,

Bill Thomas, Lambert Miller, and David McGuire, set off on their most ambitious plan: the assassination of federal judge H. Franklin Waters, Jack Knox, and Asa Hutchinson, the U.S. attorney in Fort Smith. The three federal officials had been involved in the trial of the Ginter family, the Arkansas tax protesters who had been charged with harboring Gordon Kahl after he was tracked down to their bunker and killed.

Just before they headed into Fort Smith, Ellison called the congregation together and prayed aloud: "Lord, if this is what you want, make this a trip with no problems. Let it go smooth."

But it didn't. An unexpected snow had fallen during the night. Halfway to Fayetteville, Miller, who was driving, rounded an icy curve too fast, sideswiped the car of an elderly couple, and landed the CSA van in a ditch, its radiator punctured and steaming. Snell, riding in the chase car, badgered Ellison to finish the job, but Ellison decided the snow and the wreck were signs from God to call off the plot for the moment.

A few months later, Ellison was back at it. He dispatched Noble with a briefcase full of explosives and orders to bomb a homosexual church in Kansas City, Missouri. Noble lost his nerve and skulked back to the compound.

In 1984, Ellison's machinations started to catch up with him. In April, Bill Thomas and two other CSA members were caught stealing a flatbed trailer in Missouri. Policemen who searched their car discovered an automatic MAC-10 and silencer and held them without bail.

Soon after this, Ellison lost Kent Yates, an ex-Marine who had run the compound's early-warning and defense system, the Silhouette City training course and the gun shop. Yates was a fugitive from an Arizona warrant for manufacturing automatic weapons. When Buford and his men found out that Yates was living in the CSA compound, they set up a sting, luring Yates and Ellison to a meeting with the promise of an antique magazine for their rare World War I machine gun. When the pair showed up to make the buy, the agents clapped handcuffs on Yates.

Then, on June 30, Richard Wayne Snell opened fire on state trooper Louis Bryant when Bryant, who was black, pulled him over in a routine traffic stop near De Queen, Arkansas. Snell pumped another round into Bryant as he lay bleeding on the ground. Alerted by passing truckers, troopers and police chased Snell to Broken Bow, Oklahoma, where he blasted away at his pursuers and was subdued only after he was shot five times.

Bill Buford went to Broken Bow to examine the weapons cache from Snell's car. He picked up a scrap of paper with a crude sketch and recognized the drawing as a map to his own house. It seemed that Snell had been stalking Buford.

In Snell's van, ATF found several firearms that traced back to Ellison and the CSA. A Ruger Mini-14 assault rifle, illegally converted to automatic, which Snell had fired at the police at Broken Bow, had been bought by Ellison, according to the gun dealer's records. Ellison's name was also on the purchase records of a Ruger .22-caliber pistol that, ballistics tests determined, was the weapon that had killed Bill Stumpp. Then there was a silencer with tool marks that matched the silencer found in Bill Thomas's car.

Snell recovered from his wounds and was extradited to Arkansas at the request of then governor Bill Clinton. Eventually he would be convicted of the Stumpp and Bryant murders and sent to death row.

Now the spotlight shifted to Ellison. Buford brought Knox in and stepped up his own investigation. By the end of March 1985, they had enough evidence to support warrants for a search of the compound and for the arrest of Ellison and several of his men on firearms violations. There, they hoped to find enough evidence to round out the racketeering case.

Ordinarily ATF, which exercised primary jurisdiction, would simply have raided the place, and some ATF officials were eager to do just that, but Buford knew a bloodbath when he saw one. Blasingame, Knox and Asa Hutchinson agreed the job was beyond ATF and FBI SWAT capabilities. That's when we got the call.

Buford's refusal to mount a raid had nothing to do with his personal courage, which was uncommon. He told me how he had taken to slipping into the compound alone, in the dark of night, lying on a hilltop till close to dawn and watching the CSA patrols through his binoculars. One mistake and he would have been a dead man, but he didn't make any mistakes.

In August of 1984, Ellison had actually invited Buford into the compound, one of the few outsiders and certainly the only lawman to win such an audience. Buford, another ATF agent, and Arkansas state trooper Gene Irby, who lived in Mountain Home, showed up at the gate to hand Ellison a subpoena to appear before the Muskogee, Oklahoma, federal grand jury investigating Snell. Ellison, who sometimes affected a store-bought black beret, evidently wanted to meet a war hero who had worn a bona fide green one. He sent word to the guards that Buford could enter, alone and unarmed.

As he was being escorted by ten or twelve armed men, Buford saw two long guns poking out of narrow windows and trained on his chest. Also, a sniper was drawing a bead on him from a hilltop, and a light anti-tank rocket launcher was trained on the ATF car. But once inside the house, Ellison gave Buford the VIP treatment. He wanted to hear all about Buford's experiences as a Special Forces sergeant, especially when he was running raids and recons out of Da Nang in the mid-sixties.

Buford found Ellison's playing at soldiering as offensive as his racist venom. He didn't consider war a game. He had signed on with the Special Forces at the age of eighteen because, he told me, "I'd seen a lot of John Wayne movies. I thought it was going to be a great high adventure. Well, it was pure terror." He never talked about his medals. But he kept a straight face and a civil tongue—"You gotta do what you gotta do," he said—and used the time to memorize everything he saw.

On the face of things, it doesn't make much sense for a man who claims federal agents are Satan to turn around and fawn on Buford like a groupie, but I've seen it happen time and again. People who spend their Saturdays making pipe bombs instead of going to their kids' soccer games or working on their cars don't set much store by intellectual consistency, or intellectual anything. They spew all sorts of conspiracy theories about black helicopters and the New World Order, but in their hearts, they'd love nothing more than to be a Green Beret or a Delta commando or HRT operator. They're well aware they can't pass the physicals, let alone the intelligence and psychological tests. In fact, they never succeed at anything they tackle. Mathews, Ellison, David Koresh, Tim McVeigh, Terry Nichols, Eric Rudolph, and all the rest of the haters—not one of them ever held a steady job or had a normal relationship with a woman. They get into hate because they're looking for an excuse for their failures. They try to bury their sense of worthlessness under lots of guns, lots of firepower, lots of rhetoric, and lots of hate, but they're still losers, and deep inside, they know it. What Buford was telling me, in so many words, was that Ellison was programmed to lose. This was information I knew how to use.

After I'd spent some time with Knox, Buford, Hutchinson, and a few others, Jim Blasingame and I went into his office and shut the door. I had never seen his rubbery face somber until that morning. He bore a striking resemblance to Don Rickles and had signed his share of autographs in nightspots. He wanted to talk about the children. There were sixteen women and at least two dozen children in the compound. The women had some choice in being there. The children had none. At all costs, he said, we had to avoid gunplay so long as there was a chance of hitting any of them.

I nodded. Neither of us talked about the prospects of bringing Ellison in alive, but we both knew the price we'd pay if we made another martyr. Blasingame had been the leader of the FBI team on the Gordon Kahl manhunt. He had watched the bunker burn with Kahl inside it. He knew very well how I'd felt when I saw Robert Mathews's cabin burning. Besides, the words of my friend Christian Prouteaux, the commander of France's GIGN, were never far from my mind. "All life is precious, even the life of a terrorist," he had said. "If lives are not important, then anyone can do this job. Just call in the military." It was from Prouteaux that I had developed the HRT motto, Servare Vitas. To Save Lives.

"When do you want to leave?" Blasingame said.

"We move at first light. We have a lot to do."

4

We established a forward base of operations in Branson, Missouri, an hour and a half's drive over the mountain from Bull Shoals Lake. Branson had plenty of hotels and was full of tourists on the way to the mountains. We'd blend right in without having to cook up a cover story. Ellison wouldn't hear about our presence when he drove into Mountain Home to pick up supplies.

A few more HRT members with various specialties— electronics, logistics, communications, planning—flew down to join us in completing the advance work.

Buford took the advance team on an aerial photographic reconnaissance tour of the CSA compound. Nearly thirty structures were clustered in three settlements, a plateau compound near the shore of Bull Shoals Lake, the main compound to one side, and a valley compound farther inland. All the buildings in the main compound were constructed of stone, with shooting ports cut into each structure slightly above ground level. The buildings in the outlying compounds were frame and log or mobile homes. The whole property was about eighty cleared acres nestled in a dense forest of hardwood and pine.

Buford made sketches of the floor plans of nearly every building. Inside each structure was a shallow basement that served as a fighting position. Most of the houses had tunnels that led to bunkers and pillboxes. From these emplacements, CSA defenders could set up interlocking fields of fire. Intruders would be shredded the moment they were spotted. And they would be spotted. CSA lookouts, listening posts, and patrols would pick them up long before they got near the compound's center. As I examined Buford's maps, I could see that he was right on. A frontal assault—a fast-moving, door-kicking exercise that we called a dynamic entry—would be suicidal.

And homicidal. Ellison and his people were most dangerous to us and also to themselves inside that fortress compound. If we made an approach with force, we would be facing men and women who believed themselves to be in a mortal struggle with the devil himself. This, of course, was literally true. They might kill one another, either accidentally or on purpose, to prevent those who wanted to surrender from coming out. They might kill their children and themselves, thinking that was the only way to escape Satan's grasp.

As grim as things looked, I had a plan. We would slip into the compound in the dark of night and close it up with a tight perimeter, supplementing our fifty men with FBI SWAT teams from around the South and Midwest. Then we would begin negotiations. Once we got things started, I thought we could wear Ellison down.

At least I hoped we could. He was a fanatic, and fanatics are formidable because they're willing to die. I wasn't. I couldn't afford a single casualty. And I didn't intend to start a small war in the Ozarks. I was banking on other advantages: the talent of our personnel, our training, experience, and technology. And thinking, planning and more thinking. At times like this, I flashed back to a movie I'd seen as a boy, *The Charge of the Light Brigade,* about the massacre of a brigade of British lancers during the Crimean War. I couldn't forget the incompetent commanders who led all those brave men down into the valley of death. *Why didn't they just ride around the valley and come up on the enemy rear?* I'd wondered. *There just had to be another way.* They claimed to have done it for glory and honor, but how could slaughter be glorious? When I became a man and lives were entrusted to my care, those grainy black-and-white images stuck in my mind, and I always prayed the same prayer: *No heroes. Don't make them be heroes to get this job done.*

If we planned this right and had a little luck, we could avoid a disaster. And there would be no need for heroes.

Every morning, we got up early and ran. I tried to avoid running with Horace because it was a near-death experience, with my stubby legs trying to match the pace of his long ones. Then we would gather in the motel dining room for a huge breakfast. In my opinion, anybody who worries about eggs and cholesterol has to be a commie. Horace ordered a sissy breakfast—bran, skim milk, yogurt, fruit. Was that why he could smoke me in the run? I didn't think so.

After breakfast, we held planning sessions. Or we explored the back roads and farms around CSA territory in rust buckets that Mary Ann Sullivan had hired from every Rent-a-Wreck company in the Ozarks. One day, Horace and I headed our bent-up Jeep down the main road to the compound, went down to the dead end and turned around. As we drove out, we saw a CSA member standing by the side of the road. Horace gave him the hands-palm-up, sheepish-smile, we're-just-lost look. He just shook his head, evidently thinking we were two dummies from the city, not the boys from ZOG.

Most of the time I was bent over a legal pad, sketching out tactical options. I'd learned from Delta and the SAS to draft an option for an option for an option. Long after everyone else had turned in, I was up, thinking, pacing, writing, playing out scenarios in my head, and making lists.

I spent many hours with Buford, pumping him for the smallest details. During these sessions, we became fast friends. On the surface, we may have seemed as much a mismatch as, say, Mel Gibson and Danny Glover. Or, as some of the guys might put it, Arnold Schwarzenegger and Danny DeVito. But we had a lot in common. He grew up in Kansas City, Missouri. His family, like mine, had modest means and old-fashioned values. I was a lapsed Methodist and he was a lapsed Lutheran, but I knew what Bill meant when he said there are no atheists in foxholes. He knew what it took to be a single father. When his first marriage had ended in divorce, he had gotten custody of his two children. Bill had remarried and was raising his second wife's three children as his own. I wasn't quite ready to think about dating yet, but I envied Bill's life with a loving wife, a house full of kids and dogs, and weekends in the backcountry, hunting, fishing, or just camping and staring at the night sky.

Buford and Knox tracked down a number of former members or associates who had fallen out with Ellison for one reason or another. They gave us many details about the compound, including descriptions and locations of caches of weapons and explosives. An especially valuable source of information was Randall Rader, who had turned state's evidence after being arrested in The Order case. Rader had lived in the compound in 1981 and 1982 and had directed the survival school. Then he lost a power struggle to Ellison, moved West, and switched his allegiance to Robert Mathews. Rader said the MAC-10 submachine gun with which The Order had assassinated Denver talk-show host Alan Berg had been converted to fully automatic in the CSA gun shop. He knew because he had personally sold it to Order member Andrew Barnhill.

One of Buford's prize catches was Peter John Bjerke, who had set up the compound communications system and had equipped CSA patrols and lookouts with headsets attached to portable two-way radios. Bjerke was after money and relief from a Utah warrant for parole violations and theft. He had not reformed. During one of the sessions, Horace Mewborn asked him, "Why do you guys hate blacks so much?"

"I don't hate niggers," he said. "I just think of them as I do a tractor. I think everyone should own one."

As disgusting as Bjerke was, we had to use him because he could still come and go around the compound. Still, it bothered me to have to work with such a sewer-mouth. I passed the tractor story to Ben Clarey, who gave me a big grin. "Doc, why don't you let me have a talk with that boy? I'll show him what a real tractor can do."

"I don't think so, Ben, I need him in one piece," I said. "Now don't you go changing your name to John Deere." Ben gave me his usual falsetto laugh and walked away.

Our sources told us that along likely avenues of approach Ellison's people had planted explosives that could be detonated by remote control and had booby-trapped secluded nooks where law enforcement officers might take cover as they approached to raid the place. They were building an armored car out of a truck chassis covered with steel boilerplate set at angles so that bullets would glance off it. Behind the boilerplate was an inch of concrete and another layer of steel. A World War II, English-made Lewis machine gun was mounted on top of the contraption.

Literally hundreds of assault rifles were within the compound, many modified to fire fully automatic. There were also piles of homemade hand grenades. The most fearsome device the CSA possessed, as Buford had discovered, was the light anti-tank rocket, which would knock out armored vehicles. It had replaced the flamethrower as a bunker buster in the U.S. military's arsenal. One of its rounds would take out a whole assault team.

I was particularly concerned about their night-vision capability. The CSA had a number of infrared night-vision devices that would allow them to operate effectively in pitch dark. Our night-vision equipment usually gave us a tremendous edge over bad guys, enabling us to encircle them and spring our trap before dawn. In their passive mode, night-vision goggles intensify available light many thousands of times. Using only starlight, you can operate, navigate, and even read maps. If the starlight is blocked by cloud cover or fog, you have to move to the active mode, which means turning on a built-in beam that bounces infrared beams off whatever you're trying to see. Infrared beams are invisible to the naked eye, but the CSA equipment would pick them up as if they were airport beacons. The bottom line was that we could rely upon our night-vision equipment only in its passive, starlight mode.

I contacted a European commando unit and asked to borrow a Thorn EMI handheld thermal imager. The size and shape of a telescope, it produced an image by reading thermal heat. This device was so sensitive to differentials in heat that if the individual you were observing touched his shirt for a moment, you could see the imprint of his hand on the cloth. It was passive and projected no beam. It would allow us to operate in total darkness without being detected.

Within an hour of the phone call, our friends came through. They agreed to lend us a Thorn imager on condition that we give them a detailed briefing on the operation. "Done," I said. The device was on an airliner the next day.

5

At about 9 P.M. on the evening of April 11, 1985, Larry Bonney, Bob Core, Bill Buford, Steve Wiley, Rick Warford, and I embarked on our first cross-country reconnaissance, in which we planned to chart the avenues of approach that we would use to set our covert perimeter. Though we did not intend to force our way into the compound, we had to draft an assault plan as a contingency, in case of an emergency or some sort of mass suicide.

The Hostage Rescue Team is divided into two elements, the operators and the sniper-observers. The operators are subdivided into four-man assault teams, each of which practices a specialty: aircraft, maritime, mobile assaults (intercepting suspects fleeing in moving vehicles), and strongholds. The two-man sniper-observer teams are the eyes and ears of the commander, slipping into a location unseen, establishing observation posts, and radioing information back to the commander. As we had learned from the SAS and Delta, all the teams conceive, choreograph, and rehearse their parts, making contingency plans to deal with sudden changes.

One man designated as assault leader reviews their proposed actions, accepts them or orders them revised, and incorporates their individual roles into the overall concept of the mission. Larry Bonney, the leader of the stronghold team, would perform that crucial role in this case. I knew that he would come up with a good plan that would not be bound by conventional thinking. It wouldn't hurt to have God on our side either. I told the guys that if we got in a jam, my first line of defense was Bob Core, who was a lawyer and would talk us out. If things got really bad, Bonney could pray us out.

I was not too sure how God felt about Core, a dark, muscular operator who was the HRT class clown. The whole time he was on the team, Core stayed in trouble for one thing or another, such as throwing somebody into a pool and wrecking his beeper. But he had an agile mind and was a fine strategic thinker. He would work as Bonney's number two, helping him coordinate all the elements.

On the evening of our visit to the compound, we walked out of our motels around dusk, each carrying a gym bag, and climbed into a battered van. Mewborn was our chauffeur. As he steered out of Branson for the hour-and-a-half trip to Mountain Home, the rest of us changed into our camouflage gear in the back of the van. We didn't have to worry about anyone spotting our Superman act because the van had no windows.

The day before, when we had run a road reconnaissance of the area around the compound, we had all enjoyed the scenic, winding drive through the Ozarks. What had been a pleasant country outing in the daytime became a nighttime nightmare. As we jostled blindly through the hills, the van became a motion-sickness machine. We all bitched and moaned at Horace about his horrible driving.

I will never forget the breath of fresh air that flooded that van as we slid the door open and sprinted into the woods. "That was the worst fucking ride of my life," Core announced. I won't embarrass any of us by relating who threw up. We lay in the damp grass, trying to stop the world from spinning. The cool night breeze perked us up. We tested our radios.

"Alpha One to Verne, how do you copy?"

"Alpha One, copy you five by five," Verne called back.

"Alpha One, I copy you five by five," Lonnie Reynolds chimed in. "You should have total coverage on patrol route. Suggest two com checks every hour. Call in, give your approximate location so we can verify coverage."

Reynolds, our radio technician, had scrambled up a U.S. Forest Service fire tower overlooking the valley and had erected an antenna that could not be seen from the ground, and that allowed us to communicate within a radius of several miles around the compound.

We checked our maps, verified our position, and set off. We traveled light. Core carried his Heckler & Koch MP5 suppressed submachine gun with an aim point projector for accurate nighttime firing. Wiley took his Colt Car-15. Bonney, Warford, and I packed our Browning Hi-Powers. Buford also took a semiautomatic pistol. Every man had two flash-bangs, a handy-talky, two spare batteries, and night-vision equipment. Most of the men used PVS-5 night-vision binoculars. I preferred a PVS-4 monocular because I could reconnoiter with one eye using the infrared or light-intensive capability of the device, while keeping the other eye free.

Our first objective was to spot listening posts and the avenues that patrols generally took. No matter what kind of training paramilitary operators have, they are almost always the victim of habit. A listening post on Monday night is likely to be a listening post on Tuesday, Wednesday, Thursday, and Friday. A patrol route is likely to stay a patrol route.

We also wanted to get a look at the lake shoreline nearest the CSA property, which lay about a quarter of a mile from the water. Bonney thought we could take the main compound's lower perimeter with an amphibious landing. That approach would help to minimize the possibility of being compromised by motor noise. We could leave our vehicles several hundred yards from the lake, paddle across in total darkness, pick our way to the compound's border a quarter mile from the shore, and surround the place with sniper-observer positions before the inhabitants were the wiser.

We hiked toward the lake, with Buford at the point, to see if the shoreline made it possible to land boats and to drag them into the woods to conceal them. Once we got there, I could see that Bonney might be right. "Doc, I know you think I'm crazy about using the boats, but look, this will work," he said. "It's a short paddle. We won't be silhouetted on the water, and we can hide the boats once we get here. All we have to do is have the snipers secure this landing position so we don't get surprised."

"Larry, it may be doable, but we have a lot of details to work out," I said. "We'll talk about it. I'm not saying no."

We moved on toward the valley compound, halting every few minutes to scan the area in front of us for listening posts or for a CSA patrol. Every so often we radioed Horace and Lonnie to let them know where we were.

Stopping just short of a clearing, we saw men and women walking in and out of five houses. "These are all wood-frame construction, not very defensible, and they know it," Buford said. "I wouldn't want to be in one in a firefight, and neither will they. If they go to war, they're likely to abandon this place and go into the main compound." We made some quick sketches and notes, then set off for the plateau compound.

We slipped into a thicket so that we could switch on our infrared beams to check a map and insure our sketches were right. As we emerged, I heard Wiley whisper, "Shit."

"What's up?" Bonney asked.

"My hat popped off. Hit a branch. I can't find the goddamn thing."

This doesn't sound like much of a problem, but it was. If CSA patrollers found the hat, they'd know that somebody had been on their land, and he wasn't a hunter. No hunter dared go near the place.

We went down on our hands and knees, groping frantically. Finally Wiley stepped on the hat and slapped it back on his head. "Goddamn it, will you keep your hat on," I growled. Lucky for him I didn't have a staple gun.

We advanced inland toward the plateau compound. To protect our eyes as we crept through bush, we wore clear Lexan goggles. When we came to an open field, we changed to night-vision devices and scanned the area.

"Patrol!" Buford whispered. A group of armed CSA men were heading right for us. We broke to the left and right and dived into the bush.

As Wiley ducked, the muzzle of his Colt Car-15 slammed into my right eyebrow, splitting it to the bone. I saw stars but managed to crawl deep into the vegetation. As the patrol approached, I lay silently on the damp ground and wiped the blood that ran into my eye. *What if I have to shoot?* My right eye was my shooting eye.

I reached into my left-hand pocket, pulled out a flash-bang grenade, and got ready to pull the pin. If we were spotted, we planned to throw flash-bangs, temporarily blinding our adversaries, then make a dash for a rendezvous point.

Fortunately they walked on and never noticed us. We regrouped, moved in a direction ninety degrees from the path that the CSA patrol had taken, and slipped into heavy bush.

"Jesus Christ, Wiley, I know you're interested in advancing your career, but do you have to do it by bayoneting me in the goddamned eye?" I whispered. "If you want this job, just tell me and it's yours."

"Hell, Doc, I wouldn't do it in front of witnesses," Wiley said, fishing some butterfly bandages out of his pocket. "Anyway," he said as he taped my eyebrow back, "nobody would want your job, at least until we finish this mess."

We crept toward a rise and looked down at the plateau compound. It was very much like the valley compound, small frame houses with few defenses. In the event of a siege, its residents, like those in the valley, would likely move.

We had a few more hours before daylight. "We need to spend as much time as we can over at the main compound," Buford said. "That'll be our biggest problem. Let's get over there. There are a lot of things I want you to see."

This was the most dangerous part of our recon. On the way, we stopped every few yards and turned in a full circle to check for movement in the brush. We had heard that the mines studded about were not pressure activated but triggered by a remote switch. If that was so, there was little danger we would set one off. As long as we were unobserved by members inside the residences of the compound, inside the bunkers, or on patrols, we figured we would be relatively safe.

Buford moved like a cat. He had been here several times before. I reflected that he had done it alone, with no one to come to his rescue and no special equipment, only an old pair of binoculars and his standard-issue sidearm.

"You FBI guys have all the toys," he griped. "Hell, I can't get ATF to buy me a decent flashlight. Let me look through that son of a bitch."

I handed him my fancy state-of-the-art night-vision monocular. "Here, have some fun."

He raised the device to his eye. "Holy cow," he whispered. "This is unbelievable. We had some of this stuff in Vietnam, but nothing like this. Can I take this home with me?"

"Hell, no, but I do have an application for you. We'd love to have you in the FBI. We would have to send you to New York for a while, though, to learn to be a real agent."

"No, thanks." Buford grinned, lowering the glass from his eye.

For the rest of the night, Bill and I passed the device back and forth. He was like a kid with a new Luke Skywalker light-saber.

Hell, Buford doesn't need this stuff, I thought to myself. I was proud that the three HRT operators were almost as good as he was. There was no sound of feet plodding the path, no sound at all, except for the occasional riffle of breeze.

We crawled into the compound on our hands and knees. Most of the brush had been cleared out, but a few bushes had been spared. We moved from one clump to the next, twisting from side to side, peering through our night-vision equipment to cover comrades in exposed positions. We seemed to be the only people outside. In a few houses, we could see electric lights glowing through the shades. Other houses were dark.

When you can't see well, your hearing becomes acute, especially when your adrenaline is pumping. I became totally absorbed in the rhythm of the night. Crickets and cicadas, wind ruffling the grass and the trees—the sounds knit together in a lovely orderly pattern like a night song. I can't remember how the grass felt under my hands, though I know it must have been pleasantly damp with dew, or how the earth smelled. Every part of me was tuned in on the night song, which was as loud as if I had been sitting in an orchestra pit. I listened for anything breaking the rhythm, such as feet scuffling on dirt, twigs breaking, people talking and sneezing, a match scraping across a matchbook cover. I could hear my own heart beating. I wondered if the others were conscious of their heartbeats. Was a commander supposed to be nervous? Well, this one was.

Even in the starlight, I could discern the fine structure of the stone buildings. The light-colored stones fit perfectly together because, as we found out later, one of the CSA members was a master stonecutter. I pointed to the largest building. "From the size of it, I would say that's Ellison's house," I told Buford, "and the one next to it has to be Noble's. You'd expect them to have the biggest places."

"You got it," Buford said. "The two big guys take care of themselves."

It was a beautiful night, not good for patrolling. I had hoped for rain, or at least a strong wind, to mask our movements. As I crept through the grass, I wondered what would go through the minds of Ellison's followers if they discovered ZOG at their door. I expected that they would run to their firing positions. I could almost see Ellison siccing them on us. If we were spotted, we would beat a hasty retreat, probably in a wild hail of bullets fired from every shooting port in the place.

Buford motioned for me to join him. "I really want you to see the chapel. It could be a big problem for us. We'll have to move to the other side of the compound."

Buford led us to a place in the woods where we could contemplate this so-called house of worship. We lay down in a line in the grass. Warford, always the professional, stayed to the rear of the line and constantly scanned the area all around us with his night-vision goggles. No one said anything for a while. We were almost mesmerized by this ghostly structure.

Core, as usual, broke the silence. "Hell, that's no church," he said, spitting tobacco juice. "That's a god-damned fortress. Looks like it's made more for shootin' than prayin'."

It was a solidly constructed stone building with a chapel on the first floor and a school for the children on the second floor. It had shooting ports on all four sides of the building, and more shooting ports at intervals up a tower that looked like a cross between a steeple and a chimney. Inside the tower, Buford said, a narrow stair-case spiraled to an observation post that gave good command of the back side of the compound. I sensed that this lookout was where Ellison meant to stage his last stand.

I was struck by the perverse brilliance of the design. No matter that anyone who stood close to the building would see it was clearly designed for killing. The reality would never catch up with the first news bulletins declaring that lawmen had stormed a church. Certainly, I did not want to be the FBI agent who got into a shoot-out with some good old boys in their church. I wondered if Ellison was really that politically astute, or whether it was a lucky accident. Whatever the case, I was more determined than ever to negotiate his surrender.

We lay quietly in the grass for some minutes, gazing at the chapel and the surrounding buildings. How could people with the talent to create this beautiful place, near a pristine lake, come to this end? I could imagine people living here happily, enjoying simple pleasures, hunting, fishing, and raising their families.

I imagined the children. Every day, the yard must have been filled with them, kicking up dust, playing catch, whittling. I thought about Doc. He would have loved living in the backwoods, hunting and fishing every day, splashing into the crystal clear lake. He would have gotten a kick out of seeing all those guns.

And if I had been a CSA member, he would have lis-tened to me and believed me and tried to be exactly like me, all twisted around with poison and fear. That was the horror of the place, the thought that the children were being bombarded day after day with the paranoid vision of a world in which marauding blacks, Jews, and government agents were going to break in, kill their par-ents, and kill them. What kind of people would torture their children in this way, then put them on the firing line? There were so many illegal arms in the place that any rational adult would know that sooner or later, the law was going to come down. The fortifications would protect the inhabitants from small-arms fire, but if the government were really as sinister as they said it was, then the compound wouldn't last ten minutes against a full-scale military assault. Surely some of them understood that if there were a real war with the government, they were going to lose and many of them would die, including children.

All those thoughts had to go back down in the box. My job was to get in and out without hurting any of us or them. It was time to get going.

We crawled away toward the lake. We needed to figure out exactly how long it would take to get from the lakeshore to a place of cover and concealment that would form a segment of our perimeter. This part of the trip was uneventful. No one got bayoneted in the eye, and Wiley managed to keep his hat on. The frogs, bless them, were making a racket that masked the sound of our footsteps.

We slipped out of the CSA property and headed for a bend in a country road some distance away. We would lie in wait in the woods as Horace approached in the van, then sprint for it as he slowed down. We had to cross the pasture of a neighboring ranch.

As we reached the fence, my macho commando FBI agents all expressed doubt about walking into a field with a bunch of cows. These guys had been cool as a six-pack as they had crawled around a place populated by heavily armed individuals who would love to kill them. But here we were, lying on the edge of a field looking at a bunch of cows and steers and possibly a few bulls, and they did not think they wanted to go over the fence.

"Come on, you wimps," I snorted.

I have to admit that there were a hell of a lot more cattle in that field than I'd ever seen in my career rodeoing.

"Doc, did you know there's a fucking bull out here?" Core whispered.

So this tough leatherneck Vietnam vet is scared of bulls.

"I know there's bulls out here," I reassured him. "Bulls, cows, they can't see in the dark. Don't worry about it."

His sigh of relief was so loud it probably caught the bull's attention. We continued across the pasture and arrived at our rendezvous point. As Horace approached, I radioed him to shift his lights from high to low beam at three-second intervals, so that we would not mistake him for a CSA van. It was not long before we saw a vehicle coming down the road with its lights going up and down. I borrowed Core's aim point projector, which shoots a laser beam designed to be seen only with night-vision equipment, and shined it on the windshield. Horace stopped on the shoulder, yanked off his goggles, and opened the door. We ran for the van, jumped through the door, and slid it closed.

Everybody wanted to help Mewborn. "Horace, I'll drive."

"No, I'll drive."

"No, I'll drive."

"Horace, aren't you tired?"

Nobody wanted to ride all the way back to Branson, Missouri, in the rear of the vomitmobile. I made a command decision. "Shut the hell up. Horace, you drive and look for a place we can eat."

"I hope you guys are going to clean up," Mewborn said. "I don't want to be seen with you. It'll ruin my image."

"Hell, Horace," I said, "you don't have an image, at least not one you can talk about."

Then he caught sight of my shiner. "Holy cow, Doc, did Ellison punch you in the eye?" he gasped.

"Hell, no, Wiley tried to kill me."

When we settled down for the awful ride back, Core began to reflect on his new knowledge of stock. "Doc, I didn't know bulls can't see in the dark."

"Bulls can see in the dark just fine, you turkey," I replied.

Core's face reddened.

"You dumb shit," said Warford. "You know he lies to us. Remember, he said this job would be a lot of fun."

"I should have known," Core said, nodding.

We stripped off our camouflage utilities, scrubbed off our brown and green face paint with paper towels and water from our canteens, and pulled on jeans and T-shirts. By the time we found a diner, the sun was coming up and we were the first patrons. Nobody commented on my slit eyebrow and black eye. I guess the waitress had seen a lot of veterans of bar fights. We consumed a mountain of eggs, biscuits, grits, country ham, potatoes, and just about anything else they would sell us.

Back at the hotel, I carried my gear to my room, peeled off my jeans, fell onto the bed, and conked out until around one in the afternoon. I decided I needed to get some kinks out of my body and go for a run. Why did I hate running so much? I always wondered why other people seemed to enjoy it. I would have preferred to have found a gym and pumped some iron for a while, but there wasn't one nearby. I was always being asked, "Boss, did you have a good run?" To which I would snarl, "Hell, I've been running most of my life, and I haven't had a good run yet."

I pulled on a pair of shorts and running shoes and

walked into the parking lot to stretch. I looked up to see Horace just returning from a run. Was I glad he was finished. If we had walked out together, he would have asked me to go along with him, and that would have been torture. Horace could run all day. He loved to push me into exhaustion.

"Afternoon, Verne. I think I'll go out for about twenty miles. Be back in about an hour. Get the boys together and meet me in my room. We need to talk."

"Twenty miles, huh? That should take you about a month."

"I may cut it a little shorter. Just have the guys in my room. If I'm not back, send somebody with oxygen to look for me."

I got back to my room just as the crew walked up. All of them were in shorts and running shoes too, having had the same idea.

We popped open some soft drinks. Then I spread a topographical map on my bed and started retracing our steps.

"You know," Buford said, "this would be a piece of cake if we could just get Ellison to stay in the compound and not send out patrols. We have good points to drop off trucks without being seen, and we have safe avenues of approach. But moving two hundred men around in the dark will be real tricky."

"Shit happens," Mewborn said, nodding. "It's one thing to send in a small team. It's another to send in two hundred people falling all over things, making all sorts of noise. Anything can go wrong."

"Let's use the lake," Bonney pleaded, tapping the blue part of the map. "It would take hours for the men to walk to the lake side of the compound. The odds of being intercepted by their patrols are pretty high. We have a good beach to land on, you saw that. We could set a perimeter within ten minutes of the time we land."

I looked at Buford. "Bill, does Ellison have a navy? I wouldn't want the guys sunk at sea."

"Nope, no navy," Buford said. "I don't even remember seeing any fishing boats on the shore last night. He isn't likely to have anyone on the water."

Bonney looked at me hopefully. "Does this mean you're going to let us do it?"

"Hell, no," I said. "It does look pretty good though. Let's explore it. Come up with a plan. Find out where we can get boats without attracting attention. Give me some options, you know the drill. I don't want you to do the planning yourself. You have to focus on the entire operation. Give it to Ratso. Those squids love anything to do with water."

Even if the lake approach worked out, we still had to move the rest of the men into position without being compromised. We were all leaning on the bed, looking at the map, when there was a knock on the door. This was somewhat of a shock since we didn't expect any callers. The maid had done the rooms earlier. No one in the hotel knew our true identity. Horace opened the door warily.

In walked a vision, a drop-dead blonde. She confidently marched right into a room full of shirtless male strangers.

"How're you all doing?" she said, smiling sweetly.

I'm doing a hell of a lot better than I was a few minutes before you walked in. We all just stared at her, trying to figure out who she was and how we had the good fortune to have her come to the room. Any fantasies we might have conjured up were quickly shaken when Jim Krauss, an FBI pilot, and Ron McCall, the chief of the aviation unit at FBI headquarters, followed her through the open door.

"Buck sent us," McCall explained.

We started grabbing our shirts and wishing we had showered.

McCall introduced Mary Ann Snowden, the unit's imaging specialist.

"It's good to see you guys," I said, "but we haven't asked for any airplanes yet."

Ron gave me a mischievous look. "We aren't offering you just any plane," he said. "We came down in Nightstalker. We had a job on the West Coast and were heading home. Buck called and diverted us here to help you guys."

I had heard about this bird, but I'd never actually seen it in action. In the early eighties, the electronic wizards at the FBI's engineering facility had fitted out the airplane with forward-looking infrared aerial surveillance equipment adapted from classified U.S. military applications. This allowed it to watch and record activity in total darkness. It was painted black and muffled so that it flew almost soundlessly. For years, FBI officials responsible for national-security matters had allowed the plane to be used only for long-running counterespionage missions. They had been unwilling to let the airplane be used in any criminal investigations, for fear its scientific capabilities would be divulged during a trial. Only recently had Buck Revell forced the R and D guys and the spy catchers to share their toys. No one said no to the Buckster.

"Bill, you and Bonney show them our problem and

see if they can help," I said. "Show them your proposed patrol routes and tell them about the lake idea. Verne, let's get some sodas."

"What do you know about this airplane?" I whispered to Horace as we fed coins into the drink machine. "Can it help us?"

"I've seen videotapes of some of its jobs on kidnapping cases," Mewborn said. "It's very impressive, and I hear that the girl is terrific. They call her Grits because of her drawl."

"Well, you two should get along real fine," I said. "We'll have to fly in an interpreter for both of you. Let's go see what they have to offer."

"Doc, I think we may be the answer to your problem here," McCall said as we handed sodas around. "We can establish an orbit of the compound and walk you guys right in. We can almost guarantee that you won't run into a patrol, listening post, or an ambush."

"How about the guys coming across the lake?"

"Piece of cake. We can take care of that too. About the only thing we can't do is paddle the boats for you."

"Can you stand in front of us if they start shooting at us?"

"You're on your own there, pal."

"How does this work?" I asked. "Will we be talking to the pilots or what?"

"That's mah job," Mary Ann interrupted, a little sharply. "The imager is on a turret that I operate. I'll talk directly to you. I'll tell you everything I see and move you where you want to go. Nobody can hide from us. I can talk directly to your patrols or the guys on the lake, if you want. Cuts out the middleman and makes communications shorter."

McCall gave me a warning look that I took to mean, *Don't assume a male is in charge on this one.* "Doc, Grits is real good at this. She has a ton of experience."

"I'm better than good," she said firmly. "I'm the best. Look, why don't you take a ride with us after dark? We'll show you our stuff, and you can decide to use us or not."

"Sounds like a deal," I said. "You know, Ron, you just might be Santa Claus. How come Buck got so generous with the toys?"

"Hell, everyone back there is scared to death," McCall said. "They see this as a potential war for you guys. They're going to give you everything you want. Pick you up at seven-thirty."

"Okay, you guys hit the trail," I said. "Bonney, call Ratso and give him a heads-up. Bill, can you reach out to your informants to see what Ellison is up to? I'm going to get some winks. Got a date."

I turned on the TV with the remote, laid my head on the pillow, and fell into a deep sleep. Hunger woke me around 6:30 P.M. I got up, showered, and dressed in my usual blue jeans, boots, and T-shirt, with a lightweight windbreaker to cover the Hi-Power and extra magazine that rode on my hip.

The ancient Jeep that Blasingame had given me seemed to know the way to a hamburger heaven. I ordered a monster. In my opinion a burger is really no good at all unless the juices run off your elbows and onto your pants.

As I sat there making a pig out of myself, I kept thinking about how much was riding on this job. Lives, of course. Any compromise and my worst nightmare would come true—a chase and a moving firefight in pitch dark.

My men scrambling and stumbling from bush to bush. His people running blindly before us, shooting wildly in all directions. Friendly fire casualties. Women and children caught in the cross fire. Careers. A lot of people in the upper echelons of the FBI still distrusted the whole HRT concept. If things went bad, they'd say that we were just a bunch of cowboys. The HRT would likely be disbanded and I'd get stuck in some boneyard like White House liaison until I retired. In my humble opinion, the Hostage Rescue Team was better at night and in rural operations than any other law enforcement unit in the country. But we had to have still another edge. Nightstalker just might be it.

I pulled up to my motel just in time to see Grits, McCall, and Krauss drive up. "Hey, buddy, you need a lift to the airport?" Krauss called.

The plane, tethered on a deserted section of the general-aviation airport outside Branson, was unremarkable except for its bat-black skin. But when Krauss popped open the door and waved me inside, I saw more lights than at Rockefeller Center at Christmas.

Wait till Little Doc gets a load of this. The cramped cabin looked like the arcades he adored and probably cost nearly as much. "Did you bring me out here to play video games?" I grumbled, settling into a bucket seat surrounded by twinkling gizmos.

"Yeah," Grits said, laughing, "but this is a lot more fun, and it may just save your butt. Buckle up, Doc, we're gonna give you a show."

Flying without lights, Nightstalker glided thousands of feet above the pitch-black Ozark foothills. Grits' face glowed pale green in the flicker of the thermal imager screen. I played with my joystick and squinted at the monitor. "Deah," she said, pointing to a lime-Jell-O shadow of a doe dancing across the glass. "Ovah theah, that might be a coon."

With her honey hair and voice to match, she came on like Miss Georgia Peach. One of the pilots was determined to marry her. That was fine by me so long as she saved her evenings for me. Grits had a gift. Anyone could learn to work the equipment and see everything, but she saw what was important. She had a feel for danger, and when it was coming, she said so, in time to do something about it. No hedging, no wavering, and no jargon. If you think that's easy, you've never worked in a bureaucracy.

After she coached me for a while, I began to pick out deer, standing stock-still, then bolting across a clearing. The thermal imager trained on the dense woods below detected heat, mechanical heat from an engine or body heat from a human or animal. The on-board computer converted the signals to green pixel images that appeared on a screen the size of a small television. The apparatus was so sensitive that not only deer but raccoons, coyotes, and other little varmints were plainly visible. Manipulating her joystick, she pointed out every living creature in the hills.

Nightstalker began an orbit of the main compound. The imager showed spectral images of men and women, walking and talking with one another. They looked like the ghosts in the Haunted House ride at Disneyland. I couldn't see faces, but I could make out tops of heads, bodies, and hands, gesturing as if in conversation. I could see clear outlines of shoulder weapons.

Grits pointed to a group of five individuals standing outside one of the main structures. One turned and walked toward the woods. She looked up at me and smiled.

"That guy's gotta go take a leak," she said.

"How in the hell do you know that?"

"Just watch."

Sure enough, the man went over to the woods, turned his back on the group, and fiddled with his pants. Then he returned to his conversation.

"I've been doin' this a while," she said, grinning.

The plane made pass after pass over the compound. With the ability to pinpoint Ellison's patrols and listening posts, it would be a simple matter for Grits to guide our teams into position.

She's right. This thing can save our ass.

"Get some rest tomorrow," I told Mary Ann and the pilots. "Sleep as much as you can during the day. I'm going to need you every night from now on. We'll call you Hawkeye."

Back at Quantico, Wehmeyer and the sniper team loaded up our borrowed C-130 and took off for Fort Leonard Wood in southern Missouri. The operators stayed behind to practice entries and clearing maneuvers on a layout of the CSA compound they had constructed on the athletic field. They would fly south on another borrowed C-130 in a day or so.

Mewborn, Wiley, Core, Bonney, Mary Ann Sullivan, and I drove over to Fort Leonard Wood to meet Jeff and the snipers. I always got a clutch in my heart when I saw the big bird touching down. I walked out on the pad and watched the plane make a tight turn so that its rear bay was toward me. The blast of air from the engines almost knocked me over. Mary Ann stood beside me with her blond hair blowing straight back. She made no attempt to turn away from the hot wind. The tail ramp dropped down. The men, looking like a very, very fit church softball team in their clean T-shirts and creased jeans, trotted out, bags in hand. They took turns hugging Mary Ann and shaking my hand. Then they pitched in to unload the plane.

One of them drove a Chevy Suburban out of the bay. It looked like a typical family van, but on the inside, it was a mobile emergency trauma center. Jay Mulholland, our medical coordinator, had outfitted it with everything you could possibly need to keep a person alive.

Hiding two hundred FBI agents in Mountain Home, where everybody is related by blood or marriage, was no small problem. J. T. Shaw, the local sheriff, had come up with the solution. We would pose as sportsmen. Bull Shoals Lake was dotted with fishing camps that catered to people who came from all over the world to fish for its famous striped bass.

Horace herded the snipers into a briefing room at the airport to explain the ruse. "Now y'all listen up," he announced. "Since you'll be posing as fishermen, you'll be expected to fish. And you're approved to rent boats and use them to launch your recons. Remember, this is your cover."

John Eastes raised his hand. "Let me get this straight. We're supposed to go fishing. Does that mean Doc is going to pay for the fishing poles?"

"That's right," Horace said. "But they better be cheap, and they become the property of the United States government when this mission is done."

Another hand went up.

"I understand we're supposed to fish," said Don

Bartnick. "Does that mean we're expected to catch anything?"

"Good point," Horace said. "Eastes, they do have restrictions on this lake. You can't fish with a .44 Magnum."

The place broke up. On Eastes's desk at Quantico was a photo of himself holding a giant catfish with a bullet hole through its midsection. It seems that while hunting wild pig on his uncle's property, he had walked past a stream, spotted the monster, and suddenly developed a taste for fried catfish. Having no pole, he pulled out his big revolver and shot it.

"Guys, we have a lot of hard work to do," I said. "The subjects are very dangerous. They'll kill you in a heartbeat. You are the devil. You are ZOG. And don't kill me on how much you spend. Someday I'll have to account for all this fishing equipment. Mary Ann has rented cabins for you at various camps. She'll show you the way. She has cars for you all. Lonnie has put coms in them. Be discreet, and don't get compromised."

For the next few days, they rose late, around 7:30 A.M., ate breakfast, and attended team meetings, where they went over topographical maps and photos. Horace would brief them on the latest intelligence. They ran at lunch and did about a million push-ups. Toward dusk, they threw some gear into fishing boats and went out onto the lake to scope out the area. The male camp managers bought the cover story—that we were a group of corporate managers on a seminar-and-fishing junket—but a woman manager decided it was bogus. She called Sheriff Shaw and reported that her new guests worked out during the day, did damn little fishing, and were gone all night. None of them had any women with them.

Shaw had more of a twinkle in his eye than usual when he showed up for breakfast the next morning. "She thinks you're a collection of homosexuals," he said pleasantly.

I spit out my coffee. *Wait till this gets back to headquarters.* "I don't think most of them are," I said, wiping my face. "But if that's what people want to think, fine. Just as long as they don't think we're FBI."

Intercepting Ellison while he was outside his domain would be the safest thing for everyone concerned, including Ellison. He would be vulnerable. He might surrender peaceably. If he tried to resist and started shooting, at least there would be no danger of cross fire hitting women and children.

For a few days, this seemed a viable option. One of Buford's informants told us that Ellison, Kerry Noble, and other male CSA members left the compound from time to time to cut and sell cedar. Don Glasser and his team started planning a mobile option. Buford told his informants to find out exactly when and where Ellison and his men would venture out.

Our hopes were dashed on April 15. When U.S. Attorney Gene S. Anderson of Seattle made public a ninety-three-page indictment charging twenty-three alleged members of The Order with racketeering, including armed robbery, arson, counterfeiting, and the Alan Berg assassination. That very day, David C. Tate, a twenty-two-year-old member of The Order, was driving through Ridgedale, Missouri, not far from Branson, when two Missouri state troopers pulled him over on a routine traffic stop. Tate, who had just found out he was a defendant in the case, panicked, opened fire with a MAC-11 submachine gun, killed Trooper Jimmie

Linegar, and wounded his partner, Allen Hines. Then he fled into the Ozarks on foot.

Law enforcement officers in Missouri and Kansas launched a massive manhunt and set up roadblocks in both states. Backed by four National Guard helicopters, hundreds of cops and troopers trekked into the Ozarks. Some of them stumbled upon Frank Silva, another Order fugitive, at a campground near Rogers, Arkansas, but Tate eluded the dragnet. Police commanders thought that he might be heading for the CSA. So did the local reporters and television crews, who staked out the compound gate. Ellison and his men were now on high alert, expecting the police to use the search for Tate as a pretext to get at them. Buford's informants said Ellison vowed not to leave the compound until the furor died down.

"Shit," Glasser said. "This place is crawling with ambush points. We've picked out a couple that would work just right for us."

"Well, we may get a chance yet," I replied. "Keep working on your plan. But it looks like we'll have to deal with the compound."

6

The Gospel of the Sword and Arm of the Lord 245

Lawyer and wounded his partner. Allen Hines, Then just before the battle broke out,

Law-enforcement officers in Missouri and Kansas launched a massive manhunt and set up roadblocks in

Stidt Claxon said. This place

Now everything depended on the negotiation option.

From the moment we took the CSA mission, we'd been feeding information on Ellison and his group to the behavioral science unit at the FBI Academy in Quantico. John Douglas, Roy Hazelwood, Clinton Van Zandt, and other FBI profilers had earned a nationwide reputation for developing profiles that predicted the behavior of criminals. Profiling was hardly an exact science. Like many field agents, I sometimes derided their work as a combination of voodoo and WAGs, which was FBI-speak for wild-ass guesses. But I had to admit that whatever it was they did often worked, so I made sure they were in our loop.

Their psychological profile of Ellison concluded that our traditional hostage-negotiation techniques were not going to work because they had been developed for situations in which the hostage taker was a common crook, distraught husband or boyfriend. In fact, we probably could not even use a trained FBI hostage negotiator. Douglas and Van Zandt were convinced that Ellison would refuse to negotiate with anyone he perceived as an intermediary. He may have gotten into the preacher business because he was honestly searching for the truth, but he stayed in it for the power. Power was why he had reinvented himself as God's strong right arm, the General Patton of the Christian Identity movement. Egocentric, insecure, and status-starved, he demanded, and got, unconditional praise and obedience from his people. Those who disagreed with him left.

Douglas and Van Zandt were particularly interested in Ellison's fixation with all things military. Though he had never been in the armed services, he insisted that everyone in the compound take part in military training and wear military-style uniforms. He banned cigarette smoking, drinking, drug use, or cursing. The most important thing in Ellison's life, they thought, was his vision of himself as "the commander." They believed he would only talk "commander to commander"—so someone with command authority had to act as the negotiator.

This was a bold recommendation that flew in the face of traditional FBI policy and of all the teachings at the FBI Academy or other hostage-negotiation schools throughout the world. The negotiator's job was to string things out for hours by claiming not to have ultimate decision-making authority. By definition, he could not be the boss. One FBI negotiator stretched the dialogue out so far that the bad guy finally gave up the hostages and surrendered in exchange for a cigarette. I suspect the happy ending was more a function of his addiction than FBI expertise, but we claimed credit. We always do.

I didn't like the way this was going. I sought an outside opinion, from David Soskis. Soskis agreed with Douglas and Van Zandt that the commander should negotiate with Ellison.

What about somebody else? I countered. What about Jim Ahern or Tony Daniels? Ahern, the SAC in Omaha, and Daniels, the SAC in Oklahoma, had been sent to Little Rock to help Blasingame with command and control. I was glad to see them both. Ahern and I had worked together on a hijacking squad in New York.

Daniels had been my partner on the inspection staff. Once, in Charlotte, the driver of the city bus we were riding got out and went into a restaurant for about fifteen minutes. We were the only passengers. Tony and I looked at each other and started making our way toward the front. "I'll drive and you navigate," I said. Fortunately for our careers, the driver returned. I say we would probably not have been charged with theft, because we never intended to keep it. It's possible Tony might have kept it, but certainly I wouldn't have.

I thought Daniels would be good with Ellison. Something about his gentle, weathered face and blue eyes made people want to please him. I had been to his house many times to help with some project, only to find ten or twelve other agents whom he had also conned into doing the job.

Soskis threw cold water on that idea. No, he said, it had to be somebody who was clearly in charge of the HRT, who could talk guns and tactics and all that stuff. It had to be me.

"Hell, Doc, I'm not a negotiator, I'm a tactical guy," I protested. "If I do the negotiations, I can't command at the same time. We're not sure HQ will even buy the idea. They'll probably think I've gone crazy."

Soskis volunteered to call Revell and endorse the idea. "How do you feel about not being in command of your team during this thing?" he added in that silky professional voice.

"Well, I don't like being the negotiator to begin with," I admitted, "and I certainly can't command the team if I negotiate. There will be a lot of things going on that I will have to focus on, and I can't do both. Of course, Jeff is capable of commanding without me. He really knows his shit."

"I suggest you start thinking about it and really lock onto Clint," Soskis said. "He's about as good as they come, and he will talk you through it. He and I have already talked about how to go about it. He will coach you and play Ellison for you, so you can practice. There may be one problem for you."

"One problem! Do you know how many goddamn problems I have now? One more problem is not going to amount to much. What the hell is it?"

"You can't use profanity when you talk to him," Soskis replied calmly. I hated it when he got calm.

"Are you shitting me? This goddamned bigot wants to kill blacks, Jews, cops, FBI agents, and he'll be offended by my language!"

"See, I told you this would be a problem for you."

He had me there. "I guess I see what you mean," I said as humbly as I could manage. "Why is profanity an issue for this immoral bastard? Oh, shit."

"He doesn't see himself as immoral. He thinks he's on God's side, and he wants to act with dignity. You have to be as dignified as he is, so he'll respect you."

"Son of a gun. Darn." I would never get this sissy-ass language down. Finally, I decided to give up expletives altogether. I spoke as stiffly as if I were the guest of honor at a Junior League tea.

Van Zandt, who had flown to Mountain Home to help me practice, would walk up to me and say, "I'm Jim Ellison." We would shake hands and start a dialogue. Every now and again, I slipped in a few sons of bitches, just to see if Clint was paying attention. I don't think he had much confidence in me, but he was damned if he was going to let me fail. See, there I go again.

Wehmeyer and I spent hours going over our plans and checklists to make sure that we forgot nothing.

We had to assume that after we got the perimeters set, we might be faced with attempts to escape through our lines. The CSA might try to cover a breakout with gunfire. Or they might set off explosions as a diversion in one direction while they took off through the woods in the opposite direction. The CSA might use the negotiation sessions themselves as a diversion. Jeff would constantly monitor the radio traffic from our snipers so that he would be in position to parry and block. The perimeter would not be static but fluid. It would require constant adjustment.

"Your most important job, of course, will be to provide security for the negotiators," I told Jeff. I was half-joking, but we both recognized that Wehmeyer had to think about what he would do to keep Ellison from taking us hostage and dragging us inside the compound as bait. I kept thinking of the church and its shooting slots. I didn't want anything to draw my men into that meat grinder.

One of our main concerns was emergency medical care. If Ellison tried to fight his way out, there would be casualties. The HRT had one of the best medical programs in law enforcement. Every member of the team was a trained first responder. Thirteen of our agents were trained as emergency medical technicians and regularly worked in emergency rooms and in ambulances in the District of Columbia, Maryland, and Virginia. Because of our difficult training regime, there were many injuries and lots of time to practice on one another. In addition, the FBI had contracted with Lew Jordan, a Baltimore physician's assistant, to deploy with us. We had our Suburban ambulance, but it was a long drive to the nearest hospital. Medical tech Jay Mulholland would bring in a Huey helicopter, after we had set up the perimeter, to take out the wounded and to help with observation if the confrontation deteriorated into a chase.

My next concern was communications. I called in Lonnie Reynolds and Dennis Hughes—the Radio Shack guys—so named because whenever I got a requisition for some gadget, I'd walk over to their cubbyhole and say, "What the hell is this bullshit stuff you're buying now? I could probably go down to Radio Shack and get it for ten percent of what you're asking me to approve." They didn't work cheap, but they'd done a superb job establishing a secure HRT communications net throughout the Mountain Home area. It included voice privacy, a rare feature in those days, which gave us a tremendous advantage over the CSA members, who operated on normal channels subject to monitoring and jamming. In this day of digital cell phones, what Reynolds and Hughes accomplished doesn't sound like a big deal, but in 1985, it was no less than a miracle. I'd been on surveillances in which I could look at an agent in another car and not be able to talk to him, and if I could reach him, every crook on the block could listen in.

Now I needed a bigger miracle. The net had to be expanded to accommodate a couple of hundred more people: FBI SWAT teams from Kansas City, Oklahoma City, Little Rock, and Omaha, who were coming in to take the two outlying compounds, plus two Arkansas State Police SWAT teams who would serve as a blocking force on one of the ridges. In a day or two, Dennis

Hughes, a former Navy fighter pilot who was HRT's answer to Radar O'Reilly, briefed me on their progress.

Hughes had conned the HQ technical services people out of over two hundred state-of-the-art digital voice private Motorola radios, and all of the goodies that went with them. I could talk to every one of our team leaders and individual operators if need be and to the other FBI SWAT teams and state police tactical units. If Ellison tried to monitor us, all they'd pick up was the static of two hundred and fifty radios. "But wouldn't that tip them off?" I asked. Hughes was way ahead of me, as usual. "We've been generating false radio traffic for several days now," he said. "They're hearing static day and night. They'll likely think it's interference in their scanners. I don't think it'll be a problem. With all the activity on the search for Tate, they'll pick up more of the state police traffic anyway."

Blasingame, Daniels, and Ahern would man the rear command post, located in an aircraft hangar at a private airstrip that belonged to a wealthy rancher. Horace, Mary Ann, and the Radio Shack boys had fixed it up with desks, a radio system, aerial photos of the compounds, and tables. The telephone bank was set neatly on a stack of hay bales, and more hay bales partitioned off a section for the SACs. It smelled like a Western dance. The SACs would communicate with headquarters via phone and relay any orders or changes to me.

"Doc, I can set up a sat com [satellite communications link] for you if you want so you can talk direct to HQ," Hughes offered.

I felt a chill go down my spine. Hughes's only flaw was, he didn't know when to quit.

"Hell, no! They'll be calling and bugging the shit out of me. Just keep that on standby."

Van Zandt, who always seemed to be at my elbow, chuckled. "Glad you're keeping your profanity down. You really have to work on it."

"You're right, goddamn it," I muttered. "I'll work on it. I always did play better than I practiced."

Most every afternoon and evening, the men assigned to the amphibious landing went fishing and watched the CSA shoreline for hours. Some nights, they went ashore and ran recon patrols to the compound's fence, checking out the paths they would use when they finally moved in to set the perimeter.

One moonless night, I sat on a rock with my radio, waiting for three boats to return.

"We're wrapped," Ratso radioed. His next transmission was not so confident. I heard some confused chatter between Norris and another boat, so I broke in.

"You guys lost?"

Ratso chuckled. "Yeah, we're having a little trouble navigating these fingers." With a shoreline that measured a thousand miles, Bull Shoals Lake had hundreds of finger-shaped coves. In the dark they all looked exactly alike.

Grits' soothing accent sounded in my ear. "This is Hawkeye to Alpha One. You want me to bring yoah chickens home?"

"I didn't know you guys were working."

"We're always working."

"Yeah, round them up and bring them home for me."

She addressed the lost boys. "Okay, you guys, drive in a circle, slowly. Okay, I gotcha, now straighten out."

She zigzagged them around the fingers and brought them to the dock, where I greeted them in my usual fatherly way. "Hey, Ratso. What navy were you in? Was it the U.S. Navy or some other navy?"

He grinned, shrugged, and headed for bed.

I went to a pay phone and called Little Doc. I did this every night. He always had the same question. "Did you get the bad guys yet?" Never "Be careful" or "What is it like?" I was proud that he had faith in me. He didn't wonder, *Will Dad get them?* In his mind, it was just a question of when. I'm sure I got more out of these calls than he did.

7

April 19 was our D day. Today, it's impossible to mention the date without conjuring up the fires of Waco and the Oklahoma City bombing. At the time, it was simply a gray Friday.

Wehmeyer, Bonney, Wiley, Mewborn, Buford, and I gathered in my cabin. "I think we're ready to go," Bonney said.

I turned to Buford. "Bill, any updates from inside? Do they expect us? Is Ellison still inside?"

"Hell, Danny, they always expect us. We can't really change that. They just don't know when, and they're probably hoping never."

"Horace, what about weather?"

"Weather looks great for us. They're predicting rain."

Any tactical operation is better in the rain. Heavy rain would cover the noise of our movements and would discourage the CSA members from their regular listening posts and patrols. If they went out, the rain would affect their ability to see and to hear, and their rain gear would dramatically diminish their peripheral vision. Our scent would not carry as far, so there was less chance their dogs would raise a ruckus. We had made it our business to operate as effectively in rain as on a sunny day. We trained in rain and worked in rain, we were outfitted in Gore-Tex and waterproof boots, we swam with weapons and radios. We were as used to being wet as to being dry.

After we went over our checklists one more time, I drove over to the rear command center in the hangar and joined Blasingame, Daniels, and Ahern. They'd already given Revell a heads-up. Daniels said he had about a thousand questions. "You know they're all pissing their pants back there," Daniels said. "They're really worried that you guys are going to walk into a firestorm and a lot of people will get killed."

"They're pissing their pants?" I groused, flopping down on a bale of hay. "I've been pissing my pants for weeks. Just remember, so far no one has ever been shot in the Hoover building."

"Yeah, I know, but they can't help but be concerned."

"True. You know, Daniels, if this goes to hell, I'll just blame you for it."

"That's okay. I'll just blame you too."

The phone rang.

"I'm outta here," Daniels said, waving cheerfully and scuttling out the door. "He may start asking me questions."

"Coward," I hissed.

"You got it," he called over his shoulder.

"We're good to go," I told Revell. "Our recons are finished. Hawkeye's up. I want to begin tonight, move to the rendezvous point and launch just after midnight. I want to be in place when the sun comes up. We need to have as many hours of daylight as possible after we make the announcement, in case they have some plan to break out."

Revell grilled me for the better part of an hour. "What about the LAW rocket?"

"I've told the snipers that if someone is spotted with that thing and they extend the tube to fire it, they're to be shot. I can't risk one of those nuts firing that thing into our perimeter."

"I agree with that. Why now?"

"We're not going to get any more ready. Ellison is in place. Horace promises me it's going to rain this evening."

"Are you guys still going to come across the lake in the boats? That sounds a little risky to me."

"Hell, Buck, this whole thing is risky. I'll have Grits work us across. The bird will check out the landing zone. I guarantee you we won't be compromised."

"Are you going in the boats?"

"No, I'll be in the Suburban. I need to be with the coms so I can move people around if I need to."

"I take it that as usual you will not be in the command post."

"Hell, no, I can't command from the rear."

"I knew you'd say that. I just didn't want you in the boat. I know that lake. It's pretty deep. If your guys fall out of the boats, the rest can probably wade out. But being so short, you'd drown."

"Hell, Buck, I was a hell of a lot taller before I started working for your big butt."

"Okay, sounds good to me. You have my authority to launch. I'll tell the director. I'll keep people here off your back. One last thing, about that tank they're building. Does it really have a Lewis machine gun on it?"

"Yes, but we don't think it's quite finished yet. If they get it going and come after us, we have high-energy rounds for the M-79 grenade launchers. We'll just blow the wheels off of it and then deal with it."

"Okay, do it. Let me know if you need anything. Oh, yeah, good luck."

"Thanks, we'll need it."

I hung up, walked out of the command post, and found Wehmeyer and Bonney.

"Did you talk to the Buckster?" Jeff asked eagerly. I could see the strain on his face, and Larry's too. The hardest part of these missions is waiting. You start what-iffing yourself to death.

"Yeah, he mostly talked to me."

"Well, what did he say?"

"He said to tell you that he loves both of you guys and will take the matter to the executive conference for approval. We should hear in about a week."

Four eyes and two mouths popped open. Then both faces turned beet red. Before they could start their tirade, I started laughing.

"Call the team leaders to the fishing camp in thirty minutes. Get Buford. It's a go for tonight."

We gathered in the camp's dilapidated "party room" and pulled our folding chairs into a circle. "We'll launch tonight, late," I began. "Don't jock up in the camp. We don't want to spook people when they see two hundred armed Macedonians in full battle gear. Just act like fishermen. Put your gear on at the rendezvous point. Be sure to do a com check on all channels. If you have any problems, check with Dennis and Lonnie. Don't forget spare batteries. We have chargers in the com van. We could be out here for a week or ten days, or more if necessary.

"Remind everyone that they should take extra care of their cover and be sure their cammie is good," I said. "Since we will be here for days, we'll do everything we can to keep you updated on the negotiations. That's all I have to say, except that we intend to talk them out. I anticipate the most dangerous part of the op will be setting the perimeter. Don't get compromised."

In fact, Ellison had a pretty good idea that something was up. That very morning, as we'd finalized our plans, trooper Gene Irby was making a last-ditch appeal to Ellison, local boy to local boy. Much later, I heard the whole story from Kerry Noble.

It seems that on April 18, Irby went to the gate of the compound, called Noble out, and told him that a federal warrant had been issued for Ellison. Irby hoped Ellison would do the right thing and surrender peacefully. Noble delivered the message to Ellison, then returned to the gate and told Irby that Ellison wanted to pray about it. He should come back the next day.

At about ten o'clock on the morning of April 19, Irby returned to the compound. Noble met him at the gate. They took a drive together. Noble said he had bad news. Ellison wouldn't surrender. Irby pressed Noble harder, telling him that the FBI was in Mountain Home. Roadblocks would be in place by 5 P.M. One way or another, Ellison would have to deal with the warrant.

After Noble reported what Irby had said, Ellison sent him and three other men into Mountain Home to buy supplies and look for law enforcement activity. On the way back to the camp, the CSA van was stopped at a state police roadblock. The officers recognized the men inside and refused to let them go home. "If you don't let me back in, there'll be no negotiations, and Ellison will go to war," Noble threatened. The others were sent back to town, but Noble was allowed to pass—and to alert Ellison.

I've been told the plan was devised by state police leaders and Buford and approved by Dan Kelly. Had I been asked, I would have objected. I certainly didn't want Ellison jacked up to red alert. Somehow, no one thought to tell me about it, before or after, so I had no clue that Ellison had been forewarned.

Toward midnight on the nineteenth, the HRT and SWAT units who were to hike to the compound gathered in a pasture some distance from the road and on a straight line to the edge of the CSA land. In a bustle of activity, the men ran radio and equipment checks. Every few moments, you could hear the clanks as bolts closed down on loaded chambers. A light rain began to fall. Before long, it was a downpour. Horace's weather prayer had been answered.

At 2 A.M., I dispatched Butch Roll and the Kansas City SWAT team. They had a long way to go to get to the valley compound. A short time later, Chuck Choney—I had nicknamed him "the world's largest American Indian"—took off with the Oklahoma City SWAT team, heading for the plateau compound. The CSA sentries would have to be good to see Chuck coming. He had been out in the woods tracking game while the rest of us were watching *Howdy Doody*. Buford and the Little Rock SWAT team headed out for the valley compound.

I stood by the pasture gate and waved cheerfully as the four-wheelers lurched toward the trailheads. The men's faces were so sooty with camouflage paint that all I could see were eyes and teeth. I could hear voices wishing *me* luck.

8

"Alpha One, this is Hawkeye, how do you all read?"

Grits was checking in. I picked her up on the radios that were wired into the Suburban. I had half-expected to get a call saying the bird had engine trouble, or one of the million things that seemed to go wrong with aircraft. This was wonderful. The plane worked. The radios worked. And it was raining. *There is a God,* I thought, *and he* really *hates bigots.*

"Alpha One, are you ready to turn over your little chickens to the pros?" Grits purred.

"Who said you were the pros?"

"Hon, we are the pros. After they see us work, you may be out of a job."

"Well, pro, you can have this job."

"No, thanks."

"Grits, take a tour of the compound and tell me what you see. By the way, why don't you guys work on a system that would let me see what you see?"

"You HRT guys are all alike. Never satisfied. Actually, we're working on that. Next time, we'll be a full-service bird."

"Call me back after your pass."

"We already did a pass. We're so far ahead of you. Looks very quiet in the valley compound and no activity on the plateau. You have a listening post fairly close to where the boats will land, and there's a three-man patrol about fifteen hundred meters out."

I motioned to Wehmeyer. "Jeff, get that to the boats, verify they copied."

"We copied direct, Doc," Ratso radioed from the boat launch. "Are we still a go?"

"Affirmative, proceed. You're a long way from his position," I said, referring to the sentry in the listening post. "Hawkeye will call you direct if there's a problem. He may go in to get out of the rain."

"Alpha One, this is Hawkeye. I have two of your Sierra units moving up on the LP. They should be able to see him."

Sierra Three, a sniper unit, was the first to the listening post—LP for short. "He looks cold and wet and isn't very active," the sniper said. "We can slip up on him and take him into custody if needed."

"This is Alpha One. I copy. Keep that option open. I'd rather he catch cold and go home."

"So would we."

"Alpha One, this is Hawkeye. That patrol is still making turns around the perimeter. Still fifteen hundred meters out, but they stop periodically and look around and then go straight out about a quarter mile and look around, and then walk back and continue in their big circle."

"Will they intercept any of our people?"

"Not with us here they won't. We'll just keep moving your chickens around them."

"Okay, do your stuff, and everyone listen up."

Grits guided the units along their paths, describing what she saw as calmly and clearly as if she were telling a story to some children. The most valuable thing about Grits' style was that she didn't lapse into jargon—"Turn north twenty degrees"—but used everyday English so that the men on the ground didn't have to stop and calculate their compass heading.

"Butch, you all need to turn a little bit to your right and move around the right side of that rise, do you see it?"

"Yeah, Grits, we see it, thanks."

I imagined J. Edgar Hoover spinning in his grave. He thought women should type and file papers and make coffee. "Grits," I said. "How about the guy over by the landing site?"

"He's huddled down by a tree, looking miserable."

"Alpha One, this is Sierra Three," the sniper radioed. "Do you want us to take him?"

"No, not yet."

I signaled Norris. "Ratso, what is your position and ETA?"

"We're about fifteen minutes from shore."

Wehmeyer, Bonney, Van Zandt, and I monitored the radios from the Suburban, which was crammed with gear, clothes for a long stay, maps, and a large overhead photo of the compounds. The vehicle was going to be our home, kitchen, forward command post, and tactical operations center for a while. I paced back and forth beside the door, reaching in every so often to grab a radio mike. By the depth of the rut next to the car, I figure I walked about five miles between midnight and dawn.

When Wehmeyer calculated that the boat team was a couple of hundred yards from the shore, he reminded me of the guy in the listening post near the landing zone. "We'll have to make a decision soon," he said.

"Yeah, I know, Sierra Three may have to take him. I don't want a compromise. Tell them to stand by to take him into custody."

This was not an easy call. There might be brush crashing, maybe shouting, maybe a shot fired, maybe . . .

Just then, the channel from the plane crackled.

"Alpha One, this is Hawkeye. Your boy just got real cold. He's heading back into the compound."

Yes! "Keep an eye on him to make sure," I said, "and let me know if he decides to come back."

"By the way, your boats are about a hundred yards offshore. They sure are paddlin' hard. You guys having a problem?"

"We're okay."

Actually, we weren't, though I wouldn't find that out until the next day. Norris and his team had climbed into the eight johnboats and had started paddling, only to hear the awful sound of gushing water. The Arkansas State game and fish people, who had kindly loaned us the boats, had delivered them to their launch point with the plugs pulled. None of the HRT operators had thought to check the plugs before setting out. With all the technology and planning, with all the behavioral science research, with all the weight of the FBI going into this mission, it almost failed because of eight rubber stoppers.

As water lapped around their boots, some of the men scrambled to replace the plugs while others paddled furiously. Each operator was carrying about a hundred pounds of expensive equipment—a Heckler & Koch model 93 assault rifle equipped with an infrared aim point projector for night firing, two hundred rounds of ammunition, a Browning Hi-Power with four magazines, a ruggedized, waterproof radio with two extra batteries, four flash-bangs, and a Heckler & Koch MP5 submachine gun with four magazines. Some carried M-79 grenade launchers and bandoliers of tear-gas grenades. A few carried shotguns to shoot locks off doors. Each man carried two days' rations of food and water. Over all this gear, each operator wore an uninflated life jacket like those worn by Navy SEALs. The jackets could be inflated with a bottle of carbon dioxide gas.

HRT operators, like the SEALs, trained in combat swimming with a load of gear, but nobody wanted to slog across the lake with all that stuff. They might have lost some of it, and they would certainly never have lived down the embarrassment. I cannot even imagine telling Buck Revell that the boats had sunk. Faced with such horrific prospects, the men paddled so hard and fast that someone could have water-skied behind the boats. They landed every boat safely and secured the fleet under the brush. Then they headed for the south end of the compound.

"You boys are moving real fast," Grits radioed Ratso. "Just keep going. We'll watch for bogies."

Then she addressed me. "Alpha One, looks like the patrol has had enough too. They're heading for home. You all can move along now."

By 4 A.M., all four elements reported that they were in position and their sections of the perimeter were set. Everyone was in place but the Kansas City SWAT team.

"Ask for a sit rep."

"Alpha Two to KC. Sit rep."

"We're moving, but not yet in position," Butch Roll replied. "We seem to be off course. Lost a radio and stopped to look for it. That delayed us."

"Butch, this is Doc. Forget about the radio, take your time, everyone is in, and we still have lots of time."

"We'll hurry."

"Grits, can you help out a little?"

"Sure, we were on the other side of the compound watching the water landing and the returning patrol. We'll come around and get you."

A moment passed.

"You guys are hard to pick out, help me out. Stand in a circle and hold hands."

"Hold hands!"

"Okay, at least stand in a circle so I can get a better sight on you. Helps to pick you out. What's the matter, don't you guys like to hold hands? Okay, I got you. Head out straight toward that big oak, and along the draw on the other side. You're actually right on target when you get through the draw."

"Alpha One, we're back on course. We never did find the radio," Roll radioed.

"Forget the radio. We've got lots of them, and I'm sure you can afford two thousand dollars for a new one. Let me know when you get in position."

He and his men locked down on the perimeter ten minutes later. I called the command post.

"This is Alpha One. Advise HQ that the perimeter on all three compounds is secure. There has been no compromise. We will make demand at first light."

By 4:45 A.M. two hundred FBI agents were positioned in the bush. The snipers reported activity in the main compound but none in the others. As we had anticipated, the entire population had moved into the most heavily fortified buildings.

"It's about time to wake up our friends," I said.

Wehmeyer, Van Zandt, and I climbed into the back of the Suburban. Bonney drove toward the compound, stopping at a junction near a creek. I got out of the car with my field glasses but could see neither friend nor foe. The rain had stopped and the sky was clear.

Half an hour later, Steve Wiley motioned me over to a radio carrying the sniper channel. "Doc, better come listen to this. It's Fain." Mike Fain, a former Special Forces soldier and one of the sniper team leaders, was hiding in the bush near the front gate of the compound. We had him anchor the gate because he was a rock. When he practiced endurance swimming in the FBI pool, he dived to the bottom and just stood there. No one had ever seen him get excited about anything.

"This is Alpha One, what've you got, Mike?"

"Doc, I have two armed white males walking out of the gate. They are glassing the area. They glassed right past us. Both are armed, sidearms and shoulder rifle, looks like an AR-15. They're walking this way."

"Mike, have they seen you yet?"

"No, they're looking all around, but they haven't seen any of us."

That was what we had expected. The HRT snipers took great pride in their ability to make themselves invisible in their gillie suits festooned with greenery. Once in position, the snipers dug into the earth, then covered themselves over with canvas and vegetation.

"Do you want us to arrest them?" Fain asked.

"How close is your support?"

"There are two other Sierra units about fifteen meters on both sides of me and some operators to my rear. Uh-oh, they are walking directly toward me now. I'm sure they don't see me or anyone else."

"Mike, listen. Let them get as close as you dare. Announce you're FBI and tell them to go back inside."

I'm sure Fain wondered what the hell I was doing, but he didn't ask questions. Jeff told nearby units to stand by to give Fain support.

The CSA pair walked directly toward Fain. The first, about six feet one inches tall with red hair and a beard, had a pistol on his hip. The other, about five feet eight inches, carried an AR-15 assault rifle. Fain whispered that they didn't seem to be nervous. They looked as if they were on a casual morning stroll, enjoying the morning sunlight after a night of pounding rain. In hindsight, this seems odd, since we now know that Ellison had been told the FBI was in the area. All I can figure is, they thought we were no closer than the roadblocks because no one could drive up to the compound without making all kinds of noise on the gravel road.

Fain let them get to within about fifty feet of his position.

"FBI," he called. "Go back into the compound."

The pair jumped about a foot in the air. The shorter man shouldered his weapon. Their heads turned right and left, trying to find the voice.

Another sniper to Fain's left announced, "You heard him, FBI. Go back inside." Then, to Fain's right, a third sniper echoed, "FBI, get back inside. We'll tell you when to come out."

Both men whirled first to their right, then left, then back again, finally spinning in a complete circle, but no one was there. They turned on their heels and sprinted back through the gate.

"Alpha One," Fain reported laconically, "they went back inside."

"I bet they went in to change their pants," Wehmeyer said. "Fain must have scared the shit out of them."

"That was a good move," Van Zandt said. "They'll be knocking down Ellison's door to tell him ZOG is here. I'd like to see them scurrying around. Ellison will have them going to the ramparts, and they're all terrified."

I radioed Horace at the command post to tell the SACs what had happened. "They need to tell HQ, and stand by for stupid questions."

A short time later, I was called to the radio. It was Tony Daniels.

"You guys having fun yet?"

"Just a blast."

"Listen, I told HQ about you sending the two guys back inside. They want to know why you didn't arrest them. They think you should have considered taking them into custody. You'd have two shooters out of there and you might get some intelligence from them. Do you want me to tell them to go shit in their hat, or do you want to make a reply?"

Some desk jockey was putting in his two cents, I figured, trying to look good for the brass. The question was too dumb to have come from Revell or anybody else who counted.

"Tony, who's asking the question, and are you and Blasingame comfortable with it?"

"I'm not telling you who asked the question. I don't think you have time to leave right now and go back and kill him. We're all comfortable with what you did. You're there. You have to make the calls."

"Okay. I wanted to show Ellison and his followers that we're not here to hurt anybody. I wanted to give them an order they absolutely had to follow. They had no choice but to go back inside or, in their minds, die on the spot. I want them to get used to following orders from us, and this was the first one, and they followed it. Right now, we're the faceless enemy who has trapped them, and they're scared to death. They expected ZOG to come in and shoot up the place. They were ready for war, not for this. We have to convince them that we're not the devils they were waiting for, and that we're patient and that we won't go away. This is the first step."

"Do you expect me to remember all of that stuff?"

"I know you, you took notes, and you can remember everything. If there's a problem, I'll call Buck as soon as the Radio Shack guys get a phone line established."

Dennis Hughes overheard me. "Doc, do you want Lonnie and me to start getting you a hard line now?" he asked earnestly. There he went, getting ahead of the curve again.

"No, not yet. We have to see about coms to the compound," I said. "Hell, I'd rather talk to Ellison than HQ anyway. You can start thinking about starting to work on it. Just don't think too fast, know what I mean?"

"I got ya. We'll probably have to run about ten miles of phone wire anyway. Could take a while."

"Good!"

Van Zandt was eavesdropping too. "Next time, could you say, 'I had rather talk to Ellison,' as opposed to, 'Hell, I had rather talk to Ellison'?"

"Van Zandt, do you ever miss anything? You're driving me crazy."

"Boss, I know you, and you told me to stay on your ass. Ah . . . uhh . . . stay on you."

"See, you've been around me too long. Soon I'll have you speaking in proper FBI agent's terms. I may corrupt you before you save me." I knew this was not true. Van Zandt was one of the most devoutly religious and selfless people I had ever met. And I took his words to heart. Why the hell not, as I often told him.

At 5:35 A.M., the sniper net crackled. "Got a white male walking out of the gate, waving a white flag. He looks real nervous."

"I bet he's nervous," said Van Zandt. "They must be real upset and curious. He'll be here to size us up and to get as much intelligence as he can."

We had pulled the Suburban across the creek and into a clearing on the side of the road that led to CSA's front gate. We were about a quarter mile from the gate and down in a low spot so that we couldn't be seen from the compound.

I motioned to Wiley. "Direct him down the road to Alpha One's position and hold your cover. We don't want him to see our sniper positions. I'll send an assault team to intercept him when he gets to the creek."

Kerry Noble walked out of the compound and shouted toward the woods that he wanted to talk. He was intercepted by two HRT operators, their bodies bristling with weapons and combat gear, their faces painted in camouflage, floppy brush hats drawn low over their eyes. One man covered him with a twelve-gauge shotgun while the other approached him from the front. Two other operators came up from the rear. "Don't turn around, put your hands up," one of the men commanded. Noble's hands trembled as he raised them above his head and trotted meekly toward the Suburban.

"Mr. Noble, I'm Danny Coulson. I'm with the FBI and I'm in charge. We have a warrant for Mr. Ellison's arrest and a warrant to search your compound."

Noble accepted my hand with a firm shake. He was tall and slender, with a pleasant, open face, thick red hair, and a red beard. He was not what I had expected. He did not appear to be a fire-breathing religious nut. He was courteous, intelligent, and willing to listen. I got the feeling that he really did want to talk things out. I had to assume that if pushed into a corner, he would fight to the death with the rest of Ellison's people. But if I handled it right, if I didn't push him too hard, maybe I could make him an ally.

Van Zandt had suggested that we not make an early demand for surrender, but rather that we begin with a calm, matter-of-fact conversation about our purposes and procedures. That made sense to me, especially when I thought about the LAW rocket. How do you threaten a man who has bigger guns than you have? I didn't want Noble to know we were worried. I wanted him to think that we were gentlemen. I've always found that if you treat people as ladies and gentlemen, they tend to act that way. I hoped I could draw him into wanting to help me solve this problem, gentleman to gentle-man, not warrior to warrior. At the same time, I wanted him to get the message that if it came to a fight, I had better fighters. I could see fear in his eyes as they shifted left to right, fixing on the unsmiling young men around him.

"Mr. Noble, all your compounds are completely sur-rounded," I said briskly. "There is no chance of escape. We have been here all night and we have seen your patrols and your listening posts. We don't want anyone to get hurt. I'd like to meet with Mr. Ellison."

"We figured you'd be coming, sooner or later." Noble told us that the valley and plateau compounds had been emptied and everyone was in the central compound. I nodded to Wehmeyer, who walked over to the com van.

"Mr. Noble, we'll check out your information and start to search these areas," I said. "There had better not be any booby traps in there. I don't want any of my peo-ple to get hurt by anything you left behind. I'll hold you personally responsible for anything that happens."

"I guarantee you there are no booby straps, explo-sives, or anything like that," Noble said anxiously.

Wehmeyer's voice came in on my earpiece. "Doc, teams report absolutely no activity in either of the outer compounds. I'm sending them in to clear both of them. After they're secure, we can pull those teams off and reinforce our main perimeter."

I turned to Noble, who had not heard the exchange. "Mr. Noble, would you like to walk over to the plateau compound and show us around?"

"Sure. I'd like you to see there's nothing there."

I took this as an act of good faith on his part. He wouldn't want to be close by if someone tripped an explosive. I sent word via the radio net that Alpha One and a visitor were coming up to the plateau compound.

Noble, Bonney, and I crossed our lines and entered the compound. A quick recon had already been done by a SWAT team. Noble guided us through some of the buildings. We moved with extreme caution. "I'll bet a hundred dollars there's not a single surprise in here," I radioed Jeff. "But I won't bet my men. Remember, assumption is the mother of fuckup."

"Roger that," he replied.

"Mr. Noble, I really would like to talk to Mr. Ellison," I said at the end of the tour. "Can you take a phone and some line into the compound so that we can talk?"

"I'd be glad to, but he will probably want to talk face-to-face."

"That would be better for me too, but we need to have a way to reach each other twenty-four hours a day. We need a line into your compound so we can talk if we need something." I motioned to Hughes. "Can you string enough wire for a phone line?"

"Sure, but it'll take several reels."

"Do you know how to reel out reels of wire and splice them in?" I asked Noble. "It is a long way to your compound from here."

"That won't be necessary," Noble replied. "We have wires that lead to all the compounds. We can link up right here if you have a sound-powered telephone."

Hughes nodded and accompanied Noble into the woods, returning in a few minutes with the lines in hand.

Noble said that Ellison was afraid that if he came out to the road, he would be arrested. He asked if I would go inside the compound and meet with Ellison. I declined.

I was not going to give Ellison myself as a hostage. I may be a little bit crazy, but I'm not stupid.

Bonney told Noble to go back and tell Ellison that if he'd come out, we'd guarantee his safety. "If we tell you something, you can bet on it," Bonney said. "We will never lie to you. There's too much at stake here, and the possibility of too many people dying. None of us want that. We'll work out the details so Mr. Ellison can be comfortable.

"Call us when you get inside so we can check our coms," Bonney added, as if he and Noble were already on the same side. Noble took the telephone and went back to the compound.

I sidled up to Van Zandt. "See, you silly shit. I didn't say 'son of a bitch' or one 'goddamn' during the entire conversation."

He smiled serenely. "It's early yet. I'll have to bail you out sooner or later."

"Clint, here is what I want to do," I said. "I want to meet him on the road and sit in the grass and talk. He's a fugitive, and we don't meet with fugitives and then turn them loose. But this is different. I think we should talk, and when we finish, let him go back in. If we arrest him right there, we'll have no credibility and this thing could turn real bad."

"Well, you haven't followed any rules so far, although I notice that you declined his invitation to go inside. Yes, from a psychological point of view, we'd gain a lot of credibility by allowing him to come and go. It would also help his stature in the compound."

"If you hadn't agreed, I was going to have Glasser and Wolf tie you to a tree and leave you to starve."

I called the command post and filled in Daniels and Blasingame.

"Do you have a place where you can meet so his snipers can't take a shot at you guys?" Blasingame asked.

"Yeah, Bonney and the snipers and his assault team are working on that right now. They think there's a place on the road where we can cover him, but his people can't cover us. Thanks for asking."

Larry, Jeff, and I walked around to the back of the Suburban. I took a long draw from my canteen. They did the same. I had not realized how wrung out we all were.

"What do you think?" Bonney asked. "Will they go for it?"

"Are you kidding?" I said confidently. "They're scared to death this thing will turn into the shoot-out of the century."

"I hope so."

Five long minutes passed. Then Daniels came back on the radio.

"The Buckaroo says go for it." I gave Larry and Jeff the high sign.

"He did ask if you could do it safely," Daniels added. "I said that I'd be perfectly safe back here in the command post, but I didn't know or care about you."

"Thanks. I know a guy can get hurt in the CP. Okay, we'll set it up. I'll let you know if Ellison goes for it. And Tony? Thanks."

"Don't mention it. Just make sure you keep our safety in mind." I heard Ahern and Blasingame laughing in the background.

The telephone squawked. Clint picked it up. "Doc, Noble for you."

"Danny, this is Kerry. I'm coming out to talk for him. He has some concerns."

We were now Danny and Kerry. This was a good sign.

I worked on Noble a while longer. I told him about the listening-post guy we could have taken during the night. I also pointed out that we could have arrested him for harboring a fugitive. "We've proven our good faith," Bonney said. "Now it's time for you and Ellison to trust us."

Bonney and Noble walked with me out to the spot on the road that had been selected for the meeting. The road ran slightly uphill at this location and was bounded by a ditch and a fence. The compound was a few hundred yards away.

"Kerry, this is the place," I said. "We can talk in peace here. I give you my word Ellison won't be arrested as long as he is coming to talk to Larry and me. And he must be unarmed."

Noble hesitated.

"Kerry, FBI headquarters has approved this agreement," I said. "They have never approved anything like this in the past. Kerry, go in and tell him he has my word." Noble shook hands with Bonney and me and walked up the hill. We watched him go, trying to decipher his body language. If Ellison didn't come out after all that, it meant that he wanted to fight.

We walked back down to the Suburban and waited. Hughes broke out some coffee. The field phone rang.

"Ellison wants to talk to you," Van Zandt said.

9

Okay, I said to myself. Now it begins.

"Mr. Ellison," I began formally and respectfully, as Clint and I had rehearsed. "This is Danny Coulson. I'm with the FBI. I would like to talk with you."

"I understand."

I gave him the same spiel I'd given Noble. "We have you completely surrounded. There is no escape. There's a warrant to search the compound, and we need to talk about how to go about it. We don't want to get anyone hurt."

"Do you intend to arrest everyone here? We have women and children."

"No, so far, the warrant is just for you. If there's a warrant for someone in there, we'll arrest him. I think we need to sit down and talk about this. We will work out the details and make sure no one gets hurt."

"My people are afraid that if I come out, you'll arrest me."

"I understand. They don't want to lose their leader. I give you my word you won't be arrested. Come out. We can talk, and you can go back inside."

"Do you want to come in here?" Ellison ventured.

"Not hardly." I paused, then added, "We are searching the valley and plateau compounds right now."

"I'd like to talk to you about the search," Ellison said, recovering a bit of his authoritarian voice. "I know how you tear places up. These are our homes."

"We are going to search," I said firmly. "But we won't tear anything up. Mr. Noble saw us begin the search,

277

and he can come out now and see how it's going. You can come if you want to."

"I need to talk to my wife and pray on it. I'll call you back."

I joined Wiley, Bonney, Wehmeyer, and Van Zandt in a clearing where we had set up a generator and parked the Suburban containing the medical gear. I sat on a stump. Bonney pulled up a log. The others grabbed some grass.

"They're probably using glasses to try to pick up our snipers," Wiley said. "He may be playing for time to find a hole in our perimeter. I've walked it. There isn't one. It's very important that he doesn't see anything. That way, he won't be trying to figure out the best place to break through."

"Good point," said Van Zandt. "He'll be more afraid of what he doesn't see than what he does. We want to keep up the faceless-enemy idea for now. We can show some force later."

"Doc, I sent the Hawkeye crew home," Wehmeyer said. "I told them to get some rest and to be back tonight."

"Thanks, tonight will be very important," I said. "Ellison will be looking for ways to slip out, and tonight will be his first chance."

"Doc, we want to push in closer tonight," Wiley said. "Even with SWAT, we're pretty thin. If we push in, we can tighten it up and send them back if they start out. I've told everyone that if we are probed, to challenge and send them back in. With the bird, we should have plenty of warning and can slide people around to intercept."

"Good, coordinate with the operators on the perimeter," I said. "They'll be in position to turn people back too."

"That's been done," Wehmeyer said. "Steve and I will walk the perimeter after dark to see how far in we can go."

We chatted a while longer. Then I crawled into the back of the Suburban and fell asleep. Within the hour, the phone rang. It was Ellison. "Danny, we have two women and six children who want to leave. Can they come out and not be arrested?"

"Sure. If there are no warrants for them, we'll search them and their possessions and take them to a motel. Do I send you the bill?"

"You said you'd pay," Ellison said a little huffily.

So Ellison had a strong streak of horse trader. Good. If money and material possessions still mattered to him, he wasn't quite ready to meet his Maker, and we had some leverage.

"Okay, my treat. When this is over, they can come back and live here again."

Soon, the strangest vehicle I've ever seen came clattering out of the compound. It was a short-bed truck chassis that had only a bench seat and a flatbed with no sides across the back. No hood, no fenders, no dashboard, no muffler—just a naked, ancient V-8 engine, four wheels, a seat, a steering wheel, and two headlights. Kerry Noble was driving, and two women and six little children were riding on the flatbed.

As Noble urged the Jed Clampett–mobile up the road, we stood there shaking our heads. "I'd give anything to put that truck on our airplane and fly it back to the Academy," I told Bonney.

Wehmeyer motioned for Noble to stop short of our

position. If it was a mobile bomb, we didn't want to lose our vehicles. Several HRT operators approached the truck and offered their hands to the women. Noble helped the children down. I could tell from the gentle way he handled them and talked softly to them that he was a dad. In fact, he had six children.

The women wore simple print dresses, clean and neat as if they were going to church. They never said a word. The children, from toddlers to about eleven, kept huddled together near the rear of their truck. I wondered what they were thinking. Mewborn had told us that even the young children were taught about ZOG. The older ones must have been terrified of the devils that met them on the road. One thing struck me as odd. Most children would have been fascinated with our men, who looked pretty fearsome dressed in camouflage and dripping with weapons. These children didn't give them a second glance. I guess they were accustomed to seeing their fathers and the other men in full battle gear.

Bonney told Noble to put all the bags on the ground so they could be searched. There had better not be any surprises, he said. He made Noble stand by the bags, just in case. Then Mary Ann Sullivan and several other female agents came forward to show the women to the van in which they were to ride to the motel.

"I have to go back inside now," Noble said, shaking my hand.

"Thanks, Kerry, this is a start. Everyone will be treated the same way."

"I hope so." He smiled. He clambered back into the thing and chugged back up the road toward the gate.

At twilight, Noble was back. "I'd like to talk about how we might proceed with negotiations."

"Sure," I said. "Have a seat."

Noble said that Ellison had sent him to make sure we understood that if we tried to arrest him during the talks, he and his people would resist, and that if we took him, his people would never surrender without a fight. But he did not say this in a menacing way. He delivered his lines woodenly, as if he had memorized a script. I nodded, said that I understood, and smiled pleasantly. The sun was going down and the night chill was coming upon us. The warm coffee cup felt good to my hands. Having delivered his message, Noble lingered over his coffee too. I had the sense that he wasn't too keen about going back inside.

Bonney motioned me away. Van Zandt smoothly moved in, took my stump, and began making small talk with Noble. I hoped Clint didn't throw in any *sons of bitches* while I was gone.

"We are up for a shift change," Bonney said. "I want to walk the next shift right through here. We had intended to do it down the road, but with Noble here, Clint and I think it would be a good idea to let him see some of what he is facing."

"The faceless enemy?" I asked.

"That's the point. He'll see them here and it'll scare the shit out of him, but then they'll disappear, and he won't see them again, even from the compound. He'll report what he saw. Ellison will get really frustrated that his people won't be able to see them. It might make them think twice about a breakout."

"Okay, do it."

Within five minutes, Bonney had nearly a hundred HRT and SWAT personnel parading past us and hiking into the woods. Behind the FBI units marched police officers from the Minneapolis police department, deputized as U.S. marshals, and four German shepherds, pulling on their leashes. This was our shift change, fresh replacements for the men who had been holding the perimeter since early morning.

Noble gaped at the cadres of muscular young men swathed in camouflage, toting automatic assault rifles, grenade launchers, and stun grenades. His gaze lingered on several men hauling M-60 tripod-mounted machine guns with long belts of ammunition hanging over their shoulders. This was obviously not your ordinary police SWAT team. He had the look of a child watching a parade of Martians. "Are you guys Delta?" he said finally.

"No, we're not Delta. We're the HRT."

"You sure look like Delta."

"Yeah. Delta thinks we look like Delta too." I gave him a smile and poured him another cup of coffee. Then I put on my most serious face. "Kerry, we can do this the easy way, but, if necessary, we can do it the hard way. We're prepared to defend ourselves if you attack our positions. We're not going to be fooled by a diversionary attack on one end of the perimeter that is meant to cover an escape attempt on the opposite end. You're under constant observation. If you attack us, we will retaliate with great force. It won't take long. I don't believe the CSA can sustain our attack and survive."

I added that if some fool fired the LAW rocket or even extended the tube, the whole group would be faced with a swift and awful retaliation.

Noble sat straight up with his hands open in front of his chest, as if he were stunned. "No, no, there won't be any problems like that," he gasped.

All the while, I was speaking in a low tone, slowly and deliberately. I wanted Noble to believe that I was absolutely confident that if force became necessary, we would prevail in short order, but that in my heart, I did not want to use force. I wanted everyone in the compound to walk out. I wanted to shake him out of his fantasy world in which there would be a magnificent confrontation during which God would descend to smite the forces of ZOG. I wanted him to face the cold reality of his predicament.

Only, to tell the truth, the picture I was painting in his mind wasn't reality either. This was what my literary friends would call a play within a play. I knew we would win the gunfight. I was also sure we would suffer casualties. We would have to restrain our fire because of the women and children. Our intelligence reports indicated that ten women and two dozen children remained inside. Some of the women and older boys had been trained as CSA soldiers and would likely shoot at us, but we wouldn't shoot back. I didn't want to take any lives, justified or not. Our job was to bring Ellison in alive. We had chosen the motto To Save Lives. We were about to find out if we could live up to it.

"Kerry, this has been a good start," I said. "We have shown good faith. Tell Jim he has my word he can come out. As long as he is talking in good faith, we will be patient. Kerry, don't try to slip out tonight, or break out. We don't want to ruin what we've started."

"I understand. I'll see what I can do."

He headed up the dirt road, crossed the creek, and disappeared into the compound. I crawled into the far backseat of the Suburban and fell into a sound sleep.

There's not much glamour holding a perimeter. Each

man makes his own bunker out of logs and boulders, covers the pile with his poncho, and crouches inside. This makeshift pillbox will protect him from small-arms fire and grenades but not from a direct hit by a LAW rocket. Squatting in the dark with rain trickling down your nose and bugs crawling across your neck is not what they put on "Join the FBI" posters. You know that the only thing that will break the monotony is a potshot from some dim bulb who thinks he can beat ZOG because he owns a gun and a pair of camouflage utilities.

All during the night, every man on the perimeter peered into the drizzle through his night-vision goggles. The radio channel buzzed steadily as one after another reported seeing CSA members probing our line.

"We have two moving out from the church," a sniper reported.

"You guys are real good, you even beat us on that one," Grits said.

"Just popped out of the back of the church right in front of us."

Two men, one very small, probably a boy, were running bent over with rifles in hand toward the woods, straight at our line.

The sniper called out, "That's it. Get back inside before you get yourselves hurt."

"You heard him," another sniper yelled. "Get back in there right now."

The two veered to their left as if trying to find a break in the line. "Back inside before you hurt yourselves," the first sniper commanded. Finally, the pair walked back toward the church.

After some minutes, Grits came on the operational channel. "This is Hawkeye. I have two of your signals crawling up the black side, in among the sheep. You boys've been out here too long."

Grits had picked up HRT operators Jaime Atherton and Jim McAllister sneaking through the CSA's back pasture. *Black* is commando jargon for "back." Front is *white. Green* is left. *Red* is right. Using the sheep and goats as cover, the operators were trying to get as close as possible to the compound so they could sound the alert if Ellison started to come out the rear.

One ewe nudged McAllister with her nose.

"I think she likes you," Atherton whispered.

"Yeah, she heard about my arms," McAllister replied. Everyone in the gym knew what pride McAllister took in his biceps and triceps development.

Then the fun was over. "We have three men walking out toward the sheep," Grits called. "You boys, hold real tight now. I will let you know if they get too close."

As was our standard practice, an HRT sniper-observer team, consisting of two snipers in fixed positions on the perimeter, had their night-vision goggles trained on the operators as they picked their way through the flock and toward the compound's fence. When they heard Grits' warning, Atherton and McAllister froze while the sniper team scanned the pasture. The snipers spotted the three men crouching low, moving in the direction of the sheep.

"Sniper leader to all Sierra units," a sniper radioed. "Prepare to give support to Charlie team if subjects move upon them."

"Roger."

"Roger."

"Roger."

"Roger."

Across the black expanse, HRT snipers selected their targets and clicked off their safeties. It was a moment we had all dreaded. This firefight, if it happened, would be brief—three shots. Then the real problems would begin.

Atherton and McAllister lay motionless in the cool grass for what must have seemed an eternity. All they could hear were sheep bells and rustling leaves. After a few moments, their sniper team radioed that the three CSA soldiers had turned and were walking back toward the compound. Evidently, they had decided that whatever was out in the pasture, they did not want to fight it. It was one thing to talk about pouncing upon an enemy in the dead of night, but it was another thing to do it. The operators stayed among the sheep, watching, waiting, and listening until dawn.

I woke up about five o'clock. Wiley briefed me on the episode. Moments later, I spotted Atherton and McAllister walking past the command car during the shift change.

"Hey, Jim," I yelled. "I hear that you and one of the sheep are picking out china, and Jaime is going to be the best man."

"Boss, I've gone a long time, but not quite that long," McAllister said. They sat down on a couple of my executive stumps.

"Okay. How did it go out there?"

"We got a close look-see," Atherton said. "They don't appear to be doing any work on the fortifications. Some of the bunkers don't appear to be manned, but some are. There's a lot of activity around the houses, a lot of meetings and running around. Everyone has shoulder weapons."

I told them about the boy who had come out of the church.

"Yeah, mean little son of a bitch," McAllister said. "He came out to the perimeter again this morning. He had a Mini-14 in his hand, kept yelling at us and brandishing the gun over his head, looked like he wanted to fight. I don't like the idea of having to shoot a little kid. We yelled at him and sent him back inside."

"Ellison will probably send him out again to get intelligence on where our people are," I said. "They know we won't shoot him. Just be sure you have cover if he comes out again. He's young and stupid enough to take a shot at one of you."

"I hear that!"

"Oh, yes," Atherton said. "We feel we have a duty to tell you that one of the sheep kept saying 'Baa-Burke' all night long. Almost drove us crazy."

"Yeah," McAllister chimed in. "One of the snipers saw Burke leading the sheep into the woods, and we haven't seen him or the sheep since."

They were referring to Fran Burke, who led a team of operators and was a great practical joker. The guys took a shot at him whenever they could.

"Well, Mac, maybe you can have a double wedding," I said. "I'll talk to Ellison about marrying you guys up. He's a preacher, you know. How would you feel about a ceremony in the CSA chapel?"

"Hell, I'll give away the brides," Atherton said.

Okay, we'd had our fun. Back to business. "You guys get the hell out of here before they send Soskis in to haul us away," I barked.

I turned to see Ron Kelly's shining smile. "Doc, what would you guys like for dinner tonight?"

Every good operation has to have a scrounger to find the little things that make life bearable. Ours was Kelly, a supervisor in the Little Rock office. A stocky, muscular man with a gonzo gleam in his eyes, Kelly enjoyed doing the impossible and the inadvisable.

"Man, I'd go for a pizza, and I'm sure the boys would too. Any chance of that?"

"Hell, yes. What do you want on it?"

"Have Jeff and Steve poll the teams on the radio. You really think you can get pizzas way out here in the middle of nowhere?"

"Hey! This is your man Ron. I'll get them, and they'll be hot too!"

"I don't want to know how you're going to do it."

All I know is, he did. And they were hot.

The next night, the teams wanted hamburgers. Kelly came up with two hundred of them, straight from the grill. Exactly how he got them remains a mystery as far as the FBI is concerned. But folks in Mountain Home still tell the story of the night a Huey helicopter landed in the parking lot of McDonald's. It seems a stocky stranger climbed out, ordered two hundred Big Macs and fries to go, and flew them away into the night.

Wehmeyer and Van Zandt said that Bonney and I looked like bums and that if we were going to be negotiating with anybody, we had to look professional. I was stymied. My kit bag always has a razor and shaving soap. It doesn't come equipped with hot water.

One of the operators told me about a springhouse at the plateau compound. It was forty degrees tops, but it was fresh and it woke us up. Just as we were sticking tissue on our nicks, the field phone rang. It was Ellison, ready to talk.

I looked at Bonney and said, "Let's go meet the man."

10

Bonney and I walked out on the road. Ellison stopped thirty yards from the command car and turned slowly around. "I'd like to talk to you from here for now," he called. "My people are afraid you'll arrest me."

"Mr. Ellison, I gave you my word that you will not be arrested," I said. "It wouldn't be in your best interest or mine to arrest you. We *will* not lie to you. You may not like what I have to say, but I will not lie to you."

He seemed to be somewhat reassured. I felt that he was sizing us up, hoping for some clue as to what he could expect and wondering how well our men would perform.

Of course, I was sizing him up too. Even in jeans, a casual shirt, and work boots, he was a powerful-looking man. He was about five foot ten inches tall, but he was built like a Mack truck, with wide shoulders, a thick torso, and large forearms. But he'd never pass the HRT physical tests, I could see that. At forty-four, his face was getting pudgy, and if you looked closely, you'd see that his gut was on the soft side.

His hair was brownish black and wet. He'd been bleaching it blond, with a matching blond beard, to go into town. Now, it appeared, he was trying to get it back to its natural dark brown. He looked as if he had just dumped a bottle of shoe polish on his head.

In my earphone, I could hear our snipers watching the gates telling one another they had a bead on him. "Sierra Five. I have subject scoped." "Sierra Six, ten-four on that, subject scoped here too." Ellison was also being watched

by an assault team in camouflage hiding in the bush. We
had instructed Ellison to come out unarmed, but there
was always the chance that he had a small gun in an ankle
holster. I wasn't worried about that. If Ellison made a stupid move, Bonney and I could draw our Hi-Powers and
engage him before he could do much damage. I suppressed a laugh at the thought of Bonney drawing on
Ellison like two gun-toting preachers in Dodge City.

"Mr. Ellison, can we walk up to your position?"
Bonney said. "It's a little hard to talk from this distance."

"Fine."

We started up the hill. "Doc, we have to be sure we
don't get in the view of his snipers," Bonney whispered.
Ellison solved this problem for us, walking just far
enough down the road so that his men couldn't see us.

I extended my hand. "Mr. Ellison, I'm Danny
Coulson, the HRT commander. This is Larry Bonney."

Ellison shook my hand and then Bonney's.

"Mr. Ellison, we have a warrant for your arrest, and a
warrant to search the compound," I began.

"I don't want to be put in jail with no bail," he said,
scowling. "I know how you guys work."

"I'm sure we can work something out on bail for you
with the United States Attorney," I said crisply. "First we
have to agree that we don't want anyone to get hurt, and
then we can work out the details."

"What will happen to our place? Are you going to
take it from us?"

"No, we have no interest in your home. Mr.
Hutchinson has agreed that he will not seek to seize it.
After we finish our business, we'll go away and your people can return to your land as long as they don't violate
the law."

Ellison eyed me carefully and asked if I would meet his wife. He said he had a great deal of confidence in her ability to judge character. So a corner in Ellison's psyche maintained an almost mystical faith in the intuition of women. That was an interesting complication in someone who was otherwise obsessed with manliness, as defined by firepower.

"I'll be glad to," I said. "The same rules will apply to her. We meet on the road, have a talk, and she can go back inside."

After Ellison went home, Bonney and I located Mewborn. "What do you know about Ellison's wife?"

"Which wife?" Horace said.

"He has more than one?" I asked.

"He has two. Ollie and Annie. Said it was God's plan, but a lot of the congregation got pretty upset and moved out on him. That's one reason the CSA has been having trouble paying down the mortgage."

Ellison's first wife, Cheryl, had abandoned him some years before, leaving him with five children. In 1972, he had wed Ollie, a twenty-two-year-old bank employee and church singer from Lewis Springs, Missouri. Ollie was divorced with a small daughter, and she bore six children to Ellison. After Ellison pushed his eldest daughter into marriage at the age of fifteen, there were eleven kids to be fed, clothed, and home-schooled. That would have been plenty for most people, but not Jim Ellison, who, in November of 1982, announced that he had had a revelation from God, that he was a king of the true Israel, King James of the Ozarks, and that God had told him to take a second wife. He chose Annie, a twenty-nine-year-old Minnesota minister's daughter who was separated from her husband, both of whom were

CSA members. Jim and Annie exchanged vows. She moved into the household and soon gave birth to yet another small Ellison.

"So, which wife do you think will come out with Ellison?" I asked.

"I don't know." Horace frowned. "He risked a lot to take the young one. But he probably has faith in the older one."

"Be very deferential to Mrs. Ellison," Van Zandt warned us. "If she senses you're not sincere, or you act disrespectfully to Ellison or her, all is lost and we could be here through the winter. You may find that she doesn't say very much but she'll watch and hear everything you say to Ellison, and when she gets back inside, she'll have an impression that she'll share with Ellison and the group."

"Should we shake hands with her?" I asked.

"Good question," Van Zandt said. "No. Listen, do you remember anything that happened out there that we can start to think about?"

"Aw, Bonney just talked a bunch of God stuff, and I told him that he had better come out or we would kick the shit out of him."

"You are unbelievable," Van Zandt gasped. "Bonney, how many swear words did he use?"

"Not one. Even I could not believe it."

"Don't worry, Clint," I said. "Just wanted to see if you're paying attention."

Bonney and I straightened our shirts and brushed off the dust. We were dressed, as usual, in full camouflage, including our boots and body armor. Normally, we would also have worn load-bearing vests with extra magazines and an array of stun grenades and other equipment. For this occasion, Clint advised us to strip off the extra gear. He wanted us to look as much like commanders as possible and not to appear too threatening. On his advice, we limited our accessories to our Browning Hi-Powers. A simple, elegant statement, I thought. An hour later, the snipers reported that a white male and a white female were walking out of the gate and heading up the road in our direction.

"Let's go," I said. "It's show time."

"I would like for you to meet my wife Ollie," Ellison said with great formality and obvious pride. "I value her opinions, but most of all she is a real good judge of people."

Ollie Ellison gave me a Mona Lisa smile and a slight nod. I yanked off my battered black baseball cap and tried not to stare. This was not the terrified, beaten-down gun nut's wife I had envisioned. Ollie was a true beauty, five feet seven or five feet eight inches tall, with long dark hair, and high cheekbones that reminded me of Emmylou Harris or Rita Coolidge. In a modest sleeveless print dress that hung loosely below her knees, she might have been a flower child or a Berkeley grad student off on a country weekend. I had expected a woman with furtive, downcast eyes, her shoulders slumped with the enormous burden she bore. Her husband must have told her that her judgment would be crucial in deciding whether there would be a war. The lives of every man, woman, and child depended on her, including eleven children under her own roof. We had to be her worst nightmare, ZOG warriors, men poised to launch an attack upon her home. Yet her eyes were cool and intelligent. She stood ramrod straight, shoulders back, chin up.

"It is nice to meet you, Mrs. Ellison," I said. "We have business with your husband and a warrant to search the compound. We have come peacefully and want to see that no one will get hurt."

"Will I be arrested?" she asked in a matter-of-fact way. "What about the rest of the families? Will they be arrested?"

"We have only a warrant for Mr. Ellison, but we don't know who else is inside that may be a federal fugitive," Bonney replied. "There is the possibility that others may be arrested. But right now we have only one arrest warrant."

I sensed that her questions, expressed as calmly as if she had been questioning one of her children about homework, were meant mainly to get us talking so that she could take the measure of us. I tried to answer in a way that would convince her we weren't the devils she heard about on Sundays. "Ma'am, you must be concerned about your homes," I said. "I want to assure you we have no intention of taking them. Even if we find contraband, we'll leave your homes as we found them, and you can return later."

"We don't really trust the federal government," Ellison said. "How can we be sure you're telling the truth?"

"Sir, we don't really trust the government either," I said. "We're here to do a job. If I lie to you here, the whole world will know, because you have a tremendous following and you'll tell everyone. We'll never be able to talk these things out in the future. We've allowed your people to come and go when we could have stopped them. We're proving over and over again that we can be trusted."

Ellison's eyes flicked from us to his wife and back again. "We have to go back and pray and talk."

"Yes, sir," Bonney said quietly. "So do we."

Ollie gave us a final appraising look, then turned, took her husband's hand, and walked back toward the gate.

You sure figured this one wrong, I said to myself. *That is one strong woman. I just hope she's strong enough. And that she believes us.*

About an hour later, the phone rang. Van Zandt picked it up. Ellison was coming out of the compound.

"Great," Van Zandt exclaimed. "I guess his wife thinks they can trust you guys."

Ellison had changed out of his civvies and was now dressed in full camouflage, just as we were. He evidently took this commander-to-commander idea literally. We shook hands. "Jim," I said, "this is going to take a while. I don't like standing up and talking. Let's sit on the side of the road." I motioned to a bunch of flat stones in a ditch along the left side of the road. Bonney, Ellison, and I seated ourselves on the rocks. The earth had dried out and was a little dusty. Small insects were crawling around. You generally think of negotiations between commanders in some formal setting. This was about as informal as you can get. Three rocks, three men, and a lot of tension.

Ellison leaned his back against the dirt wall, facing away from the compound. His blue eyes were rimmed with shadows. His skin was pasty gray. I could only imagine the battle that must be going on inside him. He had preached for years that he would fight ZOG to the death. Now he was sitting in a ditch with two ZOG agents and talking about handing himself and his people up to ZOG. On the ridge above us, hidden in the bush, were Jaime Atherton, Jim McAllister, and Don Brigham. I could look past Ellison and see Brigham, his face painted in greens and browns, his submachine gun pointed at Ellison's head. If I hadn't known he was there, he would have been invisible.

"Why do you guys carry Brownings?" Ellison asked, pointing to my Hi-Power. "I thought all you guys carried .45s." He was making small talk, evidently reluctant to get down to business. We humored him.

"No, we like the nine-millimeter Browning," Bonney said. "I think it's a better gun. We like it cocked and locked. Very fast."

"Isn't the .45 a better bullet?" Ellison said.

"Probably," Bonney said. "But it doesn't make any difference if you hit the right place. The Browning is much quicker and shoots faster with more accuracy than the model 1911."

"Cocked and locked," Ellison said with a knowing smile. "That's for pros."

"Jim," I said, "we would like to go over the situation with you. We have you completely trapped. We've been planning this for weeks. You're completely surrounded and tremendously outnumbered. There's no chance of escape. If you expect people to come and help you, that won't happen. We control this entire area, both on the ground, on the lake, and in the air."

The one thing I didn't say was that we had a Southern belle up in the sky, helping us all along the way. Hawkeye was still an FBI secret.

"How did you get in here without my patrols spotting you?" Ellison demanded.

"Jim, we've been coming into your compound for over a month," Bonney replied with a we-know-our-stuff smile. "Hardly a night has gone by when we haven't been watching you guys. We even followed your patrols and watched your listening post down by the lake."

Ellison's face sagged a little. "Was that you guys down by my sheep last night? Something really had them stirred up for a while, and then they calmed down. That really frightened my people. They thought you were coming for us."

"Jim, you were probing our perimeter all night," I said sternly. "You even sent a kid out last night and again this morning. He could have started a firefight and gotten himself and a lot of us killed. You have to get control of your people. Tell them they aren't getting out and we are not going away. Ever!"

Ellison's eyes darted around frantically. He was still trying to avoid coming to grips with the reality that we had him and there was no escape. He spotted a patch of poison ivy growing near the fence.

"Do you get poison ivy?" he asked.

"No, I generally don't," I said, looking perplexed.

"I used to be allergic to poison ivy." He grinned. "I cured it by eating a big bunch of it." He reached over into the brush, snapped off a poison ivy leaf, popped it into his mouth, and munched it like lettuce. "You know, in your job you must spend a lot of time in the woods. You should be sure that poison ivy doesn't get you," he said triumphantly. "You should really try to eat some. It really works." He offered me a leaf.

I shook my head. "I'll just take your word for it. Seeing how it doesn't bother me anyway, I don't see any reason to take a risk." I envisioned myself in some Arkansas hospital ward with my throat swollen shut. Not a real John Wayne image.

Finally Ellison focused on the matter at hand. Perhaps the poison ivy snack had the beneficial effect of concentrating his mind. "Danny, there are some serious problems we need to work out. We have other people in there that want to fight it out with you. They don't trust anything about the government, and they say you are still a fed."

Yes! I thought. *Now we get down to Danny and Jim and Larry.* I kept a poker face and avoided looking at Bonney for fear of tipping my hand, but the moment I heard Ellison's almost offhand remark about "other people," I knew he had made the psychological leap. I didn't know exactly what we'd said or done that had gotten to him, but the important thing was, we had. Though he could not bring himself to say as much explicitly, he was now aligning himself with us, talking about how "we" could deal with "them," meaning the hard-core radicals inside the compound. In the movies, the moment when the criminal gives in is played for high drama. In reality, the meeting of the minds to work together evolves slowly, with oblique exchanges that suggest, but never say outright, that two opposing parties are now on the same side.

The notion that Ellison would surrender also remained unspoken. At some level, he must have known that once he started down the path with us, there could be no other end to this story. But I didn't push him to say so out loud. I had to maintain a delicate balance between controlling him and humiliating him. I needed his help separating the other inhabitants of the CSA compound from their guns. We couldn't risk a factional rebellion, ambushes, and booby traps.

I had banked on the idea that Ellison was a loser and

would fold under psychological pressure. Now I had to shore him up so that he'd behave as if he were a winner as this high-stakes game was playing out. It was a matter of finding the right mix of intimidation and comfort. I wanted Ellison to be much more terrified of us than anyone inside. He had to believe that the worst thing he could possibly do would be to get into a fight with us, that he had no chance of success, and that he would bring disaster down upon himself and his family if he tried anything. At the same time, he had to keep his dignity and be a leader. If he lost his dignity in front of us, he'd also lose it with the people inside. I needed him to stay strong and see this thing through. To do that, he had to be left with a scrap of hope that surrender would not necessarily destroy the CSA. Privately I hoped it would do just that, but I couldn't let him read me. I wanted him to think of surrender as a simple event, a sort of tactical retreat on his part, not the end of his whole world.

"Jim, we're pros," I said softly, leaning in so that my forehead was inches from his. "But these pros want to end this thing peacefully. We don't want to have anyone die. There's no need."

He nodded.

"Look," I added. "Sometimes we have to tell our people to do things they just don't want to do. Just ask Bonney. I make our people do things they hate, and sometimes they hate me. And frankly, I don't care if they hate me. It's for their own good and the good of our unit."

Bonney took the cue. "Jim, I know how hard this is for you. Being a leader is never easy. It may be harder to lead your people toward life than to lead them to their deaths. You have to convince them that this is not the time to die. It's a time to go in a new direction. We're not the enemy that you thought we were. We've shown you that time and time again. We're talking with you because we have confidence in your strength and your ability to do the right thing."

"Danny," Ellison said quietly, "I don't know if I can get all of them out."

"Jim, you have to get out as many as you can," I said. "We want them all to come out, but at least be sure that all the women and children come out, and as many of the men as possible. You have to come out too. I don't want to have to fight you."

"Some of them think they can fight their way out." He sighed miserably. "There are very powerful people inside that I don't think you know are here. They absolutely want to fight it out, house to house, or to try to slip out or shoot their way out. I haven't convinced them that war would be futile. It's a real struggle."

Ellison gazed out into the forest, his forehead knotted with tension. *He must be going through hell in there,* I thought.

"Jim, you tell Randy Evans and Tom Bentley to get out here," I snapped.

He gaped. How did I know their names? He had never mentioned that he was harboring two Order fugitives. He had to be thinking I had the whole compound wired.

In fact, the info had come in over the transom. In looking for Randy Evans after The Order pulled the Brinks truck robbery, Wayne Manis had interviewed Evans's family and friends. He'd made a favorable impression on at least one person in the Evans circle.

This individual happened to catch a TV news broadcast about the siege and noticed that Evans's wife was among the women and children who came out of the CSA compound on the Jed Clampett–mobile. The person called Manis. Randy had to be inside, and his good buddy Tom Bentley was probably with him. If Bentley was there, *his* friend David Tate was probably there too.

In fact, Tate hadn't made it to the CSA. On April 20, the police dragnet had trapped him in Forsyth, Missouri, about twenty-five miles away. In November 1985, he would be convicted of Missouri state trooper Jimmie Linegar's murder and sentenced to life without parole.

But Evans and Bentley were inside, Ellison admitted, along with two other Order men, Jefferson D. Butler and James Wallington. All four were siding against Ellison and the CSA elders.

I lowered my voice almost to a whisper and locked my eyes onto Ellison's. "Dammit, Jim," I said, uttering the oath—Clint, forgive me—in hopes of getting Ellison's attention. "All this talk about slipping out or shooting your way out. Do you think you'd have a chance? You people haven't even seen our positions, and yet we turn you back. If you try to shoot your way out, who'll you shoot at? You can't see or find us. If you start a firefight, we *will* use deadly force. And you'll never even see the men that will kill you. You'll be fighting ghosts."

He said nothing but stared. I could see him crumbling. Good. Now to put him back together.

"Jim, this isn't the time or place to die," I said. "Don't let some idiot start a war. If we go to war, we've both lost. We're both responsible for our people. We've used great restraint in dealing with you. We've lived up to every bargain. Now you must lead your people out, to live for another day."

"Danny, I'm going to need some help," Ellison said slowly. "I need for Robert Millar to come over from Oklahoma to help me. All of us respect him. I need him to talk to the others. He needs to come into our home and pray and talk with us."

Robert Millar was a patriarch of the Christian Identity movement. He had founded a Christian Identity compound called Elohim City outside Muldrow, Oklahoma, near the Arkansas-Oklahoma border. Millar had been born in Kitchner, Ontario, to a father who turned pacifist Mennonite in reaction to the carnage he had witnessed on the battlefields of Europe during World War One. Somewhere along the way, Millar had embraced Christian Identity dogma and now, at sixty, was one of its most influential proselytizers. Elohim City was well known to Tony Daniels and the Oklahoma law enforcement community as a haven for all sorts of gun-crazed white supremacists and neo-Nazis.

"Jim, how important is this?" I hesitated. "I don't like sending a third party inside. What if one of your people tries to harm him or hold him hostage?" I could just see some belt-and-suspenders lawyer in the FBI legal counsel division having a heart attack over our putting Millar in harm's way.

"That won't happen," Ellison replied. "We all love him. We may disagree with each other, but we all listen to Robert Millar."

"Jim, I will have to check on that," I said. "Give me some time. I'll call you with an answer. Do you think he'll come?"

"No doubt," Ellison said, standing. The three of us shook hands.

"Good luck," I said.

Ellison nodded, walked away, and turned back to me. "Danny, I really need Millar's help."

"I'll work on it."

We radioed Daniels and Blasingame at the command post.

"I'll call Buck," Daniels said, "and tell him that Doc has another crazy idea. He'll agree to bringing Millar out here. I'll send a plane and some agents. But don't let Millar go inside until Buck gives the final approval."

11

Robert Millar strolled up the dusty road dressed as if a pretty widow had invited him to an ice cream social. He had on a neatly pressed vanilla suit, starched shirt, black tie, and shiny alligator shoes. He had an impish smile and probably weighed 120 pounds. When I shook his hand, I noticed that it was as small and soft as a woman's. How ironic, I thought, that the macho Ellison was betting that this fragile little man could win over hard cases like Evans and Bentley.

We explained the problem.

Millar nodded gravely. "There's no need for bloodshed here today. I'd like to go inside and talk with them. I think I can help you on this."

"We're very concerned for your safety," I said.

"You don't know me or my people very well," Millar replied placidly. "I'll be in no danger."

Clint took Millar aside for a cup of coffee. After their chat, Clint told me he was convinced that Millar was the key and would be safe.

I walked over to the communications van and telephoned HQ. "This is Coulson, Buck's illegitimate son," I began cheerfully.

"No, it's not," Revell's secretary said. "This is trouble. Whenever you call, there's always trouble."

The Buckster got on the line. "You know we've never done anything like this before."

"Yeah, I know it. It's risky on its face, but Ellison is getting desperate. He can't control everyone inside, and he needs Millar."

"Well, we've broken a lot of rules so far, and this sounds like a risk worth taking. Go ahead and do it. You have my authority."

I rang off and thanked the Good Lord that Buck was a gambler. If he had run every decision up the chain to the Department of Justice, we might have waited a week or more for a decision, and the window of opportunity might have slammed shut.

Bonney telephoned Ellison with the news. He arrived at the ditch puffing hard, having run nearly all the way. He greeted Millar shyly. The little man must have powerful medicine.

"I'm holding you responsible for his safety," I lectured Ellison. "If I call you and order him out, he must come out immediately. And if he asks to come out, you'll personally escort him out. Agreed?"

"Yes, I promise you he won't be harmed."

"We're going way out on a limb," Bonney pressed. "Just don't let us down."

Millar gave Ellison a fatherly hug and said, "Let's go inside and talk and pray."

Even with Ellison's assurances, I worried. The Order guys were stone killers, with probably little spiritual grounding. I cautioned Millar that I wanted him out of the compound by 3:30 P.M. and that he was to call me every half hour so I would know he was alive.

At 3:30 P.M. on the dot he called to ask for an additional half hour. Clint and I heard no sounds of distress, but we were nervous. I tossed about a million stones into the creek. Clint paced. Bonney left us and went over to hang out with his team.

Then Millar called and said he thought he was making progress, but he needed to stay the night in the compound.

"Robert has been a lot of help," Ellison chimed in, "but we need more time." The CSA members were sold, but Evans and Bentley were holding out.

"Mr. Millar can stay," I said, "but you better be sure he is protected. We don't want this to fall apart now."

I made that decision without asking anyone. I'm not sure I had a real choice. I wasn't about to walk up there and lead Millar out by the hand.

Now it was up to Millar and Ellison. I was beat. I peeled off my pistol belt and body armor and jumped into the back of the truck, welcoming sleep but dreading the next morning's ice-water bath.

At 10:05 A.M. the next morning—April 22—the phone rang. Bonney picked it up, listened intently, smiled, and hung up. "Ellison says Millar, Noble, and he are coming out. They think we have a deal!"

Much later, I found out how much I owed to Kerry Noble and Ollie Ellison. When we showed up at Bull Shoals Lake, each had been casting about for a way to escape from Ellison. Noble had never really been comfortable with paramilitarism, and Ellison's hypnotic effect on him was wearing off. He had secretly been making plans to pack up his wife and children and slip away from the compound for good when we showed up.

Ollie was desperate too. She had suffered through an abusive childhood and a bad first marriage and was struggling to raise her retarded daughter on a meager salary when Ellison, then thirty-two, handsome and confident, swept into her life and announced that he was her destiny. She was better educated than he and more broad-minded, but she needed a strong man, and he needed a helpmeet to further his ministry and care for his motherless children. Identity and *The Turner Diaries* changed everything for her. She hated the hate movement. It transformed Jim into a tyrant and her world into a prison.

When Ellison took Annie as his co-wife, Ollie fell into a deep depression and started wandering the woods for hours, praying to be saved. She thought God had forgotten her until the day ZOG warriors surrounded the compound. She went into the laundry room and stared out the window, folding clothes and sending ZOG a message. *There are real people in here. Real children.* Then the feeling came over her that God was answering her prayer. *You're not here to kill us,* she exulted. *You've come to set me free. All this madness can stop now.*

Ollie knew what she had to do. She had to enter Jim's delusion and gently guide him toward the right result. The night Robert Millar came into the compound, she sat at her husband's side and asked quietly, "Do you think Yashua"—Jesus—"has something else in mind for us? Look what He has done." Hadn't Yashua thwarted the assassination plan by sending the snow? Hadn't He sent some of Ellison's best men into town just as the road was being sealed off? Look at what He had done to the minefield. A week before we arrived, Ellison had ordered his men to plant land mines all through the property. Not long afterward, a fierce thunder and lightning storm swept the lake, and by some freak of nature, a thunderbolt hurtled down from the heavens and struck square in the middle of the minefield, making a fearful racket. The next morning, the CSA members discovered every last mine had been detonated. If that was not a sign from Yashua, Ollie said, what was?

Ellison broke down and cried. Would Ollie help him convince the FBI to let him escape? *You coward,* Ollie thought. *After all this talk about war, you're afraid.* She cradled him in her arms. "I wish my dad was here," he sobbed. "I just wanted to do something for Yashua." Then he pulled himself together and sent word out that Yashua had revealed that the CSA must lay down arms and live to fight another day. In the fullness of time, He would work a miracle so that Ellison and his people would be exonerated in the courts of Babylon.

As Ellison walked down the hill to greet us, I could see the relief on his face. Noble looked happy and Millar was cool as a cucumber. If they were planning to use the surrender as a cover for battle, they were good actors.

"Okay, we have a deal," Ellison said. "They've all

agreed to come out and surrender. We had a little trouble with one fellow, but we finally convinced him to come out. At first he said we could all surrender but he was staying in to fight. Reverend Millar talked him out of it." I found out later that Ellison and Randy Evans had argued so furiously that Ellison had punched Evans and blackened his eye. Ellison was lucky Evans hadn't hauled off and shot him.

"That's very good," I told Ellison with the formality the occasion deserved. "I personally appreciate what you have done. You've shown great leadership and strength."

I turned to Millar. "We could not have gotten this far without your spiritual help. We appreciate what you did."

Bonney and I shook hands all around. "Now we'll have a very dangerous situation," I cautioned. "Any one of your people could change his mind, and we could still go to war. We want to set up procedures so that we can do this as safely as possible. We want all the men to walk out first, with you, Jim, and Reverend Millar. They're less likely to cause trouble if you're with them. Then the women and children will come out with Mr. Noble. They can drive in your truck, or walk."

All three nodded in agreement and walked back up the road. I sent for Bill Buford, who was out with the SWAT teams, getting ready to sweep the compound for weapons and booby traps. Ellison had especially requested that the great Green Beret be the one to arrest him.

The radio crackled, and a sniper reported that Ellison was jogging out of the compound and down the road in my direction. Bonney and I rushed to meet him.

"What's wrong, Jim?" I said anxiously.

"Look, there's going to be a slight delay. I have everything ready to go, I'm ready to go but I didn't comb my hair this morning and you've got to give me time to comb my hair."

This is absolutely unbelievable. We were coming to one of the most critical phases of this operation. Two deadly forces had been standing facing each other with some of the heaviest firepower ever assembled in a civilian law enforcement operation. Evans or Bentley or any of the others could change his mind and start a firefight. And the whole thing was being held up because Ellison had to fix his ratty-looking mat of black-brown hair.

"Jim, that's fine," I said as straight-faced as I could manage. "Go back up, comb your hair, and let's get this thing over with."

As he walked away, I exhaled sharply, turned my back on him, and hit the talk switch on my radio. "This is Alpha One. Mr. Ellison has just advised me that the surrender will be delayed. It seems that he hasn't had time to comb his hair. He'll bring his people out once he has attended to his hair." Bonney and I walked back down to the cars. Everybody was sitting around shaking his head and wondering what would happen next.

Before long, a sniper reported that a large group of individuals were forming up in the compound. Lew Jordan, our physician's assistant, walked over to me and handed me a kitten.

"What's this for?" I said.

"Well, we've all heard that Ellison says he can turn himself into a field mouse and escape. If he does it this time, let the cat go on him."

"Thanks, but I don't think we'll need it," I said, laughing. "What I need right now is a hairdresser. Want to go inside and spruce him up?"

"No thanks, boss," Jordan replied, taking his new pet off for milk.

Steve Wiley had positioned practically the entire sniper-observer team and many of the operators in a line along the road leading from the compound to my command post. We were still a long way from home. I had learned a long time before that you never really have control of a dangerous fugitive until you have your hands on him, and he's down on the ground. Even then you may have a tussle.

As Ellison and his warriors walked out of the gate and made that fateful right turn down the road toward our position, they could see a clearing, thirty or forty feet long, dotted by clumps of bush and trees. Suddenly a monster covered in green vegetation and bearing an M-14 rifle rose out of the grass. Five yards farther, another monster arose, this one holding an assault rifle. Every five yards other monsters appeared, all faceless, all brandishing terrible weapons. Not one of Ellison's men made a move to break away. They walked hands on head, glancing nervously over their shoulders. Did any of them give any thought to making a run for it? We'll never know. It would have taken some kind of courage to charge into the bush-men, and no one felt up to it, at least on that day.

Ellison, now dressed in civvies—a blue windbreaker, a Ban-Lon shirt, khaki pants, and street shoes—walked out with Millar. Ellison's head was high and his stride was brisk. He clearly enjoyed being the star of the show. "You guys follow that Danny," he shouted. "He's a good one."

I offered Ellison my hand. "Congratulations, Jim, you did a heck of a job." I still believed that he followed a

The scene of the murder of New York City
police officers Foster and Laurie.

WANTED BY THE FBI

BANK ROBBERY; INTERSTATE FLIGHT - ATTEMPTED MURDER; ROBBERY

TWYMON FORD MYERS

DESCRIPTION

Born, November 27, 1950, Bronx, New York; Height 5'7" to 5'8"; Weight, 170 to 180 pounds; Build, heavy; Hair, black; Eyes, brown; Complexion, medium; Race, Negro; Nationality, American; Occupations, garment worker, laborer; Social Security Number used, 052-46-0042.

CAUTION

MYERS ALLEGEDLY HAS BEEN IN POSSESSION OF FIREARMS IN THE PAST. HE REPORTEDLY IS CLOSELY ASSOCIATED WITH PERSONS WHO ARE HEAVILY ARMED WITH EXPLOSIVES AND A VARIETY OF GUNS. CONSIDER EXTREMELY DANGEROUS.

The FBI wanted poster for Twymon Myers.

Bruce Brotman and I make an entry into an apartment looking for Twymon Myers and Joanne Chesimard.

The scene of the shootout with Twymon Myers.

Bill Baker (right), my partner in the New York field office, arrests bank-robber/hostage-taker John Wojtowicz (center) in Flatbush. The 14-hour standoff was the basis for the film *Dog Day Afternoon*, starring Al Pacino as Wojtowicz. *(Corbis/UPI)*

Richard Girnt Butler, founder of the racist, anti-Semitic organization Aryan Nations. We faced two terrorist groups inspired by Butler's sermons of hate—The Order, and the Covenant, Sword and Arm of the Lord. *(Michael Nichols/Magnum)*

Kerry Noble (with
rifle, months before
the siege) and
Jim Ellison.

The Covenant, Sword and Arm of the Lord chapel.

A swastika and cross in
the CSA chapel.

ATF agent Bill Buford (left) and FBI agent Chuck Mastin (right) in the pulpit of the fortified chapel at the CSA compound.

The cover of the CSA's *Christian Army Basic Training Manual.*

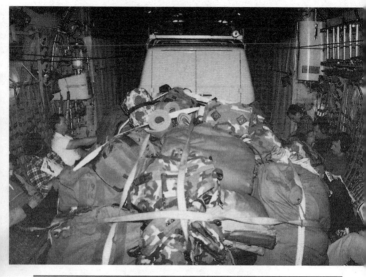
First class on the HRT special: inside the C-130
on the way to the CSA compound.

On the phone with Jim Ellison.

With Jeff Wehmeyer (center), Larry Bonney (right), and the CSA's tank.

On the CSA's truck.

Jim Ellison (in white) and Kerry Noble (right) meet Larry Bonney, Bill Buford, and me to negotiate their surrender.

The Atlanta prison.

Prisoners on the roof during the riot.

Briefing Attorney General Ed Meese and Director William
Sessions after the release of all the prisoners.

The surrender ceremony: with Charlie (fourth from left)
and Leon Blakeney (far right).

My worst nightmare: my friend Bill Buford bleeding badly
from multiple gunshot wounds during the shootout
with the Branch Davidians at Waco.
*(Rod Aydelotte/*Waco Tribune Herald*/Reuters)*

The bomb site in Oklahoma on the ground and from the air.

Briefing Attorney General Janet Reno
and Director Louis Freeh.

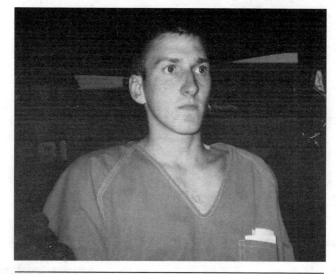
Tim McVeigh in FBI custody.

perverse philosophy, but I gave him credit for sucking it in and standing up when it counted.

"I hope we did the right thing," he replied.

"Of course it was right," I said. "Everyone's alive. And there's still hope for what you believe in and what I believe in. We learned a lot about each other too."

Bill Buford stepped up and shook Ellison's hand.

"Bill, it's good to see you again," Ellison said. "You and I are on opposite sides, but we admire your war record and what you've done for our country."

"You're doing the right thing here," Buford said. "This thing could have gotten ugly. You've shown you're a leader here."

"We're all leaders here," Ellison replied solemnly. "If I had to be arrested, you're the people I'd want to surrender to."

Buford's blue eyes twinkled. He was close to bursting out laughing, what with Ellison's airs and his ridiculous hair. But he merely smiled, causing Ellison to glow like a kid who was about to snag Cal Ripken's autograph. *Is there anyone in the world that doesn't admire Bill Buford?* I thought.

"We're not going to handcuff you in front of your people," I told Ellison. "Let's just walk down to the car."

"I really appreciate that," Ellison said, and meekly followed Buford toward a car that would take him to jail.

"Hold it," I called. As Buford and Ellison turned, I stuck out my hand once more, and Bonney offered his. Ellison grasped my hand in both of his, then shook Bonney's hand.

"Jim, good luck," I said softly. He looked at Bonney and me, nodded, then turned back toward Buford and walked down the hill.

After a few minutes, Noble, eight women, and a group of children emerged from the compound with bags. As they walked down the hill past me, I noticed a boy of about fourteen. This was the same boy who had probed our line and brandished a rifle at my men. I had never seen such a look of hatred on anyone so young. He was about the same age as Little Doc, who was still a baby to me.

"Look at the face on that one," I whispered to Bonney. "Have you ever seen such anger? We, or someone else, will have to deal with him in five or six years."

"You know, Doc, somehow we ended up on the same side with these people today," Bonney said. "Another time, another place, and they would kill us in a minute. We should never forget that."

"I was just thinking the same thing," I said. "We cornered a bunch of rattlesnakes. I believe if we had given them any chance of escape, they would have shot it out and fled."

We began sweeping the main compound. The HRT assault teams and specialists in explosives ordnance disposal went in first, cautiously probing each building for stragglers, mines, and booby traps. After an hour and a half, they pronounced the compound "clear," meaning safe, and set up a perimeter to keep out the media and any CSA members or sympathizers who might have been hiding in the forest. I got to a telephone and called Little Doc.

"We wrapped it up," I said.

"Yeah, we've been watching it on TV," he said excitedly. "But I didn't see you on TV."

"That's right. Nobody's gonna really know I was here. All anyone should know is that the FBI did its job. We don't want the team to take credit."

The next day, we did a thorough search. Assault rifles converted to fully automatic were stacked like cordwood, and there were hundreds of hand grenades, many fashioned from beer cans. Some were hand-lettered with the slogan, "This Bud's for you." Just as the informants had said, a truck chassis was well on the way to becoming an armored car.

The thirty-gallon drum of cyanide puzzled me. Eventually Ellison and Noble explained that it was meant for fomenting urban anarchy, like in *The Turner Diaries*. Ellison planned to use it to poison the water supplies of New York and Washington, D.C. This, he reasoned, would bring on the revolution.

During a lunch break, an FBI agent was leaning back against a tree and happened to look up. "Oh my God, there it is," she shouted. "Up there in the tree." A LAW rocket was lashed to a high branch. A couple of ATF agents scrambled up the tree, cut it loose, and passed it down a human chain. Everyone crowded around. Few had ever seen a live LAW.

Buried under a flower bed were 155 ounces of gold Krugerrands worth $50,000. There was also a cache of jewelry stolen from the Texarkana pawnshop where Snell had murdered Bill Stumpp. Evidently, Ellison's followers did not entirely trust the Lord to provide.

All told, we recovered a pile of arms that would be the envy of any Middle Eastern terrorist group, and I'm certain that we found only a fraction of the weapons and equipment that had been stashed around the property. *The Turner Diaries* advises urban guerrillas to bury arms in fifty-five-gallon drums. I still wonder if the CSA had sunk an arms cache so deep it wasn't picked up by our metal detectors.

Late in the day, Wehmeyer and I decided to take a break. We went back to our fishing camp, showered, grabbed a couple of rods and a johnboat, and went out on that marvelous lake. After many hours, we hadn't had a bite. "You know, we couldn't buy any luck," I grumbled.

Jeff smiled. "I think we bought all of our luck yesterday."

BOOK FOUR

RIOT

The State Department caused this son of a bitch.
Let's send their asses down in the tunnels.

—Danny O. Coulson,
November 23, 1987

1

After we left the Ozarks, Jack Knox and Bill Buford went back to Little Rock and wrapped up the racketeering indictment against Ellison. Asa Hutchinson and Steve Snyder, his assistant, moved the case through the courts with remarkable dispatch. By the end of July 1985, Ellison had been tried, convicted, and sentenced to twenty years in prison.

After a few months behind bars, Ellison decided he wasn't cut out to be a martyr. He made a bargain with J. Michael Fitzhugh, Hutchinson's successor as U.S. attorney in Fort Smith, to spill secrets on the whole crazy-right network. It seemed to be a good deal all around. Ellison ended up with a reduction of his sentence to ten years, and the government got unparalleled insights into the players in the white separatist movement. Also, it pretty well guaranteed that if Ellison had a relapse after he got out of prison, he'd have to work solo because none of his old buddies would ever trust him.

Whatever happened was out of my hands now. The team and I resumed our training regimen at Quantico. It was only a matter of time before some creep poked his head out of the mud and they'd send us out again. Doc and I settled back into our nightly routine of Dad's short-order cooking, homework, and sports. We hit Chinese a couple of times a week. Doc even ate a few vegetables.

After one of our workouts in August 1985, we pulled in at the gas station near our house just as the ugliest car in America, a yellow Pontiac station wagon that Doc

317

called "the Big Banana," was gassing up. "Hi, Danny. Hi, Doc," Debbie Conner called. "Hey, Doc, have you finished that book I gave you?"

God knows Debbie had enough to do, what with taking care of three kids and commuting to her low-paying, no-security substitute-teacher job, but she always found time to talk with Doc about the problems he was having in school. She was one of the few people on the planet who could get him to read to the end of a book. Like many thirteen-year-old boys, he had too much energy to spend time reading and studying when there were baseballs to throw and soccer balls to kick.

I slipped Doc a couple of dollars and pointed him at the Baskin-Robbins. "Here, go buy yourself a double." Debbie and I flopped down on a bench. She was making small talk about something, probably Jeff's basketball team or Jenny's dance class, I can't remember what. I was popping off wisecracks as usual and she was giggling. She said nobody at the school had a mouth like mine. "I'm not disrespectful, just direct," I said. "There's a difference."

Then I looked at the perfect oval of her face, and I stopped yakking. There was something about her I hadn't seen before. Maybe I'd been obsessed with my job and single fatherhood, or maybe lack of sleep and too much of my own cooking had messed up my vision, but now I just had to tell her.

"I think," I said, dead serious, "you think it's just a friendship, and you and your kids will have your life, and Doc and I will go our separate ways and we'll just visit as friends. But one day, it's going to be different."

She stared. She didn't say anything. But her lips curved and her green eyes were soft when she said good-bye.

A couple of weeks later, Debbie called me with good news. She'd just gotten the teaching job she had been after, a permanent position at the Oak Hill elementary school in Fairfax County, just three miles from her neighborhood and only about a mile from our town house.

"They're lucky to get you," I said. "Listen, how about if I take you to dinner? I have to go down to the Academy on Sunday night to meet the new operator candidates. You can come along and then we'll go out. I know a great place in Quantico."

Okay, so our first date wasn't the Jockey Club. But it was in my price range. Besides, men offered Debbie fancy nights out all the time. She said she never accepted because she didn't want to be some guy's ornament. She told me later I was the only guy she knew who cared about her thoughts, her ideas, and her hopes.

She was right about that. I'd known for a long time that she was smarter than me about a lot of things. On the other hand, I couldn't deny that I thoroughly enjoyed walking into the HRT reception room and watching heads swivel to see the commander coming to work with a drop-dead beautiful blonde on his arm.

"Hey, Tony." I motioned to Tony Betz. "I need some help. Meet Debbie. Take care of her until I get this meeting over with. Then we're going to dinner."

Tony's eyes lit up. It was probably the first job I had given him that he liked. As he shook Debbie's hand, he looked over his shoulder at me. "Do I get to go to dinner too?"

"Not hardly. You're cute, but you're not invited."

While Tony gave Debbie a two-dollar tour of our building, I did my "welcome the poor bastards who'll be going through hell for the next two weeks" act. Afterward, I found Debbie in the room where HRT guys gathered after the working day ended. She was surrounded by Betz, Bill Luthin, and Mike Wolf, who had started on a pitcher of beer and were regaling Debbie with war stories. She was laughing and talking to everyone who stopped by. This girl would fit in here. Not one bit intimidated by a mere bunch of crazy commandos.

"You hungry, or do you want to ruin your reputation and hang out with these guys," I asked.

"I'm hungry," she said. "You did promise to feed me."

I almost had to pull her away from the table. "Did you have fun?"

"I had a blast, but let's eat."

We drove into Quantico to the Globe and Laurel, which was owned by a retired Marine major (natch). I had been hanging out there since I was a new agent in 1966. Many a time had the major's wife loaded up a car full of agents, me included, and raced us back to the Academy just in time to beat the curfew.

We ordered steaks and a decent bottle of wine. Well, it didn't have a screw top. It was great, having a quiet, grown-up evening without having to nag anybody about finishing his vegetables or not flicking carrots across the room with the salad fork.

It felt right. We decided to do it again. And again and again.

2

Deb helped me get through the moment I had dreaded from the time I took command of the HRT. In April 1986, I got my orders to rotate out of the team and become an ASAC in the Washington field division. This was a promotion and a giant step up the career ladder. I was determined to snag my own field command, and you couldn't be a SAC unless you had been an ASAC.

Still, it was terribly depressing to leave the team and the men who had become like brothers to me. About the only thing that made it tolerable was that I was leaving it to David W. "Woody" Johnson, and for a while there, I was not overjoyed to see his shining face. I felt like a kid who goes to a birthday party and has to hand a new red truck to his best pal.

Woody had all the right stuff. He was well educated, with a bachelor's degree in chemistry, a master's in criminal justice, and postgraduate courses at the Kennedy School of Government at Harvard. He had learned tactics while commanding a Marine combat unit in Vietnam and as a member of the Washington Field Office SWAT team. His counterespionage assignments had taught him the ins and outs of the intelligence community. He wasn't popular at HQ, where the drivers called him "cantankerous" and "difficult." These epithets were badges of honor in the field. He was also tall and handsome. I consoled myself with the idea that a lesser man would be insanely jealous of this paragon.

Woody's only serious flaw was that he was nice. "You have to have the courage to make these guys uncomfortable," I told him, by way of parting advice. "As much as you care about them, you may have to leave them in the rain or snow for days, or ask them to swim in freezing water or climb mountains. Just remember, that's what they're trained to do."

My job at Washington field was largely administrative, but I tried not to complain. The cases were high-profile. The agents were the cream of the crop. When Dana Caro, the SAC, retired, I got to be acting SAC for a spell. Most important, I got home nights and weekends. Doc was getting into his teens. He needed me to be around more than ever.

Over Thanksgiving weekend in 1986, Debbie and I farmed out the kids and Doc's dog, Max the Second, to friends, piled our gear into my four-wheel-drive Isuzu Trooper, and headed into the Shenandoah National Park for a few days of hiking and climbing.

Our little vacation lasted until the afternoon of Sunday, November 30, when a Bronco with state police insignias on the side bounced up the nearly impassable road to our cabin. Two Virginia state troopers clambered out. The older man nodded curtly and gave me a cold, wary look and said, "You Coulson?"

I nodded. "Sure am."

"We have an important message for you. You need to call Mr. O-toe."

"Thank you." I grimaced. "Sorry, Deb. I've got to go into town and find a phone."

"It's okay," she said, smiling. "I know."

Indeed she did. Debbie had met John Otto, the executive assistant director, and she had heard the story of his nickname, the Hulk. He was slight of build and could be an absolute charmer with outsiders, but he'd never used any charm on me. His tirades were legendary and his capacity for profanity unmatched. He was one of the FBI's truly tough guys, and few dared to cross him. I drove down the mountain and found a pay phone.

"John? Coulson. What's up?"

"What's up is we're giving you the Iran-Contra case."

President Reagan and Attorney General Ed Meese had informed the White House press corps five days before that Reagan national security adviser John Poindexter, his predecessor Bud McFarlane, and National Security Council counterterrorism specialist Lieutenant Colonel Oliver North had secretly arranged to sell arms to Iran, hoping to free American hostages held by the radical Islamic fundamentalist regime. Moreover, they had used the Iranian payments to buy arms for the Contras in Nicaragua, in violation of a congressional prohibition on shipping munitions to the CIA-backed guerrilla army that was striving to overthrow the Communist Sandinista regime. Reagan claimed he hadn't authorized the covert schemes. Meese had launched an inquiry into whether the NSC staff or any others had broken federal laws.

"Oh, no, I'm not taking that case," I said. "I've already spoken to Buck about it and he's decided to give it to somebody else because I'm still acting SAC in Washington."

"Listen, goddammit. I've spoken to Webster about it. You've got the case. We've ordered Doug Gow in from Houston, Texas, to take over the Washington Field Office, and you need to get your ass back here."

"Is there any debate on this?"

"No. Get down here. We're going to have a meeting at FBI headquarters with your unit and with your staff at approximately seven o'clock tonight. Where in the hell are you anyway?"

"The Shenandoah Valley."

"I suggest you drive real fast. Are you with Debbie?"

"Yes."

"She's the only thing you've done right since I've known you. Never could see what she saw in you. Give her my love."

"Are you going to give me your love?"

I could feel Otto starting to hulk out. "Hang up the damned phone and get back to Washington right now."

As I pulled up to the cabin, I saw that Debbie had already packed up and had all of our bags and camping gear stacked out on the front porch. "I knew we were leaving." She smiled. "If it wasn't important, they wouldn't have sent the state police up on top of this mountain to get you. Get in the car. Let's find a newspaper and I'll drive home."

We called the case Operation Front Door. I told the agents under me to follow the facts, no matter how high they led. They went right to the National Security Council and started conducting interviews, accessing computer files, and sequestering documents. Some of the files we seized were so sensitive that none of us was cleared to read them. I had to get a higher security clearance just to flip through them. I couldn't even tell Director William Webster about them. He wasn't too happy with me, but being a by-the-book kind of guy, he went out and got the necessary clearances.

On December 19, 1986, Lawrence E. Walsh, a former federal appeals court judge, was named independent counsel for the Iran-Contra scandal. By the time I began reporting to Walsh, we had a good first cut on the facts. One agent's diligent questioning led to a crucial discovery, the famed PROF notes, computer E-mail messages among North, Poindexter, and McFarlane that North thought he had erased. Our computer tech people unerased them. The PROF notes gave us a day-by-day picture of the NSC staffers as they concocted the Iran arms sales and Contra supply schemes.

Our aggressive approach was possible only because the case was being run by the FBI. Not one single Department of Justice lawyer was giving us directions. If it was logical and Constitutional, we did it. That's not the way it works nowadays. Justice Department lawyers call the shots and FBI agents cover leads. Sometimes the lawyers dither for so long that the evidence has wandered off by the time the agents get there. Anybody who doubts this has only to look at Janet Reno's campaign finance investigation, the Olympics of vacillation.

Just before Christmas of 1986, I had to go out of town. Debbie took Doc to the movies with her kids and noticed that he was limping badly. She told me about her concern when I returned. I took him to the doctor.

The diagnosis was terrifying. Doc had a congenital back problem that was getting worse. If he didn't have immediate surgery and fusion of his spine, he'd be crippled for life.

There were tests, and forms to fill out, and more tests, and more forms. One icy day in early January, I drove Doc to Georgetown Hospital in Washington, D.C. The doctors assured us that he would be as good as new, but we were all frightened. Any operation that involved the spine had to be dangerous.

I knew about waiting. Waiting out a crisis, or waiting for a murderer to arrive at a location so that I could arrest him. This was absolutely the worst. Doc spent about 90 percent of his time in motion. I hated to think about how he would deal with life if he wasn't 100 percent recovered.

Doc emerged from the operating room locked in a body cast from his chest down to his knee. He was ashen. As he came out of the anesthesia, he opened his eyes. "Dad, this really hurts," he gasped.

I tried to smile confidently. "I know, but the worst part is over. Everything went perfectly, and you'll be good as new."

Please, God, make that true.

Doc bounced back a lot quicker than any of us expected. Before long, he was dashing around as if he had on a suit of play armor.

Around this time, I was talking to Debbie about getting a bigger place when I stopped short and said, "You know, this is crazy. Why the hell am I thinking about buying a house for Doc and me? We should just get married and buy a house for all of us."

Debbie shook her head and laughed. "Why's it taken you so long to figure this out?"

We were married on April 14, 1987, in a simple Methodist ceremony in Herndon. We didn't invite any friends, just Debbie's parents and the kids. Little Jessie had on a white, wide-brimmed hat and starched dress. As she leaned over the communion rail to get a look at our faces, she flipped upside down and tumbled over the rail.

The minister never missed a beat. He reached down with his right hand, picked her up, and continued the service until we got to the I-do part. To this day Jessie claims that Jeff pushed her.

The Independent Counsel operation was the most frustrating assignment I'd ever pulled. The problem was lawyers. Judge Walsh was a scholar and a gentleman of the old school, but he seemed to have a weakness for packing every nook and cranny with people who had law degrees, as if those pricey pieces of paper had anything to do with common sense or human decency. Keith DeVencentis, our case agent, circulated a fake memo outlining the Walsh operation's "investigative priorities." It went like this:

Hire more lawyers.
Please the press.
Please the Congress.
Please the people.
Hire more lawyers.
Get T-shirts for the grand jury.
Seize every document everywhere.
Number every document.
Copy every document five times.
Hire more lawyers.
Get more office space for lawyers.
Ignore the documents.
Ignore the FD-302 reports of interviews.
Hire more lawyers.

Don't get me wrong. There were some pros like Chris Todd and Michael Bromwich, who had been assistant U.S. attorneys in the Southern District of New York, an office justly renowned as the finest prosecution force in the nation. But Walsh also hired a bunch of hotshot novices drawn by the glamour of the case and the chance to make

names for themselves as the Watergate prosecutors had.
Some had been in civil practice and had never prosecuted
a case in their life. They seemed to be fixated on collecting
scalps, as if maxing out on numbers of defendants and
charges would secure their fortunes in Washington.

We had a furious internal debate over whether to
prosecute low- and middle-level CIA people who had
run afoul of the law or regulations while engaged in dangerous, thankless assignments in Central America. For
example, our investigation found that some CIA employees had been loading a helicopter with medical supplies
for a Contra camp when they received a desperate call
that the guerrillas were under attack by Sandinista
troops and about to run out of ammunition. The CIA
men added a few cases of bullets to the cargo and threw
them down to their buddies at the camp.

I spent a tedious morning listening to one of Walsh's
aides making an ardent pitch for charging the CIA
employees with violating the law against fraud by wire,
on grounds that their cables back to Langley reported
delivering medicine but not ammunition. After an hour
or so, I'd had enough. "You've gotta be kidding me," I
snarled. "What interest in justice are we serving by
indicting men who made a snap judgment in the heat of
battle, just trying to save the lives of their friends?
Where's the justice in that? If that's all we have to do,
then maybe we ought to fold our tents and go home.
Besides, if we're going to start indicting members of federal agencies who don't fully and completely report
every single thing they do to their headquarters, then
we're going to have to start indicting virtually every FBI
office and every other federal agency's field offices in the
United States."

Walsh's eyes flicked at me, and I thought I saw a slight smile. I couldn't be sure. He was famous for his poker face. The aide fell silent and we never heard about his proposed indictment again.

My triumph was short-lived. My faction of small-*c* conservatives such as Todd, Bromwich, Bob Swartz, David Zornow, and Audrey Strauss, and most of the FBI agents as well, lost the crucial battle of the case. We argued that any indictments ought to be confined to specific crimes that had been well defined by statutory and case law—obstruction of justice, for instance, lying to Congress, theft of government funds, and tax violations.

On the other side were Guy Struve, Walsh's partner at the blue-chip Manhattan firm of Davis, Polk and Wardwell, and John Keker, a former public defender from San Francisco and one of the best trial lawyers in the country. They wanted to charge North, Poindexter, and others with a criminal conspiracy to violate the Boland amendment.

"The Boland amendment? Shee-it. What kind of crime is *that* supposed to be?" I sputtered in exasperation at one meeting. "We're wasting our time even thinking about ideas that no court would uphold, especially where we have clear-cut violations of the criminal statutes."

Walsh gave me another one of his inscrutable smiles, but in the end, he went with Struve and Keker because, as he later wrote, he found the reasoning behind the Boland conspiracy theory "elegant and sophisticated." He was a gambler, and he lost, though not in a way any of us had anticipated. The Boland conspiracy charges were dismissed because Walsh couldn't convince the Reagan administration to declassify the documents that constituted much of his evidence. North and Poindexter were convicted on lesser offenses, but these convictions were overturned on appeal.

In fact, nearly all the other major players eluded Walsh's dragnet. On Christmas Eve, 1992, President Bush pardoned Bud McFarlane, former defense secretary Caspar Weinberger, former assistant secretary of state Elliott Abrams, and three former CIA officials. With mixed feelings, I watched the prosecution run out of steam. I thought we had done a service in reminding the country that the Constitution applies to the White House and that national security personnel can't lie to Congress or wage a secret war. But it galled me that the Independent Counsel operation had spent $37.6 million, a good bit of it to indulge young lawyers who wanted to debate esoteric legal theories, at a time when criminal justice and social service agencies across the nation were begging for money and the number of unsolved murders in this country had just hit an all-time high.

Though we differed on various aspects of the case, working with Lawrence Walsh was an honor. He followed the evidence where it took him and knew that it was as important to clear the innocent as to pursue the guilty. He had nothing in common with the Independent Counsels we see today. They pursue individuals. He pursued crimes.

By the time Walsh officially closed up shop in February 1993, I was merely a spectator. In August 1987, I was promoted back to FBI headquarters, where I would work in the Inspection Division.

3

I had just returned from a tour in Nebraska and was walking down the seventh-floor corridor around noon on November 23, 1987, when I heard someone snap, "Coulson! Stop there."

I turned and saw Assistant Director Floyd I. Clarke, head of the Criminal Investigative Division, striding toward me. "How quick can you get to Atlanta?"

"Today," I said. "What's going on?"

"The Marielitos have blown. They've taken prison officials as hostages and they've torched part of the prison. We need you down there as soon as possible."

I wasn't surprised. When anyone asks how come law enforcement people hate the State Department, this is exhibit A. At noon on Friday, November 20, 1987, State had abruptly disclosed an immigration agreement with the Castro government that would allow the deportation and repatriation to Cuba of as many as 2,700 "undesirables," mostly convicted criminals and mental patients who had been detained since the Mariel boatlift of 1980.

The news hit the detainee population like a bomb. These were desperate men who had endured seven years of prison in the States only to be told they might soon be sent back to Cuba to bleed and starve to death in Castro's jails. On the night of Saturday, November 21, about a thousand Cubans held at the federal detention center at Oakdale, Louisiana, rioted and took twenty-eight guards as hostages. The next day, seventeen detainees escaped from a facility in Laredo, Texas.

The largest concentration of Marielito detainees,

1,394 in all, were in the federal penitentiary in Atlanta. It was amazing that they stayed calm as long as they did, but a couple of hours before Clarke braced me in the hall, they erupted, using homemade machetes and clubs to seize buildings and capture 124 hostages.

Woody Johnson and the entire HRT had been dispatched to Oakdale, moments after it blew. The HRT could not be redeployed to the Atlanta crisis, though it was bigger and potentially more deadly.

That meant that any tactical operations in Atlanta would have to be carried out by SWAT operators. Clarke had already arranged for 400 men with tactical training—the Atlanta Field Office's 25-man SWAT team plus 240 SWAT agents from Chicago, New York, Washington, Miami, Birmingham, Knoxville, Savannah, Detroit, Philadelphia, and Pittsburgh, plus about 150 men from the U.S. Marshals Special Operations Group and the U.S. Border Patrol. "You'll be in charge of them all," he told me. "Everybody works for the FBI on this one."

As tactical commander for the crisis, I was to whip together a cohesive tactical team to contain the rioters inside the prison while the negotiators plied their trade. Also, I would devise an emergency rescue plan, which would only be activated if the detainees started executing people and if we were ordered to move in and save anyone we could.

Containment was manageable, but an emergency rescue was a problem that would stymie HRT, Delta, and SEAL Team Six combined. I was supposed to solve it by patching together units whose experience and training levels ranged from twice-a-week raids to once-a-month practices. The job was a big-time blivet. But as I'd learned a long time before, blivets are my destiny.

The good news was, I'd be reporting to Weldon Kennedy, the FBI SAC in Atlanta, and the on-scene commander for the federal government. Weldon was a big, plain man who had grown up on the family ranch a little north of Waco, served in the Navy, then signed on with the FBI in 1963. He wasn't an HQ favorite because he wasn't a driver. The people who worked for him in the field loved him because he made decisions fast and stuck by his people.

I grabbed a ticket from the travel office, drove home, and started throwing body armor, tactical clothing, gun belts, and a gas mask into my kit bag.

"You and the kids go on to your folks for Thanksgiving," I called to Debbie, who had rushed home from school. "I'll join you there if I can. Can't promise."

"I know," she said, smiling as usual.

Debbie drove me to the airport in silence. I didn't really notice how quiet she was because I was thinking through my checklists. She tells me that if I had been able to read her mind, this is what I would have heard: *So he's been home for twenty-four hours and he's off again. And all I have to do is put Max and Katy in the kennel, load four kids and all their junk into the car, and dodge eighteen-wheelers for eight hours or so until we arrive in lovely downtown Pinehurst, North Carolina. Meanwhile, here's Danny in full crisis mode, his eyes lit up like the Strip in Vegas. If I didn't know better, I'd think he was off to see a mistress. Come to think of it, maybe all those prisoners are horny women terrorists. Oh, well, every day is an adventure. I wouldn't want him to be mooning over me instead of thinking about how to stay alive.*

At National, I leapt from the car, waved, and shouted, "I'll call you." Well after I was airborne, I remembered that I had been chauffeured to the airport by the strongest, smartest, most beautiful woman in the Washington metropolitan area and I hadn't even kissed her good-bye.

Fortunately, the woman had only one fault: lousy taste in men.

On the drive in from the Atlanta airport, the cab-driver pointed to a plume of smoke that deepened the twilight haze. "The Cubans are burning the place down," he said. "Hope whoever's in charge will keep those bastards inside. People here don't want those sons of bitches running in the streets."

At the Atlanta Field Office, I found a message from Weldon. "I need you first thing in the morning. Get some rest. We'll all be bushed in the morning, and you'll need to be fresh."

I didn't need any convincing. In my line of work, you never know when you're going to get another shot at a mattress. I walked next door to my hotel and hit the sack.

Weldon picked me up at six on the morning of the twenty-fourth and drove me to the prison. I'll never forget the moment when we pulled into the parking lot. I could hear what sounded like the roar of a million bumblebees. I could smell and feel the electricity in the air. The prison complex, which sprawled over twenty-eight acres, was bigger than many towns. We walked up the administration building steps and down a broad corridor to Warden Joe Petrovsky's office, which had been converted to a crisis-management command post. Weldon and his assistants had taped butcher paper on all the walls and were trying to keep orderly lists of leads and developing information on the names and possible locations of the hostages. A quick glance told me we had only a rough idea where the Cubans and their captives were massing. "It's chaos in there," Weldon said, nodding grimly. No one really knew what part of the twenty-two-building complex was controlled by the prisoners and what was no-man's-land.

I felt a fist pound my shoulder and heard a gravelly drawl. "Nice of you to make it to Weldon's party. Did you come to play?"

I whirled around and came nose to nose with a man who's about as close to a legend as any agent I've ever known. "Hey, Leon, what's happenin'!" I said joyfully, whacking him back.

"We're up to our asses in crazy Cubans, that's what's happening," said Leon Blakeney, the leader of the Atlanta office's SWAT team, giving me the full force of what he called his "west-Texas speech impediment." "We can get this thing resolved if we can ever figure out who's in charge and start some negotiations."

That was Leon, cheerful as a kid at the beach, though one look told me he hadn't slept in the thirty hours since the crisis began. He was encrusted in soot and dirt and his eyes looked like maraschino cherries. Come to think about it, if he'd had one more cherry-eye, I would've taken that big, square, neckless, stumpy-legged body for a slot machine. Only I doubt I would've yanked on that huge right arm. Leon's viselike grip had taught manners to more than one fugitive. If I was going to be in a fight, Leon was the last guy I'd want to see on the other side. He was a crack shot too, though like most good tactical guys, he considered it beneath him to use his gun any-

place but on the range. He had outfoxed dozens of
vicious fugitives, including three men on the FBI's Ten
Most Wanted list, without firing a shot.

Leon's arrest of Bruce Carroll Pierce, the Kentuckian
who had assumed leadership of The Order after Robert
Mathews died at Whidbey Island, was a textbook example of the principle of surprise, speed, and violence of
action. Just before we surrounded Mathews's cabin at
Whidbey, Pierce had left the island and set off on a
cross-country odyssey with his son Jeremy, a van and
motor home full of munitions, and a galloping case of
paranoia, which was not irrational: some of his fellow
Aryan soldiers suspected him of being a snitch, and the
entire American law enforcement establishment was on
his tail. Thank God some unwitting cop didn't pull him
over for speeding.

In March 1985, Pierce, was camping in the Blue
Ridge Mountains and had arranged to collect his mail at
the house of an elderly woman in Rossville, Georgia. On
the evening of March 26, as Pierce stepped across the
threshold, Leon burst through the kitchen door and
jammed his MP5 submachine gun into Pierce's Adam's
apple. Pierce didn't have a chance to pull the three
handguns he was wearing, much less go for the eight
grenades, automatic weapons, and explosives in his van.
Convicted as the triggerman in the murder of Alan Berg,
Pierce was sentenced to 252 years in prison.

We found chairs, and Weldon and Leon filled me in
on the events of the twenty-third. The riot had begun
between 10:15 and 10:45 A.M. when Cubans assigned to
work in the Industries Building, where mattresses were
made and textiles processed, started setting fires. As the
fire alarms sounded, they broke out caches of home-

made swords and clubs, captured thirty or forty Bureau of Prisons employees, confiscated their handcuffs and radios, and locked them in a tool cage. As the fire spread, the Cubans thought better of burning them alive and marched them to another building.

The riot spread. The Cubans ran helter-skelter, handcuffing guards, releasing other inmates, tearing down walls and steel gates, and setting more fires. A tower guard shot and killed a Cuban who was threatening to slit the throat of a BOP employee. Five other Cubans were wounded by gunfire from towers. The tower guards laid down their weapons when the rioters threatened to kill the captured prison workers.

By 10:50 A.M., 124 BOP people were trapped inside the prison. The Cubans controlled most of the central buildings including the cafeteria, which was at the end of the corridor from the warden's office in the administration building. Fortunately, quick-thinking guards had locked down the heavy steel-barred doors between the cafeteria and the rest of the building. If they hadn't, the rioters would have surged through the broad main corridor and out the front door of the prison.

The detainees grabbed the guards' walkie-talkies and started using them to call one another and BOP officials.

The problem, as Dee Rosario, a Puerto Rican–born agent who was the government's lead negotiator put it, was that it was not at all clear that any Cuban had real authority to negotiate for all the rioters. Dee and BOP officials talked to various detainees all afternoon. The minute they thought they had a dialogue going, somebody else would butt in and claim to be the boss.

Many of the Cubans were rational and serious about attaining their goal, but there were a few wild cards.

One was Jose Meza Rodriguez, a murderer nick-named Uno because he had once cut off one of his testi-cles and thrown it at Castro. His body was hideously scarred. The thick scar tissue on his abdomen had formed a sort of crevice, which he deepened by picking at it with sharp objects until he could shove a coat hanger an inch or two into it. He enjoyed tricking new guards by pretending to be stabbed. From time to time, he sliced pieces of fat off his body and mailed them to the warden. He'd been put in the rubber room for a spell but managed to get hold of a shard of glass and tried to cut off the other testicle. I wondered how we'd deal with Meza in a physical confrontation. Obviously, inflicting pain wouldn't work. A swift kick to the crotch was unlikely to have any effect upon him.

Another scary guy was El Loco. Cuban jailers had shut him and another man into a cell and welded the door shut, leaving only a small opening to admit food and water. Some weeks later, so the story went, guards noticed only one inmate. Eventually, they cut the door open and found a pile of bones. Some say El Loco killed his cellmate for his rations. Others say he ate the cell-mate too. We'd probably never know, but either way, we didn't like the idea of our people being on the same side of the bars with him.

To find out where the hostages were and how they were being treated, Weldon sent agents to the East Gate, where a steady stream of American inmates and a few detainees were turning themselves in so they wouldn't be punished for participating in the riot. The debriefing reports gave cause for optimism. The rioters were holding seventy-nine hostages in the chapel and the American dorm. The Cubans calling the shots seemed to understand they needed to keep their captives alive, so they were making sure everybody was well treated and protected from the head cases.

Those in immediate danger were not, strictly speaking, hostages, but rather sixteen guards who had barricaded themselves in E cellhouse when the alarms sounded. This cellhouse, located some distance from the other buildings, was the prison's maximum-security wing, where the meanest, most deranged Marielitos were locked down in solitary confinement. All afternoon, the rioters tried to get to E but were repelled by tower guards, who said they'd gas or shoot anyone who approached the doors. Even when the Cubans dragged two hostages into the yard and threatened to kill them, the guards refused, knowing there would be a far uglier scene if the psychos in stir were unleashed on the sixteen guards.

Studying the prison layout, Leon observed that E cellhouse was on the far right of the fat T-shaped outer wall. A section of prison yard in between the wall and the cellhouse's back door lay in a blind corner and couldn't be seen by rioters clustered toward the center and bottom of the T. Leon came up with a rescue plan, which Weldon approved at 5:30 P.M. Leon and the SWAT team borrowed two fire trucks and pulled them up at the outer wall. One thirty-foot ladder was raised to the top of the outer wall. The second fire truck's boom lowered a second thirty-foot ladder over the wall and set its feet into the blind corner. The two ladders made an X, crossing just above the top of the wall.

As Leon and the SWAT operators arrayed themselves along the top of the wall, ready to shoot any rioters who interfered, the guards unlocked the door, descended a fire escape, bolted across the yard, scaled the inside ladder, slid sideways to the outside ladder, and scrambled to earth. "I thought some of 'em might have some trouble with those ladders," Leon told me. "They were at least twenty feet off the ground and they wobbled. I was afraid somebody might look down and freeze. Well, they didn't have a bit of trouble. They went up like squirrels and down again."

As the last guards scrambled to safety, Leon heard voices ringing out across the yard. "Over here! Come on, get us out of here!"

He swiveled to his left and saw some medical personnel he had befriended on earlier visits to the prison. Twenty-six doctors, nurses, aides, and prison employees had locked themselves into the prison hospital and barricaded the heavy steel doors with everything they could find.

Leon went back to the command post and put the matter to Weldon, who asked, "Can you get to them?"

"We can do it by lowering ladders into the yard, same as we did for E cellhouse. It's only a short sprint from the hospital entrance to the wall."

"Can you be a hundred percent sure you won't be seen?"

"No. The detainees have a good chance of observing us. They can see that part of the yard. They'll be a long way away from the actual rescue. We can get the people in the hospital out of there before anybody gets to them. But if the detainees get mad and start killing the other hostages, there won't be much we can do to help them."

Weldon set his jaw. "We can't do it," he said. "We can't risk the other hostages. I'll go talk to the warden." His mouth turned down at the corners, and he trudged off. Leon decided then and there not to let Weldon near the hospital. He was carrying enough of a burden without seeing the faces and hearing the pleas of those trapped inside.

"They had just seen us rescue people," Leon told me sadly. "They knew we could get them. They couldn't figure out why we weren't doing it for them. It struck in my craw bad that we couldn't go in there and get them. But Weldon was right. We couldn't get at them without risking everybody else."

The next night, the hospital's phone lines went dead. We wouldn't know what had happened to the staff and the pharmacy until the crisis was over.

By dusk, the air was choking with smoke. The fire had spread from the Industries Building to the food service warehouse. The rioters set the recreation building on fire. National Guard helicopters equipped with forest-fire-fighting buckets were brought in but were unable to douse the fires, which consumed all three buildings by nightfall.

During the night, the Cubans released three hostages with health problems. As another gesture of good faith, they sent out Polaroid pictures of the hostages being held in the American dorm. At two o'clock in the morning of the twenty-fourth, the prison safety director and his assistant appeared at the East Gate. They had been presumed killed in the fires. Two Cubans had hid them from the other detainees, at considerable risk to their own lives, and had then led them to freedom.

But that was the end of the good news. The rioters controlled the food services area, which meant they had enough food for six to nine months. They also had the commissary, which held plenty of cigarettes, clothing, and little luxuries. "They're happy as a pig in shit in there," Leon said. "They're set for the long haul. They could hold out for a year if they had to."

The Bureau of Prisons had master keys to everything—but the rioters had jammed many locks with dental plaster. Others had been welded shut with acetylene torches the rioters had discovered in toolsheds. If we tried to storm the place, we'd have to cut, saw, or blast our way through walls or gates, then sprint a hundred yards or so, breach more steel gates and doors, then guide the hostages back through a gauntlet of prisoners wielding machetes, shivs, and bludgeons.

All that made a deliberate rescue plan out of the question, which put unbelievable pressure on negotiators Dee Rosario and Pedro Toledo. Realizing that the detainees were still fragmented into cliques, Dee and Pedro came up with a plan to maneuver them into picking the leader *we* wanted—someone rational enough to listen and authoritative enough to sell a deal to the various factions. They flipped through the detainees' rap sheets and picked out two or three men who seemed more intelligent and amenable to persuasion. They started enhancing their prestige by allowing them to distribute mail or make announcements.

One man in particular had caught Dee's eye. Carlos "Charlie" Marrero, twenty-nine, had lived in Cuban prisons on and off since he was twelve. After he landed in the Mariel boatlift, he was incarcerated in Atlanta as an undesirable. He was a survivor, very tough, but also bright—he had taught himself English while imprisoned. He was handsome and had a presence that caused other prisoners to defer to him. Dee started cultivating him subtly. He spent hours talking to him through the bars of the cafeteria door and gave him a Bible—probably the first gift Charlie had ever gotten. Now if Dee could just get the other Cubans to anoint Charlie as their spokesman . . .

I still had to come up with an emergency rescue plan in case Dee's plan didn't work. It would be a bloody last resort, but things wouldn't go better if I failed to think it through right now.

As Leon and I talked, we heard a loud boom. Then *boom! boom! boom!* A battering ram, fashioned of several heavy pieces of lumber, was pounding the steel doors of the hospital. Then came a series of ever more frantic calls from BOP officials, culminating that night with a plea from Mike Quinlan, the director of the whole agency. Would Kennedy reconsider a rescue at the hospital?

Weldon beckoned Leon and me out of the command post and onto the steps leading up to the prison. We stood in the rain as Weldon smoked one cigarette after another. "What do you think, Doc?" he said quietly.

"The rescue itself is feasible," I replied. "Leon proved that already. We can get them out just fine. It's the other seventy-five or eighty you may lose if we try. Besides, we've got a big problem with the media. They're right across from the place we'd have to set our ladders. They'd be broadcasting us before we even got over the walls."

"Boss, when the Cubans see us on TV coming over that wall," Leon said, "they're going to believe that we're coming after all of the hostages, or there's an assault to put down the riot."

Weldon continued to puff on his cigarette as the light rain fell on us. He looked like a locomotive. "Can we possibly get to the other hostages and get them out too?"

I shook my head. "Absolutely not. The SWAT teams that are coming haven't even had time to do any planning, or rehearsals. Hell, we don't even have the breaching capability to get in yet."

"The BOP officials are furious," Kennedy said. "They want the people in the hospital out and they're ready to take the risk. They say they're very concerned that if the prisoners get the pharmacy and the drugs, the whole thing will spin totally out of control."

"Weldon, think about this," I said. "The Cubans haven't harmed any of the hostages. From what we've heard, they've assigned inmates to guard the BOP employees. They're actually protecting them. The most dangerous period for a hostage is usually the first twenty-four hours, when the initial violence takes place. When this thing went down, the guards were grabbed, not killed. If we lose the hospital, the Cubans are likely to treat those hostages just like the others."

Kennedy took a long last drag. "Do we agree on this?"

"Absolutely," Leon and I chorused.

Kennedy walked back into the command post and told the BOP officials the hospital rescue was impossible.

Nobody dared yell at Weldon Kennedy to his face, but as two BOP people brushed past us, one said loudly for our benefit, "I can't believe they won't go in. If they were goddamned FBI agents, they'd go in. This is bullshit."

"Man, are they pissed!" Leon said.

I shrugged. "Let's just hope we're right. If this thing turns to shit, they'll say that we could at least have saved twenty-six."

"Right," Leon said. "When you sit down at a poker

table, you play the cards you're dealt, and that's just the way it has to be."

The hospital rescue wasn't the only source of friction. BOP officials wanted to relax the deadly force policy so that any inmate who attempted to break out of prison would be shot on the spot.

My jaw dropped. "Even if they're just running away?" The standard deadly force policy says we can shoot only if someone poses an imminent threat of death or grievous bodily harm.

Weldon nodded. "Apparently there are people at the BOP in Washington who're afraid these raging maniacs will break out and run through the streets of Atlanta, killing everybody who gets in their way."

"Well, that scares me too," I said, "but we can't start shooting unarmed people in the back."

"I'll issue an order that says that we're going to stick by our standard deadly force policy," Weldon said. "If anyone charges one of our people with a weapon, he'll be ordered to halt. If that fails, flash-bangs will be thrown, and if he isn't turned back, then deadly force can be used to protect the lives of personnel. If somebody escapes, we'll pick him up later. We're not going to shoot anybody just because he's fleeing."

As I sat down and started assessing our tactical assets and deficiencies and making checklists, someone on the desk yelled, "Doc, you have a call from headquarters."

I grabbed a phone. "Danny, this is Buck. Floyd's on the phone. Have a minute?"

"Sure," I said jauntily. "What can I do for you?"

Buck spoke first. "We know you're a little thin down there. What can we get to help?"

"We can do okay," I began. "The SWAT teams can

learn how to do close-quarter battle, but I do need some help. Could you ask for Delta's breachers? And while you're at it, we could use Delta sniper-observers too."

Our ability to breach prison walls was about zero, I explained. Military counterterror teams and the HRT used shaped charges made of military plastic explosive to blow locks on steel gates and make those neat rectangular holes in solid steel. FBI SWAT had nothing more sophisticated than acetylene torches. It would take us at least half an hour to cut through any steel doors or reinforced wall, and cutting through multiple obstacles would take hours.

Given the numbers—four hundred of us versus roughly thirteen hundred of them—I needed every last SWAT man as an operator. Without snipers in stationary observation points to report on the movement of the Cubans and the hostages, we'd be at a severe disadvantage in terms of tactical intelligence. Besides, if the Cubans walked out a group of hostages and started to execute them, only trained snipers could make the long-range surgical shots needed to neutralize them.

Buck didn't hesitate a minute. "I think we can get them for you. Anything else?"

"While you're at it, ask for Delta's medical team. They're the best. They can pop a chest, do trauma surgery right on the spot. If we have to go in, a lot of people are going to get hurt. Likely some of us."

"Tell Weldon we're working on this for you guys," Buck said. "I'll get back to you."

I called Jeff Wehmeyer and Fred Kingston, who had transferred to SOARU when their HRT stints were up, and asked them to fly down to help with training and contingency planning. The next thing on my list was a secure radio network. Each SWAT team had arrived with its own radios, procured by its field division. One division's channel one might be another's channel six. The common channel four on all Bureau radios gave us the ability to communicate between divisions, but it was in the clear and could be heard by the media or anybody else. The Marshals Service and Border Patrol had radios that couldn't talk to any FBI radios. We needed radios with at least two channels, one for the four hundred tactical people and another for the hundred or so administrative people. I called Floyd and asked him to send some technical services people down to the prison with every digital voice privacy radio they could get their hands on.

Sometime later, Dee alerted us to big trouble brewing. Among the rioters were a number of veterans of the Angolan war. That made them half-crazy anyway, and what was pushing them over the edge was the sound of the Atlanta police helicopters flying over the prison and taking surveillance photographs. The Cubans had used choppers in airborne assaults in Angola, riding them in low and fast, machine-gunning everyone in their paths. The deafening whop-whop-whop of the helicopter blades meant one thing to them: incoming. They stormed the chapel with bottles of acetylene and threatened to blow the hostages and themselves sky-high.

Weldon stopped the flights. For the rest of the afternoon Dee was on the phone or at the cafeteria sally port, trying to pour oil on the troubled waters. Whatever he did worked. The Cubans released eight hostages that afternoon and during the night.

Toward nightfall, Leon was alerted to another urgent problem. A BOP guard manning one of the doors had spotted some Cubans with acetylene tanks. They were heading down to the basement, where there were doors that opened into an intricate system of ventilation and utility tunnels that honeycombed the earth underneath the prison. Their plan was to plant the tanks underneath our command post, open the valves, light the escaping gas, and turn the whole place into an inferno.

We called in a bomb tech and asked if the gas in the tanks would blow like that. The answer came back a resounding maybe. "It doesn't burn that hot," he said.

"That's a stupid answer," Leon snorted. "How hot can *you* take it? Not very hot is still hot, far as I'm concerned."

We called officials at the Atlanta Fire Department to find out if a fire in the administration building could be controlled. The answer was no. They furnished us with charged fire hoses—fire hoses under pressure—and instructions to run them around the warden's-office/command-post area. They promptly started leaking water. For the duration of the riot, we were constantly slipping and stumbling around on water-slick surfaces.

Je-sus, I thought, *not only do we have to create a perimeter and prepare to do a rescue, but also fight a damn fire under our butts too. There's got to be a better way.*

I turned to Weldon. "We've got to deny the inmates access to the tunnels. Otherwise, they can run all over the place. Hell, they can get right under us and burn us out, and who knows where else they'll come up?"

That was the other problem. The guards had told us that at least one tunnel ended up outside the wall. The Cubans were probably under there as we spoke, scurrying around like ants, looking for the magic tunnel that would take them to freedom.

"Leon and I'll recon the tunnels, assess how we could clear them, and figure out where to post SWAT teams to keep them from getting under the admin building and burning us out."

"Do it. Just be careful," Weldon said.

A strange look came over Leon's face, almost as if he felt sorry for me. I glanced down to see what he was staring at. It was the Smith & Wesson .357 Magnum revolver in the drop holster on my right hip. I gave him a sheepish shrug. I'd given up my trusty Browning Hi-Power when I'd left the HRT. I'd been promising myself I'd get another, but I hadn't gotten around to it.

"You gonna go down there with that six-shooter, Doc?" Leon said almost gently. "Seems to me your lack of firepower could be a hazard to both of us, seeing as how we won't have backup." Leon produced a Sig Sauer semiautomatic pistol, which had a sixteen-round magazine, and four extra magazines. "You best properly arm yourself if you're going to go into this goddamn tunnel with me."

We took a last look at some architectural drawings the BOP had posted in the command center. The tunnel system had been changed around so many times that the drawings from 1902 were not likely to be accurate, but they were all we had. The system was divided into main arteries that ran the length and breadth of the institution, augmented by numerous small tunnels that ran perpendicular to the main tunnels. All these underground passages were crisscrossed with conduits and large pipes that had once carried live steam. A few tunnels were lit with bare bulbs. Most were dark.

"Ready for a little sight-seeing?" Leon said.

"May as well get started."

We put on body armor and fitted our small flashlights with red lenses that provided enough light to see directly in front of us but didn't broadcast light. Then we headed for the basement.

As we climbed down the ladder that led to the utility-tunnel entrance and crept into the dark, I could hear the bumblebee roar again, the sound of raw energy crackling through the complex. If we ran into some Cubans on a quest for the magic tunnel, all that energy would be spent trying to kill us.

"Well, the good news is, most of the inmates haven't figured out these tunnels yet either," Leon whispered. "They don't know any more about the tunnel system than we do. And they're probably scared to death about running into us."

"Great. That makes me feel a lot better. If we're down here looking around, so are they."

We had to crawl on our stomachs for a while. To get through one ancient steam duct, I had to remove the body armor, push it ahead of me, and wiggle like an earthworm. *This wouldn't be a great place to meet a guy with a machete,* I thought. *Oh, shit.* At that very moment, I heard a jumble of Spanish. The Cubans were doing a recon in the tunnels too, and there were a whole lot of them.

I motioned to Leon and pointed directly down the tunnel. He crawled up to my position. We lay in the darkness listening and watching.

"Do you speak Spanish?" I whispered.

"Not much. If we run into one of these guys, I'll just grab him and choke him till he passes out, and we'll drag him back upstairs to a translator."

This was a joke, which Leon tossed out to relieve the stress of the moment. However, as I started thinking about the thing from the tunnel pouncing on an astonished Marielito, I started chuckling quietly to myself. I laughed harder and harder. I was like a kid who gets tickled in church, and the more he tries to stop, the harder he laughs. That got Leon started. We lay in the dark a few yards from people who would cut our throats in a heartbeat, and both of us were almost choking with stifled laughter. We gave each other a look, scuttled backward like crayfish to a place where we could stand, then spun and sprinted to the access ladder to the basement, climbed to the trapdoor, and threw ourselves into the basement. We sat on the dusty floor, doubled over with laughter for about five minutes. The joke really wasn't that funny. I guess we were just so scared that when the tension broke, it swung out of control.

Finally, we wiped our eyes and headed back into the tunnel. Leon kept his jokes to himself. This time, we made it to the ventilation-system tunnels. They were shaped like funnels, with six-foot-wide openings that sloped inward until we were belly-crawling again. As we approached an intersection, we caught a glimpse of some Cubans exploring an intersecting tunnel. We shrank back against the walls, and they passed by unknowingly. At another juncture, some inmates spotted us. We froze, our hands near our weapons. Incredibly they turned and ran.

"Gawdamn," Leon whispered. "Why you think they did that?"

"Maybe they think there was a bunch of us."

"Let's keep 'em thinking that way."

"Hell, Leon, if I saw your ugly mug coming out of a dark tunnel, I'd run too."

"Ugly? Ugly! Actually my wife thinks I'm pretty handsome."

"Well, you'd better hang on to that one and never buy her any glasses, or you'll be history."

After hours we emerged at the trapdoor, blinking at the bare lightbulbs in the basement like a couple of moles, only smellier and not nearly as cuddly.

"They could do it," Leon told Weldon. "They could drag acetylene tanks anywhere in there. They could blow us right out of here."

I posted SWAT team members at key access points and intersections. One section went to Washington Field Office SWAT, another to Chicago SWAT. This was one of the most distasteful assignments that I ever gave out to any FBI agent under my authority. The tunnels were dark, damp, and dirty. The job could place them in extreme danger.

These agents performed tunnel duty with dedication and good cheer. They named themselves the Tactical Underground Reconnaissance Detail, or TURD. They proudly displayed a sign with their name on it over the door to the holding area next to the entrance of the tunnel they were assigned to patrol. They developed a mission statement—to locate and apprehend the Subjects Hiding in Tunnels. Or SHITs. In other words, the TURDs were looking to protect the rest of the institution from the SHITs.

Somewhere in the warrens, they found an artificial Christmas tree and set it up. It was their way of saying that they'd stay there as long as they were needed.

4

The next day, Wednesday, November 25, a false media
report almost sent the Cubans over the edge. A local
television reporter spotted a SWAT team, decked out
like ninjas in full body armor and automatic weapons,
walking into the administration building to relieve
other SWAT teams who had been watching various
access points for more than twelve hours. It was a routine shift change, but the reporter didn't want to let the
facts get in the way of her scoop, so without checking
with Weldon or anybody else, she went on the air live
with speculation that a government assault appeared
imminent.

The Cubans, who were watching television, started
screaming, "There will be rivers of blood. Heads will
roll." They told the negotiators they had assembled a
group of hostages in the American dorm, poured inflam-
mable liquid on the floor, set the open cans nearby, and
held Bic lighters aloft. They declared they would incin-
erate everybody if there was a rescue attempt.

Dee called Charlie to the cafeteria sally port. They
locked themselves inside for the better part of three
hours. "If we were going to assault today, do you really
think we'd stage it in a place where the TV cameras
would see us?" Dee said. "We've spent all this time
working on a deal for you. Do you think we'd throw all
that out the window and assault you guys and put everybody's life in danger? It would be stupid on our part to
do something like that. If we're going to do it, you'll
know we're doing it. But I'm telling you, we're not going

353

to do it, unless you hurt those people in there, and then all bets are off. Now, do you believe me or not?"

Finally Charlie uncrossed his arms, nodded, and turned to leave. "Okay. No problem. For right now, I'm going to believe you. *Hasta luego.*" He unlocked the door to his side of the sally port and let himself back into the cafeteria.

Dee let out a long sigh, signaled for the BOP guard, and returned to the command post. Before long, the tower guards reported that the Cubans and hostages were dispersing peaceably. After this, Leon and I always alerted Dee or Pedro of any shift change or other movement of the tactical teams, so they could tell Charlie or some other Cuban and avoid another dangerous misunderstanding.

Weldon realized that Dee's magic might not work the next time. He had to prepare for a scenario in which a rioter hauled a hostage to the cafeteria door or the yard, made demands, and cut the hostage's throat. The standard deadly force policy observed not only by the FBI but by all other federal forces not only permitted but required any law enforcement officer watching this scene to shoot to kill in defense of life. Yet by taking the shot, the officer might touch off a melee on the other side of the bars.

Kennedy summoned all federal personnel and announced that he was modifying the deadly force policy with a new rule. In the case of a staged execution, he declared, "Only one person can authorize you to shoot to kill, and that is me. You don't have the green light unless I give it. And I am not going to authorize you to shoot and jeopardize the remaining one hundred twenty hostages. It may be the hardest thing we'll ever have to do, but we may have to stand there and watch a hostage being killed."

I spent the rest of the day with Jeff, Fred, and the SWAT team leaders, blocking out the tactical plan. We assigned two or three SWAT teams to each of the four areas where hostages were being held. A rescue proposal would be formulated for every location. Since the prison had been built, many haphazard remodelings and additions had completely changed the infrastructure, so the teams had to check all BOP architectural drawings and sketches for accuracy by interviewing prison employees who worked in those sectors. Once they had authenticated the floor plans, they would use engineer's tape to lay them out on the field behind the prison. Guards would walk them to make sure they were right.

Meanwhile, Jeff and Fred launched a crash course in the advanced close-quarter battle techniques we'd learned from Delta and the SAS. We were asking a lot of the SWAT agents. We'd had years to practice these skills. These men had days—maybe hours. But they were quick studies, and before the day was out, I felt confident they'd perform well if we had to go into the prison for any reason.

Sometime during the day, HQ called with good news. President Reagan had signed a formal waiver of the Posse Comitatus Act, which proscribed the use of the military for civilian law enforcement purposes. The only White House caveats were that Delta snipers fire only after the emergency rescue had begun, only in defense of rescuing personnel, and only with the permission of Weldon Kennedy.

The Delta advance team arrived Wednesday night,

and the rest of the contingent showed up Thanksgiving morning.

The Delta snipers, whose first priority was to gather precise intelligence about the identities and movements of the hostages, were positioned anyplace they could get a look at one of the target buildings. Wearing blue jeans and FBI jackets, they climbed into guard towers, where they commanded a sweeping overview of the complex with their binoculars, night-vision equipment, and rifle sights. They set up observation posts throughout the prison, in windows overlooking the yards and at every juncture where "our" territory abutted "theirs." We punched a hole in the wall of an office so that a team of SWAT and Delta men could peer into the adjoining area of C cellhouse. One Delta sniper was placed behind one-way glass in an office that overlooked the entrance to the American dorm.

The Delta Technical Detachment installed small, battery-operated closed-circuit TV cameras with motion detectors and alarms throughout the complex, on the tops of walls, in the stairwells, in basements and corridors in no-man's-land. BOP employees monitored the closed-circuit television transmissions and scribbled down names and locations of hostages.

All the information about movements and hostages and Cubans was logged. The SWAT team leaders were given an intelligence update every hour. If we had to go into the prison at any moment, we'd have a good idea where every hostage was.

Our spook types smuggled some of their hocus-pocus eavesdropping stuff into the prison. If we tell you how they did it, we'll have to kill you. I can say this much: we began to get good, precise information about the rioters' plans.

The inmates, meanwhile, busied themselves fashioning swords by the thousand, not only to thwart us but to protect themselves from rival factions. One of the Delta sniper teams was stationed right next to the C cellhouse laundry, which had been converted to a machine shop. They watched and photographed the inmates standing before the grinders day and night, making intricate and effective swords, and also sharpening the kitchen's long steel stirring paddles into short spears.

One evening Leon and I went down to watch the show. As we stood in the darkness, I felt a chill go up my spine.

"Leon, do you know how to sword fight?" I whispered. Without taking his eyes off the inmate putting the finishing touches on a three-foot-long sword, he whispered back, "Naw. Don't have to. I'll just shoot the son of a bitch."

Of course, he was kidding. He took Weldon's no-shooting edict seriously. Whenever we approached the cafeteria door or some other contact point for a chat with a Cuban, we had to remember to stand back because a sword could slide through the bars before we could react. Our body armor stopped certain kinds of bullets, but not razor-sharp pieces of metal.

On Thanksgiving afternoon, our hopes were raised, then dashed, when the Cubans agreed to release fifty hostages in exchange for permission to hold a live press conference. We made elaborate preparations, but at the last minute, the Cubans showed up with only three hostages. Dee and Pedro wouldn't budge, even though they had to watch the Cubans hustle the three hostages away from the door.

During the night, while Weldon was at home getting

some sleep, a behavioral science specialist from Quantico instructed Dee and Pedro to speak with the inmates in English. The Cubans went ballistic. Early Friday morning, they forced all the hostages in the American dorm to bunch up in a circle, surrounded them with gasoline-soaked rags and paper, and started screaming at them. Weldon arrived in the middle of the uproar. He got as angry as anyone had ever seen him. He charged down the hall, found Dee, and shoved him up against a wall, storming, "Why did you allow this?"

"I didn't have the rank to refuse," Dee replied meekly.

"Well, it won't happen again," Weldon seethed. The negotiations went back to Spanish. Dee and Pedro spent hours trying to calm things down. The Cubans finally eased up on the hostages, but the talks were derailed for several days.

Meanwhile, we were rehearsing and refining our rescue plan. One of my main concerns was how long it took to move from our last place of cover and concealment, which we call Phase Line Yellow, to the hostage locations. I calculated that it would take at least twenty minutes to get to the American dorm, where most of the hostages were held, from the nearest Phase Line Yellow position, a doorway leading from a tunnel. We had to get closer.

The architectural plans showed a tunnel leading from the administration building subbasement to an electrical switching room in E cellhouse. The switching-room door was just fifteen or twenty yards from the American dorm. Guards said the tunnel had been blocked off with steel bars years before.

We worked our way down to the tunnel entrance. It

was covered with bars as thick as my forearm and wire mesh so heavy that it broke our bolt cutter. We had two choices: cut through the bars and mesh, or find another route to the switching room. Either way, we had to work quietly. Some Cubans and hostages were directly above us. If they detected our presence, we'd have a real problem. They could stream through the tunnel, overwhelm our inner perimeter, and take more hostages—us.

The Delta breachers had a thermal device that would cut through the bar, but when we tested it in the field near the prison, it sounded like a train in a tunnel. The SOARU guys came up with a hydraulic device for taking down walls, but it was noisy and also slow.

"How about a cutting torch, like from the hardware store?" Leon said. "Bet we have one at the FBI garage."

Sure enough, we did. It was quiet and powerful. Leon cut through the bars like carrot sticks. Come to think of it, Leon always did look more like a welder than an agent.

"Good job. Where did you learn to use that thing?" I said.

"This could be my retirement job, you know. Actually, I think sometimes we tend to get too sophisticated with this high-tech equipment. I'm just a simple boy from Texas."

"Well, you're simple and you're from Texas."

I posted a SWAT team at the tunnel entrance. Then Leon and I tiptoed through it to the metal door that opened into the switching room. Good news. The Cubans hadn't found it, and the BOP key worked. One twist, and the door swung open.

A faint ray of light seeped through the dense steel mesh that covered the narrow transom windows.

Shadows of Cubans walking out in the yard were projected against the back wall. Leon and I crept up to the corner of one window, peered out, and stared at the backs of Cubans leaning against the building, a few inches from our faces.

The main door to the American dorm was in spitting distance. With any luck at all, rescuing personnel could be inside the door to the American dorm before the alarm was raised. Of course, once we were inside, we would still have to deal with enraged rioters swinging sabers. I said a silent prayer. *Please, God, let the negotiations work.*

5

On the night of Sunday, November 29, Leon and I decided to reclaim a chunk of no-man's-land: the auditorium located directly above the cafeteria. I went to the Delta commander and borrowed two MP5 submachine guns equipped with infrared lasers and PVS-5 night-vision goggles. We set out at about two o'clock in the morning, a time when most people are in their deepest sleep. Even so, the chatter of the Cubans in the cafeteria made a loud din.

We set out with the ten-man U.S. Marshals Special Operations Group and a BOP guard familiar with the passageway. We doused the hinges of the metal door to the auditorium with penetrating oil and waited a few minutes for it to seep in. The guard slowly turned the key in the lock and eased the door open. The auditorium was as dark as the inside of your belly. I couldn't see anybody with my night-vision goggles, but I couldn't be sure there wasn't a whole gang of Marielitos curled up asleep on the floor, underneath seats or around corners.

I never told Debbie what happened next. "When we go in, lock us in, because if there's anybody there, we don't want them to come screaming through this gate after you," I told the SOG commander. "If there's a problem, don't come in. Don't open this door for anything." He nodded, eased the door shut, and turned the key. The dead bolt clicked shut.

Looking back on it, I have to admit that getting locked into a room where I might stumble into a wild-eyed bunch of rioters with swords might not sound like a great idea. At the time, though, I was totally focused on making sure the Cubans stayed contained. The marshals were professional, courageous, and well-disciplined, but if several hundred rioters rushed that door, they wouldn't be able to turn them back. The Cubans would flood into our side of the prison, and a lot of people would get very dead. We had to cut our losses.

Besides, as I saw it, there were three possibilities, none of them all that bad. One, the auditorium would be empty. Two, the place would be mobbed, and we'd be captured. The Cubans hadn't killed other hostages, so they probably wouldn't execute us.

Three, if a few people were in the auditorium, they might feel imperiled and attack us. In that case, we would shoot. Our weapons were equipped with silencers. With night-vision goggles, each of us could put a couple of rounds between someone's eyes and make no more sound than a little pop-pop, like a couple of salt shakers falling over on a table. We might be able to slip in and slip out without anybody knowing it, but if we couldn't, our equipment would keep us alive.

Anyhow, that was the theory. I thought it made good sense, and so did Leon. He didn't tell his wife right off, either.

We took a few steps inside. Through my goggles, Leon looked like a green ghost. He took one side of the auditorium. I took the other. We didn't speak. In this dead-quiet cavern, even a whisper could give us away.

We tiptoed down the aisles, looking between the rows of seats. Leon gave me the thumbs-up and pointed to the balcony. I pointed to myself, then pointed up to the stairway leading to the balcony, indicating that I would go up and clear it while he stayed down below. I padded up the stairs, stopping to listen every few steps. Why was the hair on the back of my neck standing up? Must have been something I ate.

The Blakeney luck was as good as the Coulson luck, and they were both holding. The balcony was clear too. I scurried back downstairs and gave Leon the thumbs-up. All clear.

We tiptoed over to two doors covered with barred gates on either side of the stage. The guards had told us that they led to stairways that descended to the cafeteria. We could hear the Cubans talking, laughing, and clinking plates and glasses. The doors were bent from being pounded, but they had held. We jiggled them. They were locked good and tight.

Just then, I kicked an empty Coca-Cola can and sent it airborne over about ten rows of seats. It sounded like a garbage can lid landing on concrete. The clatter scared the shit out of both of us. Leon crouched, scanned the spot where the can had landed. The damn thing was still spinning.

"It's okay," I whispered. "I kicked a can."

I could hear a great sigh of relief rush from Leon's lungs. "Didn't you guys do all of that secret stealth-movement stuff on the HRT?"

"Yeah. But you've got to admit even Tom Dempsey would be proud of that field goal."

"Yeah, sure," Leon said doubtfully.

Then we cleared the third floor. Later, we would return to put a closed-circuit TV camera there, giving us a clear view of the entrance to the chapel, which the Cubans were using as their command post.

We crept to the heavy steel door we had entered and knocked twice. The marshals returned two knocks. Leon knocked three times, our signal that we were clear and not in the company of a couple of hundred Cubans. The marshals clicked open the door and let us out.

"This place is clear," I said. "Can you guys get someone to hold the entire auditorium twenty-four hours a day? We need to hang on to it."

"Can do. We'll take care of it."

About eleven o'clock the next morning, the Cubans discovered that we owned the auditorium. Many of them came up to the barred doors, gesturing violently and screaming at the marshals in Spanish. They made no real attempt to break down the doors. They seemed intimidated by the SOG men, who were dressed in blue tactical uniforms, heavily armed, and looking real nasty.

Around midday, Jose Meza Rodriguez, who had been appointed Charlie's enforcer, appeared at the gate. He called to Leon, who happened to be nearby, and pointed behind him. His henchmen had three handcuffed prison guards in tow and were stretching their throats, swords poised at their jugular veins. The hostages had to cut their eyes to look at Leon, but they said nothing and held themselves as erect as possible.

Meza Rodriguez demanded that we remove all our tactical people from the auditorium. If we didn't, he would kill the three hostages right then.

Leon gave Meza his full west-Texas-speech-impediment slow treatment. "Now, Meza," he said, grinning as if they were good old boys arguing about whose car was faster. "Yew don't want to dew that. Ah'll jest kill yew. Ah could absolutely kill all yew guys afore you git down the stairs."

"I got a bomb," Meza hissed. "Get out here or I blow everybody up. Right now. I keel jew too."

"Whu-u-ut?" Leon said, taking advantage of Meza's bad English. "Cain't unnerstand you."

"Bomb," Meza repeated. "Keel you. Blow jew up."

"Huh?"

This went on until a couple of more fluent Cubans jumped in as translators.

When Leon still appeared befuddled, Meza disappeared down the stairs, then returned with a fire extinguisher with some match heads stuck in the hole where the hose had been attached. The thing had been filled with acetylene gas.

"Thass not a bomb," Leon said. "Thass a fire extinguisher."

"Bomb," Meza repeated. "Blow jew up."

"I cain't see it here in the dark. Who's got a flashlight?" Leon said, though he had a flashlight tucked in his vest. This ploy bought quite a bit of time. The Cubans ran out, hunted through all the cafeteria drawers, and returned with flashlights.

"Okay," Leon said. "Lemme look at it over here."

By this time, Meza was so flummoxed that he nearly passed the thing through the bars to Leon. One of the smarter Cubans stopped him.

"Aw, that's not a bomb," Leon opined. "I don't think it'll blow us up. Look, Meza, let me send it to our people. They can tell us if it's a bomb."

Meza growled, but he had a small smile on his face. He was bluffing and he knew Leon had called his bluff.

"Meza, go back down there," Leon said with exaggerated patience. "All yew're gonna do is get yewerseff killed."

"Jew too," Meza snarled.

"Hell, I'd be better off dead than on this miserable sumbitch job," Leon said amiably.

Through all this shucking and grinning, the guards stood erect, their shoulders back, no doubt wondering what would happen when Meza got fed up with Leon for refusing to take him seriously.

But Meza finally looked at Leon, grinned himself, shrugged his shoulders, and walked away with his "bomb."

Actually, Meza was not the scariest guy in the pen. That honor went to American prisoner Thomas Edward Silverstein, the most notorious killing machine in the federal penal system. "He's a complete animal," a guard told us. "He'll kill anyone with a badge. Six foot two, two hundred pounds, blond hair, blue eyes. He doesn't get exercise privileges much, but he's in great condition. He does push-ups and sit-ups all day in his cell."

Silverstein, thirty-five, had been sent up the first time for bank robbery in Los Angeles. While in the federal pen in Marion, Illinois, he murdered a fellow inmate and drew a life sentence. He wanted to reach the highest level of the Aryan Brotherhood, a prison gang affiliated with Aryan Nation, and that required killing a federal official. One day, as Silverstein was being escorted from his cell, a confederate slipped him a knife. He turned on his guard and began stabbing him. As the guard crumpled to the floor, Silverstein placed his hand on the carotid artery on his neck and continued to stab him until there was no more heartbeat. For that coldly calculated act, Silverstein drew another 150 years.

He was transferred to Atlanta and held in total isolation. Whenever he had to be moved, he had to put his arms through a small portal in his cell door and allow his hands to be cuffed behind him. His legs were shackled in the same manner before the key was turned. Then he was escorted by four guards.

During the first days of the riot, we had no information on Silverstein's whereabouts. Knowing of his hatred of all authority, we were afraid that the Cubans would release him, and he'd go after the hostages, requiring us to launch our emergency rescue plan.

As it turned out, Silverstein terrified the Cubans, all except Meza, who stared him down when he went into the food-storage room and tried to take a whole Virginia ham back to his cell. Dee urged Charlie to give Silverstein to us, pointing out that this psycho could destroy all his hopes of a solution.

On the morning of the thirtieth, Weldon summoned me to his office. Some BOP guards posted outside the barred exit tunnel that led outside the wall reported that they had heard Silverstein in the tunnel. Some of our people had seen Silverstein too. They thought he was working with a core drill, a tool for drilling concrete. He appeared to be trying to tunnel to the outside.

"Doc, I'd like you to go to the tunnel, talk to the guards, and, if it's feasible, go into the tunnel and get Silverstein," Weldon said. "I know it's a long shot, but if you can get him out, we can all breathe a little easier."

"Sure," I said. Meeting Silverstein in a dark tunnel was as good a way as any to get my heart pumping.

Leon was out on a break, so I asked Jeff Wehmeyer and Fred Kingston to go with me. Each of us grabbed an MP5 and put on body armor before we descended to the basement. Eight to ten guards were there, armed with shotguns, safe behind the heavily barred gate. Yet they were all wide-eyed and obviously terrified. When I told the one with the keys to open the gate and let us pass, he became almost hysterical, as if we'd proposed diving into a shark tank.

"You can't go in there," he said. "Silverstein's in there."

"I know, that's why they sent us down here," I said. "Just unlock the gate, and then lock it behind us. We'll just go have a look-see and we'll be right back."

At the tunnel's mouth, we saw a ventilation pipe about two feet in diameter that ran the length of the tunnel. It carried voices from the depths of the tunnel. The guards had heard Silverstein, all right, but he was some distance away.

The tunnel was eight feet high and twelve feet across. We formed a reverse V, with Kingston on the left, Wehmeyer on the right, and me in the center. We wanted to be sure that we didn't walk past a hiding inmate who could ambush us from the rear. About thirty yards in, we noticed water on the floor. The tunnel sloped down, at first gradually, then more steeply. Finally, we reached a point where everything in front of us was completely flooded. Helicopters had dropped tons of water on the fires; it had filtered down and filled the lowest tunnels.

Silverstein was somewhere on the other side of the subterranean pond. Unless he was a fish, he wasn't coming out through this tunnel, and we weren't swimming in. When we returned empty-handed, the guards actually looked relieved. We weren't. We still had to get Silverstein.

A couple of hours later Silverstein was spotted on the hospital roof. Two Cubans who surrendered shortly thereafter told us why. Silverstein had a new escape plan. He was building an ultralight aircraft. Leon, whose hobby was clay-target competitions, guffawed. "Let him go," he said delightedly. "I could just see him coming over the wall, with me yelling, 'Pull!' " We found his "plane" after the riot was over. It looked like something out of a cartoon. The frame was made from a couple of lawn chairs. Mailbags covered the wings and seat. The motor was ripped from a Weed Eater.

Around seven o'clock that night, Leon and I went to the cafeteria doors and called for Charlie. He appeared at the door, accompanied by an interpreter and a tall, flamboyantly dressed Afro-Cuban we called Big Guy. We said we wanted Silverstein. Charlie and Big Guy nodded.

A couple of hours later, I was talking with the negotiators when a deputy marshal called me to the cafeteria gate. There stood Big Guy. "Boss, boss. Come quick," he yelled. "Boss, boss, Silverstein."

I looked to my right and saw about a hundred Cubans, screaming and brandishing machetes in the air. I couldn't understand what was going on at first. Then I realized that the Cubans had Silverstein hog-tied.

"I need five guys," I told the SOG commander. I had them in about thirty seconds. The five marshals, a BOP guard, and I entered the cafeteria sally port. The guard locked the inner door behind us, then opened the outer door.

We stood face-to-face with the Cubans, who were still hollering and waving their weapons. They could have taken us hostage at that point, but they had more important business. Silverstein was being carried toward us, facedown, by four of the inmates, each holding one of his limbs. Three pairs of handcuffs encircled his wrists. Two pairs of shackles held his legs. I drew my sidearm but held it down at my leg. The marshals left theirs holstered.

They threw Silverstein at us and turned and ran away. The marshals picked him up and ran back into the sally port, through the doors, and up the steps toward a cellblock that we controlled.

Unfortunately, on the way up the stairs, the deputy marshals didn't raise Silverstein up high enough. They were carrying him just as the inmates had, one on each arm and leg, and they bumped his head on the stairs. *It's really a shame that this individual had to suffer that accident,* I thought. I felt bad about it for days.

Silverstein didn't notice a thing: the inmates had given him drugged coffee. The Mickey Finn had enough tranquilizers to stun an ox, but it only made Silverstein woozy, so Meza and his boys jumped him. That was an act of great heroism, because Silverstein was armed at the time and would have killed anyone he suspected of betraying him.

Back in the command post, I told Weldon, "If the negotiations don't go well, we'll tell the Cubans that we're going to send Silverstein back in, and boy, is he pissed."

A half-smile inched across Weldon's broad face. "That would certainly get my attention."

Late that day, Woody and the HRT arrived in Atlanta. The Oakdale riot had ended late on the afternoon of the twenty-ninth, with the safe release of the hostages. The Cubans had surrendered in exchange for assurances that their paroles and extraditions would be handled fairly. Fernando Rivero, the FBI's lead negotiator at Oakdale, arrived with details. Dee, Pedro, and Fernando put conditions similar to those in the Oakdale deal on the table. The government would establish a special INS board to review the detainees' cases individually.

Things were looking up, but we needed to get rid of a few distractions. One was Radio Mariel.

This was the Cubans' name for the loudspeaker system they'd rigged up to broadcast messages over the wall. Their families signaled back with banners that could be seen from the hospital roof. The ability to communicate with the outside world seemed to energize the Cubans. Leon asked some electrical engineers how to short-circuit the electricity. They advised us to run cables from two large portable generators to the electric-systems room underneath the cafeteria. The theory was that touching the cable ends to certain terminals would blow out the system. Leon's SWAT team spooled out hundreds of yards of cable and crept into the basement systems room at two o'clock in the morning. They revved up the generators and hit the terminals. "Not even a lightbulb flickered," Leon groused.

6

The negotiations stalled out on Wednesday, December 2. To intensify the psychological pressure, Dee and Pedro asked us to resume low-altitude helicopter flights over the prison. The noise set off the Angola vets, who renewed their threats to stage mass executions. Around ten-thirty that night, the prison's Catholic chaplain, who was one of the hostages, came to the cafeteria door with a petition signed by forty-three other hostages begging us to knock off the flights. We complied.

By now, Dee, Pedro, and other negotiators were meeting with Charlie and the other Cuban spokesmen face-to-face, at a table outside the cafeteria doors. We had built a floor-to-ceiling plywood partition in the hall-way behind the table so rioters in the cafeteria could see their negotiators but not down the hall to our command post.

We found out from our hidden mikes that the Cubans had somehow gotten the idea that if we tried to rescue the hostages, we'd be armed only with riot batons and tear gas. It would be their sabers and shivs against our sticks, not a bad match, and the worst that would happen to them would be a knot on the head.

No wonder these talks are going nowhere, I said to myself. *It's time to pop their bubble.*

As a negotiation session dragged on, Charlie looked over his shoulder at me and said, "I need to go to the bathroom."

"Wait right there," I said. "I'll make arrangements for you."

I slipped behind the barrier and rallied the New York SWAT team, "Get all your gear on, all your weapons, and line up on the right side of the hallway." Then I went to the Marshal SOG commander and asked him to do likewise. In a couple of minutes, I had a hundred armed men dressed head to foot in black uniforms, body armor, and ballistic helmets, ripping with submachine guns, shotguns, assault rifles, and all sorts of electronic gear.

"Stand there at port arms," I ordered. "And look nasty."

I went back to the table and motioned to Charlie. "Come on, let's go." I put my hand on his shoulder, real friendly like, and walked him around the barrier. As he turned the corner, he jumped six inches and his mouth fell open. He didn't say a word, but as we walked that gauntlet, he kept looking left and right, eyes big as Frisbees.

I escorted him to the entrance to the bathroom, guided him between two of the biggest marshals in the United States and stood there while he did his business. As he turned around and washed his hands, I said, "Charlie, we have to talk."

He nodded, almost meekly.

"Charlie," I said, "you guys have brought sabers to a gunfight. Let's think of resolving this thing peacefully. I understand why you don't want to go back to Cuba. But if we have to make an entry to rescue hostages, we're not coming in with batons and tear gas, and we're not going to do battle with you. You'll be facing the full weight of four hundred tactical operators, all armed as you see them here. They'll use deadly force to protect their lives and the lives of the hostages. If you attack us with your sabers, we'll shoot you."

The sweat was pouring down Charlie's face as I walked him back to the table.

"I think I need to talk to the others," he said.

I could see in his eyes what he meant. He'd turned the corner.

Our side had still another card to play, as Leon and I found out when Weldon summoned us to his office. "We've just found out that all of the Cubans won't be going back," he said. "The State Department has established some sort of criteria for their return, and some of them will be allowed to stay. If we can get to their records, we can find out which ones will be staying."

"Uh-oh," I said. "Here we go again. And just where are those records?"

Weldon smiled. "No-man's-land." The Immigration and Naturalization Service office was in a cubbyhole off the floor above the auditorium.

I looked at Leon, who was rolling his eyes. "Let's do it."

We went to the Marshals' SOG and asked for backup. This time we didn't need night vision. The lights in the auditorium were on and really bright. We climbed the steps to the third floor, found the INS door, and did the soak-the-hinges bit. The documents showed that Charlie and the other detainee leaders were not among the group slated for immediate deportation. In fact, Charlie was scheduled for release in three weeks. Dee and Pedro gave Charlie and his pals the good news.

They called a huddle, then nodded agreement.

To help cement the deal, Weldon flew in Bishop Agustin Roman of Miami. Roman spoke to the Cubans through the cafeteria door, and his speech was broadcast throughout the entire prison. He touched them in ways no one else could.

The Cuban negotiators agreed to the terms of the surrender. The formal agreement was signed at one o'clock Friday morning and witnessed by Bishop Roman. Twelve minutes later, the first of the hostages appeared at the cafeteria sally port.

I stood close by as the hostages filed in. I didn't want to miss the chance to look into their eyes as they walked out to freedom.

Afterward, the hostages said that they had in fact been treated well. On three occasions, they felt they might be killed, but most of the time, they had been fed and handled with dignity. That was a credit to their own professionalism. The BOP people had obviously been decent to the detainees in their everyday dealings, and the Cubans had returned the favor. In fact, Charlie had assigned Meza Rodriguez to protect them from other crazies like El Loco and Silverstein. Charlie had definite management potential: he had transformed Meza from part of the problem to part of the solution. Meza, immensely proud of his newfound responsibility and status, ran his "protection detail" with zeal and dedication.

The medical staff had been treated courteously and had carried on as usual, treating wounded or ill prisoners and hostages. Most of the prison had been trashed, but the hospital was pristine. Not a vial or bottle was out of place in the pharmacy. The Cuban leaders, it turned out, had been as worried about losing control of the crazies as we were. They had refused to let the rioters have free run of the hospital and pharmacy and had demanded prescriptions as usual.

Charlie insisted that he would only surrender his sword to Leon and me. Some kindly jailer must have let him watch a lot of Civil War movies. We handed our guns to other agents and went through the sally port. The door was locked behind us. An FBI photographer poked his lens through the bars of the door as we approached Charlie.

Charlie, who was immaculately groomed even in his gray prison sweats, made a great show of presenting us with his sword. He snaked his arm around Leon and gave him a flirtatious squeeze as the three of us posed for the camera. I could see the blood rising in Leon's face, but he squinted and gave the camera a look that was somewhere between smiling and baring his teeth. Then we shook hands and returned to our side.

The rioters left the cafeteria, dispersed, then lined up at the East Gate. Each man was searched for weapons, handcuffed, and led to a bus to be transported to other federal prisons. Many of them were shipped to the federal prison at Talladega, Alabama—where in 1991, they would riot once more, and the HRT would be called in to rescue ten hostages.

Meza Rodriguez was one of those sent to Talladega. Eventually he was deported back to Cuba.

Charlie was also sent back to Cuba for taking part in the riot. Dee saw him on a television documentary about Cuba, free and apparently thriving in Havana.

After the last prisoner left, the tactical units conducted one last exercise. They carried out their rescue plans. They followed the avenues of approach they would have used in a real rescue and walked through their target buildings just as they had practiced. The HRT took the American dorm. The plan worked exactly as it should have.

Not bad, I said to myself. *We could have pulled it off.*

But a few of them might have gone home in pine boxes, and some of the hostages and Cubans as well, if not for Dee Rosario and Pedro Toledo. They received the Attorney General's Hispanic Award for Valor, which they richly deserved. As I had often preached to the HRT, life was not a video game. There were no restart buttons on operators. If we lost one, it was forever. The best tactical option was always, always, a surrender achieved by negotiation. Better to talk for weeks, for months, than to have to drag out a single body of a hostage or one of your own.

I found a telephone and called Debbie.

"It's finished," I said. "The negotiators resolved it."

"Yes, I know. We saw it on TV."

"I'm coming home tonight. Sorry I missed Thanksgiving. The kids okay?"

"Everybody's fine. Kids, Max, Katy, Mom, and Dad. How are you?"

"Bushed. Just gotta pack and say good-bye to Leon and Weldon, and have lunch with Jeff and Fred. Hey, Deb?"

"Yes?"

"Love you."

"I know."

BOOK FIVE

ASSUMPTION IS THE MOTHER OF F***-UP

Your greatest fear should be that you will be given a failed tactical mission from another unit. You will forever be tarred with the brush of their failure.

—CHARLIE BECKWITH,
Delta Force commander

ASSUMPTION IS THE MOTHER OF F***-UP

1

I put a little more time in at HQ and then made a break for it.

In the spring of 1988, the Portland SAC job opened up.

"Hell, I'd walk out to the West Coast for that job," I told Tony Daniels, who shared the commute from Virginia with me. More important, a man with mental problems had a fixation on Debbie and the girls and seemed to show up wherever they were. We had reported him to the authorities in Fairfax County, but there was no law against showing up in a public place. I thought about dragging him out into the woods, but an FBI agent wasn't supposed to take the law, or lack of it, into his own hands. The idea of putting three thousand miles between him and us was very attractive.

"They might as well pick you as anyone. I'll talk to Buck."

Did I mention that Tony, in addition to getting promoted to deputy assistant director in the criminal division, was a saint?

Everybody was happy about the move except for Jessie, who was five. One night after her bath, she came downstairs and climbed up into my lap. That's the way she started important conversations.

"I want to ask you a question about Oregon," she said gravely.

"Okay. Fire away."

"I want to know if they have stars out there in the sky."

"Well, I've never been there. But I know one thing for sure. When you get there, there'll be at least one."

She giggled and rolled her eyes. "No. I mean in the sky!"

"Actually there are millions, and you'll be able to see them clear as a bell."

"Oh, good, I was really worried about that."

"Don't worry. Have I ever kidded you?"

"All the time."

"Well, I'm not kidding this time. You'll see. Now get to bed."

After she disappeared up the steps, I turned to Debbie. "What was that about?"

"She just saw *Star Wars*," she explained. "The opening line was, 'In a galaxy far, far away.' You told her that Oregon was 'far, far away,' so she's pretty sure we're heading for outer space."

Jenny announced to her second-grade buddies that we were moving because "my dad's gonna be king of Oregon." I had told her I'd be in charge of all the FBI for the state of Oregon. Jenny's translation was that if I was in charge, I had to be king. We all went to Burger King and staged our own coronation. I was King Dan for a day.

After I had the Portland office team up with the local cops to bust a major drug dealer, the people in the neighborhood he'd been terrorizing poured out onto the streets to thank us and give us information about other gangs.

Those people got me to thinking about why I'd joined the FBI in the first place. I'd been all fired up about seeing that the Constitution and the Bill of Rights were living documents. I'd wanted to make a difference in the lives of ordinary Americans. Well, here was the way.

Despite its pristine image, Oregon was crawling with drug dealers. Decent, hardworking folks were being denied their rights, not by an oppressive government, as the Founding Fathers anticipated, but by criminals like that scum-sucking crack dealer we'd just busted. These people had been prisoners in their homes, peeking out from behind barred windows and doors. They couldn't sit on their front porches or stoops and visit their neighbors for fear of being struck by a stray bullet from a drive-by shooting. They couldn't stroll down to a newsstand to buy a paper. Their kids couldn't play sandlot ball. They were afraid to walk to church. Where was their freedom of assembly, their freedom of speech and religion?

I talked to the police chief and the sheriff. They had avoided the FBI in the past; they thought we were arrogant, high-handed glory hogs. That was hard to argue with, but I humbled myself, not an easy thing for me, and charmed and pleaded until they agreed to set up a drug task force with our office. We had computers, radios, cars, and a small budget for extras. They had experienced officers who knew the city. Before long, we were retaking whole neighborhoods, and we drove the price of cocaine up dramatically.

Our violent-crime initiative came to the attention of HQ, though not in the way I'd had in mind. I received a letter of censure for using profanity while arresting a couple of fugitives.

The first was a bank robber who was hitting banks with a lever-action thirty-thirty carbine, the kind you've seen in John Wayne movies, and sticking the barrel into tellers' mouths. After he pulled this sadistic trick a few times, we got together with the Portland cops and tracked him to a trailer park. The bank robbery squad and the SWAT team staked the place out, waiting for him to show up. Charlie Mathews, my ASAC, and I supervised from a car parked a short distance away. Late in the evening, I came down with a roaring thirst, so Charlie and I drove to the 7-Eleven for a Slurpee. As we pulled into the parking lot, we spotted our suspect paying for a bag of groceries. We radioed the agents at the trailer park, but we couldn't let him leave. His car was blocked by steel posts in front and cars on either side. Charlie slammed on his brakes and slid our car sideways behind his, trapping him. I sprinted to the passenger side, shoved my M16 into his cheek, and said, "FBI. Don't fuckin' move or I'll blow your head off."

Charlie opened the driver-side door, rolled him onto the ground, and stood him up against the car while I cuffed him. By this time, the other agents had arrived, so we turned him over to them. One of the young agents turned his head for a split second, during which the robber spun and ran. I chased him, knocked him down, and said, "You fuck, don't you run from us." He settled down after that. SACs rarely make arrests themselves, so naturally the story made the rounds at the office.

Then something like it happened again. The SWAT team and I drove down to Salem on a case we were working with the local police. We intended to arrest a drug kingpin who lived in a compound surrounded by a tall hurricane fence with heavy, remote-controlled gates.

The SWAT guys had gotten hold of an electronic device that would open the gate, but the suspect saw us coming on a closed-circuit-TV hookup. He leapt out of a second-story balcony on the back side of the house and scrambled for the woods. I was out back, leaning on a tree, so I vaulted a rail fence, tackled him, snapped, "You asshole," and cuffed him.

Not long after that, I found myself under internal investigation. An anonymous letter came in saying I'd chased two fugitives and beat them up. I don't know who trumped up the charge, because neither the defendants nor their lawyers made any such accusations, and U.S. Attorney Charles Turner told HQ he'd never had complaints of FBI brutality from any defense lawyers. In the end, I was exonerated, and I thought this ridiculous episode was over until I got a call from Floyd Clarke saying he was going to censure me for my bad language. I was pissed off big time, or as they say at HQ, deeply distressed. The message seemed to be that I had done wrong to make the arrests in the first place. In fact, I think they preferred driver SACs who sat in the office and read teletypes instead of going out with the agents. I tore the letter up and threw it in the trash. I probably should've framed it, because those guys were as dangerous as any crooks I'd run across in New York, and I doubt they would've stopped in their tracks if I'd said, "Pardon me, sir, would you please comply with my instructions?" Violent criminals have a language of their own, and I've found we can often avoid shooting by barking an order they understand, like, "You motherfucker, move and you're history."

Of course I would never have gotten into trouble if the FBI had had the foresight to send Clint Van Zandt with me on all my assignments. He was just about the only person in the Bureau who could make me clean up my language.

In May 1989, I picked up Jenny and Jessie on the last day of school. "Well, that was great," Jessie said. "Where are we going to go to school next year?"

I felt a pang. The poor kid had bounced around a lot for a six-year-old. "Well, at least for now, you're going to go to Lake Grove Elementary School again."

"That's great," she said.

We would move many more times. The kids would have to leave all their friends, all their teachers and coaches, and go back to being the new kid on the block in some distant city. I can't even remember how many times we had planned family events only to cancel them because I had to fly away to some job someplace. But they were always good sports about it.

Except when I was ordered back to HQ in December 1991, just in time to spend Christmas on the road.

The villain of the piece was Bill Baker, my former partner and best friend. Baker had been promoted to assistant director of the Criminal Investigations Division. He began campaigning to get me to move back to be his deputy in charge of terrorism, violent crime, and civil rights.

Jeff, Jenny, and Jessie pleaded not to go back to Washington because of the man they feared. I asked to be transferred anywhere else in America. But Baker was determined. "I really need you," he said. "You're the only one I trust to handle a real crisis." I wasn't sure about that, but I had to admit that he knew that flattery would get him anywhere. After a lot more coaxing and arm-twisting, I gave in. Actually, I didn't have much choice. The FBI isn't a democracy.

It was hardest on Jenny, who rushed into the bathroom, slammed the door, and burst out sobbing the minute she heard the news.

I waited for about five minutes, then knocked meekly. "Aw, Jenn, we've got six weeks," I called. "You gonna spend them in the bathroom?"

Eventually she emerged, sniffing and rubbing her swollen eyes, and went out in the yard to see if she could kick the air out of some soccer balls. It would be a while before she was as dangerous as her mother.

2

"You know," Debbie radioed me on her CB, "if I could get my hands on Bill Baker, I'd cut his nuts off." We were driving in a caravan—kids, dogs, bird, and all—through a ferocious snowstorm in northern New Mexico.

"Cold as it is, he wouldn't notice," I radioed back.

We got to Washington just in time for Baker's gala retirement party. It turned out that he couldn't stand working for "the empty suit" or "His Goofiness," as we later called Director Sessions. Baker took a cushy job with the Motion Picture Association.

I understood why he left. But there I was, stuck in headquarters, second banana to a legendary workaholic named Larry Potts. Pottsy, as he was known, was the busiest executive in the FBI. He was directly responsible for every FBI criminal investigation in the world. Most of the people who had held the position seldom bothered to find out about the cases they supervised, but

Potts immersed himself in even the smallest details. This was a habit of years in the field, solving tough cases in which a single fiber or receipt could be the key. Potts had made his reputation in 1989 and 1990, by finding and stopping Walter Leroy Moody, a vengeful crank whose mail bombs killed Eleventh U.S. Circuit Court of Appeals judge Robert Vance in Alabama and Georgia civil rights lawyer Robert Robinson. By the time Potts was through with Moody, there was almost nothing the FBI didn't know about him. Potts had bugged Moody's cell, flipped his ex-wife, traced his life history, and tracked every nail, battery, and snippet of wire in the bombs back to its retailer, wholesaler, and manufacturer.

Larry brought the same passion for detail to the CID job. To make matters worse, he often found himself the butt of the perverse game of gotcha, an HQ tradition in which the sultans of the seventh floor quizzed us underlings about trivia, like, "What color was the getaway car in St. Louis?"—as if they were going to go out and look for it.

Or, as Sessions once asked me, "Dan, this is your director. How's that case going in Phoenix?" I was new to the game. Case in Phoenix? There were hundreds of cases in Arizona. As my mind whirled through their names and Sessions crowed, "Ha, gotcha on that one," the answer came to me. "Are you talking about the father and son from Phoenix who were kidnapped while they were diving in Mexico?"

"Yep, that's the one."

"Yes, sir, we're working with the Mexican federal police on that." I went on to give him a detailed recounting of the case.

Potts was called upon to play gotcha about ten times a day, which meant that I or one of the other deputies had to know all the details, too, and keep him constantly briefed. Since my branch oversaw all violent crime, civil rights, and terrorist cases worked by the FBI, I had to know everything about hundreds of high-stakes cases like the investigation of the Los Angeles police officers whose beating of Rodney King had ignited the Los Angeles riots, the kidnapping and murder of Exxon executive Sidney Reso, and the 1988 terrorist bombing of Pan Am flight 103. When the other deputies were on travel, I handled white collar crime and drug section cases and chaired the undercover review committee.

Potts drove us all mercilessly, but it was impossible not to like him. We never became close personal friends, and we never socialized because our days were so long and stressed that, at night, we rushed home to our families. Still, I came to have a deep respect for Larry Potts's professionalism. I've never had a boss who worked harder or had more devotion to his job. Also, he was modest and irreverent, with a Tom Sawyer grin and a way of tweaking drivers with sly asides that they might not understand, but the rest of us did.

I stole every moment I could find to work on the new Operation Safe Streets initiative, which involved FBI and state and local anticrime task forces all over the nation. It was an expansion of the task force we had created in Portland. The name had come from the Washington, D.C., Field Office, which was aggressive and innovative in using federal statutes to go after violent criminals in the nation's capital. Ever notice how the best ideas come from the field? They always do, in my book at least.

The biggest problem Safe Streets faced was getting past the Dr. Nos at headquarters. One executive told me that the Bureau could not do much about street crime because it was a "medical problem." To which I had replied, with my usual tact, "Yeah, when they shoot your ass, it becomes a medical problem. Well, I don't think we're prepared to tell the American public the FBI can't do anything about violent crime." We had done a pretty fair job in Portland. When I got back to the field, which I hoped would be soon, I intended to amaze him.

In the meantime, I had to take care of HQ business. By the ton.

I became a pretty fair speed reader. Somewhere in the great drifts of paper that settled onto my desk might be one or two reports I couldn't afford to miss. These described critically important matters requiring immediate action or contained the kind of thorough, insightful reporting essential to keep us ahead of new criminal threats. The rest of the stuff was make-work produced by the unwilling for the incompetent about the unnecessary. Field agents wrote voluminous reports full of details that were useful in solving and prosecuting crimes. But most of that minutiae was forwarded to HQ for the wrong reasons, as fodder for the seventh-floor gotcha games.

I got so I looked forward to the dog days of August. The city was built on top of a swamp, and in the summer, it remembers, especially in August, when it's like standing behind a bus in a steam bath. The whole federal city empties out. You can drive across the Potomac River bridges in lonely splendor. With all of Congress and most of the top Justice and FBI brass on vacation, you can get all kinds of really useful things done. You can have a second honeymoon. Take your wife to any restaurant in town with no reservations and no tie. Fire a cannon down Pennsylvania Avenue and not hit a single lawyer, a waste of a good cannonball.

Well, that part's a damn shame.

In August of 1992, though, all hell broke loose.

I woke up around four o'clock in the morning on August 21 with my neck hurting like a son of a bitch. It was all downhill from there.

The hot-knitting-needle stabs in my spine, which the doctor attributed to my habit of jumping out of helicopters with forty pounds of gear, were the least of it. We had to get up early because Debbie had to go in for a series of tests. She had been having severe abdominal cramps and bleeding, which she had ignored as she tried to comfort Jenny and Jessie, who were now panicked.

The man who had terrified Debbie and the girls before we went to Portland was now stalking the kids' soccer games. Often he came right up in front of Jenny and Jessie and snapped their pictures, never saying a word. To their great credit, they excelled at their sport despite him. We contacted local authorities, but they said they could do nothing because no violation of the law was involved. Never mind that he scared the wits out of our children, not to mention us.

Debbie refused to think about her own health. "We like to have a lot of stressful things going on all at once," she laughingly told friends. But the pain got worse. Her doctor didn't know what it was, but he was sure it wasn't just nerves. I made jokes all the way to the doctor's office. I couldn't let her see how I felt. She was braver than me. *God, if you're listening,* I prayed, *make her okay and I don't care if you twist my neck clean off.*

"Did you ever notice that ninety percent of your neck problems go away as soon as you leave headquarters?" Debbie observed. My doctor noticed the same phenomenon and advised me to relax.

Right. I'd relax as soon as I knew Debbie was going to be okay. And as soon as we got back to the field.

After the tests, I dropped Debbie back at the house and headed downtown to shovel the paper out of my in-box before it looked like a Montana blizzard. It was close to one-thirty in the afternoon by the time I got off the elevator on the fifth floor.

I should have known there was trouble the minute I saw Potts and Mike Kahoe, the chief of the violent crime section, boarding an elevator that was going up. That could mean only one thing: they had been summoned to the seventh floor.

"Did you guys get called up to the principal's office?" I cracked.

Larry didn't smile back, which was strange. No matter how bad things got, he had always managed a grin and a wink. Something really terrible must be going on.

"A deputy marshal has been killed in a shoot-out in Idaho," he said. "Come on up to Gow's office."

I dumped my jacket on my chair, grabbed a notebook, and headed for the elevator bank. As I walked into the office of Associate Deputy Director Douglas Gow, Potts and Kahoe were leaving.

"We're going to get SIOC set up," Larry said, referring to the Strategic Information and Operations Center, the HQ crisis command post. "The marshals are asking for help. They still have guys pinned down out there."

Gow was on the phone. He motioned me to a chair. In a moment or two, Henry Hudson, director of the U.S.

Marshals Service, arrived with two assistants. Hudson briefed us in a low, urgent voice.

A short time before, an unplanned encounter between six U.S. marshals and a federal fugitive in the Idaho panhandle had gone bad. Deputy Marshal Bill Degan had been shot dead in a gunfight with a former Green Beret sergeant and Christian Identity survivalist named Randy Weaver, who lived in a backwoods cabin in Boundary County, Idaho, about a hundred miles north of Spokane, Washington, and forty miles south of the Canadian border. Locals in nearby Naples (pop. 150) called the place Ruby Ridge.

3

The case against Randy Weaver, Hudson explained, had started off with a gun deal. In October 1989, Weaver had sold two sawed-off shotguns, which were illegal, to an ATF informant for $450. That didn't strike me as the crime of the century. Apparently, ATF agents Herb Byerly and Steve Gunderson didn't think so either, because they waited around until June 1990 and approached Weaver with a deal. They knew he had attended meetings at the Aryan Nations compound in Hayden Lake. If he informed on some suspected firearms-law violators who were hanging around Aryan Nations, they'd see he got off light on the shotgun case.

Like most Identity zealots, Weaver called the government ZOG and believed hell's most loathsome fiends
wore ATF badges, so, not surprisingly, he didn't play. In
December 1990, a grand jury in Boise indicted him for
making and possessing an unregistered firearm. On
January 17, 1991, a male-female ATF team posing as a
couple with a stalled car flagged down Weaver and his
wife, Vicki, near the road to their cabin. When Randy
got out to help, he was arrested. "Nice trick," Weaver
told the agents. "You'll never do that again."

After he was released on bond, Weaver didn't return
for a pretrial hearing on February 20. He holed up on
the mountain with Vicki, their children—Sara, sixteen, Sammy, fourteen, Rachel, ten, and Elisheba, ten
months—and Kevin Harris, a twenty-four-year-old
whom the Weavers treated as a foster son. Federal judge
Harold Ryan in Boise issued a warrant for his arrest, and
U.S. attorney Maurice Ellsworth had Weaver indicted
for failure to appear.

It fell to the U.S. Marshals Service to serve the arrest
warrant. Chief Deputy Ron Evans, the chief operating officer in the Idaho marshal's office, assigned the case to senior
deputy Dave Hunt. There was no way to sneak up on the
cabin, which Weaver had built as a stronghold against the
looters and pillagers of the Tribulation. It was on a rise, with
a 360-degree view of the surrounding forest. Randy and
Vicki, their three older children, and Harris went about
their daily chores with rifles in hand and pistols strapped to
their waists. "Weapons was a hobby, and my children
enjoyed weapons" was the way Weaver later explained the
family arsenal. Whenever a vehicle crunched along the
gravel and dirt road, everybody took defensive positions in
the rocky ledges overlooking the cabin.

There was a brief discussion of going up to the cabin under a white flag and trying to reason with Weaver, but chats with Weaver's friends and neighbors convinced the marshals that idea was too risky. Ed Torrence, whose property adjoined the Weaver spread, said Weaver had declared that if federal agents showed up on his property, "I'll take some with me." Another neighbor named Bill Grider quoted Weaver as saying, "If a man enters my property with a gun to do me harm, you can bet I'm going to shoot him to protect myself."

Grider agreed to be a go-between and deliver Hunt's letter asking Weaver to come in peacefully. The response was a letter signed by Randy, Vicki, Rachel, Sammy, and Sara declaring, "You are the servants of lawlessness and you enforce lawlessness. You are on the side of the One World Beastly Government. . . . Whether we live or whether we die, we will not obey your lawless government." That letter caused the marshals to wonder if Randy and Vicki Weaver were contemplating an apocalyptic fight to the death. Their fears that the Weavers were planning a suicide-by-cop, as our behavioral scientists call the phenomenon, were bolstered by a letter Vicki sent the U.S. attorney's office, in which she quoted the "Declaration of War" Robert Mathews had published just before he died at Whidbey Island. "Do you hear the approaching thunder? It is that of the awakened Saxon. War is upon the land. The tyrants [*sic*] blood will flow." Also, Frank Kumnick, a Weaver friend and leader of a local Aryan Nations church, told the marshals that the Weavers entertained "ideas of martyrdom." Evans was keenly sensitive to the martyrdom pitfall, having been in North Dakota when Gordon Kahl had embarked on his quest for immortality by killing two marshals.

Hunt tried negotiating with Weaver through friends and family but to no avail. Weaver was in no mood to talk. Besides, Hunt didn't have much to bargain with. Only the U.S. attorney's office could reduce charges. Ellsworth and Ron Howen, the line prosecutor in charge of Weaver's case, opposed any kind of deal. In fact, in October of 1991, Howen sent Evans and Hunt a letter over Ellsworth's signature ordering them to stop trying to negotiate with Weaver, on grounds Hunt was violating Justice Department ethics guidelines. This was a crock. Talking to a dangerous individual about surrender didn't violate any standard and made good sense. But the marshals didn't challenge Howen at that time.

Hunt hoped a hard winter on the mountain would drive the family into town, but it didn't. As spring approached, the pressure mounted on the marshals to do something about Randy Weaver, who was becoming an embarrassment. "Feds Have Fugitive 'Under Our Nose,'" said the *Spokesman Review* of Spokane. "Marshals Know He's There but Leave Fugitive Alone," *The New York Times* echoed. TV personality Geraldo Rivera sent a crew to Idaho, conferring something like folk-hero status on Weaver. Also, the Weavers' neighbors, a family by the name of Rau, were complaining that the Weavers were harassing them and if the marshals didn't do something about it, they would. At this point, the last thing the marshals needed was a shooting war on the mountain.

In February of 1992, Henry Hudson, the former U.S. attorney in northern Virginia, was sworn in as the new director of the U.S. Marshals Service. No sooner had he moved into his office than Mike Johnson, the U.S. Marshal for the state of Idaho, brought the Weaver case to him, calling it a "powder keg."

Hudson, a man of intellect and judgment, didn't have to be told anything twice, and unlike many people in Washington, he actually tried to solve problems instead of hoping they'd die of old age. He told Hunt to ignore Howen's directive and give negotiations another try. When that failed, Hudson called Ellsworth and pleaded with him to drop the charges, then reindict Weaver in a sealed indictment. The ploy, Hudson reasoned, would give the Weavers time to cool off and drop their guard. Weaver could be arrested whenever he came into town. Ellsworth refused, responding that the idea raised ethical problems. Then Hudson asked Ellsworth if he could talk to the judge directly, to explain how dangerous the arrest would be. Ellsworth and Howen opposed that idea, so Hudson backed off.

Hudson would never say "I told you so," but I will. If the prosecutors had listened to Henry Hudson, the armed standoff that has caused this country so much grief, in my view, would never have occurred. The course he proposed was just and prudent. The prosecutors should have paid attention to what he was saying. But then, they seldom do.

The only card Hudson had left to play was trickery. He told Evans and Hunt to work with Deputy Marshal Art Roderick, chief of the headquarters enforcement division domestic operations branch, to devise a way of trapping Weaver. They came up with a plan for an undercover sting that they called Northern Exposure after the popular television series about eccentric characters in the Alaskan outback. It was expensive, elaborate, and slow, but at that point, Hudson was willing to pay whatever it took to get Weaver off the mountain safe and sound. The marshals planned to buy a piece of property adjoining the Weavers' spread. Two deputies, male and female, would pose as a married couple clearing the land for a cabin. Sooner or later, so the thinking went, Weaver would be lulled into complacency and wander over for a visit—alone—at which point he could be handcuffed.

After Hudson gave the green light in April, the marshals spent the summer working out logistics for the sting, gathering intelligence, and conducting physical and video surveillances on Ruby Ridge. When Hudson's aides pulled out an aerial photo of the mountain, I could see that they weren't exaggerating about the difficulty of the terrain. Weaver knew what he was doing when he positioned that cabin.

On August 21, Hunt, Roderick, and four other deputy marshals—Bill Degan, Larry Cooper, Frank Norris, and Joe Thomas—drove out to Ruby Ridge in the early morning to conduct a reconnaissance around the periphery of the Weaver property.

Things spun out of control at about ten o'clock in the morning, just as the marshals completed their recon and were about to head down the trail to the Rau family house, where they had left their Jeep. Weaver's dog started barking and lit out for the marshals' position in the woods. The marshals started running down the mountain with the dog in pursuit, and Randy and Sammy Weaver and Kevin Harris close behind him.

Hudson said that one of the marshals killed the dog because it attacked him. The shot touched off an exchange of gunfire in which Degan was killed. Roderick, Cooper, and Norris stayed with Degan's body. Hunt and Thomas made their way down the mountain to the Rau house and called the Boundary County sheriff's office, which alerted the Idaho State Police Critical Response Team. Hudson said the CRT was on the way to rescue the three still on the mountain, but he feared they might still be pinned down by gunfire. He wanted us to deploy the HRT to make sure they got out and to arrest Weaver for Degan's murder.

As the marshals' briefing went on, something Delta Force commander Charlie Beckwith had told me kept flashing through my head: "Son, don't be afraid that your superiors will give you what appears to be an impossible mission. You and your boys will figure out a way to do it. Your greatest fear should be that you will be given a failed tactical mission from another unit. You will forever be tarred with the brush of their failure."

Charlie gave me a lot of advice in my life, and all of it was right on point. I wish he had been wrong about this one. The gunfight on Ruby Ridge was exactly what he meant. What had happened and why was not clear to me on August 21, and to this day a lot of questions have not been answered satisfactorily.

But I had no doubt about one thing. A nest of rattlesnakes had been stirred up, and a bunch of FBI agents were going to have to wade into the middle of them. Ruby Ridge was about as dangerous a mission as the CSA. Maybe worse, since this one started with a dead marshal. Jim Ellison had a bigger pile of weapons, but he hadn't committed a hanging crime and he wasn't an ex–Green Beret. I'd trained with Special Forces at Fort Bragg, and I knew the Green Berets to be the most efficient killing machines our tax dollars could produce. They specialize in operating against superior forces in rugged rural environments. There are none better at setting ambushes and at concealing themselves, and they're deadly with virtually any kind of weapon, including their bare hands. Hudson and his men believed that Weaver had explosives training and access to explosives. Some speculated that he had dug fortifications and spider holes, secret firing positions something like foxholes, all through his property.

"I'd like to go out on this one," I told Gow.

Gow looked at me as if I were crazy and shook his head. "You don't do that anymore."

But this is what I do, I protested silently. I'd run operations in the woods. I'd set up a damn fine perimeter around cabins many times. I'd negotiated successfully with a man whose brand of Identity was as irrational and aggressive as Weaver's. Dick Rogers, who had succeeded Woody Johnson as the HRT commander, had commanded a tank company in Vietnam, so he knew what it was to plunge into unfamiliar and treacherous terrain where hostile forces lurked. Floyd Clarke, who was now the FBI deputy director, had worked with Rogers closely in the field and had great confidence in him, especially after he commanded the successful rescue of ten prison guards at the federal prison at Talladega, Alabama, in August 1991. But Rogers hadn't been a SWAT or an HRT operator. He didn't bring the experience of a Woody Johnson to the job. He'd never been in the middle of a significant law enforcement operation against an armed fugitive in a rural environment. I thought it wasn't fair to him or the team to expect him to make up for all that with on-the-job training in the wilds of northern Idaho. But it was clear to me that Clarke and Gow weren't going to change their minds.

I went back to Potts's office just as he was calling

Rogers to order a full-scale HRT deployment. The team would fly to Spokane in two Air Force C-130s, then caravan to a forward command post near Ruby Ridge. Then Potts sent word to SOARU to assign a negotiator. Normally, the job would have gone to Clint Van Zandt, Quantico's lead negotiator at the time, but he had been sent to Florida on another case. Frederick Lanceley, chief of the crisis negotiation training unit, was deployed with the HRT. SWAT teams from Salt Lake City, Portland, Seattle, and Denver were dispatched to the scene. While the HRT formed a perimeter around the cabin, the SWAT teams would secure the rear and the roads near the cabin so that Weaver sympathizers couldn't get to the cabin or attack the HRT on its flanks.

I telephoned Gene Glenn, the SAC in Salt Lake City, who was about to board a flight to Idaho. As the senior FBI official in the region, he would be the on-scene commander for Ruby Ridge. I passed along the information Hudson and his men had given us and told him the danger was not to be underestimated. My opinion, based on what we knew about Weaver's behavior, was that he had more than a few loose wires. While people would commonly shoot a cop or an agent in the heat of passion, we seldom ran across people who would chase federal officers and murder them as they were fleeing. Also, most people who had just been in a firefight with law enforcement didn't stick around. So why was Weaver still in his cabin? Why hadn't he headed deeper into the woods? After all, the Canadian border was only forty miles away. An Identity believer who thought ZOG was in his backyard might very well attempt some sort of apocalyptic last stand, taking down as many of Satan's warriors as he could.

Green Beret strategy was to hit and move, stay in the woods, and create confusion. A good special ops man could keep it up for days. I warned Glenn to be on guard against an ambush near the bottom of the trail or even as the HRT operators were getting out of their trucks at the rear staging area. Randy Weaver knew his mountain by day and by night, and we didn't. He might even have called in reinforcements from the Identity or militia movement.

To underscore the extreme danger, Potts, with some help from me, drafted a set of rules of engagement for the HRT. We thought rules of engagement were needed because, contrary to what usually happens, we at HQ had a more complete threat assessment than the HRT or any other FBI personnel heading for the scene; we knew that Weaver and Harris had been the aggressors in the gun battle with the marshals and wouldn't hesitate to go on the offensive against the FBI. We wanted to make sure our people were told they could shoot to defend themselves or others. This sounds obvious, but in fact, some of them had been involved in standoffs in which they had been ordered not to shoot in the face of an immediate threat. In Utah in 1988, the HRT and several SWAT teams had surrounded the cabin of Adam Swapp, a heavily armed survivalist suspected of bombing a Mormon temple. Swapp and his confederates blasted away at the agents, who had been told to take cover but not to return fire, no matter what, for fear of hitting women or children in the cabin. None of our people was hurt, but a police officer was killed by a shot from a member of the Swapp household—a boy in a wheelchair, firing from a window.

Potts's rules for Ruby Ridge said that any armed adult

seen outside the Weaver cabin or on Ruby Ridge should be considered an immediate threat and could be the subject of deadly force. This language was written to refer to Randy Weaver, Vicki Weaver, Kevin Harris, and any allies who made the scene.

We placed a call via cell phone to Rogers, who had taken off about 6:30 P.M. en route to Idaho aboard the FBI Saberjet aircraft with his advance team—Steve McGavin, Les Hazen, and Dale F. Carnegie—and Duke Smith, the deputy director of the Marshals Service. Potts went over the rules of engagement with Rogers, then passed on additional intelligence that had come through HQ.

After Potts signed off, I headed down to the SIOC, the large, windowless room a few doors away from my office on the fifth floor. The submarine, we called it. I took the four-to-midnight shift. One of the CID unit chiefs would relieve me for the midnight-to-eight shift. Potts would take the day shift.

SIOC duty is the most dreaded job the Bureau has to offer. The person in charge of the shift has tremendous responsibility but little real authority. The FBI system is very much like the Navy's. The captain of the ship, not the admiral in the Pentagon, is in command. This crisis was two thousand miles and three time zones away. Sitting in the submarine, with no way to see or hear what was actually going on on the ground, and no way to catch the nuances from the conversations with the advance team, the marshals, the sheriff's office, and whoever else was around, all Potts, I, or anybody else at HQ could do was try to make sure the field commander followed Bureau policy and didn't make bad decisions. That is, if any of us at HQ knew that decisions were about to be made. More often than not, we didn't.

I called Debbie and told her not to wait up. "I'm going to be late. How're ya feeling?"

"I'm okay."

"That's good."

"I just want to find out what's wrong with me and get it fixed." This was as close as she ever came to saying out loud she was worried. Debbie usually wouldn't admit she wasn't feeling well if you held a gun to her head.

"I know. Me too. It'll work out. You'll be fine. See ya later."

This was one of those meaningless conversations married couples have to say they care. I tried to sound positive, though I was scared to death. The tests wouldn't be in for days. Waiting was torture, but there was nothing we could do about it.

Sometime that night, some marshals and HQ personnel showed up with surveillance videotapes they'd taken during the preparations for Northern Exposure. These corroborated source reports that the Weaver household was an armed camp. Randy, Kevin, and the older kids could be seen walking around the yard carrying guns. At one point in the tape they ran out of view of the camera. The marshals interpreted this to mean they had heard a car and were running to their fighting positions.

I didn't doubt what the marshals were saying about the danger posed by the family, but something didn't jibe. I looked at the videos several times and finally figured it out. It was the dog. The dog that Hudson said had attacked his men was bounding about the yard. He was a big yellow Labrador retriever, not much older than a puppy by the look of him.

After the marshals left, I told one of the agents manning the direct line to Idaho, "I want an autopsy on that dog." There was a little chill in the command post. I could sense people thinking, *Why does he care about the dog?* I told them I wanted the autopsy report for the homicide investigation we'd have to conduct concerning the circumstances of Bill Degan's death. We had to start fact-finding right then. Seldom do you get a second chance to gather forensic evidence, especially when you're dealing with a decomposing corpse.

I had another reason. I had raised and trained a lot of Labs and other dogs. Labs could be pretty protective, but they were not generally aggressive out in the open. They usually would not attack unless they were cornered, or unless they were protecting someone who was cornered. I couldn't imagine that young retriever actually attacking a marshal. I could see him barking and chasing a marshal, but not lunging like a Rottweiler or Doberman trained as a guard dog.

4

I left SIOC around two o'clock in the morning of Saturday the twenty-second, after we got word that the Idaho CRT had gotten to Roderick, Cooper, and Norris and were bringing them and Degan's body down the mountain. I fell into bed next to Debbie and crashed. The kids' laughter woke me up at about eleven o'clock. I mainlined a few cups of coffee and headed for HQ, arriving close to one o'clock in the afternoon.

Potts was running SIOC, but he was dead on his feet. He didn't share my philosophy about grabbing sleep when you could. He had worked in his office all night and had then taken over the day-shift SIOC command. Finally somebody convinced him to go home. I took the con.

Just before 7 P.M. I was handed a fax. It was an operations plan drafted by Rogers and the HRT and approved by on-scene commander Glenn. To put the plan into action, Glenn and Rogers needed a sign-off from Potts, or me.

As I read the fax, my jaw locked. *My God, we've got a problem,* I said to myself. *Well, this is just not going to happen.* I thought thoughts that would've earned me about a hundred letters of censure, the cleanest of which was, *These dumb shits. Have they got their heads up their ass or what?*

What I had in my hand didn't resemble anything that the HRT or any law enforcement agency should do. It was a military assault plan. The execution paragraph said the snipers would form a perimeter around the compound. Then two armored personnel carriers would roll forward and loudspeakers would be used to order the occupants to surrender. If the Weavers ignored the order for two days running, the ops plan said, "The APCs will begin dismantling the outlying buildings by ramming them. If no compliance, tear gas will be deployed into the main house." Then the HRT would assault the house, arrest the adults, and take control of the children.

This so-called plan violated every tenet of crisis management drummed into us at the FBI Academy. The first principle is "isolate, contain, and negotiate." Glenn's fax mentioned none of these things. The second principle is "play for time." String things out and let fatigue work for us; emotions on both sides have to have time to subside to let rational thought become possible. We never, never set deadlines for hostage takers because that only escalates the crisis. Only bad guys set deadlines.

I'd made a religion of these ideas, and so had our best crisis managers, men like Weldon Kennedy and Tony Daniels. Reading Glenn's fax, I realized that not everybody considered them values to live by. Glenn was an honorable man but a generalist thrown into the role of on-scene commander by virtue of geography. He hadn't been through the crisis management course, which was a shame. Under Webster, all SACs had to go through stressful tabletop training exercises, working through crisis scenarios with their SWAT teams, negotiators, legal advisers, and technical people. In the Sessions era, the Bureau fell away from that requirement; there were more in-service seminars about how to deal with the media than about handling armed standoffs.

Given Glenn's inexperience in these matters, I could see how he might have been overwhelmed by the well-oiled machine that is the HRT. At a crisis site, the team puts on a show of efficiency and discipline. Commanders are always looking to succeed, so they tend to give HRT recommendations great weight. While everybody else is scrambling around like sprayed bugs, the team is up and running with contingency plans, maps, sketches and diagrams, communications nets, electronic surveillance emplacements, and intel briefings. It's not that its members are knuckle-draggers spoiling for a fight. Because they know they may be thrown into a fight whether they like it or not, to survive they have to be prepared. Besides, as a group, tactical operators tend to be aggressive, fearless, and infectiously confident. Without this supreme self-assurance, they wouldn't have the gumption to enter a crisis site and engage an adversary in close-quarter battle. Anyone who watches the HRT operate can't help but believe that it will be totally successful. Even the most skillful negotiators suffer by comparison because they have to take a little time to sit back and size up the opposition. In the first hours of a crisis, they can seem irresolute. Their diffidence may cause an inexperienced commander to let things slide out of kilter and tilt toward the tactical people.

What really fried me was that somebody in the HRT had put this ops on paper in the first place. *They know better.* Had everything I'd said and done and stood for been lost on these guys? How many times had I said that a tactical assault is always the last, worst option, that every nonviolent, nonconfrontational alternative has to be thoroughly explored, no matter how long it takes? I understood the temptation to *do something.* Those of us in the tactical business tend to look at ourselves as a hammer and the rest of the world as a tack, but that's an impulse we have to resist in the interest of saving lives. What the plan boiled down to was this: we'd gas the place and rip it up until everybody inside was too hysterical to think straight, and then HRT operators would go into close-quarter battle with women and children. The agents would be reluctant to fire upon children, though the children would likely fire at them. Why hadn't the authors of this plan thought through to the likely conse-

quences of their proposed actions? I couldn't feel worse
if my own children had come up with some self-destruc-
tive scheme. I still thought of the HRT as my second
family.

I was actually somewhat relieved when I learned,
some months later, that Rogers had come up with the
plan without consulting the operators. Several of them
told me that, like me, they were stunned when they read
it. Most ops plans were worked out among the men, but
this had simply been given to them for implementation.
They confided to me that they had resolved among
themselves to walk off the mountain if they had been
ordered to go forward with this recipe for a massacre.

Another thing I didn't find out till much later was that
a poisonous dynamic had developed between Glenn and
Rogers on the one hand and negotiator Fred Lanceley,
who was excluded from the meeting in which Rogers
and Glenn put the finishing touches on the ops plan.
After that, Lanceley simply withdrew and kept his own
counsel.

Why didn't those of us in SIOC know any of this?
Nobody on the scene told us. We had what the military
calls an UNK-UNK—unknown-unknown—problem,
meaning we didn't know what we didn't know. The HRT
operators were too locked into the hierarchical HRT
command structure to think about back-channeling their
reservations, and Lanceley was too reticent. If I had it to
do over again, I'd make sure we at HQ had a way to find
out about dissenting views at the scene. I'd make sure
the negotiators had a persistent, obstinate spokesman
like Van Zandt as a counterweight to the tactical commander. Clint had never been shy about telling me when
I was about to make a bonehead move. I'd grumble that

HRT guys had to risk their lives to get their job done while the greatest risk that a negotiator faced was having a heart attack from too many doughnuts. But I always listened, and he was usually right.

Actually, if I could do it over again, I would have gone to Ruby Ridge myself, but you have to play the cards you're dealt. My cards put me in the submarine, two thousand miles from the command center, trying to figure out how to spike an incredibly dangerous ops plan by remote control. A string of short, sharp Anglo-Saxon words came to mind, but I'd have to save them for the next time I saw Debbie, who was a lot tougher than the headquarters weenies. Also, I didn't want to write anything down that would get Glenn even more rattled than he was. I gritted my teeth and faxed back what I hoped was a calm, measured response advising him that HQ was "not prepared to approve the plan as submitted."

"There is no mention of a negotiation strategy to secure release of individuals at the crisis point," I wrote. "There is no mention of any attempt to negotiate at all. SAC Salt Lake is requested to consider negotiation strategy and advise FBI HQ."

Later that night I received a fax from the command post in Idaho. It was the negotiations plan I had insisted upon. It had been written by Fred Lanceley, who had been brought into the loop to deal with my orders. Lanceley proposed to go up the mountain in an APC, tell Weaver that there were warrants for himself and Harris, and leave a field phone so they could continue to talk about how to end the standoff peaceably. Then Lanceley and the APC would withdraw.

I faxed back an immediate approval. At the same time, I pushed Glenn to move immediately to have HRT sniper-observer teams surround the cabin. Weaver had to be contained, or he could run around that mountain setting up ambushes and booby traps and wreaking all kinds of havoc.

Toward dusk, Rogers called to say the sniper teams were about to move in to set the perimeter. *It's about time,* I said to myself. At the same time, I was worried. "This is going to be the most dangerous part of the operation," I told the other agents in the command post. "If they're going to shoot at agents, it'll be now."

Later that night, I received a short message that an HRT helicopter conducting reconnaissance over the Weaver cabin had come under fire from the Weavers or Harris. An HRT sniper had returned fire at Randy Weaver and Kevin Harris, possibly wounding one or both.

5

A more detailed account came in the next day.

The sniper-observer teams got to their positions between 5:07 P.M. and 5:22 P.M. Idaho time. A mixture of rain and snow was falling, so they had to strain to see anything at all. Lon Horiuchi and Dale Monroe, sniper-observer team Sierra-4, who were on a ridge about six hundred feet from the cabin, saw a slight figure who was probably ten-year-old Rachel emerge from the cabin, then go inside. Then they saw a man come out on the porch, check some drying ponchos, and go back in.

At 5:58 P.M. the FBI helicopter took off for a reconnaissance run near the cabin. Inside were HRT pilot Frank Costanza, Dick Rogers, Deputy Marshals Service Director Duke Smith, and John Haynes, commander of the U.S. Marshals Service Special Operations Group and a veteran of the Atlanta prison riot.

As the helicopter clattered overhead, Randy and Sara Weaver and Kevin Harris, all armed with rifles, came out of the cabin and ran toward the rocky ledge. The snipers took this as a danger signal, having been briefed that previous surveillances had shown that the Weavers used the rocky outcropping as a defensive position against approaching vehicles.

The three ran behind the outbuilding known as the birthing shed and then came out into view. Horiuchi focused on one of the men—he could not make out who it was—who was carrying a rifle across his chest in the high-port position. Horiuchi thought he looked as if he were scanning the sky and preparing to shoot at the helicopter. Horiuchi fired. The man slid around behind the shed, out of Horiuchi's view. Horiuchi did not think he had hit him. He had, in fact, wounded Randy Weaver.

After ten or twenty seconds, all three people emerged from behind the shed. The first two—Randy and Sara—made a dash for the cabin. Randy ran through the door first, leaving Sara behind. Kevin Harris was a few steps behind them. Because of the poor visibility, Horiuchi thought this was the same man he had shot at before, the man he believed was threatening the helicopter. He decided to fire again before the man could reach the house. He reasoned that once the man was inside the house, he was in a protected position. The HRT snipers couldn't fire at anyone shooting out of the house, for fear of harming the children inside.

Horiuchi fired just as the man ran into the doorway. He thought he saw him flinch. Then he heard screaming and assumed he had hit the man.

A few minutes after that second shot, two armored personnel carriers lumbered up the hill. One dropped off a field phone about twenty yards from the cabin. Speaking through a bullhorn, Lanceley made his announcement. "Mr. Weaver, this is Fred Lanceley of the FBI. You should understand that we have warrants for the arrest of yourself and Mr. Harris. I would like you to accept a telephone so that we can talk and work out how you will come out of the house without further violence. I would like you or one of your children to come out of the house, unarmed, pick up the telephone, and return to the house."

There was no response.

The next morning—Sunday, August 23—Dick Rogers rode an armored personnel carrier up the hill and addressed the Weavers with a bullhorn. Nobody in the cabin responded. That evening, when there was still no word from the Weavers, Rogers prevailed upon Glenn and Bill Gore, the SAC from Seattle, who had arrived to help with command issues, to let him move the outbuildings to improve visibility and enhance the safety of the HRT operators if a tactical assault was ordered.

Before the APCs moved in, HRT operators swathed in body armor went into the buildings on foot, to make sure no one was inside. An operator entered the birthing shed and radioed, "There's a body in here." It was Sammy Weaver. The boy had been mortally wounded

during the gunfight with the marshals. The marshals told
us they had no idea he had been hit.

I felt sick. I think we all did. He had been an armed
and dangerous child, but still a child.

By now, agents in Idaho had debriefed the marshals
who had been on the disastrous reconnaissance. They
said that they had been well out of range of the cabin,
but the yellow Lab started barking and following the
scent of Roderick, Cooper, and Degan. They started
running down the mountain followed by the dog, Kevin
Harris, who was carrying a 30.06 rifle, Sammy Weaver,
with a Ruger Mini-14 rifle and a .357 Magnum, and
Randy Weaver, toting a shotgun and a nine-millimeter
pistol.

Upon reaching a fork in the trails known as the Y, the
three marshals took cover in the bush. As Sammy
Weaver and Kevin Harris ran into the Y, Bill Degan rose
up slightly, pointed his weapon at them, and called out,
"Stop. U.S. marshals." Cooper said he saw Kevin Harris
wheel around and shoot Degan in the chest. As Harris
raised his gun to shoot a second time, Cooper said he
fired a three-round burst, which he thought had hit
Harris, who disappeared into the bush.

Then, Cooper said, he heard two shots to his right,
near Roderick's position. He saw Sammy Weaver in the
Y, yelling, "You son of a bitch." Then Sammy faded into
the brush. "Coop, I need you," Degan shouted. As
Cooper moved toward his friend, he heard bullets
whizzing past him from the right side of the Y, where he
had last seen Randy Weaver. Desperate to clear a path to
Degan, he fired a second three-round burst in the direction of the incoming fire, assuming he was shooting at
Weaver. He didn't actually see Randy Weaver at this

point, but he said that after he fired his second burst, he spotted Sammy Weaver retreating toward the compound. Cooper knelt beside Degan, who was gurgling and barely conscious. He threw off his pack and placed his fingers to Degan's neck, searching for a pulse. The downed man's heart was beating weakly. Then it stopped.

Roderick, a short distance away, didn't see Kevin Harris shoot Degan but heard the shot. He said he saw the dog turn toward the gunfire, then look back at him; fearing the dog would draw the Weavers and Harris to his position, he shot him in the back. As he dived into the woods for cover, he heard heavy gunfire and Cooper radioing for help. Roderick radioed Hunt, Thomas, and Norris, who was a medic, then jumped into the path to try to get to Cooper and Degan. He felt something pass over his abdomen, looked down, and discovered a bullet hole in his shirt.

From the direction of the cabin, the marshals heard an explosion of gunfire, a woman wailing, "Yahweh," a man cursing, and a child's voice screaming, "You tried to kill my daddy." The marshals assumed the commotion was over Kevin Harris. Now we knew it was Vicki and Randy grieving over the death of their son.

Hearing the gunfire, the marshals thought they were still under fire from the Weaver clan. Roderick, Cooper, and Norris decided to stay with Degan's body while Hunt and Thomas pressed on to the Rau cabin to call for help. Fearing ambush by the Weavers, the Idaho State Police CRT waited till nightfall to extricate the three marshals hunkered down at the Y. It was a chilly, moonless night, with a cold front moving in. Since only two men had night-vision equipment, they walked slowly, making a human chain with their arms. Every few feet, they looked for booby traps and signs of ambush. They reached the Y at 11:21 P.M. Bearing Degan's body, they snaked down the trail again and were off the mountain just before one o'clock in the morning.

The debriefing cleared up something that had been puzzling me from the start. Hudson had told us the marshals shot the dog because he attacked them, but that story didn't square with the autopsy report that had found the dog had been shot in the anus. As the marshals on the scene told the story, the first shot was fired by Harris and it hit Degan. Cooper fired at Harris. Roderick shot the dog to keep him from leading Weaver to his hiding place in the bush. It wasn't that I thought Hudson had intentionally misled us. The pandemonium that breaks out in the first moments of a law enforcement crisis is no different from the fog of war. Hudson was a victim of that initial confusion, as were we all.

As I drove home in the early-morning hours of August 24, I tried to put myself in Randy Weaver's shoes. I was feeling a lot more empathy for him than I had in the first hours of the crisis. Here was a guy holed up on the mountain, waiting for the Tribulation, charged with what I believed to be a thoroughly insignificant offense. He was arrested by the ATF in front of his wife. He was pressured to become a government informant. A bunch of guys in camouflage showed up and killed the family dog in front of his son. There was a firefight in which his only son was killed. I didn't doubt the marshals' assertion that Kevin Harris had fired the first shot, but it was entirely possible that Sammy Weaver had fired after he saw the dog shot in the back. Randy Weaver had done some terrible things, broken some laws, indoctrinated

his children to believe that God wanted them to hate
and fear.

But what had started this crazy business? A lousy ATF
case involving two guns that had nothing to do with
crime in the United States. A bench warrant for nonap-
pearance. What was the point? At the same time that we
were trying to find more FBI agents to send into high-
crime areas to reclaim our streets, we had a federal
agency chasing after a mountain man who had produced
a couple of sawed-off shotguns.

This guy is just a poor soul, I said to myself. *Surely we
can offer him some kind of deal to get him to come in.*

That night or the next day, Glenn submitted
another proposal to assault the cabin, on the premise
that the children had to be protected from their
mother. This idea was apparently based on a profile of
Vicki Weaver submitted by Van Zandt, who was back
at SOARU. Van Zandt urged the use of third parties
instead of government negotiators, suggested that the
family's resolve would actually be hardened by aggressive HRT tactics, and speculated that Vicki Weaver
might kill her daughters and herself if she felt the government was closing in on her. Clint told me later he
was trying to argue for backing off to give the Weavers
some breathing room, but Glenn apparently seized on
his speculation about murder-suicide to revive the
assault option.

I rejected the new assault plan, writing a memo that
said pointedly, "What kind of documentation exists to
support that conclusion? . . . You should constantly monitor your technical coverage [eavesdropping devices hidden in or near the cabin] to determine if the SOARU
assessment [predicting suicidal tendencies] is valid and

to update your option planning. . . . Have close friends and family of Vickie [sic] and Randy been interviewed to determine their attitude regarding the children? Is the assessment of SOARU [Van Zandt] based on FBI data and interviews?"

At the bottom of the memo, I scribbled some points that I hoped would help Lanceley and the other negotiators extend the olive branch to Randy and Vicki Weaver:

> Something to consider
> 1. Charge against Weaver is Bull S. . . .
> 2. No one saw Weaver do any shooting.
> 3. Vicki has no charges against her.
> 4. Weaver's defense. He ran down the hill to see what dog was barking at.
> Some guys in camys [sic] shot his dog. Started shooting at him. Killed his son. Harris did the shooting. He is in pretty strong legal position.

For the next days, no one stirred outside the cabin. Lanceley, Rogers, and others went up and down the hill in the APCs, calling out with the bullhorn, asking to speak to Vicki Weaver, who was considered the family's anchor.

Autopsy photographs of Sammy were brought to my office. I locked the door and sat in a chair and looked at them. Sammy was really little more than a baby. I could not help but think of our own children. Why had his father sent him to war on the government? What could we have done to prevent this?

On August 26, the HRT decided to send a robot up to the cabin with a field phone for Weaver to use for negotiations. Incredibly, no one had remembered to remove the twelve-gauge shotgun that was attached to the robot. The function of the shotgun was to disrupt an explosive device by blowing apart its electronic system or to blow the lock off a door. It was not meant to be used against people. Why hadn't the HRT detached it before sending the robot up the hill? Sheer carelessness is all I can figure. Understandably, Weaver refused to approach the robot or to touch the phone. Instead, he screamed to the HRT agents, "Get the fuck out of here."

The breakthrough came on Friday, August 28. Weaver shouted that he would like to talk to Bo Gritz. Gritz was a former Green Beret who had become a leading spokesman for the militia and survivalist movements and was running for president on the antigovernment ticket in 1992. As it happened, Gritz had showed up among the crowd outside the Ruby Ridge command post to announce that he had drawn up a warrant for the "citizen's arrest" of Gene Glenn, William Sessions, Henry Hudson, and Governor Cecil Andrus of Idaho.

Glenn asked SIOC to approve using Gritz. We okayed the idea in a heartbeat. If Randy Weaver admired Bo Gritz the way Jim Ellison looked up to Robert Millar, we might have found the way in.

Gritz approached the cabin window around dusk. When he asked if everyone inside was okay, Weaver said, "No. My wife was shot and killed last Saturday."

It turned out that Lon Horiuchi's shot at Kevin Harris had pierced the wooden door and crashed into the face of Vicki Weaver, who had been leaning out of the cabin, holding the door open from the other side and beckoning the three to get inside. She died almost instantly as the round passed through her carotid artery and vein, causing massive blood loss. The round exited the other side of her head and struck Harris in the arm.

Gritz was taken aback, but he talked for a half hour or so, then said good-bye, found Dick Rogers, and told him about Vicki. She died, Weaver said, with baby Elisheba on one hip and a .380 semiautomatic pistol on the other. Rogers sent word to Glenn in the command trailer.

When word of Vicki Weaver's death reached the submarine, there was a terse announcement, then a hush. The news hit me like a ton of bricks. This entire operation was snakebit. But even though the original charges were nonsense, I still couldn't understand why Weaver was putting his family in harm's way. Most rational men will do everything in their power to keep their families safe. If he wanted to go to war with the government, why did he have to involve his entire family? There was no need for this. We had to find a way to get the rest of them out.

Over the weekend, Bo Gritz went back to the cabin several times, accompanied by Jackie Brown, a Weaver family friend, and Jack McLamb, a retired Phoenix policeman and militia leader who was helping Gritz with his presidential campaign. Between the three of them, by midmorning on Sunday, August 30, they convinced Kevin Harris to come out.

Gritz and Jackie Brown talked Randy into letting them take Vicki's body down the mountain. Weaver still refused to come out, insisting that he and the girls would be killed. But things were looking up. Gritz, garrulous and over-the-top, seemed to be pulling Weaver out of his stupor, and McLamb's reassuring manner calmed the Weaver girls.

When I walked into Potts's office that afternoon, he was on the phone with Glenn and Robin Montgomery, the SAC from Portland, who had flown in to help Glenn manage the crisis. They were forwarding yet another proposal to inject tear gas into the cabin. They said they believed the negotiations were at a standstill and they wanted to bring the situation to an end.

I couldn't believe it. We'd made so much progress. We'd started with blood on the ground and passions roaring. Now the violence had ceased. We had a guy who had established a dialogue and who could come and go from the cabin at will. We had come miles down the road. And they wanted to gas the cabin.

I lunged for Larry's speakerphone so fast I almost got whiplash. "This doesn't make any sense," I snapped. "Why do you want to do this if you have a possibility of getting them out? Besides, they have gas masks."

"Gritz didn't see any" was the reply.

"I don't care if he saw them or not," I said. "Every survivalist has a gas mask. Mathews had them. Pierce had them. The CSA had a million of them. It's a rite of passage. You go out and get a gun and then you get a gas mask. They are going to have gas masks. The only one we'd gas would be the baby. You've got the guy he admires most in the world in there. You throw tear gas in there, and it'll be a disaster. They're gonna come out shooting, and we're going to shoot a man with three little girls. Well, we're not going to do this."

Potts agreed. The cabin would not be gassed.

On Monday morning, August 31, Gritz and McLamb went back into the cabin. Gritz had two things to put on the table. Ellsworth and Howen had agreed to let Weaver tell his side of the story to a grand jury. Gerry

Spence, the flamboyant Wyoming defense lawyer, would represent him. By the middle of the day, Weaver had agreed to surrender.

The news of the surrender came as a relief but brought no joy. A marshal, a boy, and a woman had lost their lives over two sawed-off shotguns.

6

The HRT C-130s lumbered home to Andrews. The aerial photos and maps came down from the SIOC walls. The Weavers and Vicki's folks, the Jordisons, buried their dead. It could have been worse, I told myself. If anybody had green-lighted any one of those tactical assault plans, we'd be going to a whole bunch of funerals.

I went back down the hall to my office and to my day job and attacked the mountain on my in-box.

At least it was over.

I had no idea.

Henry Hudson and the marshals wanted to see Randy Weaver and Kevin Harris charged with the murder of a federal officer, Deputy Marshal William Degan. So did we.

Ellsworth and Howen had more ambitious ideas. The Boise prosecutors, especially Howen, who had prosecuted a number of people associated with the Aryan

Nations, wanted to portray Randy Weaver as a key player in a terror underground of white hate cells popping up all across the Northwest.

Howen drafted a sweeping conspiracy indictment that accused Randy Weaver, Kevin Harris, and the late Vicki Weaver of having plotted since 1983 to lure government forces into an apocalyptic battle. The indictment would assert that the Weavers' 1983 move from Iowa to Idaho, and just about everything they had done since, had been part of this calculated plan to provoke a firefight. The indictment's list of particulars, known in legalese as "overt acts in furtherance of the conspiracy," included such sinister things as building "a remote mountain residence/stronghold"—really just a sad little shack—swiping the Rau family's water tank, and destroying surveillance cameras hidden in the woods by the marshals.

Hudson was appalled. He had spent twenty years as a prosecutor before President Bush tapped him to run the Marshals Service, and he liked to keep his cases direct and to the point. "The more you put into an indictment," he said, "the more you have to prove."

He spent a long Sunday afternoon pleading with the Idaho prosecutors to concentrate on bringing Bill Degan's killers to justice. "This is a homicide case pure and simple," he argued. "To try to elevate it into a major white supremacy case does nothing but cloud the issue."

The reaction in the Bureau was unanimous, from case agents Joe Venkus and Gregory Rampton in Boise to everybody in the Criminal Investigations Division at HQ. None of us believed that a guy who eked out a living cutting timber had the cunning, patience, or foresight to concoct an elaborate, long-running conspiracy. He had met with other ideological extremists at the Aryan Nations, but last time I checked, freedom of association was still in the Constitution.

The indictment wasn't even factually accurate. It accused the Weavers and Harris of firing at the helicopter carrying Geraldo Rivera's TV crew, yet there was precious little evidence to back up this claim. Even sloppier, or more cynical, was the charge that Randy Weaver, Kevin Harris, "and an unidentified female, probably Vicki or Sara Weaver," had tried to shoot at an FBI helicopter. There was no "probably" about the identity of the female seen in the yard—all the FBI snipers on the perimeter said it was sixteen-year-old Sara, not her mother. No one on the ground thought Vicki Weaver had taken a shot at the helicopter.

A Justice Department report would later describe the overstatements and misstatements in the indictment as "the result of overzealousness, or perhaps poor judgment, but not malice, on the part of the prosecution." As far as I was concerned, absence of malice was no excuse for a government presentation that anybody with common sense would regard as shoddy and vindictive. By its words, the U.S. attorney's office confirmed what Weaver's lawyer, Gerry Spence, had been saying—that the government was determined to demonize a white supremacist for exercising his Constitutional rights to hold unpopular beliefs.

"This is the most outrageously absurd theory of a prosecution I've ever heard," I told Potts. "Weaver is already in a pretty strong legal position. Any decent lawyer will turn this case into toast."

Potts nodded. We actually knew more about Weaver

than would be admissible in court, and we did not believe there was any conspiracy. If we didn't believe the conspiracy theory, and the marshals didn't believe it, even though they had lost a man, how were the prosecutors going to get a jury to believe it?

Potts called main Justice and got us in to see Mark Richard, the deputy assistant attorney general in the Criminal Division, and Jim Reynolds, chief of the section in charge of terrorism-case prosecutions.

"We have an obligation to charge a man with a crime he committed and not to charge him with a conspiracy that exists only in the minds of the prosecutors," I said. "Because you're charging him with something he didn't do and the jury won't buy it, the assaulting-a-federal-officer charge will be rejected too. They'll lose the whole thing."

We got nowhere. Richard and Reynolds acknowledged they had some qualms about the scope of the case but insisted that they could not overrule a U.S. attorney. The conspiracy indictment was handed down by the Boise grand jury on October 1, 1992.

Then Ellsworth and his aides really piled it on. They announced they intended to seek the death penalty. This decision gave main Justice another shot at the case, since under the policy of the department, a U.S. attorney could not seek capital punishment without the express written permission of the Attorney General.

Again, Justice officials bowed to Ellsworth's wishes. I did not believe the death penalty was appropriate in this case, since the Supreme Court had ruled it should be reserved for aggravated murder cases, where there was a clear-cut case of premeditation, for instance, or heinous acts such as torture. Besides, how would a jury of

Montanans feel about a government that proposed to orphan three young girls, one an infant, after having killed their mother by accident?

But Potts and I didn't slug it out at the department. Once the conspiracy count was in the case, we figured Weaver's chances of acquittal were about 99 percent.

7

Over Christmas of 1992, the doctors, and now there were a bunch of them, pronounced themselves baffled by Debbie's condition. Finally she was ordered into the hospital for a biopsy. They wanted to see if she had ovarian cancer. They said there was a good chance it was nothing to be alarmed about. They just had to check it out.

Right. I was alarmed. Debbie was a rock, as usual. I kept up the jokes and acted as if I were absolutely sure that cancer was not in the picture, to keep her from knowing how scared I was.

They operated after Christmas and removed a tumor on her ovary. We got the word three days later. It was benign.

"See, I told you it would be okay," I told her. "I knew all along." Boy, was I full of it, but I sure had hoped.

Larry Potts had been going through hell too. His little girl had been hospitalized with a mysterious ailment that was attacking her joints and kidneys. Eventually, they narrowed the diagnosis down to an extremely rare autoimmune disorder that could have been touched off by anything from an extreme allergic reaction to an unidentified virus. All they could do was give her massive doses of cortisone and pray.

Days at headquarters, meanwhile, were about like the inside of a pinball machine. The place was in an uproar about Director Sessions, a former federal judge from San Antonio who had been plucked from obscurity by former Attorney General Ed Meese and who was now self-destructing. On January 15, 1993, Attorney General William Barr, as his last act in office, had released a scathing report produced by the Justice Office of Professional Responsibility. The director was charged with abusing the perks of his office by forcing his security men to run errands for himself and his wife, concocting business meetings to justify their personal travel on the FBI jet, misusing his chauffeured limousine, and billing the Bureau $10,000 for a fence at his home.

Sessions would be fired by President Clinton—but not for six nerve-racking months. He would be replaced by Louis Freeh, a forty-three-year-old federal judge in New York who had built an impressive reputation as a relentless adversary of organized crime, first as an FBI agent and later as a federal prosecutor with the prestigious Southern District of New York. I played a bit part in Freeh's selection: I mentioned his name to Michael Bromwich, my old friend from the Iran-Contra case. I told Bromwich that Freeh was a guy who should be considered, especially since the Senate seemed to like federal judges as prospective FBI directors. Bromwich dropped Freeh's name to a White House official. Little did I dream that my fate would become entwined with his for years to come.

On February 26, 1993, Middle Eastern terrorism reached our shores. Shortly after noon that day, a truck containing a low-tech urea nitrate fertilizer bomb went off in the parking garage of the World Trade Center, killing six people and injuring more than a thousand. We threw nearly every agent on the East Coast into the fray. Four of the bombers, expatriate Muslim extremists, were arrested within weeks. Agents in our New York office determined that the mastermind was Ramzi Yousef, a fanatical Jihad warrior who traveled on an Iraqi passport and had trained in explosives with the Afghan guerrillas. We put him on the Ten Most Wanted list and posted a $2-million reward for him. Two years later, an acquaintance enticed by the reward led U.S. and Pakistani authorities to Yousef's hideout in Islamabad. The Bureau's work on the World Trade Center investigation saved untold thousands of lives, because by the time he was caught, Yousef was linked to Osama bin Laden, a Saudi multimillionaire who underwrote radical Muslim terrorist cells all over the world. Yousef's laptop computer contained plans to blow up a dozen U.S. airliners simultaneously.

The agents who solved the World Trade Center case and neutralized the terrorist cells behind it didn't receive the recognition they deserved because the biggest catastrophe in FBI history was building on the Texas prairie, like one of those twisters that starts out as a cloud the size of your hand.

8

130 NO HEROES

On February 28, two days after the World Trade Center bombing, Dana Caro, my old boss at the Washington Field Office, and his wife, Eunice, dropped by for coffee and some leisurely Bureau gossip. I was in the kitchen getting cups when Dana called out, "Danny, you better come see this. It's awful." He had flicked on the television in the family room to catch the afternoon sports scores, only to light on a special news bulletin displaying a scene of carnage.

An ATF agent, dressed in a raid jacket, froze in a half-crouch as bullets exploded out of the roof beneath his feet. Another agent scrambled down a ladder in a rain of automatic-weapons fire. Others could be seen dragging their dead and wounded out of the kill zone. The news anchor said there had been a shoot-out between the ATF and a heavily armed apocalyptic cult who lived in a commune named Mount Carmel, on the plains a few miles out of Waco. The congregation, called the Branch Davidians, was a splinter off the Seventh Day Adventists. Its leader was a onetime rock musician who had changed his name from Vernon Wayne Howell to David Koresh. ATF suspected the cult of illegally stockpiling machine guns and explosives in anticipation of the battle of Armageddon.

Dana shook his head in consternation. "What the hell did they run into?"

"I don't know, but it was brutal," I said, leaning forward to try to see if I could spot my old friend Bill Buford from the Little Rock ATF office. "There's one thing for certain, if this was a planned operation, I'm sure Buford will be in the thick of it. I hope he's okay."

"Guess you'll be going in to work soon," Debbie said.

"The FBI will be called into this thing, you know," Dana agreed. "They always call us." He had retired a few years before, but for old FBI agents it's forever "us."

The phone rang. Debbie answered. "Told you so. It's SIOC."

It was Beverly, the SIOC technician who had been at my right hand during the Ruby Ridge crisis. "There's a situation in Waco. Mr. Potts wants you in the office right away."

I grabbed my keys and my windbreaker, gave Eunice Caro a hug and Dana a slap on the back, pecked Debbie on the cheek, and did the old "I'll call you" shuffle. I could feel Dana's eyes on me. He wished he were getting into that FBI car with me.

On the drive into the city, I listened to the radio bulletins from the scene. Around 9:30 A.M., seventy-six ATF agents seeking to serve a warrant for automatic weapons, explosives, and other illegal armaments had pulled up to the Branch Davidian compound in cattle trailers. As they ran toward the compound, they were sprayed with thousands of rounds that came right through the doors, walls, and roof. The Davidians even threw grenades at medics trying to get to the downed agents. The agents returned fire whenever they saw a Davidian with a weapon, but because children and other innocents were inside, they didn't fire blindly through closed doors and walls. Four ATF agents—Steven D. Willis, Robert J. Williams, Conway LeBleu, and Todd McKeehan—were killed. Twenty others were seriously injured. ATF agents killed two people and wounded four others, including

Koresh. Two cult members were shot at close range, evidently executed by other cultists.

My thoughts returned to Charlie Beckwith. Here we go again, getting sent in to deal with another agency's mess. The prairie was soaked in blood, and now we were supposed to bring peace to a war zone.

By the time I pulled in at HQ, Potts was in the office and had lined up a crisis management and negotiations team. This time it was apparent from the start that a tactical solution was out of the question. Jeff Jamar, the SAC in San Antonio, was on his way to Waco to serve as on-scene commander. Jamar was well regarded as a field commander. Three other solid SACs—Bob Ricks from Oklahoma City, Dick Swensen from New Orleans, and Dick Schwein from El Paso—would back him up in the command center. Negotiations would be coordinated by Gary Noesner, a senior hostage negotiations specialist based at Quantico.

One seasoned negotiator was already in Waco. Byron Sage, who ran our Austin office, had driven there as soon as the news broke on the radio. He relieved Lieutenant Larry Lynch of the McLennan County Sheriff's Department and ATF agent Jim Cavanaugh, who had been on the phone since the shooting started, negotiating a cease-fire with Koresh. Dick Rogers and the HRT advance team had taken off for Texas.

I settled into the submarine and started reviewing news footage of the gun battle. Sure enough, Bill Buford had been right in the middle of it. He was badly hurt, but doctors at the local hospital thought he would live. He had been leading a team up ladders and onto the second-floor roof when rounds from an M16 and an AK-47 ripped into his legs and hip. He fell off the roof, breaking several ribs. As he lay bleeding and helpless, the Davidians had strafed the ground around his head with machine-gun fire. An ATF medic had thrown his body across him and protected him for nearly two hours until the cease-fire took effect.

My heart ached for Buford. Not because of his wounds—he would survive those. His body was as tough as an old bobcat's. What you never get over is losing your men. Three of the young agents killed—LeBleu, McKeehan, and Williams—were on Buford's twelve-man team, and three other members of the same team were wounded.

I've always believed you make your own luck. The U.S. government did just that at Waco. As just about everybody on the planet now knows, it was nearly all bad.

The more I found out about the ATF raid, the more outraged I was that anyone in authority had signed off on it. ATF's own affidavits, filed in support of the search warrant that provided legal justification for the raid, estimated that the cult had spent nearly $200,000 on weapons and ammunition in the past year and a half. The arsenal held nearly three hundred assault rifles, many of them converted to machine guns, and hundreds of thousands of rounds of ammunition. A United Parcel Service deliveryman said he had delivered to Koresh two cases of "pineapple-type" hand grenades and black gunpowder. Another source claimed the Davidians were trying to make a radio-controlled aircraft to carry explosives. Most fearsome of all were two fifty-caliber Barrett rifles, whose half-inch-diameter rounds could penetrate a truck. Positioned at the U.S. Capitol, a Barrett could rain effective fire on the White House.

The discovering-the-obvious award had to go to an ATF spokeswoman in Texas who told reporters after the failed raid, "The problem we had is we were outgunned. They had bigger firearms than we had."

Well, yes, but they knew that going in. ATF's entire rationale for the raid was the cult's firepower. ATF officials said they suspected that Koresh and his male followers, whom he called the "mighty men," were going to drive into town and shoot up some public place like a restaurant, provoking a showdown with law enforcement authorities.

ATF officials also knew that Koresh was waiting for them. ATF undercover agent Robert Rodriguez, who had been posing as a neighbor and prospective convert, was visiting Koresh about forty minutes before the raid when a cult member rushed in to say he had encountered a local TV cameraman out on the road. The KWTX crew had been tipped to an impending bust and was looking for the compound to film it. "Neither the ATF nor the National Guard will ever get me," Koresh told Rodriguez. "They got me once and they'll never get me again."

Then he gazed out the window and repeated, "They're coming, Robert, the time has come."

Which, from his point of view, might not be a bad thing. David Koresh claimed that he was the new Messiah, Jesus Christ come back to earth to usher the chosen through death's door. He had recently prophesied that the beginning of the end would come before Passover of 1993. Who could doubt his divinity now, with hordes of black-clad raiders descending upon the plain?

Rodriguez had rushed to warn the senior ATF managers on the ground—Philip Chojnacki, the Houston SAC, Chuck Sarabyn, his ASAC, and Ted Royster, the Dallas SAC—but they had brushed him off because, as they later explained, Rodriguez had not actually seen the Davidians breaking out arms.

"The element of surprise does not mean they don't know you're coming. Only that they can't take control," said ATF intelligence chief David Troy.

I don't pretend to understand what Troy was trying to say, but for my money, if you have time to get a rifle into your hands and draw a bead, you've got control. Over the fifty-one days of the siege, it would become very clear who was in control at Waco, and it wasn't the U.S. government.

ATF officials insisted that they had to assault the compound because Koresh never left it. Furthermore, they said they wanted to raid the compound rather than pick Koresh off outside because they wanted to separate the cult from its arsenal. I wasn't convinced either premise was sound. ATF had assigned eight agents to live in an undercover house near Mount Carmel but they didn't conduct the kind of intense, twenty-four-hour surveillance necessary to determine Koresh's habits. Adequate surveillance logs weren't maintained, and no one even had a good photograph of Koresh. Jeff Jamar obtained the first photo of him from his Texas driver's license after the FBI took control. As for the second point, I didn't think the intelligence supported the assumption that the cult was as dangerous without Koresh as with him.

If I had gotten the ticket to arrest Koresh, I would have done exactly what I had done at the CSA. I would have sent Horace Mewborn and an intelligence group to

Waco to develop as much information as possible about Koresh's daily movements. I would have set up round-the-clock surveillance using cameras and aircraft and ground personnel and technical equipment. The FBI special operations group surveillance team would have been posted near all entrances to the compound. We would have established a covert command post that would keep twenty-four-hour-a-day contact with all of the activities of the agents. Everything we learned from the surveillance and interviews of police and former members would be digested into daily intel summaries. Surveillance might have determined that he was vulnerable when he went to the video store, to get ice cream, or to visit the Mag Bag, where he stored arms. In that case, I would have used an HRT assault team to plan a mobile ambush to arrest Koresh. If he showed no signs of leaving the compound for weeks on end, I would have waited. If we got Koresh but his followers barricaded themselves in the compound, we'd form a perimeter of HRT sniper-observers and negotiate. With Koresh out of the way, the chances of getting the other Davidians to walk out would have been much greater. At least we would have given our negotiators something to work with. They could have offered the hope that if everybody behaved, they would soon be reunited with their Messiah.

As things now stood, what leverage did our negotiators have? None. After the raid and the deaths of the ATF agents, we had nothing to put on the table. Koresh had two choices. He could lead his people out and go to prison, where he would probably be brutalized by other inmates and then go to trial for capital murder in a state that executes murderers.

Or he could stay in the compound and be God.

9

For the first three days, we had hope. On the morning of February 28, during his first conversations with negotiators, Koresh disclosed that he had been shot in the hip and left wrist. The negotiators offered him medical assistance, which he refused. We hoped that time and fear of infection would wear him down. At 2:29 P.M. Koresh said he would send out the children and end the confrontation if he was allowed to broadcast his religious views. The negotiators agreed. Koresh's message went out on Dallas station KRLD at four o'clock in the afternoon and was rebroadcast several times later in the day. That night, Koresh sent four children out.

At about eight o'clock the next morning, March 1, President Clinton, briefed by acting Attorney General Stuart Gerson, said he understood the FBI would negotiate an end to the standoff and that he should be advised if the Bureau wanted to escalate to an assault. ATF officials had been reluctant to relinquish control of the case but were overruled by Treasury officials, who handed formal responsibility for resolving the crisis to the FBI at about 9:30 A.M. The full HRT was on the ground by close to noon.

Jeff Jamar and Potts issued rules of engagement that were the standard deadly force policy, period. The HRT was told to avoid getting into a situation where a shoot/don't-shoot decision had to be made. Throughout the fifty-one days of the siege, not a single FBI weapon was discharged. The strategy was by the book: keep the negotiators talking to Koresh, use the HRT to set a perimeter, have behavioral specialists and intelligence people find out as much as possible about the beliefs and fears that drove Koresh and his congregation. FBI agents would eventually find and interview nearly every former Davidian in the world.

Still, as Marine commandant P. X. Kelley once said, life is full of lousy choices. We would make plenty of them before the siege was resolved. The first, on March 1, was to bring in armored vehicles. I hated the very idea. I felt strongly that whenever you use military equipment, the signal you send to the American people is that you are making war on U.S. citizens. On the other hand, the HRT operators had to be shielded if they were to work their way toward the compound's walls. The Davidians stood sentry in a tower that had a 360-degree view of the prairie. They had night-vision scopes and their fifty-caliber guns could blast apart any vehicle we had. We could not responsibly send our people within striking distance of them, not without armor.

We asked the Army for nine Bradley fighting vehicles, configured without gun barrels. HRT operators started driving them around the compound shortly before five o'clock that afternoon. The sight enraged Koresh, who told negotiators he was going to blow the Bradleys "forty to fifty feet in the air." We weren't sure he couldn't make good on his threat. God knows lots of LAW rockets and Soviet-designed rocket-propelled grenade launchers were on the black market. We went back to the Army for two Abrams tanks and five combat-engineer vehicles that could withstand a direct hit by most hand-held rockets. There was no debate about the necessity of using these vehicles. We had to insure the safety of our agents.

By the end of the day, the negotiators had spent seven hours on the phone with Koresh, his top lieutenant Steve Schneider, and a few others. Ten more children had been released, for a total of fourteen. Moreover, Koresh was promising that he and everybody else would surrender on March 2 if his message concerning the end of the world was played to a nationwide radio audience. The Christian Broadcasting Network and KRLD agreed to carry it, between one and three o'clock.

We were elated. Everyone in SIOC and at Jamar's command post worked late into the night, making elaborate preparations for the surrender. We made arrangements for medical care for those who needed it, for a safe facility for the children, for arresting those thought to have participated in the shoot-out, and for evidence technicians to collect material at the crime scene for the murder charges that would be filed against Koresh and others.

Two children emerged shortly after 1 A.M. on March 2. At 8:10 A.M., two more children and two elderly women came out, delivering Koresh's taped message. A few hours later, Koresh's wife, Rachel Howell, gave us the first head count of those remaining inside: forty-three men, forty-seven women, and twenty children.

As agreed, Koresh's sermon went out over the air at 1:30 P.M. At 3 P.M., the appointed hour for the surrender, we watched the exits where he said he would appear, carried out on a stretcher and surrounded by women and children.

Nothing happened. Four o'clock passed, then five o'clock. At 5:45 Steve Schneider took the phone, preached and read the Bible until the negotiators broke in, demanding to know where Koresh was. Schneider left the phone, then returned and said God had told Koresh to wait.

A short time later, a negotiator was on the phone with one of the adults when a little girl got on the line. "Are you coming to kill me?" she asked. The negotiator swallowed hard and said we were not there to hurt anybody but to help her and her mommy and daddy to come out and asked her to please come out. Neither she nor her parents made it.

At our request, Dr. Park Dietz, a professor of psychiatry at UCLA School of Medicine and a frequent consultant at Quantico, traveled to Waco on March 1 to give us a personality assessment. After listening in on Koresh's conversations with the negotiators and reading up on the history of the cult, Dietz concluded that Koresh would never leave the compound nor allow those he cared about to leave. In Dietz's opinion, he valued his power over others more than life itself. He was extremely manipulative and proud of it. He had grandiose visions of himself as a great prophet who would be persecuted and killed, like the Biblical prophets.

Moreover, Dietz was struck by reports that Koresh often had sex with girls as young as ten. He preached that God wanted him to be, as one former cult member said, "a sinful Jesus so that, when he stood in judgment of sinners on Judgment Day, he would have experience of all sin and degradation." After ordering the men to become celibate, he commandeered their wives and daughters, a number of whom bore his children. Koresh had told negotiatiors he feared prison because child molesters were often gang-raped.

Dietz concluded that Koresh might have a mass suicide-homicide in mind. The only hope, Dietz said, was to convince him that God did not want him to die yet, and that, by living, he might actually acquire more followers and more power. Meanwhile, we should try to drive a wedge between him and his followers by shaking their faith in his authority.

Three more children came out on March 3, 4, and 5, but then no more. Koresh told negotiators the rest were his biological children. Also on March 5, the Methodist Children's Home notified us that a note had been found, pinned to the jacket of Joan Vaega, a seven-year-old who had been released March 2. The note, from Joan's mother, was addressed to the girl's older sister Ursula in Hawaii. It said that by the time Ursula read the note, the mother would be dead.

Over the next weeks, twelve more adults came out, the last on March 23, but we found they had been expelled for drinking or insubordination, or because they were old and weak. As Dietz predicted, Koresh gave up those who didn't matter to him.

Splitting Koresh from his remaining followers was to prove impossible. Whether or not Koresh really believed all the things he said, the Davidians believed in him. No matter how many times I replay the scenarios in my head, I come back to the same dilemma. How do you get to people whose whole purpose in life is to die? This sounds like lunacy to us, but one thing will put it in perspective. Think about your own faith. How strongly do you believe? The Davidians believed as strongly as you do. Kind of scary, huh?

Long before David Koresh came on the scene, the Branch Davidians had been waiting around to die. The sect traced its origins to Bulgarian immigrant Victor Houteff, a radical Seventh Day Adventist who formed a farm commune outside Waco in 1934 to await the Second Coming of Christ. Houteff died in 1955, leaving his widow, Florence, to carry on the vigil. She forecast that the world would end around Easter of 1959. When it didn't, the congregation memorialized the date as the Great Disappointment. Most of the sect splintered off with Ben Roden, who claimed to be the reincarnation of King David of Israel. The congregation, now known as the Branch Davidian, acquired property outside Waco and built the Mount Carmel compound. Roden died in 1978. His widow, Lois, became the group's spiritual leader and prophet.

A long-haired twenty-three-year-old high school dropout and rock guitarist named Vernon Howell started hanging around Mount Carmel. Howell, though dyslexic, had a gift for memorizing and spouting Scripture, especially the Book of Revelation, whose murky prophecies obsessed the Davidians. Some believe he seduced sixty-seven-year-old "Sister Lois." After she died, Koresh staged an armed coup. In 1987, he and half a dozen other young men decked themselves out in combat fatigues, blackened their faces with greasepaint, and ambushed Lois's son and heir, George. The younger Roden survived the attack but suffered a mental breakdown and was institutionalized.

Howell took control of Mount Carmel and changed his name to David Koresh—David for the biblical king, Koresh for Cyrus, the ancient Persian king, and also for Death; he thought the sound imitated the human death gurgle. Koresh got very good at twisting the congregation's fixation with earthly death to satisfy his desires for power and pleasure. He declared that he was the Lamb of God, the risen Messiah, whom the Book of Revelation said would appear to marshal the faithful at the end of time. "If the Bible is true, then I'm Christ," Koresh said. To be worthy of heaven, God's chosen had to fight a terrible battle against the forces of Satan—meaning, said one former Davidian, federal agents, whom Koresh called "Babylonians" or "Assyrians"—and suffer agonizing deaths. Koresh talked of renaming the compound Ranch Apocalypse. One day, when Koresh was in a belligerent mood, a negotiator remarked, "Do you really think we're going to start firing indiscriminately up at that place?" Koresh replied, "I sure hope so."

He controlled his followers by haranguing them for hours on end, brainwashing them in classic fashion by depriving them of food, sleep, and bathroom breaks. People who challenged his authority were sometimes forced into the sewage pit. To prepare his flock for war, Koresh played videos like *Full Metal Jacket* and *Hamburger Hill*.

The children of the cult called him "father" and were taught to worship and fear him. According to former cult members, Koresh spanked children as young as eight months old until they bled. He starved his three-year-old son for two days, and forced him to sleep in a rat-infested garage. Children released in the early days of the siege told of being beaten with a paddle called the Helper. That parents could stand by and let their children be abused said a lot about how far gone they were.

As the picture of Koresh was developed by our intelligence people, behavioralists, and agents who interviewed everyone who stood still, I came to believe that he was as close to pure evil as any human being I had ever heard tell of—devious, calculating, self-absorbed, charming, and completely sadistic.

In endless meetings, we sifted and resifted options and different negotiation strategies. Koresh made promise after promise to come out and then broke them.

In discussions among Jamar, Rogers, and those of us at HQ, the HRT developed an emergency assault plan to be used in case a murder-suicide pact began to unfold. The only thing we could do was to make holes in the building and throw some tear gas and flash-bangs around as distractions for those who might come to their senses and try to flee. Dick Rogers and I talked about how frustrating this was. It was not a good plan, but it was about the best we could do without having our own agents massacred in an attempted rescue mission. In case the adults decided to poison everyone, including the children, Rogers acquired enough anti-cyanide kits to provide a lifesaving dose for every child and a few of the adults. The medics kept them at the ready at the forward command post. The HRT operators were ordered not to go near the building on foot, no matter what they heard or saw. We feared that Koresh and his people might try to lure the HRT men inside and ambush them. Koresh often spoke of traps and snares.

In contrast to the Weaver siege, which was run by people in the field and a skeleton August weekend crew, everybody who was anybody had a say in the Waco crisis. It was a typical committee deal. Big rooms, big egos, lots of power. But no one had any good ideas about how to handle this madman. I certainly didn't. Floyd Clarke was in the saddle at HQ. Jamar and the other SACs working in the Waco command post held telephone conferences several times a day.

Late in the ordeal, Justice officials began to migrate to SIOC to discuss options. They didn't have any good ideas either. After Attorney General Janet Reno was sworn in on March 12, she immersed herself in the details and asked dozens of questions, mostly about the welfare of the children. No one doubted that they were her main concern. Of course, they were everyone's concern. The adults were volunteers. The children were victims.

As at Ruby Ridge, friction developed within our ranks, with the negotiators sometimes at odds with the tactical people or the commander and top managers. For example, on March 12, Gary Noesner told Koresh that because they had had a "very good dialogue" during the night, the electricity would remain on. A half hour later, Jamar ordered the electricity shut off for the duration of the standoff. Jamar wanted to show the Davidians that the FBI, not Koresh, was in control. On March 21, the negotiators secured the release of seven adults. Shortly afterward, the HRT used armored vehicles to drag cars away from the compound. The tactical team contended that the vehicles formed a dangerous obstruction, but the negotiators believed that moving in with armor signaled to the Davidians that their concessions had been meaningless.

We now know that most of the disconnects between the HRT and the negotiators were the unintentional result of Jamar's "stovepipe" management style. Jamar or the SACs backing him up met with the tactical team, or the negotiations team, but seldom both at once.

The negotiators never argued they could have resolved the standoff peacefully if they had been in control. As Byron Sage put it, "Was there tension between the negotiation effort and the tactical effort? Yes, there was. Did it ultimately affect the outcome of this incident? No, it did not."

I don't think anything that our people did on the scene had any effect on the decisions that David Koresh made. We were just supporting players in his drama.

Around the middle of March, it was clear the talks with Koresh weren't going anywhere. He was subjecting the negotiators to what they called Bible-babble until their ears ached, but he wouldn't connect on a rational level. The negotiators tried to put some daylight between Koresh and Steve Schneider by prodding Schneider about Koresh's boast that he had taken Steve's wife, Judy, to his bed and that she had borne Koresh's child. Schneider didn't take the bait. This was not really surprising, since Schneider was in way over his head. He had only recently been promoted to Koresh's number two. That job had been held by Perry Jones, a sixty-four-year-old father and grandfather to a number of Davidians until February 28, when he killed himself by putting a gun in his mouth. Schneider had given Koresh everything, including his wife. As Byron Sage put it, "He'd relegated himself and his manliness to his commitment to David. Once you've done that, it's a very difficult thing to convince yourself, hey, you've made a mistake."

On March 15, Sage and McLennan County sheriff Jack Harwell met with Schneider and Wayne Martin, a Davidian who was a lawyer, on the road leading out of the compound. The plan was to try to inject a little spine into Schneider, but it failed. Schneider didn't show for a second face-to-face meeting with Sage two days later.

Jamar and Sage decided to turn up the heat. Sage got Koresh on the phone and chewed him out. He told him he had a record of reneging on his promises. If he were truly the Messiah and a leader, Sage stormed, it was time for him to lead his people out of harm's way. Koresh left the phone to go to the bathroom and put Schneider on the line. Schneider gasped that he had never heard anybody talk to Koresh like that before. After that, Koresh began referring to Sage as "Mr. Byron."

The next night, Sage broadcast the tape of the conversation over loudspeakers so that the inhabitants could hear David stammer and waffle when challenged. Meanwhile, Jamar ordered the HRT to move in with tanks, move obstructions, and shrink the perimeter. On March 21 the loudspeakers started blasting the compound with loud music. Tones and irritating noises such as Tibetan chants were added to the repertoire the next day.

Dick Rogers and I have ended up on the opposite sides of a number of issues, but I have to say here that two accusations have been unfairly leveled at him and the HRT. The public has been given the impression that the idea of blasting the compound with irritating noises came from the tactical commanders. That's just not true. Actually, as a Justice Department internal review later found, the noise bombardment was suggested by Park Dietz and seconded by some of the negotiators, Sage among them, in an effort to disrupt the sleep cycle of Koresh and his "mighty men" so that they could not think straight. There were indications from electronic listening devices the HRT had slipped into the compound in milk deliveries that Koresh was getting stronger. The whole Waco crisis team feared that Koresh and his inner circle were plotting to burst out of the compound, firing at our lines while holding the children as shields. They thought this because the Davidians sometimes hoisted children up to the windows as the tanks rolled near the walls to tow away vehicles. Also, men occasionally walked out of the compound and straight at our sniper positions as if they were probing to see what we'd do. On occasion, HRT operators threw flash-bang devices near them, to drive them back into the compound.

Nor is it true that HRT initiated the idea of injecting tear gas into the compound to clear the buildings. On March 22, in preparation for a crisis-management-team strategy session, the negotiation team submitted a memo opining that Koresh and his core group would not give up anytime soon. The negotiators felt that the odds of group suicide were not great. They thought that the standoff would eventually be resolved peacefully, but since Koresh had no incentive to bargain, they suggested speeding things up by introducing tear gas "to incrementally escalate stress within the compound to bring the standoff to an orderly and positive resolution." The tear gas idea met with no objections at HQ but was placed on the back burner.

On March 29, Jamar allowed Koresh to meet with attorney Dick DeGuerin, who had offered to defend him against the murder charges. This was an unorthodox move, and some of the negotiators opposed it because it took some pressure off Koresh, but Jamar was ready to try just about anything. Over several sessions, DeGuerin extracted a promise that Koresh and his flock would surrender after Passover, which fell on April 6.

But they didn't. On April 9, Schneider emerged from a meeting with Koresh with a letter that declared, "I am your God. I love you for My mercy's sake. I see your evil and pride and yet you fear me not. Do not fear the fear of man, fear me, for I have you in my snare. . . . Fear me and the hour of my judgment, for it has come. . . . Learn from David My seals or, as you have said, bear the consequences. I forewarn you the Lake Waco area of Old Mount Carmel will be terribly shaken. The waters of the lake will be emptied through the broken damn [*sic*]. The heavens are calling you to judgment."

This message and four similar ones were signed "Yahweh Koresh." Translated, that meant "God Death."

At our request Dr. Murray Miron, professor of psycholinguistics at Syracuse University, analyzed the letters. He called them the products of "rampant, morbidly virulent paranoia." Koresh was neither going to surrender nor commit suicide, Miron said. "In my judgment," he reported, "we are facing a determined, hardened adversary who has no intention of delivering himself or his followers into the hands of his adversaries. It is my belief he is waiting for an assault. . . . He intends to fight."

A second and somewhat contradictory opinion came from Van Zandt and Dr. Joseph Krofcheck, a psychiatrist who had worked with the FBI on a number of hostage negotiations. Their analysis concluded that Koresh was a paranoid psychotic "willing to kill, to see his followers die and to die himself." He might have in mind a "magnificent end," they warned, by springing a trap that "could take the lives of all of his followers and as many of the authorities as possible."

Information coming out of the compound supported either view. An adult who was expelled by Koresh told us that his promise to surrender on March 2 had actually been one of his apocalyptic murder-suicide plots. The plan was for men to carry Koresh out on a stretcher, then toss grenades by the handful, killing themselves, Koresh, nearby women and children, and all law enforcement people in range. Everybody left in the compound would then be killed or commit suicide. Koresh backed out at the last minute, the Davidian said, claiming God had told him to wait.

Bruce Perry, chief of psychiatry at Texas Children's Hospital and an expert in post-traumatic stress, interviewed the children released by Koresh. He reported that most of them had heard talk of a suicide compact. These children referred to their parents as "dead," Perry said. They believed the compound would be annihilated by evil forces, everyone would perish, and they would all be reunited in heaven. Kiri Jewell, a girl who had lived in the compound with her mother until a year before the ATF raid, confirmed this, saying that during her residence at Mount Carmel, children were taught how to kill themselves by putting a gun down their throats. Kiri had been removed from the compound by her father, who got a custody order after learning that Koresh had molested the girl when she was ten.

On the other hand, some of the experts and our own in-house behavioral science unit thought Koresh was actually too selfish and materialistic to kill himself. After all, he had not gone through with the March 2 scenario, and he sometimes chatted with negotiators about book and movie deals. "An antisocial personality has an extremely low suicide rate," as Gary Noesner put it. "They are users of people, not abusers of themselves." Byron Sage thought that "we were dealing with a psychopathic personality that did not want to die. Would he organize a situation in which he would sacrifice his people? That was a possibility. We felt he himself was not a suicide, that he could orchestrate events up to but not necessarily including a suicide. Normally people like this look for that last-minute exit-stage-left situation."

Floyd Clarke and Larry Potts went to Waco on April 7. Jamar again raised the issue of CS gas—tear gas. He felt some urgency to move Koresh off the dime because of the increasingly foul conditions inside the compound. Jamar thought it was only a matter of time, a short time, before the open cesspools spread disease through the compound. If that happened, the young and the weak would go first.

Clarke, Potts, and the rest of us took his point. Koresh could hold out practically forever. He had at least a year's store of MREs—military meals-ready-to-eat—on hand, plus huge tanks of water. He would never be hungry or thirsty. He would eat and drink first. After all, he was God. We knew we'd end up sending in food for the children, and he'd appropriate it. A man who would have sex with little girls and beat toddlers wouldn't hesitate to starve them, nor to exploit their pain to gain sympathy for himself. Suppose Koresh demanded regular access to television, and we conceded. What would the world see? Sick, hungry children.

Furthermore, the snipers had been out on the line for thirty-eight days, peering through their scopes, watching for the first signs of a breakout. This was stressful duty. If we had to pull them out for rest and retraining, we had no one who could replace them, because no SWAT unit or any other law enforcement team could use their weapons with the surgical precision necessary to shoot a Davidian charging our lines with an AK-47 in one hand and a baby in the other.

None of us were enthusiastic about tear gas, but

nothing else of a nonlethal nature was available to us. As
HRT commander, I had argued for studies of nonlethal
knockout gases, but research into this subject was only in
its infancy. As things stood, no anesthetic gas could be
administered in a controlled way. A dose strong enough
to knock out a grown man would kill a child or old person. Rogers and I talked about using a water cannon, but
it would have the force of a wrecking ball. It might cave
in the building and kill those inside. All the toxicology
tests we had seen indicated that CS gas would not
endanger the children. We thought it a better option
than letting the crisis drag on for more months.

Sessions, Clarke, and Potts briefed Attorney General
Janet Reno and her aides on the tear gas option on April
12, exactly a month after she was sworn in. The strategy
developed by Jamar and Rogers contemplated using
armored vehicles with spray booms to insert gas into the
compound, section by section, then finish the job with
cold tear gas cartridges dispatched with grenade launchers. We would announce our intentions first so that the
people inside could clear out. The idea was not to gas
the people but to make large parts of the compound
uninhabitable. The gas would be shot in a liquid, which
crystallized in the air and turned to a fine dust that settled to the floor. Anyone who entered the room for days
afterward would stir up the dust and get a dose of it in
the eyes and mouth.

Reno asked for opinions from medical experts about
the effects of CS gas on children, pregnant women, and
old people. She also wanted to hear from the military. A
second briefing, on April 14, featured a panel of military
experts on CS, including Dr. Harry Salem, chief scientist
for life sciences at the U.S. Army Chemical Biological

Defense Command. This session persuaded Reno that tear gas wouldn't do permanent damage to the people in the compound and wouldn't ignite. CS gas in crystal form would actually put out a small fire.

The same day, Dick DeGuerin told Jamar that Koresh had set a new timetable for surrender. He would come out after he had written a manuscript that interpreted the Seven Seals, the mystery of God's plan for the world's end, referred to in the Book of Revelation. Since Koresh's dyslexia prevented him from writing himself—he dictated to a follower, usually Judy Schneider—this effort could take months, if it was ever completed at all.

Reno considered the gas plan for two days more but, depending on whom you talk to, either disapproved it outright or shelved it. She worried that Koresh might set off a bomb or hold children up in the windows and threaten to shoot them.

She asked us to prepare a detailed statement describing the negotiations, conditions in the compound, and the rationale for tear gas. On April 17, after receiving this document, Reno approved the tear gas plan, to be executed on Monday morning, April 19. She briefed President Clinton on April 18, explaining that the talks were stalemated, the FBI could not sustain its high alert level indefinitely, and as time passed, the danger to those inside and outside increased. The children in the compound were living in unsafe, unsanitary conditions and might be suffering abuse. The President told Reno he supported her decision.

That afternoon, the HRT operators drove their armored vehicles close to the compound walls and towed away the rest of the cars, including Koresh's prize

Chevrolet Camaro. Koresh called the negotiators and raised hell, warning, "If you don't know what you're doing, this could be the worst day in law enforcement history." As the operators kept at their task, the snipers saw children being held aloft in the windows and a cardboard sign that said, "Flames Await."

10

Early on the morning of April 19, Byron Sage went to the HRT team forward command center, a house about three hundred yards from the compound. He called the compound at 5:59 A.M. A man answered. Sage asked for Steve Schneider. The man said Schneider was asleep.

"Wake him up. This is extremely important."

When Schneider finally came to the phone, Sage said sharply, "Steve, I have something I need to tell you, and you need to listen to this. Can you hear me?"

"I'm listening," Schneider said groggily.

Sage read a prepared text that went about like this: "We are preparing to introduce a nonlethal gas. It's tear gas. We are not going to enter your compound. This is not an assault."

Schneider didn't respond. Sage read his lines again.

"You're going to put tear gas into the compound," Schneider said in a flat voice.

Sage repeated the message a third time. He heard a

click. He took the microphone attached to his bullet-proof vest and started broadcasting the text so the rest of the Davidians would know why the armored vehicles were approaching the building. "This is not an assault," he announced. "We're introducing a nonlethal tear gas which will render the compound temporarily uninhabit-able. It is not an armed assault. Do not shoot. We are not entering your compound." He added that people who came out of the compound would be escorted to the end of the driveway, where a Red Cross flag had been erected, and would receive medical treatment.

At 6:02 A.M. as Sage spoke, HRT operators in two combat-engineering vehicles rolled up to the living quarters. The CEVs on the front left side punched holes in the first-floor windows and sprayed CS gas inside in two fifteen-second bursts. These rooms were chosen because they were farthest away from where we thought the children slept and also because they were next to an underground bunker formed from an old school bus. The intention was to prevent people from streaming into the bunker, where they might suffocate from over-crowding.

At 6:04 A.M. a sniper at Sierra One radioed the word, "Compromise," meaning he had seen gunfire coming from the building. Then heavy firing erupted. Other snipers and operators reported seeing sparks on the skins of the CEVs as they were pelted by automatic-weapons fire. Rogers, sitting in an Abrams tank on Double E road, heard the firing and ordered the opera-tors to suppress the gunfire by gassing the whole com-pound. Rogers would later be criticized for escalating the confrontation, but in fact, he was following orders. The plan approved by Reno provided that if the agents were fired upon by the Davidians, the HRT would saturate the entire structure.

The HRT brought in the Bradleys, and operators used grenade launchers to fire hundreds of tear gas cartridges, called Ferret rounds, at the compound. At 7:09 A.M. the operators reported they'd delivered all their rounds, but except for the left side, they hadn't penetrated the walls. Jamar told Rogers to intensify the gassing. Rogers sent CEVs to punch holes in the walls and fire more Ferret rounds. The supply of rounds was exhausted at close to 9:30 A.M. Nearby field offices were asked to send more tear gas cartridges to the scene; these arrived around 11:30 A.M. Meanwhile, Rogers deployed CEVs to knock holes in the rear walls and open an escape route. The last tear gas rounds were delivered into the building at about 11:40 A.M., according to the HRT log.

At 12:07 P.M., the infrared tape on Nightstalker, which was circling above the compound, captured images of fires igniting at three separate points in the compound. At almost the same moment two snipers reported seeing smoke at separate points. At 12:10 P.M., an HRT operator saw a man wearing a dark mask and toting a rifle moving back and forth behind a piano, as if pouring something, then kneeling as if to light a fire. Flames shot up.

Sage saw three fires flickering, then roaring. Clutching the microphone, he pleaded with Koresh, "Don't do this to those people. This is not the way to end it. David, don't be a destroyer, be a savior, lead your people out of there." Sage repeated this message over and over. He appealed directly to the other Davidians, pleading with them to walk toward his voice. He felt the heat of explosions on his face. He waited for the children to come out, but none did.

From his vantage point, Rogers saw plumes of smoke rising from the right side of the compound, from the center, and toward the back, then watched in horror as the entire compound lit up. He waited for the people to come flooding out. But they didn't. The fire began to consume the building. He heard gunshots and thought people who wanted to escape were being shot.

Rogers radioed his men that the first question to ask every person who emerged was, Where are the children? He saw Renos Avram on a roof, rolling in pain, his clothes afire. A Bradley moved toward him. Avram waved the agents off, then jumped off the building, put his hands up, and walked toward a Bradley. Then Rogers saw Marjorie Thomas come out of the building, her clothes burning. A Bradley door opened. Three operators dragged her to the side of the tank, rolled her around, beat the flames out, and took her to the medics.

Ruth Riddle ran out of the compound, then ran back inside. An operator then chased her, struggled with her, and dragged her out of the building. He told me later that the heat was so intense that he feared that his stun grenades, attached to his leg, would ignite and blow huge chunks of his leg off. She said, "Who are you?" He said, "Where are the children?" She shook her head.

In all, nine adults—three women, six men—survived the fires. Every HRT operator who encountered one of them told the same story. They had screamed at them, where are the kids, what did you do with them? None of them answered.

Rogers drove up to the front of the compound. He signaled the fire trucks to approach. He had kept the trucks away until now, to prevent the firemen from being shot, but the building was collapsing and he thought no Davidian snipers would be left. He told the firemen to douse the area around the buried school bus. If the Davidians had tried to save the children from the gas, they might have thought to hide them there.

Rogers put on his gas mask, grabbed his M16 and his ballistic shield, got out of his tank, and headed for the construction pit, where he knew there was a tunnel that led to the school bus. Sixteen operators followed.

Rogers and his men jumped into the construction pit and waded through waist-deep water, filthy with human excrement, toward the entrance to the tunnel, which was in the half of the pit that was covered with tar paper and plywood. It was pitch black under the makeshift tar-paper roof. The men found their way with lanterns and flashlights mounted on their M16s. Brushing off rats swimming in this stinking pool, the agents got to the plywood door to the tunnel and knocked it in. This was a risky move. It might have been booby-trapped. Fortunately, it wasn't. The men ran down the underground passageway, shouting that they were coming and holding their shields high. They slowed down as they reached the L-shaped corner of the tunnel, a perfect trap. On the other leg of the L, there was a second wooden door. They broke it down and rushed into the bus. No children were there. The operators pulled off their rebreather packs. The air was cool and fresh. It was coming in from the tunnel mouth, which was well away from the fire. If the children had been in here, they would have survived.

At this moment, Rogers told me later, the enormity of the tragedy hit him, and he felt a wave of nausea sweep over him. The bus/bunker was the last place the children could be. They were lost. He and the other men stood silently in the bus; there was nothing to say. Then they clambered back outside. The fire was raging, as hot as a refinery blaze. Ammunition exploded for about four hours. A search later determined about four hundred thousand rounds were in the building, plus well over one hundred weapons.

I was in the submarine, watching the whole thing on the bank of television sets and following the actions of Sage, Rogers, and the others via telephone linkup with the command post. I paced about the big room—the small command center where I usually sat was occupied by Reno, Clarke, Potts, and a few other big shots. Reno left shortly after 10 A.M. to make a speech. I stayed in the big room—more pacing space. Shortly after noon, I saw wisps of smoke and thought, *Okay, they're burning the evidence, and now they'll be coming out.* A minute or two passed. *Okay, let's go,* I hissed under my breath. I saw Renos Avram run out onto the roof. *Where were the others?*

Where were the children?

The SIOC was totally silent. Everyone was glued to the images on the television sets. Someone said that the HRT was going into the bunker to get the kids. Then the call came from Rogers that the kids weren't there.

I stared at the televisions a while longer and finally called Debbie.

"I saw it," she said. "You must feel terrible."

"Yeah. It was horrible. It was the worst thing I've ever seen."

I still couldn't believe it. As humans we probably fear death by fire more than anything else, yet this group chose it. And they kept their own children in that inferno. I knew Koresh was cruel, but I hadn't imagined that all the other people inside the compound had lost the most basic human instinct after survival—the parent's drive to save the life of a child.

The medical examiner concluded that seventy-five people died in the fire—fifty adults and twenty-five children under the age of fifteen. Five more Davidians were killed during the February 28 raid—two from ATF shots, one, Perry Jones, a probable suicide, and two others apparently murdered by other Davidians.

David Koresh was found in the communication room. He died of a gunshot wound to his forehead. Nearby was the body of Steve Schneider, who had put a gun in his mouth and fired. We'll never know whether Koresh asked to be shot or whether someone killed him. A number of people in our ranks suspect he tried to save himself at the last minute, and Schneider killed him in a rage, then committed suicide.

The autopsy reports on the children formed a terrible chronicle of the compound's last minutes. Joseph Martinez, eight, died of smoke inhalation. Audrey Martinez, thirteen, was buried alive and died of suffocation. Abigail Martinez, eleven, died of a gunshot wound to the head. "Doe 33," an unidentified three-year-old boy, was stabbed in the chest. "Doe 51A," a two-year-old girl, died of smoke inhalation. "Doe 53," a five-to-six-year-old girl, was shot in the heart. "Doe 57," a six-year-old girl, suffocated. "Doe 62," a one-year-old girl, died of blunt force trauma to the head—she was bludgeoned to death. "Doe 67-2," a seven- or eight-year-old boy, was buried alive. "Doe 67-8," an infant, died of a gunshot wound to the head. And on and on they went. I couldn't finish reading them.

In response to accusations that the FBI started the
fire, the Texas Rangers sent a third of their hundred-
man force to handle the arson investigation. They, in
turn, assembled a team of specialists from local fire
departments around the United States. The conclusion
of all was that the fire was arson, set at three separate
points, fueled by accelerants such as kerosene, gasoline,
and other petroleum products.

It fell to federal prosecutors Ray and Leroy Jahn of
San Antonio to work with the Rangers and make a case
against those involved in the deaths of ATF agents
Willis, Williams, LeBleu, and McKeehan. This husband
and wife, who acted as a prosecutorial tag team, were
legendary in the federal system. They had convicted
Charlie Harrelson, the assassin of Judge John Wood, the
first federal judge to be murdered in modern memory.

Leroy is just about as Texan as any woman can be.
She worked her way through college giving guided tours
of the Alamo in English and Spanish. She had grown up
hearing her dad tell the story of the mayor who had frantically telegraphed the governor for help because the
prisoners in his jail were rioting. When the mayor met
the train and saw a Texas Ranger standing on the platform, he gasped, "I have a riot here, and they're sending
me one Ranger?" "One riot, one Ranger," the Ranger
said. "Let's go."

So when she met with the Rangers for the first time,
Leroy said, "Listen, fellows, I have just one thing I want
to mention. We all know your motto—One Riot, One
Ranger. Frankly I'm a little surprised that the Rangers
would send thirty-three of you guys to work this case.
I'm starting to lose a little confidence in you." From the
back of the room an old Ranger slid back in his chair,

pushed his white Stetson back on his head, and said, "Wa'al, you have to understand, ma'am, that what we're dealing with here is the Son of God."

That broke the ice. The Jahns and the Rangers put together an indictment charging a dozen surviving Davidians with various offenses, up to conspiracy to murder the ATF agents.

It was an uphill battle. By the time the trials took place, popular opinion was strongly against anybody from the government. You only had to hook into the Internet and type "Waco" to see your computer screen light up with a thousand conspiracy theories, all painting the government as a diabolical force that had murdered the Davidians on account of their radical religious beliefs.

Ray Jahn's simple, powerful presentation salvaged the case. "This is a country of laws and not men," Jahn summed up. "This is a country in which you can believe anything you want to, you can worship a golden chicken, you can worship a golden calf, you can worship David Koresh, you can believe anything you want to, ladies and gentlemen, but it does not justify your physical acts. . . . Whether it's a car bomb in the United Nations building, whether it's a car bomb in a barracks in Lebanon, religious zeal does not justify criminal activity."

The jury rejected the most serious charges, conspiracy to murder federal agents. In a compromise verdict, it convicted eight of the Davidian defendants of lesser offenses, and a ninth defendant, Kathy Schroeder, pleaded guilty. Five of those convicted, all believed to have been Koresh's enforcers, the "mighty men," were sentenced to forty years each in prison.

The vindication in that Texas courtroom could not

alleviate the profound sadness that all of us have felt since the fires of Waco. Nor has it changed the minds of the many Americans who are now convinced that the FBI launched a military assault on a religious compound.

We paid—and are still paying—a heavy price for deploying tanks, even though they were necessary to protect our people. Waco galvanized the extremist movement. It became a rallying cry and recruiting slogan for the antigovernment fringe, which designated April 19 as Militia Day.

It was no coincidence that the worst domestic terrorist attack in our history occurred on April 19, 1995. As all the world now knows, condemned mass murderer Tim McVeigh made a pilgrimage to Waco shortly before he assembled the two-ton fertilizer bomb that destroyed the Murrah building in Oklahoma City and took 168 lives.

For years afterward, the last thing I thought about before I fell asleep and the first thing I thought about when I woke up in the morning was Waco. Night after night, I tried to think of what I could have done differently. On a purely intellectual level, I was not surprised by what happened. I knew that David Koresh and his people were all about death. I had read the transcripts of his talks with the negotiators, the transcripts from the bugs, his letters, and the expert opinions. Not one ray of hope was on any of those pages.

But in my heart, I could not accept that here was something we just couldn't fix. I am a total optimist. In my business, you have to be. Hope is the foundation for everything we do. Plus, I have a big goddamn ego. I think, *My plan's going to work. It's got to work.* I'm just not prepared when it doesn't, even when I know better. If I let myself think, *This stuff might not work*, I'd never try it.

At Waco, I couldn't think of a thing that might work.

Not long ago, Jeff Jamar said to me, "If I had it to do over again, I would make some different decisions."

"Hell, Jeff," I told him, "if I'd been on the scene, I would have made some different decisions. If we had ten different commanders, we would have had ten different sets of decisions. These things are not math problems, where there are always right and wrong answers. We can't say to ourselves if we had done this one thing or that differently, we might have been successful. Just understand this. Koresh did not name his place Ranch Mercy, Ranch Salvation, or Ranch Hope. He named it Ranch Apocalypse."

I met up with Bill Buford at the memorial service for the slain ATF agents in Washington, D.C. I spotted him from across the grounds. He looked the same as he had years before, when we had partnered up in Arkansas, fit, strong, and confident—and as if he had been born in the wrong century. I'd always thought he should have been a U.S. marshal in around 1865. After the ceremony, Horace Mewborn and I waded through the multitude of agents and their families who were offering Bill words of comfort. When he spotted me, he broke away from the well-wishers and walked toward me. I reached out my hand and took his. He threw his arm around my neck and hung on for a minute. There were tears in my eyes. I don't know about his; he was always stronger than me. "Danny, I wish this had turned out like Arkansas."

"So do I, Bill," I said. "You did the best you could, and

you held your people together. I don't know if I could have done that."

We talked for a few minutes, and then we both turned and walked away. Little needs to be said between two men who have been through so much together.

The ATF has been criticized mightily for Waco. In various after-action meetings, I've had plenty to say about the ATF executives who ordered brave men and women into a suicide charge. But I've also said this. None should fault the courage of the men and women who followed their orders and, through scores of heroic acts on that terrible day, held their ground in the face of overwhelming fire. As Bob Ricks said to me afterward, "You know, Doc, this thing got screwed up by their leaders, but these men and women showed great courage under fire. I only hope that our agents would be as brave in the same situation." Many ATF agents risked their lives to save the lives of wounded comrades. Though their ammunition was practically exhausted, they didn't run. They stood and fought until a truce was declared. I believe that had they broken ranks and fled after the first volleys from the compound, Koresh and his people would have pursued and murdered them.

Those men and women performed as heroes because incompetent leaders put them in a desperate situation. I could only pray that, in the future, law enforcement leaders would do everything in their power to see that no one had to be a hero to get the job done.

Preoccupied with Waco, we paid little heed to the
Randy Weaver–Kevin Harris prosecution. That was not
good because—as I found out when I came up for air
after the Waco disaster—the U.S. attorney's office in
Boise on one side and our Salt Lake City and Boise
Field Offices on the other were getting along about like
two strange bulldogs. The prosecutors accused the
agents of being uncooperative and inflexible. The
agents said the prosecutors were arrogant and abusive.
Both sides were probably right. The prosecutors were
also complaining that some FBI lab work had been slow
and substandard. Supervisors in the HQ Criminal
Investigations Division were accusing the prosecutors
of proposing to let the Weaver defense team use the
discovery process to conduct a fishing expedition into
FBI sources and methods that were irrelevant to the
charges against their client.

To give just one example, there was a battle royal
when the U.S. attorney's office proposed to give the
defense an HRT contingency plan, composed during the
last day or two of the standoff, that laid out an emergency rescue of the children if Vicki Weaver started to
kill herself and them. The plan contained details of the
HRT's explosive-breaching techniques. These techniques were never used at Ruby Ridge, so they seemed
irrelevant to the criminal case. Yet to reveal them could
compromise their use in the future and could also give
amateur bomb-makers a handy how-to guide. When the
dispute landed on my desk, initially I opposed handing

over the entire plan. When the prosecutors and defense lawyers continued to press for it, Mike Kahoe and I worked out a compromise, which Justice officials eventually accepted. I personally went over the documents, blacking out the technical data on breaching and other sensitive sources and methods, then sent the paperwork to the Justice Department for transmission to the defense team.

The squabbles and delays within government ranks continued. Judge Edward Lodge became so infuriated that he slapped the FBI with a contempt citation and a fine of $5,160. We could afford it, but we got the point.

When the trial opened on April 13, 1993, Gerry Spence ripped through the prosecution case like a McCormick reaper. He didn't bother to put on a single defense witness. Spence made an imposing figure, with his flowing silver hair, deep mellow voice, and Western-style fringed leather jacket, but his flamboyant rhetoric was overkill in this case. The government's case was so shot through with holes that Weaver would have walked if he had been represented by Pee-Wee Herman. Judge Lodge threw out two counts of the indictment for lack of evidence and remarked dryly that what little evidence the government possessed actually helped the defendants. On July 8, 1993, the jury acquitted Weaver and Harris of the alleged conspiracy and all other serious charges. Weaver ended up with an eighteen-month sentence and a $10,000 fine for failure to appear at trial on the old gun case.

Randy Weaver joined the pantheon of heroes of people who believe that the federal government uses black helicopters and surgically implanted computer chips to subjugate God-fearing white citizens. Conspiracy theories abounded—for instance, that Vicki Weaver had deliberately been targeted for assassination by the FBI and that the helicopter had flown over the Weaver cabin as a ploy to lure Weaver and Harris out into the yard so that the HRT snipers could kill them.

Spence called upon Boundary County prosecutor Randall Day to charge FBI agents with murder and handed the Justice Department a stack of allegations of government misconduct.

As the public uproar grew over the Ruby Ridge and Waco debacles, Attorney General Janet Reno ordered thorough internal investigations of both incidents. That's exactly what she should have done, but I got a funny feeling when the investigations took off in sharply different directions.

In the case of Waco, Reno said her objective was "to study what happened at Waco, to learn from our experience, and to make changes so that as we go forward, we can be as prepared as possible to deal with future situations." Although she was a key player in the incident, Reno retained control over the fact-finding inquiry by putting her special assistant Richard Scruggs in charge of it. His report was completed by October 8, 1993, warp speed by Justice Department standards. The assessment of the FBI's performance was done by a Bush administration veteran—Edward S. G. Dennis, a former assistant attorney general in charge of the Justice Department Criminal Division—but it didn't cause Reno or the FBI any discomfort. Dennis concluded that while the bureau "did not achieve their objective, which was to resolve it without the loss of life . . . I did not believe that that was for want of a reasonable plan given what they knew at the time." As Reno herself put it in a

House Judiciary Committee hearing in 1995, "We all mourn the tragic outcome. But the finger of blame points in one direction—it points at David Koresh."

In contrast to the low-key, collegial Waco inquiry, the Justice Department's Ruby Ridge inquiry was adversarial to the point of downright hostility. It was conducted by Barbara Berman, a lawyer in the department's Office of Professional Responsibility, and four other career Justice attorneys. The fact-finding was delegated to a team of twenty-eight FBI agents supervised by Robert E. Walsh of the FBI Inspection Division.

It was clear to me that the Ruby Ridge inquiry was going to be a lot more than a study of what to do better when Bob Walsh called me in October 1993 and said the matter was being handled as a criminal investigation and I would be given a Miranda warning advising me of my rights. I agreed to the interview and waived my right to counsel, but I insisted on submitting a signed, sworn statement about my role. I had seen too many criminal investigations in which FBI agents conducted interviews and then paraphrased their subjects inaccurately because they were unfamiliar with the complicated subject matter or had their own spin on the case already.

The Berman task force sent its report up the line at Justice on June 10, 1994. It was a 542-page litany of errors and mistakes in judgment at every level of every federal agency involved in the case. No one in the chain of command escaped blame, including me.

The heaviest scrutiny fell on Lon Horiuchi, the only FBI agent to discharge a weapon. Outside the conspiracy-minded extremist right, Horiuchi's first shot wasn't an issue. He made a convincing case that he had believed the man in his scope—Randy Weaver, as it turned out—was about to shoot at the FBI helicopter. Since the shooter could have downed the chopper with a single well-placed shot to the pilot or the engine compartment, Horiuchi's shot was solidly within the bounds of the deadly force policy, which says, "Agents are not to use deadly force against any person except as necessary in self-defense or the defense of another, when they have reason to believe that they or another are in danger of death or grievous bodily harm."

There were deep divisions within the Justice Department about the legality of Horiuchi's second shot. This was the shot meant for Kevin Harris as he was about to disappear through the cabin door, the shot that killed Vicki Weaver. Berman and the other task force lawyers argued that it was illegal and unconstitutional because Harris, in retreat, could not have posed an imminent threat to anyone. Moreover, they said Horiuchi was reckless for shooting into the wooden door, knowing that a woman and children were in the cabin and could be behind the door. ("We believe that the shot was unnecessarily dangerous and should not have been taken," the task force concluded.) Berman recommended that the Justice Civil Rights Division, which has jurisdiction over police brutality and abuse-of-authority cases, investigate Horiuchi for possible prosecution for use of excessive force.

Michael Shaheen, head of the Justice Office of Professional Responsibility, and other senior OPR attorneys disagreed with Berman's group. If the first shot was justified, they said, so was the second, fired just twenty to thirty seconds after the first. To find otherwise, they concluded, "places an impossible burden on law enforcement officials who, facing extreme danger, must

make life-and-death decisions instantaneously." Harris
had already shot Bill Degan, and there was no reason to
believe he wouldn't shoot at another law enforcement
officer. After all, he didn't throw down his gun and fling
up his hands after Horiuchi's first shot. Horiuchi was justified in believing that the man in his scope was not running away from anything but rather running toward a
more fortified location from which he could fire on the
helicopter. Horiuchi was not required by law or regula-
tion to hold his fire while a dangerous man improved his
shooting position.

In October 1994, the Civil Rights Division lined up
with Shaheen, declining to prosecute Horiuchi on
grounds there was no evidence he had criminal intent to
break the law. After more internal reviews, Deputy
Attorney General Jamie Gorelick accepted the Shaheen
and Civil Rights Division views as the official position of
the Justice Department. Freeh did likewise. Vicki
Weaver's death was pronounced a tragic accident. Lon
Horiuchi was exonerated.

I was relieved to see Horiuchi cleared. I had selected
him for the HRT. I knew him to be a man of honor who
was grief-stricken over the death of Vicki Weaver.
Horiuchi had not fired into the doorway but along a line
parallel to the house's front face, and his shot hit his
intended target, Kevin Harris, who had shot and killed a
U.S. marshal and who was then acting in a threatening
manner. It was unfortunate that the door hid Vicki from
Horiuchi's view. I'm sure he would give anything to call
his bullet back, but since he couldn't, his only consola-
tion had to be that his peers believed he had discharged
his weapon in good faith, to save lives.

It wasn't going to be easy to recruit good people for

the HRT after the tortures of the damned suffered by Horiuchi, whose every move was dissected and debated under the harsh light of hindsight. Task force lawyers with no practical experience upon which to draw were quick to criticize him. They had no conception of how it felt to have to decide whether another human being would see the next day. The only life-and-death decision I'd ever seen departmental attorneys make was when they hit the brakes of their BMWs as they sped down the freeway.

The second focus of the Ruby Ridge postmortem was on an extremely serious command failure. On the morning of August 22, Gene Glenn and Dick Rogers gave the HRT and the FBI SWAT teams some hastily improvised, poorly written rules of engagement that could be read as an order to shoot on sight. These "special rules of engagement" were issued without the knowledge of us at HQ and represented the worst of the UNK-UNK disconnects between the SIOC and the Idaho command center. The rules issued by Glenn and Rogers advised the tactical personnel that "if any adult male is observed with a weapon prior to the [surrender] announcement, deadly force can and should be employed, if the shot can be taken without endangering any children. If any adult in the compound is observed with a weapon after the surrender announcement is made, and is not attempting to surrender, deadly force can and should be employed to neutralize the individual."

In other words, the Glenn-Rogers rules of engagement came perilously close to rules of warfare, in which government forces are permitted to fire offensively as well as defensively. Such language had never before been used by the FBI, because in a civilian law enforcement context, offensive shooting is nothing less than murder. The deadly force policy isn't just something we memorize. It's what we are. It's anchored in the virtues to which we all aspire: self-restraint, personal account-ability, courage, common sense. We look at its words as a brightly lined circle around our authority. Inside the cir-cle, we have plenty of room to move. Whenever I'm faced with a shoot/don't-shoot decision, I ask myself, can I manage this threat without using deadly force? If I'm strong, well trained, and close by someone who is about to draw a gun, I may grab him and knock the daylights out of him. If I am inexperienced, or if my adversary is some distance away, I may have to resort to deadly force. The facts are the same, and each decision is a legally and morally justifiable choice, based on my assessment of the threat and my abilities. What I can't do is step out-side the circle. If I cross the bright line and shoot a man who has a gun slung over his shoulder, or one who's unarmed and running away or who's down on the ground and not threatening anybody, I become a mur-derer. If I order another person to violate the deadly force policy, he must disobey me.

The tactical people at Ruby Ridge understood all this very well. Though no one back-channeled a protest to those of us in the submarine—HQ got word of the Glenn-Rogers rules only after they were revoked, toward the end of the standoff and after Vicki Weaver died—all the tactical operators made conscious deci-sions to ignore them. When interviewed by Walsh's team, every single HRT member said that he had con-sidered his actions governed solely by the U.S. Constitution, the deadly force policy, and the HRT motto, To Save Lives. The proof is that Randy Weaver and Kevin Harris are walking around today. If the HRT had interpreted the Glenn-Rogers rules as a shoot-on-sight order, Weaver and Harris would be dead as stumps. Most, if not all, the HRT sniper-observers who formed the perimeter around the cabin had their scopes trained on both men for some minutes and could easily have picked them off. Yet not one of the snipers fired. When Horiuchi saw one of them moving as if to draw a bead on the helicopter, then and only then—when he was sure lives were in danger—did he pull the trigger.

The SWAT operators weren't tested with a real shoot/don't-shoot choice as the HRT snipers were, but they also told the Walsh team they had agreed among themselves to disregard the Glenn-Rogers rules. As Denver SWAT coordinator Gregory Sexton later testified, he felt he'd been given an order that amounted to, "If you see them, shoot them." He said he told his team, "We were not going to go up on that hill and basically have a green light on anyone." When I heard about Sexton's dissent, I was proud. I had picked him as one of the HRT first fifty. When he transferred to Denver and picked his own SWAT team, clearly he tapped men who shared our values—men such as Donald Kusulas, who told the Senate terrorism subcommittee in 1995, "We did not go up there as assassins, and we're not a bunch of mindless sycophant lemmings waiting to jump off a cliff when somebody tells us to. And we have integrity, and we have minds that can think, and I think the American public can expect that we won't do this."

I've since been told that some of the SWAT men were so astonished by the Glenn-Rogers orders that the rumor spread that the language must have come from the White House because no FBI agent would write down anything that stupid. That was wishful thinking. We had nobody to blame but ourselves for this mess.

In fact, the business of assigning blame became the ugliest part of the whole sorry affair. The finger-pointing started right after the existence of the Glenn-Rogers rules first became publicly known, during the Weaver-Harris trial. Gerry Spence, Weaver's lawyer, had obtained them during the discovery process and used them to good effect, telling the jury, "Here you had federal agents come into a little county in northern Idaho, suspend state law, and then say they had the right to eliminate anyone with a gun."

At the Weaver trial and later, Glenn and Rogers acknowledged issuing the flawed rules but insisted that the wording had been cleared with Larry Potts. Potts said it had not. I think they were all telling the truth, insofar as they understood it. The problem was, they were talking past each other and making assumptions that turned out to be wrong. All of us, including me, violated the cardinal rule: "Assumption is the mother of fuckup." It was a mistake that would cost us all dearly.

It's true that Larry Potts wrote some rules of engagement for Ruby Ridge, but they weren't the ones Glenn and Rogers issued. Several things support Potts. First, Potts took notes of the cell phone call he made to Rogers on the evening of April 21, as Rogers and the advance team were flying to Idaho. These notes reflect that the rules of engagement he dictated to Rogers provided that the tactical operators were to "make every effort to avoid contact with children. When contact is made and they are armed, will not fire unless it fits normal FBI firing policy of threat to life. Adults who are seen with a weapon are to be considered an immediate threat and appropriate action can be taken."

I was in Potts's office during the call, and my memory squares with his notes. I'm not sure whether Potts said the tactical people "may" or "can" shoot if threatened, but it was one of the two. I'm sure I didn't hear any discussion about telling the tactical people that they "shall" or "should" shoot. If I had heard that kind of talk, I'd have jumped in and objected. It wouldn't have occurred to me that the commanders were trying to override the deadly force policy and issue an illegal shoot-on-sight order—I can't believe any FBI agent could think like that, and in fact, Glenn and Rogers later testified that they meant only to supplement the deadly force policy, not supplant it. I take them at their word. I've never met an FBI agent who doesn't regard the deadly force policy as pretty close to holy writ. But I expect I would've protested the use of *should* on grounds it muddied a situation that cried out for clarity. I don't think *should* means *must;* to me, *should* connotes a measure of individual choice. But what exactly does *should* mean? Reasonable people disagree. We couldn't expect our snipers to haul out dictionaries while they were squinting out into the mist and sleet, trying to stay alive. As far as I was concerned, saying *can* or *could* was just fine. Everybody knows what *can* means. *Can* means can. It puts us just where we ought to be. It means every life-or-death decision is the individual agent's to make, based on the law and the facts as he sees them.

Potts's version of events was also corroborated by HRT supervisor Steve McGavin, who was in the cabin of the FBI Saberjet with Rogers, listening in on the other side of the call. McGavin told the task force that when the advance party landed in Idaho, he wrote out in long-hand the rules of engagement as dictated by Potts. Rogers reviewed them and told him to scratch out *can* and insert the words *can and should*. No reason was given. McGavin did as Rogers ordered.

Neither Potts nor I nor anybody else at SIOC went over the rules with Rogers word by word after he got to Idaho. This is where the UNK-UNK set in. We didn't know he had changed the wording and didn't know to ask what the wording was because it didn't dawn on either of us that a mid-level FBI official would dare change an order from a superior.

At nine o'clock on the morning of August 22, Rogers briefed the HRT using his *can and should* construction, then presented that version to Glenn, who approved it. Glenn didn't see any red flags, probably because he'd never been on a SWAT team, had seldom, if ever, been faced with a shoot/don't-shoot decision, and wasn't familiar with rules of engagement, a term of art peculiar to the Bureau's tactical components. Glenn told the task force he thought Potts had approved the rules Rogers gave him because of a telephone conversation he'd had with Potts in which Potts told Glenn he and Rogers had worked out some rules of engagement, and they could be used. Another UNK-UNK: Glenn didn't double-check the wording of Rogers's rules with Potts, and Potts didn't ask Glenn to read back what Rogers was proposing. Potts told Glenn that the wording Rogers showed Glenn was fine, not knowing that Rogers had changed it.

To support his argument that HQ approved the Rogers language, Glenn told the task force he had faxed the Rogers language to SIOC on the evening of August 22, when I was the senior duty official. He said that they had been the second page of the now notorious ops plan that proposed using tear gas and tanks against the compound and then assaulting it. So, Glenn's argument went, it stood to reason that I had also read the rules of engagement with the *can and should* language. Since I hadn't registered an objection, Glenn reasoned, I must have approved the language.

I am damn sure about this: I read a fax that guaranteed carnage, but I never read a fax or approved anything that said tactical operators *can and should* shoot at anybody. By the time the Berman task force got around to asking me about it, fourteen months had passed, and I wasn't able to identify the exact fax that had come into my hands. The SIOC logs show receipt of a fax of an operations plan faxed from the Ruby Ridge command post at about 6:40 P.M. on August 22. But the logs don't show how many pages SIOC received. At various times, Justice attorneys have shown me not one but three different versions of the ops plan, all similar in nature. Two were two pages long; one was three pages. I don't know that any one of them is the exact document that came across my desk on August 22, 1993.

So, as far as I can see, there are three possibilities. One, only one page arrived on my desk. Two, in the reams of paper grinding through the SIOC fax machine, the first and second pages got separated. Three, I received all the pages but failed to read the second page because I was so busy slam-dunking the first page with its awful gas-and-assault ops plan. If that's what happened, I made a serious mistake. I felt terribly depressed when I realized that I might have missed a chance to save us all from a great deal of anguish. But I'm not at all sure I ever had that chance.

In the end, Berman and her task force didn't believe me or Potts. "It is inconceivable to us that FBI Headquarters remained ignorant of the exact wording of the Rules of Engagement during that entire period," their report said.

It was tough to swallow that accusation. I have my faults. I can be profane and cocky. I don't suffer fools gladly. But I don't lie.

Besides, the idea that I'd approve those stupid rules makes no sense in view of the fact that I had actually prevented the HRT from being sent into the compound with submachine guns to do close-quarter battle with men, women, and children. I can't imagine how anybody could think I would have said, "No, you can't gas the cabin. No, you can't knock down the outbuildings with the tank. No, you can't assault the cabin. You can't send FBI agents to engage children in a gunfight. You must negotiate an end to this. Oh, by the way, you can shoot Weaver and Harris on sight."

The whole matter was kicked into yet another internal review, this one for the purposes of determining who at the FBI should be disciplined. It would not be concluded until 1995. I desperately wanted to close the chapter on Ruby Ridge, but it wasn't going to happen.

In the meantime, I was trying to get on with my life.

The good news was the Coulson luck had struck again. In August 1993, I was named SAC of the Baltimore Field Division, covering the states of Maryland and Delaware. If the twenty or so months I had spent at HQ rated right up there with the worst experiences of my life, the Baltimore job was one of the best. The staff was a field commander's dream team—experienced, competent supervisors who generated tremendous energy and direction, agents who were highly educated, street-smart, and motivated. There were plenty of real crimes to be tackled—major heroin and cocaine trafficking organizations and a Chinese organized crime kidnapping case where we rescued about a hundred hostages being held by heavily armed Asian hoods.

Best of all, it meant I got to the field without having to uproot my family again. God knows I owed them. I'm not sure how I would have weathered the stressful months of the Ruby Ridge and Waco crises and the political firestorms that followed without their stalwart support. Debbie and our four have always believed that the FBI would do the right thing, but it couldn't have been easy to be the child of an FBI agent as the newspapers and the network news portrayed us as out-of-control killers.

BOOK SIX

TEXAS

But the real value of our attacks today lies in the psychological impact, not in the immediate casualties. For one thing our efforts against the System gained immeasurably in credibility. More important, though, is what we taught the politicians and the bureaucrats. They learned this afternoon that not one of them is beyond our reach. They can huddle behind barbed wire and tanks in the city, or they can hide behind the concrete walls and alarm systems of their country estates, but we can still find them and kill them. All the armed guards and bulletproof limousines in America cannot guarantee their safety. That is a lesson they will not forget.

—The Turner Diaries
by Andrew MacDonald
(pseudonym of William Pierce,
founder of the National Alliance)

1

The man who said you can't go home again wasn't from Texas.

For a while, I believed it. Then Mama died.

In March 1994, Pop called and said she had to go to the hospital. She had been wasting for some time, with lung cancer from years of smoking and a brain tumor. I jumped on a plane and flew down.

Mavinee didn't recognize me at first, but then she said, "Oh, it's you, Danny." I held her hand and we talked a bit. "I feel better," she said. Then she dozed off.

I stepped out of the room for a few minutes and returned to find her on life support. She had gone into cardiac arrest. I sat down and held her hand and watched the little dial that measured her breathing as it got fainter and fainter. Then Pop and Doc walked into the room, and a moment later, the monitor went into that flat-line drone. *How did she know?* I wondered. The nurse said it was fairly common for people who seemed unconscious to wait to die until loved ones had gathered round the bedside.

Her passing forced me to confront that Pop was getting on too, though he acted more like a forty-year-old than a man in his seventies. Pop was Texas to the core, as if he had fought with Travis. What you need to know about Texans is that they are just about the friendliest people you could ever meet, as long as you don't cross them. They're all a little crazy. What other culture could spawn men that would stand 123 strong against Santa Anna's 5,000 regular troops and do it in a chapel with no back door? This only makes sense from the Texas point of view, which is, since Texas is heaven and we're there, it stands to reason that we're immortal.

As much as I would have liked to head for home, there was no sense in even thinking about asking for a transfer back as long as Buck Revell was the SAC there. After leaving HQ, Buck had his pick of field commands. He picked the Dallas Division, which covered the entire top half of the state, and guarded his vast turf like a medieval shogun.

Soon after Mom's death, Revell got an employment offer he couldn't refuse—working for himself. He threw a retirement party the like of which nobody had ever seen, a three-day Buck-o-mania fest that involved golf outings, parties, and a rodeo, during which some poor horse hauled Big Buck around the ring. "I can't come down for the party," I told him, "but I'll be glad to handle your prostate surgery." He declined. Probably got a better offer.

Even then, I didn't put in for the Dallas post. I didn't want to move the kids again. And I'd only been in Baltimore about a year. I was really enjoying the work there. My professional life and family life were just about perfect.

But I'm a Texan, and Texans belong in Texas. When I found out that Louis Freeh wasn't pleased with any of the names that had been submitted to him for the post, I couldn't stand it any longer. "Hell, I'll go," I said. "But I'll have to talk to my family."

We had a meeting. Debbie was all for it. She was sure she'd lived her previous life in the Southwest. The girls were good to go. It made no difference to Doc, who at twenty-two was working and attending a community college in Oregon. The only naysayer was Jeff, who was in his senior year in high school. "I promised you could finish high school here, and I'll keep my promise," I told him. "I'll go first and live with Pop. You finish your senior year, and I'll come back and get you guys."

We agreed that I'd go ahead on my own. In September 1994, I drove south and moved into the spare bedroom at Pop's house in Fort Worth, the house I'd grown up in. We'd buy a house when Debbie and the kids joined me in June 1995, after school let out for the summer.

The first week I was in Dallas, I called a meeting of all the supervisors. They showed up early, in their Sunday best and jumpy as a herd of cats in a rocking-chair factory. I could understand why. The FBI had a tradition of endless management meetings that accomplished nothing because we had a lot of people who liked hearing the sound of their own voice, whether they had anything to contribute or not. Also, they were still vibrating from Buck's bulldozer management style. They didn't think I was going to be much easier to deal with. I had a reputation as a crazy HRT commander. They thought I'd walk in the door and bark at them to drop and give me fifty. The story had gotten around that back at HQ, I'd made the congressional liaison staff work out in the gym every day. "When you're negotiating with some congressional staffer," I'd told them, "I want you to have it in the back of your mind that you can reach across the table and beat the shit out of him." Mushy does as mushy is, I always say. Of course, beating the shit out of a congressional aide isn't anything to write home about.

I walked into the meeting with a cup of coffee and

said, "I'm very glad to be here. This is a great division and one I've wanted to be in since I joined the FBI in 1966. There are three things you should know about me. First, I will not tolerate your being late for a meeting. If you're late, you can expect the rest of the supervisors to come looking for you. Second, I don't like surprises unless they come from you. I'm available twenty-four hours a day. If you have problems with one of your cases or anything else, I'd better hear about it from you before I hear about it from the Bureau, the U.S. Attorney, or the news media. You bring me a problem and we'll deal with it together, but if somebody else brings me one of your problems, I'll deal with you first for not telling me. Third, I hate long meetings. I don't like long-winded people. My attention span is not very long. I believe the best meetings last no longer than a cup of coffee, and this one's half-empty, so I suggest we get started. Who's first?"

I pointed to one man and said, "You, twenty-five words or less, what do you have to tell me?" We went around the room and were done before the hour was out. "One more thing," I said as I adjourned the group. "I don't like people who are taller than me."

Everybody walked out smiling and shaking their heads. I overheard one of them say, "I've never seen anything like this before, but I think I like it."

As I settled into the job, my first priority was making sure the office's civil rights program was up to speed. One reason I had gone into law enforcement was that I believed in its professionalism. Other young people in the sixties joined the civil rights movement or the anti-war movement. I wanted to carry an FBI badge because its agents had a reputation for treating everyone with dignity, even criminals. I was driven by the racial hate I'd seen in its rawest, most malevolent form—for instance, when I used to drive to east Texas to hunt birds and wild pig with Clay Williams, a young black man who worked on Pop's loading dock with me. We weren't afraid to be seen around Fort Worth together, but once we hit the boondocks, Clay said, "Danny, stop, I'm gonna have to drive now. I don't want some cracker to see you driving me down the road." Everyone knew that black men drove whites, not the other way around.

Once, when we left late in the afternoon and it was going to be well past suppertime before we got to my uncle's ranch, where we hunted, I suggested that we stop at a café. "You crazy?" Clay gasped. "Me sittin' at a table with a white boy? You trying to get me hung?"

"Okay, okay, park around the corner and I'll go in and get some burgers to go," I said.

"You *are* crazy," he sighed. "I'll park and I'll go in. But you pay."

"I think I'm starting to figure this out," I said. But I wasn't. I didn't want to pick a fight, so I obeyed him. All the same, I was burning with fury that I couldn't drive around with my friend in my own car without fear of being stopped by some redneck with a gun and a mean disposition. I promised myself then and there that, someday, things would be different.

In Dallas, as in Baltimore and Portland, I tried to make sure we vigorously pursued all allegations of police brutality, in line with the federal statute banning violence under color of law. To fall short would undermine everything else we wanted to do; to be effective, law enforcement must have the confidence of the community it exists to serve. That means brutality charges must be proven or disproven quickly and credibly. I don't know how many times I'd gotten calls from chiefs of police and sheriffs who wanted a team of FBI agents to get to the bottom of a misconduct charge. If they had a bad cop, they needed to know right away. If they had a good cop who had been wrongly accused, an FBI finding would be perceived as fair and impartial, and the officer could be exonerated without controversy.

I was pleased to find that the Dallas Field Office reflected changes in society at large. Minority agents, once assigned to menial tasks like driving the Hoov and other executives, were now handling the full range of responsibilities in the field office. Mike Lee, who had worked for me in Washington, was now supervising the Special Operations Group squad. Daryl James and Yalonda Griffith were chasing and catching white collar criminals. Leard Pennywell was the scourge of the crack gangs. Garrett Floyd in Fort Worth had amazing sources who reported on drugs and violent crimes and was one of our best interviewers. Wilbur Gregory, the office's general counsel, became one of my most valued advisers. Henry Garcia and Art Caneda handled any kind of cases or problems we threw at them.

Like every other city in America, Dallas was infested with drug dealers and the violence that went with them. Crack was all over the black neighborhoods. Black tar heroin in capsules was turning up in middle- and upper-middle-class neighborhoods. A youngster no longer had to stick a dirty needle in his arm to get a buzz. He could pop a capsule and get high—and dead.

It bothered me when a small number of unfortunate overdose deaths of teenagers in middle-class neighborhoods caused a media frenzy. These deaths were tragic, but for some years, drugs and gang violence had been killing poor kids with scarcely a line or two in the papers.

I decided to expand our Safe Streets program. I added more people to task forces with state and local agencies. We concentrated on busting up the gangs who dealt crack and the smuggling rings who brought drugs up from Mexico. We weren't going to clean up Texas overnight, but, as I liked to tell younger agents, solving a big problem is like eating an elephant. One bite at a time.

Just after New Year's Day, 1995, FBI HQ wrapped up its internal review of the Ruby Ridge matter. Louis Freeh called me to say that I was to receive a letter of censure. I had failed to make sure that Glenn and Rogers issued the rules of engagement approved by Potts. Larry Potts was being censured too; we were supposed to be supervising the crisis, yet neither of us called Glenn to double-check the rules of engagement, letter by letter, before they were issued.

The only comfort I could take was that Freeh believed Potts and me when we said that we hadn't approved the changes Rogers had made to the rules of engagement. Glenn and Rogers were punished more severely than the rest of us because they violated Potts's direct orders and issued rules of engagement that could be interpreted as illegal shoot-on-sight orders. Glenn was censured, stripped of his field command, and suspended for fifteen days. Rogers was censured and suspended for ten days. He accepted a voluntary assignment to a non-tactical field management job.

The good news out of the whole mess was that Freeh had found the ideal man to replace Rogers—Roger

Nisley, who had helped found the HRT back when he was a crisis-management and SWAT instructor at SOARU. I admired few men more than Nisley. He believed in the things I believed in—common sense, careful planning, and above all, saving lives—and didn't tolerate creeping commandoism. Nobody would ever stick him with the touchy-feely label. He could do the run-jump-shoot drill better than most of our young hotshots, but he valued negotiators as I had and would restore them to parity with the tactical guys.

In fact, Freeh institutionalized the changes Nisley was making by creating a new entity, the Critical Incident Response Group, as a one-stop-shopping outlet for all the Bureau's crisis-management tools, not only the HRT and SWAT teams and negotiators, but also behavioral scientists and profilers, surveillance teams, air operations, and command-post specialists. Every SAC and every field office would be required to participate in an elaborate crisis exercise at least once every two years.

Though I was relieved to see the HRT—my baby!—in safe hands, I was devastated by the letter of censure. Outsiders think it's a hand slap, but inside the Bureau, it's a terrible, humiliating blow. I'd expected to get beached sooner or later for a screwup in some white collar crime case I hadn't followed closely, but I never dreamed I'd face accusations of command failure in a crisis-management situation. I'd been involved in more crisis and tactical situations than any other executive in the history of the FBI. Agents under my command had rescued or negotiated the release of over 250 hostages, a hundred since Ruby Ridge.

No good deed goes unpunished, I said to myself. If I hadn't come down on Glenn and Rogers with both feet and kept them from assaulting the cabin, who knows how much blood would have been shed?

But I took it. I hate whiners. I never put up with excuses from my people, and I wasn't about to let myself off the hook. I'd trusted Glenn and Rogers to follow orders. I wouldn't ever make that mistake again, about anybody. I wasn't going to sit around and wring my hands, worrying about how the censure would affect my career. I called a meeting of the whole field office, explained the procedure to the four hundred or so men and women I commanded, and accepted responsibility for the letter of censure. I wanted them to hear about it from me. Remember, no surprises.

Then I moved on. We had druggers to catch, white collar crooks to expose, and our share of domestic and international terrorists who needed attention.

2

All my plans were put on hold on April 19, 1995, by the Murrah building bombing. One hundred sixty-eight lives, nineteen of them little children, had been snuffed out. Five hundred other people had been injured, some of them badly maimed. With the children who had been orphaned and the families that had been shattered, the toll was incalculable.

This was the big one I'd trained for my whole career,

which I'd hoped would never happen. Now that it had, a flamethrower couldn't have kept me away.

The OKBOMB case, as it was named in Bureau shorthand, would become the largest FBI investigation conducted to that date. It was a classic example of the FBI machine at work. Before it was over, agents would conduct twenty-six thousand witness interviews and collect untold thousands of records, telephone toll calls, and videotapes.

The public face of the FBI was Weldon Kennedy, at that time the SAC in Phoenix, who arrived shortly after midnight on April 20 to become the on-scene FBI commander and official spokesman. As part of his post–Ruby Ridge, post-Waco changes, Freeh had done away with the practice of making the nearest SAC the on-scene commander. He insisted on filling that post from a core group of SACs with training and hands-on experience in crisis management. I believed this move was long overdue, but it was not well received by most SACs.

Also—and this part was unspoken—Freeh, a notorious micromanager, wanted a commander he knew and trusted. Weldon had been assistant director in charge of administration when Freeh and his clique arrived. Weldon wasn't the typical FBI executive yes-man, but he was at ease with Freeh, and Freeh with him.

Freeh's choice put both Weldon and Bob Ricks, the Oklahoma City SAC, in a difficult spot. At first, the rest of the law enforcement community read it as a vote of no confidence in Ricks. Moreover, it dredged up stories about Ricks's role at Waco, where he had worked in the command post, supervising the negotiators and handling most of the press briefings. Some even speculated that the bomb had been meant for him, though the FBI office was not in the Murrah building but several miles away.

Kennedy and Ricks were adults and pros, so they got past the first awkward moments and buckled down to get the job done. Kennedy played Mr. Outside, dealing with the press, maintaining good relations with other federal agencies, and setting overall strategy. Ricks was the inside man, retaining control over the hunt for the bombers. I took charge of collecting evidence at the site and whatever else came up.

This arrangement worked to everyone's satisfaction. Weldon was good on-camera, projecting the compassion, authority, and integrity that seemed to reassure the public that the FBI was going to do this right. Inside the command center, he made tough calls with a calm, self-effacing manner that defused conflict. No one from the other federal agencies was in any mood to put up with a prima donna from the FBI. Four of the dead were special agents of the U.S. Secret Service and two were U.S. Customs agents. DEA had lost an agent and four female support workers, one of whom was six months pregnant. Three ATF employees had been injured. These agencies needed to have a real role in the hunt for the bombers, and we needed them. God knows there was no shortage of work. Weldon gave their executives managerial responsibilities in the command center and assigned their agents to teams covering leads.

Mid-level weenies from the Department of Justice saw Weldon's less kindly side. Anyone who delayed or questioned a decision was told very quietly how things were going to be. If he still didn't get it, and a lot of folks from Washington don't, Weldon unleashed Louis Freeh on them.

For instance, on the afternoon of April 20, Oklahoma City fire chief Gary Marrs came to Weldon to settle a disagreement with James Lee Witt, the director of the Federal Emergency Management Agency. The fire department wanted to dig into the rubble aggressively, arguing that if the survivors weren't rescued quickly, they would surely die of their injuries or shock. State health department officials took their side. FEMA specialists worried about crushing victims in the scramble. They proposed to go more slowly, using high-tech sensors that could detect the presence of a living body. These gadgets sounded great in theory, Marrs said, but drilling holes for the probes and inserting them would take hours.

Weldon called officials from the two factions into his office and, after a few minutes of listening to them pound on his table, ended the meeting with "Gentlemen, we need to move this thing along." That meant he had ruled in Marrs's favor. Within the hour, the searches were accelerated. As Weldon put it to me later, both sides had good points, but he thought no one from FEMA had as much hands-on experience as the local fire and rescue people. "They do this all the time," he said. "They're actual practitioners as opposed to studiers and assisters. If they don't know what they're doing, then we're in trouble, but I'm banking that they do."

Witt had run the Arkansas Disaster Assistance Agency when Bill Clinton was governor and had then come to Washington as a Friend of Bill. He kept saying, "I just talked to Leon," until I blurted out, "Who the fuck is Leon?"

"Leon Panetta, the president's chief of staff," Weldon whispered.

"Well, I was pretty sure it wasn't Leon Blakeney," I hissed back. "I can't stand these name-droppers."

Clinton had given Witt a letter authorizing him to "coordinate and direct other federal agencies." He brandished that language in everybody's face until Weldon called Freeh, Freeh called Reno, and Reno called the White House, insisting that somebody tell Witt to back off. Eventually, he did.

Ricks's soft-spoken manner disguised one of the keenest investigative minds in the Bureau. In the first hours after the bombing, he had the command post up and running, its walls lined with butcher paper so that supervisors and senior agents like Erroll Myers, my old friend from the BLA case, had plenty of room to start drawing up lists of suspects, associations, and leads. Anything we needed from the state law enforcement agencies, we got because of Ricks. Just about everybody in law enforcement in the area liked and respected him for his decency and collegiality.

As for me, I was doing what I did best, getting down in the muck and dust with the agents, making sure they had what they needed to put together the pieces of this huge, awful puzzle. It sounds depressing but I considered it a rare privilege to be able to work alongside such brave men and women, all laboring ceaselessly, in selfless anonymity. Some would eventually be recognized publicly for their work. Others would not, but they were all heroes in my book.

I was in awe of the rescuers who teemed about the wreckage, slippery from the pelting rain, seemingly oblivious to the danger. Rebecca Anderson, a nurse, died after being struck in the head by a piece of rubble. Yet her comrades kept at it, day after day and night after night, for weeks on end, long after there was no longer any hope that more victims could be found alive.

Our Evidence Response Teams carried out equally sad, dirty, and dangerous tasks. Crawling around the unstable building and sifting tons of pulverized debris was bad enough. Even worse was standing by at the morgue, watching autopsies and taking custody of shrapnel. When the blast went off, tens of thousands of slivers from the Ryder truck and the blue and white plastic drums that held the explosive charge screamed through the air, embedding in whatever they encountered. Many human bodies were shredded by these deadly projectiles. We had to find as many of the slivers as we could to test them for explosive residues and embedded bits of timing or ignition mechanisms.

Special Agent Monica Segedy, a member of the Dallas ERT, had to fight to get to the bombing scene. She was six months pregnant. Moved by what Monica regarded as misguided chivalry, Steve Largent, her supervisor in the Fort Worth resident agency, told her she was staying home. "How can you do this to me?" she pleaded, her blue eyes snapping. "There are things I can do up there. I can answer phones, I can set out leads, I can handle administrative things. This is my team, and I have to go with them."

As I was driving through the storm to Oklahoma City, Jim Adams, my ASAC, and Largent called my cell phone on Adams's speakerphone to talk logistics. Largent told me about his exchange with Monica. "Boy, is she pissed," he said.

"Should we mention it to Matt?" I asked, referring to Monica's husband, FBI agent Matt Segedy. "He has an interest in this."

"Hell no, he can't control her and he has a gun," Adams replied. I could hear a shudder in his voice.

"Okay, send her," I ruled. "She's pregnant, not sick. Let's just check on her while she's here. Got to admire her spirit."

The DEA office had been dumped down onto the ground in the front of the building. By late on the afternoon of the bombing, Monica was at the blast site, helping DEA agents search the debris for their files, seized cash, and other evidence. Monica was climbing around on the rubble when she found a picture of a DEA agent and his wife. Was he also among the dead? She looked up, and there he stood. He had been three blocks down the street when the bomb went off. She handed him the snapshot, saying a silent prayer of thanks that she and her team did not have to pull his body out of the rubble.

After the DEA office was squared away, she joined the rest of the Dallas team inside the crater, collecting particles from the center of the blast. So much for administrative duties and answering phones.

By the next day, the twentieth, Monica was at the morgue, dressed in operating-room overalls and surgeon's gloves, methodically removing slivers of blue plastic, steel, and wood from bodies, then bagging and labeling them. Special Agent Kathy Lumley, who had an eighteen-month-old son, had a terrible time handling the bodies of the children. Monica got through those autopsies all right, but she had to force herself to stay in the room when the body of a woman who appeared to be about eight months pregnant was rolled in. Monica flashed back to the delight Matt and she had felt when she learned of her pregnancy, then looked at this woman and child, lost to this world. Through it all, agent Deb

Eckart, a former nurse who had seen many autopsies, stood by Monica and Kathy, whispering encouragement. Monica told me later that Deb had taught her to repeat to herself, *We're here to do a job. That's what we're here to do. I can do this.* No one was surprised that she did.

Hoover, you complete idiot, I mused, *how many years did we turn down female applicants because you and those toadies in D.C. thought that women couldn't do this job? Hell, Monica could kick your ass and look beautiful doing it!*

In the movies, the star gets to make the big break in the case, but in real life, the solution never springs from the imagination of one inspired investigator, or even an elite group. Rather, the truth emerges from countless hours of hard, often boring labor logged by countless men and women who just do their jobs. There's nothing flashy about what they do, nothing dramatic, but they don't miss much.

Ricks, the Oklahoma City Division supervisors, and OKBOMB case agent Jim Norman, a member of the Oklahoma City division's terrorism squad, shared the mind-boggling job of coordinating the work of hundreds and hundreds of other agents and police officers, lab technicians, psychologists, photographers, fingerprint examiners, telephone-records specialists, computer specialists, pilots, file clerks, artists, concerned citizens—the list went on and on. They fended off the inevitable backseat driving from HQ with amazing good grace. Louis Freeh decreed that they were to get any kind of support they needed. Leads sent to other offices were covered immediately, with the personal attention of the SAC in that city.

Dave Williams, the FBI lab's lead explosives investi-

gator, proved the no-good-deed-goes-unpunished rule.
Dave pointed us in the right direction when, early on the
morning of April 20, we were staring down into the
crater and he told me he thought the bomb had been
made up of four thousand pounds of ANFO—ammonium nitrate fertilizer and fuel oil. I took notes on our
conversation and immediately briefed Kennedy and
Ricks. They passed the information on to agents in
Oklahoma and Kansas who started canvassing area
agriculture-supply houses for large sales of ammonium
nitrate to first-time customers.

I was deeply troubled when, two years later, an investigation of the FBI laboratory by Mike Bromwich, then
the Justice Department's Inspector General, accused
Dave of working backward and tailoring his estimate of
the construction, composition, and size of the bomb to
fit the inventory of evidence recovered from the property of Terry Nichols, who would become a defendant in
the case. If he had done that, it would have been highly
unprofessional. But he didn't. I know exactly what Dave
Williams said and when he said it, and it was before
either of us had even heard of Terry Nichols. Nichols's
name didn't surface until midday April 21, and his house
wasn't searched until around seven o'clock on the
evening of April 22.

Dave Williams had spent the better part of two
decades looking at bomb scenes, so I was not surprised
to learn that his initial impression was right on the
money. Subsequent investigation proved that Tim
McVeigh and Terry Nichols had bought exactly four
thousand pounds of ammonium nitrate from a farm co-
op in Kansas. Steve Burmeister, head of the FBI lab's
chemical residue recovery team, found ammonium

nitrate crystals on a piece of the Ryder truck. Witnesses came forward to say that McVeigh and Nichols had acquired a lot of fuel oil and also racing fuel, which is used to enhance ANFO bombs.

The Department of Justice charges ended Dave's career as an explosives specialist. He was reassigned to general case work. It's a shame that a man of such great energy and ability has been lost to this country. We all took Dave's opinion as an educated guess to get us started down the right investigative track, not a definitive scientific conclusion that could be used at a trial. We all understood that it would take chemical analysis to establish the bomb's composition definitively. I asked for Dave's off-the-cuff opinion the way I consulted our family doctor, who could usually tell us, long before the lab results came back, whether a kid had strep throat or bronchitis, or the flu, simply because he had spent his entire adult life looking at kids. Dave devoted his career to looking at homemade bombs. He gave us a good early indication of what we were dealing with, at the moment when the bombers were still roaming around the country and could very well have set off another one. It may be that he didn't draft his reports with as many legalistic hedges as he should have, but I'd rather work a bombing with Dave Williams than any Justice Department lawyer I've ever known.

Other heroes of the OKBOMB case are the field agents who ran down lead after lead to the last thread of data. From one single scrap of data—the vehicle identification number (VIN) on the axle of the bomb truck—these agents constructed a chain of evidence solid enough to hoist a ship's anchor. Evidence specialist Jim Elliott traced the VIN truck to Elliott's Body Shop, a

Ryder rental outlet in Junction City, Kansas. Salina, Kansas–based agent Scott Crabtree quickly drove there to interview proprietor Eldon Elliott, mechanic Tom Kessinger, and bookkeeper Vicki Beemer.

Eldon Elliott, it turned out, was as good a witness as we could have hoped for. His business was mostly vehicle repair; he didn't rent that many trucks. Moreover, he had dealt with the man who rented this particular truck two times, each from a distance of no more than two feet.

Elliott said that the first call from "Robert Kling" had come in on April 14. He reserved a twenty-foot truck to be dropped in Omaha. The next morning, Kling showed up in person to complete the transaction. He was the only rental customer who came in the shop that day. Moreover, Kling did something strange. Instead of slapping down a credit card for the $80 deposit, he paid the entire rental fee in advance—$280.32 in cash.

Elliott spent several minutes with Kling, filling out paperwork, so he got a good look at him. He was a white male, about his own height, five feet ten, twenty-seven to thirty, average build, right-handed, with a military-style crew cut, no facial hair, no accent. Elliott said it was possible the man had worn camouflage-colored clothing—many of his customers were soldiers moving here or there—but he couldn't be sure.

Elliott saw Kling a second time when he arrived to take the truck, shortly after 4 P.M. on April 17. He was one of two customers that day. Kessinger said he also recalled Kling. He thought he had a companion, a white male, about thirty, five feet seven to five feet eight, white, with straight, dark hair slicked back, a tattoo on his upper left arm, and a baseball cap with distinctive blue-and-white stripes. At first Elliott said he didn't recall a second man, but after hearing Kessinger's description, Elliott agreed with Kessinger that another man had been present. Elliott could remember little about the second man.

Every bit of information on Kling's rental form turned out to be bogus—there was no such home address, no such destination, and as far as we could tell, no Robert Kling fitting Elliott's description. The date of birth—April 19—reinforced my theory that there was some kind of connection to Waco.

On the morning of April 20, Crabtree asked Elliott and his employees to meet him at Fort Riley, a large army base outside Junction City. There, they brought in FBI artist Ray Rozycki. Working with Elliott, Beemer, and Kessinger, Rozycki made sketches of both men. They would be entered into our files as "Unsub One" and "Unsub Two." Flyers distributed to the press used the more familiar name for an unidentified subject, "John Doe One" and "John Doe Two."

Agents spread out all over Junction City, showing the sketches to everybody with a pulse. Toward evening, we had another lucky strike. Lea McGown, proprietor of the Dreamland motel, recognized "Unsub One" as the man who was registered in room 25 from April 14 to April 18 and had used the name Tim McVeigh. He had listed his address as 3616 North Van Dyke Road, Decker, Michigan. He had been driving an old yellow Mercury Marquis with an Arizona license plate.

In Oklahoma City, three people who had been near the Murrah building just before the explosion identified "Unsub One" as a man they had observed near the building's front entrance between 8:40 and 8:55 A.M.

Leads were sent out to check records on McVeigh in every state. Agents in Michigan found a license for Timothy James McVeigh, born April 23, 1968, address 3616 North Van Dyke Road, Decker, Michigan. A prior license in Kansas gave his address as P.O. Box 2153, Fort Riley, Kansas. The Van Dyke Road address was the farm of James Douglas Nichols and his brother Terry Lynn Nichols. Terry Nichols had previously lived in Marion, Kansas, an hour's drive from Junction City.

A team of agents went to Decker. A relative confirmed that James Nichols was a friend of McVeigh's. One person said that James possessed quantities of fuel oil and fertilizer and had built bombs in 1994. Other people said that Nichols was often strident in his antigovernment views. Neither of the Nichols brothers looked like our sketch of John Doe Two, but they had to be found and interviewed.

Meanwhile, a picture of Tim McVeigh was starting to come together, and he looked like trouble from just about every angle. A young man named Carl LeBron called the FBI office in Buffalo when he saw the sketch of John Doe One on television. He was sure it was his old friend Tim, with whom he had worked at a local security business. Lebron told agent Eric Kruss that McVeigh held extreme right-wing views and was furious with the actions of the federal government at Waco. In fact, LeBron said, Tim had made a pilgrimage to Waco in March of 1993, just before the siege's fiery end. LeBron said Tim had been drifting, but he had a recent address for him in Kingman, Arizona.

Tim McVeigh grew up in Pendleton, New York, not far from Buffalo. His parents were William McVeigh, a swing-shift worker in a radiator factory, and Mildred

McVeigh, a travel agent. The marriage had broken up in the 1980s. Mildred and her youngest child, Jennifer, had moved out, leaving Bill with Patricia, the eldest, and Tim.

People in Pendleton remembered Tim as a teenager obsessed with guns. He got through high school without any serious problems, but then his life started coming apart. He dropped out of a local business college after one semester, then worked for a few months for the security company.

The Army stopped his drift for a while. He signed up in May of 1988, went to basic training at Fort Benning, Georgia, and was assigned to the First Infantry Division—the Big Red One—at Fort Riley, where he was a tank gunner. Tim thrived in the structure of military life. By all accounts, he was a good soldier, hard-working and enthusiastic. He attained the rank of sergeant, served in Operation Desert Storm, and received a number of commendations, including a Bronze Star. But he hit a wall when he tried to sign on with the Green Berets. The stringent strength and endurance tests defeated him. He washed out on the second day of a twenty-one-day tryout. Deeply disappointed, he mustered out of the Army on December 31, 1992.

The machine was grinding, this time not slowly. On the evening of April 20, after the license and Dreamland motel records gave us Tim McVeigh's true name, FBI agent Walt Lamar asked the National Crime Information Center for all mentions of McVeigh or Kling. The NCIC is a vast computerized database, maintained in a bank of mainframes at FBI HQ, that contains 8 million files on suspected terrorists, fugitives, missing persons, people who had made threats against the President, stolen cars, stolen license plates, stolen guns, and criminal histories of violent offenders. It is queried more than a million times a day by law enforcement agencies nationwide.

Early the next morning the answer came back from Washington that an Oklahoma state trooper had run a check on one Tim McVeigh shortly after the bombing. Mark Michalic, an Oklahoma City–based ATF agent who was running leads out of the command center, set about to find the trooper. Working the phones, Michalic learned that Oklahoma state highway patrolman Charles Hanger had arrested a Tim McVeigh at 10:22 A.M. on April 19 on Interstate 35, just north of Perry, Oklahoma, some seventy-five miles out of Oklahoma City. The bomb had gone off about seventy-five minutes before. If this Tim McVeigh was our man and if he had been heading north out of Oklahoma City on his way to Kansas, he would have been at the exact spot where Hanger stopped him. We weren't ready to celebrate yet. We had to know more.

When we did, Charles Hanger ended up on everybody's list of heroes. When his internal alarm bell went off, he didn't make one false move. Hanger pulled McVeigh over because his 1977 yellow Mercury Marquis didn't have license plates. A state trooper had been shot and killed during a traffic stop recently, and Hanger wasn't taking any chances, so he ordered McVeigh to unzip his jacket slowly. Instead of trying to kill the trooper or country-boy him, McVeigh panicked and blurted out, "I have a gun." Hanger found it, a .45-caliber Glock semiautomatic pistol, and also McVeigh's knife. He handcuffed McVeigh, put him in his backseat, drove to the Noble County jail in Perry, and booked him on a motor vehicle infraction and carrying a concealed weapon. McVeigh said almost nothing, but he gave the Nichols address in Decker as a reference.

Michalic called Noble County sheriff Jerry Cook to find out what had happened to McVeigh. As the agent waited tensely, Cook went to check, then returned to say, yep, McVeigh was still in custody. His bail hearing was coming up in an hour or so.

"Spin that boy around and put him back in your hotel," Michalic said as calmly as he could manage. This was yet another amazing stroke of luck. In most jurisdictions, McVeigh would have been in and out of the slammer in hours, not days. Michalic put his hand over the receiver and whooped, "We got him!" The entire command center erupted in cheers.

Just then, Williams, Adams, and I walked in the door after a visit to the blast site. Ricks waved to me. "McVeigh's in custody in Perry, Oklahoma. The dumb son of a bitch got caught for not having a license plate."

"Are they going to hold him?"

"Yeah, but we have to move fast. He's about to make bond."

Weldon joined us. "We have to get some agents up there fast," he said. "We need to get him into federal custody before somebody tries to kill him."

"Do you guys want me to take some agents and get up there?" I said.

They both nodded. Ricks spoke first. "Get out to the airport. I'll have a helicopter waiting for you."

"Get your gear," I told Adams and Williams. "We're going to Perry to get McVeigh. Dave, you'll take care of evidence. Jim, you and I will plan the move."

Ricks was back on the phone but glanced up as he saw us heading for the door. "Bring him back to Tinker Air Force Base. We can arraign him there. They have excellent security."

"Okay, get me whichever agents you want and make sure one of them's from ATF," I said.

As we drove toward the airport, Adams just sat there shaking his head. "I can't believe that we got a break like this. I thought we'd be in a manhunt for months."

"Right." I nodded. If this guy took *The Turner Diaries* as gospel and thought he was some sort of warrior patriot in the new revolution, why had he surrendered meekly to a lone state trooper who thought he was arresting Joe Blow? All I could figure was, he thought he'd covered his tracks so well that it would take us months to get on his trail. He had underestimated us. Not a smart thing to do.

"Don't forget we have to get him into our custody," I added. "We'd better not count our chickens yet. We still don't know if this is a conspiracy or what. Somebody may want to blow him up and us along with him."

The radio crackled. "We have an exact location on the car." That meant McVeigh's Mercury, which Hanger had left by the road when he hauled McVeigh off.

"Give it to us," I said, pulling out my notebook.

"One mile south of Billings exit, I-35, sixteen miles north of Perry, located on the side of the road."

When we got to the airport, we spotted the agents Ricks had picked for the trip. As we shook hands, Williams stood apart, looking worried. I thought that he'd be upbeat, like the rest of us.

"Jim, what's the matter with Dave?" I asked.

"He hates helicopters."

I started to laugh. Jim had flown on plenty of choppers as a Marine artillery officer in Vietnam; at
Quantico, he had taught SWAT teams the art of helicopter rappelling and extraction. Me, I just loved helo
rides. I never spent a dime on roller coasters; the years
on the HRT had given me so many helo ops that some of
my fillings had shaken out.

I threw my arm around Williams's shoulder. "Don't
worry about the trip. Almost half of all helicopter rides
end without a crash."

Williams rolled his eyes. "Oh, thanks a hell of a lot.
That makes me feel real good."

"That bomb crap that you deal with scares the shit out
of me," I said. "How can you handle a bomb and be
afraid of a helicopter?"

Williams shifted from foot to foot like a pimply
teenager about to ask a girl to dance at the prom. "I'll do
the bombs. You do the helicopter stuff."

Just then the helo pilot and his crew chief walked up.

"Hi, Doc. We can leave immediately after warm-up,"
the pilot said. "The only problem is, we haven't put the
doors on the bird. We can leave without them if you
want. You'll all be buckled in, but it might get a little
breezy."

I turned to my party. "Okay, mount up. Buckle up real
tight and put on your coats if you have them."

Williams's face sagged. "No doors. That's just great."

I grabbed a seat facing rearward on the port side,
right next to the opening where a door would have been.
Adams got into the seat in the center row facing me.
Directly across were case agents Jim Norman and Floyd
Zimms, a drug squad veteran who had a way of getting
people to talk to him. In the famous picture of Tim

McVeigh being led out of the Perry courthouse, Zimms is the bald-headed, bearded man on McVeigh's left elbow. Norman is the bearded guy with the hat on McVeigh's right. *I hope the Hoov is watching,* I thought, chuckling. Hoover didn't allow beards and would have busted any SAC who did. This was a different FBI from the one that I'd joined, and I liked it.

The other passengers jumped into the remaining seats. Williams was left with the seat next to the starboard opening. For a man who didn't like to ride in a helicopter, it was just about the worst seat in the house. The helo lifted off the ground and headed north along I-35. I gave the location of McVeigh's Mercury, our first stop, to the pilots and sat back to enjoy the ride.

At 12:34 P.M., we spotted McVeigh's yellow rust bucket just where it was supposed to be, on the east side of I-35 headed in a northerly direction. The pilot came on the air. "There it is. I'll set down right off to the side on the grass."

Do I have to say that Williams was the first one off the chopper? No sooner had my feet touched the ground than my handheld radio started squawking. Weldon was reminding me to get major case prints from McVeigh—like I'd forgotten Arraignment 101. Weldon just looked easygoing.

An Oklahoma state trooper and a Noble County deputy sheriff showed up to take us into Perry. We took off with a roar. Soon, the speedometer needle was pegged at 120 miles an hour.

"Dave, is this any better?" I asked brightly.

Williams nodded. "A lot better."

The car hadn't even pulled to a stop at the old town square when we heard chants. "Baby killer." "Murderer."

McVeigh's arrest had been broadcast on the radio and TV. A throng of people had come to vent their anger. At least I hoped that was all they intended to do.

I opened the car door and stepped out into the square. Adams was right behind me. We had nothing on that identified us as agents or cops, just our usual jeans, boots, and collared pullover shirts. A man who appeared to be in his late seventies walked toward me. He was dressed in blue coveralls and a white straw hat. "You boys from the FBI?"

"Yessir!" we said in unison.

He looked at me, dead serious, and said slowly, "If you have any trouble with the evidence"—*evidence* being three separate words—"just put that boy out the back gate and we'll handle him for you."

I looked back at him, not daring to smile. He was in no mood for banter. "Thank you, sir, but our case is very strong."

As we walked into the courthouse that housed the sheriff's office and jail, Adams paused to scan the crowd. "They don't look very happy," he whispered. "We need to get him out of here ASAP. I'd like to use the helo for the move. I don't want to get into a convoy. The media will follow us out of here, and everyone will know where we are every step of the way. It could get real messy."

"Call the CP and have the helo set up nearby. Ask the deputies for a good place. Let's hope this goes quickly."

Sheriff Cook turned over his office to us so we could make phone calls back to the command post. Shortly after we arrived, he delivered a message from a local lawyer who wanted to represent McVeigh and wanted to come in and talk to him. That wasn't the way it was supposed to work. The subject can invoke the right-to-counsel privilege but a lawyer can't.

"Sheriff, tell the lawyer that if Mr. McVeigh asks for him, he can come in and talk," I said. "But right now he hasn't asked for a lawyer."

The process took longer than any of us had wished. County Judge Danny G. Allen had to dispose of the state case before we could take McVeigh into federal custody. While we were waiting, Jim and I bought raffle tickets for a meat smoker from some of the sheriff's employees. I never did hear if I won that smoker.

Williams took possession of McVeigh's effects, including the clothes he had been wearing at the time of his arrest—a T-shirt with a picture on the back of a tree dripping blood and a quote from Thomas Jefferson: "The Tree of Liberty must be refreshed from time to time with the blood of patriots and tyrants." On the front, there was a picture of Abraham Lincoln and the quotation, "Sic Semper Tyrannis"—"Thus ever to tyrants"—the phrase John Wilkes Booth had shouted after he shot Lincoln in the head.

My cell phone buzzed. It was Ricks, requesting extra snapshots of McVeigh, a straight-on head-and-shoulder shot with a light background in addition to the usual mug shots. His people were putting together a new photo lineup and wanted to have similar poses to make sure it was fair.

No sooner had I signed off with Ricks than my cell phone jumped again. "Danny! This is Weldon." As if I didn't know. "You are authorized to arrest McVeigh on probable cause on federal charges," he said. "The United States attorney has given the authorization."

"Okay, will do. We just have to get the judge to let

him go, and we want a shot at interviewing him up here."

"Go ahead and give it a try."

While we were waiting for the judge to move down his docket, the sheriff's deputies brought McVeigh to us. That was his face on the wanted flyer, all right. Eldon Elliott's description to the artist had been right on the money. Norman and Zimms introduced themselves as FBI agents. "Do you have any idea why we're here to talk to you?" Norman asked.

"Yes," McVeigh answered, his blue eyes flat as a piece of paper. He stared at the wall and didn't even blink.

"What do you mean by yes?" Norman bored in.

"That thing in Oklahoma City, I guess."

Exactly, they said. At that point, McVeigh said he wanted a lawyer. Norman gave him an advice-of-rights form and asked him to read it aloud, which he did. Then Norman asked for personal description information. McVeigh reeled off his name, date of birth, height (six feet two inches), and weight (160 pounds). For some reason he refused to provide his place of birth, saying, "I will just give you general physical information."

When Zimms told him he'd be taken back to Oklahoma City to answer to the bombing charges, he seemed startled.

"What are you concerned about?" Norman asked, hoping to get him talking.

"My safety," he said.

What did he mean?

"You remember what happened with Jack Ruby?" he said.

He asked to be taken out of the building through the roof instead of through the door. Norman looked him straight in the eye and said, "Enough people have been killed and hurt." No one was interested in seeing him injured. He'd be given ample protection.

I'm sure the people in the Murrah building would have liked to have been taken out by the roof, I thought to myself. They never had a chance and now we had to make sure Tim McVeigh was safe. *Sometimes this sure is a strange job,* I thought. *We may be protecting the greatest mass murderer in the history of the United States.*

Mark Gibson, the Noble County District Attorney, joined us in the sheriff's office. I told him it seemed to me that the judge was not in too much of a hurry to dispose of the state charges. The longer we were in that courthouse, the more time anybody had to plan a rescue or a murder. Gibson promised to relay the message.

My cell phone went off again. "Weldon, if you don't stop calling me, people are going to start talking about us," I said.

"I know, I know. The Bureau"—meaning HQ, meaning Freeh—"is very concerned about getting him back to Tinker. They're afraid that someone will take a shot at him."

"Hell, I'm concerned too," I snapped.

"Do you want more help?"

"No, that'll take too long. We have a plan. The helo is in place and is protected by the state police and the sheriff's department. We just need to get his ass out of here and we'll be fine.

"Weldon?" I added. "Don't worry. This is what you pay Adams and me for. This is what we're trained to do. Just get ready for him at Tinker. I'll contact you when we're wheels up."

Adams's plan was, like all his best work, simple and therefore idiot-proof. The roofs of the buildings along the square would be cleared. Troopers and deputies would move the crowds back. We'd walk McVeigh out to a van owned by the sheriff's wife. The front door wasn't ideal, but there was no other suitable exit. Then we'd drive like a bat out of hell for the helo pad just outside of town, with an escort of patrol cars, front and back.

Gibson caught up with me in the sheriff's office. "Danny, the judge would like to see you."

I followed him up the stairs. Judge Allen met me just outside his chamber. "I understand that you would like to get Mr. McVeigh out of here."

"Yessir, Your Honor. We're very concerned about his safety and the safety of everyone in this courthouse. We don't know who is involved with him in this thing, but he has a military background and others may have access to rockets that can be launched at the windows of this building. I can't protect him here. We'd like to get him to Tinker as soon as possible."

The judge nodded wisely and seemed especially interested in my remark about rockets slamming into his courthouse. He handled the paperwork meticulously and released McVeigh to our custody at 5:06 P.M. Norman and Zimms put cuffs on him. He was now in federal custody.

I ran down the stairs and found Adams. "Jim, do your last checks on the perimeter. I'll call the CP and tell them we're on our way."

We hustled McVeigh to the lobby but kept him well away from the door so no one could see him. Cook had the van driven right up to the front entrance. It had the look of a vehicle that had logged about a hundred thousand miles hauling kids to soccer and baseball. Adams and I were first out the door and climbed into the back seat. Norman, Zimms, Williams, and the other agents pointed our prize into the middle seat, and we sped away.

The rotors were turning when we pulled up to the airport. McVeigh started to get out. I put my hand on his shoulder firmly and pulled him back down. "Tim, I expect you to act like a gentleman on the helicopter ride," I said in a low voice. "I don't expect any trouble from you. Act like a gentleman and you will be treated like a gentleman. If not, then you will be very sorry. Do you understand me?"

He looked me straight in the eye. "Yes, sir, I understand."

I had arrested my share of badasses in my life. Robbers. Killers. Cop killers. This was one of the most compliant suspects I'd ever seen. What could be going on in his mind? I hadn't a clue.

We loaded him into the middle seat in the chopper. I rode to his right rear; Adams faced him, riding backward, the other agents flanked him. We strapped him into the seat and lifted off, this time with the doors on. Williams must have given a prayer of thanks. I looked at my watch and wrote in my notebook: "6:10 p.m. Wheels up. Subject in custody."

I looked out the window and saw the sheriff's deputies waving. The pilot turned us north as we started our ascent. I allowed myself a brief reflection. *This is what the FBI is all about. A big case. People cooperating. Leads all over the country. A little luck. And we have a solved case in two days. The great big FBI machine scores again.* I was proud to be a small part of it.

All of a sudden a shudder went through my body. The pilot was ascending to a normal cruising altitude. If someone wanted to kill this turkey, a heat-seeking or laser-guided shoulder-fired rocket would be just the ticket. The Afghan rebels had gotten plenty of them for their war against the Soviet Union, and some of them had made their way into the international black market in arms. We needed to get real low, real fast. A chopper flying up at several hundred feet is an easy mark, but at tree level it's here and gone before you can train a rocket on it.

I ripped a piece of paper out of my notebook and scribbled, "This guy's buddies may have access to military ordnance. We don't want a Stinger up our ass. Take evasive action." I passed the note to Adams, who shoved it under the pilot's nose.

Ten seconds later the chopper went into a diving turn and headed for the deck, still in a northerly direction. We skimmed along at over 120 knots, leapfrogging trees and fences. The pilot followed the contour of the ground, going behind tree lines and staying away from I-35. I chuckled to myself. Williams was getting the ride of his life.

Jim never took his eyes off McVeigh. He wanted to be ready in case McVeigh forgot our gentlemen's agreement. McVeigh looked straight out the windshield for the whole trip, never showing any emotion. I guessed he was more worried about a possible date with the executioner than a wild chopper ride. That's what I would've been thinking about, anyhow.

At Tinker, the Oklahoma City FBI SWAT team was

standing on the tarmac as we touched down. Team leader Chuck Choney, who had been one of my operators at the CSA, took McVeigh by the arm. "Everything's all set up," he called to me over his shoulder. "We'll put him in the Suburban. We have a car and driver for you. We're cleared all the way to the courtroom. It'll be a fast ride."

Standing by a Chevy sedan was our driver, Tom Linn, his head encased in a ballistic helmet, an MP5 submachine gun slung across his chest. Adams and I jumped into the backseat and noticed a pair of chopsticks sticking out of the headrest. Tom turned and smiled. "Sir, I have to inform you that I'm Oriental. And today I feel a little suicidal. I suggest you buckle up."

He only had to tell us one time. We zoomed off in pursuit of the Suburban. Adams couldn't resist. "Tom, what are the chopsticks for? You hungry?"

Linn kept his eyes on the road as we careened around corners. "I teach machine-gun schools, and when my students pass, I give them chopsticks. Sort of an incentive, you know."

We were holding on for dear life. This was more thrills and spills than the chopper. "I've got a better idea," I shouted. "Tell them if they don't pass, they have to ride in the backseat of your car."

How do you like your Bureau now, Mr. Hoover? The most wanted man in America was roaring along in the care of an enormous Indian in full body armor, a Chinese-American who thought he was Junior Johnson, a couple of guys who looked like ZZ Top, a short guy from Texas, and a stocky—make that extremely stocky—biker from Ohio. Not a fedora or a wing tip in the bunch.

In spite of the thrill of Linn's driving, as we got close to the Tinker brig, I breathed a sigh of relief. We were in a secure military base. All that remained was an arraignment. At 8:35 P.M., the federal magistrate called the case, and the criminal justice process was under way.

3

The Mercury was a mother lode of evidence. Late on the afternoon of the twenty-first, it arrived in Oklahoma City. Lab chemist Steve Burmeister and Dallas ERT agent William Eppright III cleaned it up better than new.

Eppright found a large sealed envelope on the front seat. It was stuffed with clippings and photocopies of extremist publications and books. Among them was a page from *The Turner Diaries*. This was no surprise. I remembered well the loving detail with which the book described how to make a truck bomb using only common ingredients, ammonium nitrate fertilizer and fuel oil, boosted with stolen dynamite and hidden inside a stolen delivery truck. If you followed author William Pierce's recipe, you'd end up with a bomb that could take down the Murrah building. I didn't doubt that that was exactly what had happened. "Turner" and his pals had bombed the fictional FBI building at 9:15 A.M., just after the start of business, to maximize the number of casualties. The Murrah building had been blown up at 9:02 A.M.

McVeigh had sliced out part of page sixty-two, which told how the terrorist cell, exhilarated by the chaos at the FBI building, went on to rain mortar rounds upon the U.S. Capitol. This section was marked with highlight pen:

> But the real value of our attacks today lies in the psychological impact, not in the immediate casualties. For one thing our efforts against the System gained immeasurably in credibility. More important, though, is what we taught the politicians and the bureaucrats. They learned this afternoon that not one of them is beyond our reach. They can huddle behind barbed wire and tanks in the city, or they can hide behind the concrete walls and alarm systems of their country estates, but we can still find them and kill them. All the armed guards and bulletproof limousines in America cannot guarantee their safety. That is a lesson they will not forget.

The clause "but we can still find them and kill them" was marked especially brightly, as if someone had run the marker over the words two or three times.

McVeigh had been reading and proselytizing others to read *The Turner Diaries* since at least 1988. He had carried it around during field trials in the Army. He sold it at gun shows, sent it to high school friends, and gave it to his younger sister, Jennifer.

He seemed to be trying to imitate Pierce in his own

writings. In February of 1992, he sent a letter to the *Union Sun and Journal* newspaper in Lockport, New York, which ranted, "Do we have to shed blood to reform the current system? I hope it doesn't come to that! But it might." That screed was close to what "Earl Turner" said after he blew up the FBI building:

> It is a heavy burden of responsibility for us to bear, since most of the victims of our bomb were only pawns who were no more committed to the sick philosophy or the racially destructive goals of the System than we are. But there is no way we can destroy the System without hurting many thousands of innocent people—no way. It is a cancer too deeply rooted in our flesh. And if we don't destroy the System before it destroys us—if we don't cut this cancer out of our living flesh—our whole race will die.

In *The Turner Diaries*, the extremist cell turns violent when the Bureau of Alcohol, Tobacco and Firearms starts confiscating people's guns. The book was written before Waco, but Pierce used his radio program and Web site to inveigh against the federal government, especially the Bureau of Alcohol, Tobacco and Firearms, calling Waco a deliberate "massacre" by a "criminal government."

Tim McVeigh's driving obsessions were the ATF and Waco. Michelle Rauch, who had visited the Waco police lines for a student journalism project in March of 1993, had interviewed Tim McVeigh there. She had videotapes of him sitting on the hood of a car emblazoned with stickers like "Fear the government that fears your guns" and "Is your church ATF approved?"

Shortly before the bombing, Tim wrote a letter to the ATF and left it on his sister Jennifer's computer disc. "ATF," he warned,

> all you tyrannical motherfuckers will swing in the wind one day, for your treasonous actions against the Constitution and the United States. Remember the Nuremberg War Trials. But . . . but . . . but . . . I was only following orders! . . . Die, you spineless, cowardice [*sic*] bastards!

Other documents found in McVeigh's car helped fill out the picture of a young man eaten up with fury at a world he imagined to be implacably hostile. On one document, McVeigh had marked these words:

> The U.S. Government has declared open warfare on the American people. . . . However, the enemies of freedom, who are the enemies of America, must be made to know that we will not only resist their evil agenda, their imposed decadence, and their oppression, but we will physically fight! They must know that we will not shrink from spilling their blood.

Another marked phrase, attributed to seventeenth-century philosopher John Locke, said:

> I have no reason to suppose that he who would take away my liberty, would not, when he had me in his power, take away everything else; and therefore, it is lawful for me to treat him as one who has put himself into a "state of war" against

me and kill him if I can, for to that hazard does
he justly expose himself, whoever introduces a
state of war and is aggressor in it.

Near a quotation from Founding Father Samuel
Adams—"When the Government fears the people, there
is liberty. When the people fear the Government, there
is tyranny"—McVeigh had written, "Maybe now there
will be liberty."

On the back of a copy of the Declaration of
Independence, McVeigh had written, "Obey the
Constitution of the United States and we won't shoot
you."

As the pile of evidence mounted, Ricks put John
Hersley in charge of preparing the case against
McVeigh. A member of a drug squad, Hersley was especially good at organizing and directing big, complex conspiracy cases. Ricks expected that the best defense attorneys in the country would fight to represent the
OKBOMB defendants. He trusted Hersley to make sure
nobody cut corners legally or made inadvertent errors
that could be exploited by the defense team. "It doesn't
do any good to solve it if you can't bring it into court,"
Ricks said. "With John Hersley, I knew in the end we'd
have a product that we'd be proud of. We'd be questioned and challenged, but it would stand up." Equally
important, Hersley exuded confidence. People who got
rattled by pressure made mistakes or caused others to do
so. We couldn't afford to lose this case and let Tim
McVeigh out on the streets. He had the look of a man
with a lot of unfinished business.

4

At Lisa and [illegible] and Maria Nichols and [illegible] [illegible] Nichols [illegible] up at the [illegible] police department [illegible] introduced himself to Detective Dale King and [illegible]

Over in Herington, Kansas, agents from the Kansas City office were closing in on Terry Lynn Nichols.

Nichols had grown up on family farms in Michigan, the first near Lapeer, and later on, outside Decker. His parents, Robert and Joyce Nichols, had gotten divorced. His older brother, James, was now running the Decker farm. Terry worked for James at times but chafed at his brother's domineering ways.

In 1980, Terry had married Lana Padilla, a realtor who lived not far from the farm. His efforts to make a living foundered, and so did his marriage. He joined the Army in 1988. Padilla moved to Las Vegas with their son, Josh.

Nichols met McVeigh during basic training at Fort Benning. After that, they moved to Fort Riley together. They went their separate ways when McVeigh shipped off to Saudi Arabia for Desert Storm. Saying he wanted to spend time with Josh, Nichols returned to civilian life in late 1989. After McVeigh got out of the Army, the two men resumed their friendship, traveling the gun-show circuit together, selling military surplus, stuff like shovels and ammo cans.

In 1990, Nichols went to the Philippines and acquired a second wife, seventeen-year-old Marife Torres, whom he met through a mail-order bride service. They had a baby daughter, then quarreled. Marife went back to Cebu in September 1994, but returned to Kansas in March of 1995.

At three o'clock on the afternoon of the twenty-first,

as I was cooling my heels in the Perry courthouse, Terry and Marife Nichols and their one-year-old daughter, Nicole, showed up at the local police department. Nichols introduced himself to Director Dale Kuhn and said he'd just heard his name on the radio in connection with Tim McVeigh. He wanted to know why.

Kuhn replied that the men who knew the answers happened to be standing just outside the door. They were Stephen Smith, Jack Foley, Mike Gillespie, and Tom Price, all based in our Kansas City office. They had tailed Nichols all day. Kuhn introduced Nichols to them. They said they weren't quite sure why his name was being broadcast either, but they thought it had to do with McVeigh. Would he like to discuss it?

He did. Smith and Foley took Nichols into the basement. They didn't arrest him, but gave him a Miranda warning. They asked Nichols when he had last seen McVeigh. April 16, Easter Sunday, he said. McVeigh had called from Oklahoma City and said his car had broken down and he needed a ride back to Junction City. Nichols said he drove there and fetched McVeigh because McVeigh had his television set.

"In my eyes, I didn't do anything wrong," he added quickly, "but I see how lawyers can turn things around." He said he shared McVeigh's antagonism toward the federal government, refused to use a social security number, and refused to pay federal income taxes.

Nichols hung out with the agents until midnight. Maybe he figured he could somehow establish his innocence by appearing to be open about himself and his friendship with McVeigh.

He figured wrong. Nichols seemed to be making it up as he went along, and he said things that did not make a lot of sense. Also, when asked whether McVeigh had ever said anything that hinted at a bombing, Nichols said, yes, that McVeigh had told him, "You will see something big in the future." Nichols claimed he'd asked, "What are you going to do? Rob a bank?" To which McVeigh had responded, "No, but I've got something in the works." In hindsight, Nichols said, McVeigh could have been talking about the bombing.

Nichols obliged the agents by signing a consent form to search his house and truck, even as he worried aloud that the agents might mistake innocent household items, like cleaning solvents, for bomb-making materials. He volunteered that he had bought a hundred pounds of ammonium nitrate from an agricultural co-op in Kansas. He said he was planning to sell it at gun shows, as "plant food." He said he had thrown the stuff on his lawn right after the bombing because he realized it looked suspicious.

Late in the evening, the agents received a fax routed through the command center. Lana Padilla, interviewed by agents in Las Vegas, had handed over a letter dated November 22, 1994, which Nichols had written as he was about to travel to the Philippines to try to convince Marife to return to him. Nichols asked Lana to give the letter to McVeigh if something happened to him. The letter said that McVeigh was on his own now. "Go for it!" it exhorted. Scott Crabtree, who had just arrived with Dan Jablonski, asked Nichols what "Go for it!" meant. Nichols just sat and stared.

Shortly after seven o'clock the next evening, Mary Jasnowski, a supervisor in the Kansas City office, and several other agents searched Nichols's house in Herington. Like McVeigh, Nichols was a pack rat. That was bad for him and very good for us.

Larry Tongate found five rolls of sixty-foot Primadet nonelectric blasting caps in the basement. JoAnne Thomas discovered a receipt for forty fifty-pound bags of ammonium nitrate fertilizer in the desk.

Other things, ordinary household items—an electric drill, receipts for storage lockers, a prepaid telephone calling card, a Wal-Mart receipt—turned out to be extremely valuable pieces of the puzzle.

Tongate found and carefully labeled a Wal-Mart receipt for an oil filter. McVeigh had bought the oil filter on April 13 from the Wal-Mart in Arkansas City, Kansas. The receipt showed that on April 15, Nichols had returned the oil filter to a Wal-Mart not far from his home in Herington. Both McVeigh and Nichols left prints on the receipt. Though the transactions in themselves were innocuous, they established that Nichols had been lying when he claimed he had not spoken with Tim McVeigh in the months before meeting him in Oklahoma City on April 16.

The fertilizer receipt from the Mid-Kansas Cooperative Association on September 30, 1994, was equally telling. FBI fingerprint examiners found two of McVeigh's fingerprints on it. Co-op records showed the purchase had been made by a "Mike Havens." The same name had been used again, on October 18, for the purchase of another two thousand pounds of ammonium nitrate. Checking motels near the co-op, agents found a registration card with the name Mike Havens and the fingerprints of Terry Nichols. In other words, Tim McVeigh and Terry Nichols had bought four thousand pounds of ammonium nitrate in a three-week period. For plant food to be sold at gun shows? Sure.

Back at the FBI lab, Burmeister was running batteries of tests on scraps found in the crater. Most had been washed clean by the rains, but Burmeister was able to identify ammonium nitrate crystals embedded in a piece of plywood that had lined the interior of the Ryder truck's cargo compartment. The crystals had been driven into the wood by enormous force.

If, as we now believed, the truck bomb had been composed mainly of ANFO, ammonium nitrate and fuel oil, a high-explosive booster would have been needed to set it off. ANFO, used in highway work, construction, and mining, is a stable explosive with a relatively slow velocity of detonation. The explosive chain has to begin with a small amount of high explosive with a fast detonation velocity.

Burmeister found the likely answer on McVeigh's clothing. Nitroglycerin was in the left-hand pocket of the jeans McVeigh had been wearing when he was arrested, and PETN, a high explosive used in detonation cord, was in the right-hand pocket and on his T-shirt. McVeigh's lime-green earplugs showed traces of nitroglycerin, PETN, and a third high explosive, EGDN, a component of some types of dynamite.

The telephone calling card discovered by JoAnne Thomas was made out in the name of "Darryl Bridges." It had been bought through an ad in *The Spotlight*, a publication of the far-right organization Liberty Lobby. Once its complex codes were unraveled, it opened the door to a trove of records that shed light on McVeigh's travels and contacts. Dallas agent Joe Gray, a telecommunications and computer specialist, performed heroic work during this crucial aspect of the investigation. One of the few people in the FBI who understood the mys-

teries of the scores of national and local phone companies that now serve our communications systems, Gray
tackled the immensely complicated task of decoding the
long strings of data that identified the calls charged to
the card. Then he and other technical specialists contacted hundreds of Baby Bell companies in order to
locate corroborating records of the telephones on the
receiving end of McVeigh's calls.

The resulting computer analysis, which took months
to complete, showed that McVeigh had called Nichols at
3 P.M. Easter Sunday from an Amoco station near the
Nichols residence in Herington. That fact put to lie
Nichols's assertion that McVeigh had called from
Oklahoma City to say his car had broken down. The
most likely story was that McVeigh and Nichols drove
from Herington to Oklahoma City in a caravan, positioned McVeigh's Mercury near the Murrah building for
use as a getaway car, then drove back to Junction City in
Nichols's truck. This scenario explained the sign found in
McVeigh's car. "Not abandoned," it said. "Please do not
tow, will move by April 23. (Needs battery and cable)."
Agents who checked the battery determined that it was
just fine.

The calling card showed that McVeigh had called
dozens of people and businesses like chemical companies and racetracks. We contacted them all. A salesman
in Ennis, Texas, said he had sold more than 160 gallons
of nitromethane racing fuel in October of 1994 to someone who looked like McVeigh.

Why nitromethane? A bomb-maker's recipe book
called *Homemade C-4*, advertised in extremist publications, advised buying ammonium nitrate from agriculture supply stores and mixing it with nitromethane rac-

ing fuel. Records from the book's publishing house, Paladin Press, established that McVeigh had bought a mail-order copy of the book in May 1993, shortly after Waco.

All these connections, and dozens more, formed a compelling argument that Tim McVeigh and Terry Nichols were the main players in the OKBOMB conspiracy. Still, forensic evidence, physical evidence, analysis, and circumstantial events could only take us so far.

We had to find an insider: a live human being with firsthand knowledge of the conspiracy.

5

Bob Ricks and I asked McVeigh's father, Bill, to fly out to Oklahoma City to meet with us. He arrived on Sunday, April 23, with an escort of agents from the Buffalo office. One, Gary Delaura, was one of my old friends from the New York bank-robbery squad.

Bill McVeigh looked like the simple working man he was. That he flew all that way to talk to us told me that he wanted to do the right thing. His eyes told me how terribly wounded he felt to hear his only son called a baby killer. I sensed he felt guilty, though Lord knows, none of us considered him responsible for the actions of his grown son.

As a father of sons, my heart ached for this man with

his big, rough hands. As an FBI agent, I had to get him to cooperate with us. He needed a friend. I was going to be that friend. He was going to open his heart to me. And his memory. I wanted to know the names of every one of McVeigh's friends, acquaintances, and enemies. I wanted to know where McVeigh had been, every day, every hour, for the last two or three years. I wanted to find John Doe Two, if there was one. And John Doe Three, Four, and Five, if the conspiracy was bigger. I knew how I felt about my own sons, and now I had to convince Bill to give me information that might help send his son to the executioner. It wasn't going to be easy, but I'd do what I had to do to get the truth, no matter whom it hurt.

We showed Bill to an easy chair next to a coffee table in Ricks's office. Ricks and I settled into two more easy chairs, as if we were shooting the breeze about whether the Bills and the Cowboys would make the play-offs.

Was McVeigh a good student? Average. But, his father added, "Tim never missed a day of school." He began to glow as he talked about McVeigh's perfect attendance record. We plied him with questions about McVeigh's teen years.

Extracurricular activities?

No, not really.

Sports?

No.

Clubs?

None.

Band?

No.

Did he have a girlfriend?

Not that his father knew of.

How about the Army?

He did really well there. Made sergeant, won a lot of medals. He was really disappointed that he didn't make Special Forces. That seemed to change him, and he lost interest in the Army.

And after he got out, jobs?

This and that. He'd been moving around. He could never seem to stay in any job for long.

Was he angry about anything?

Waco, that's for sure. He talked a lot about the government's brutality at Waco.

Who were McVeigh's best friends? Whom would he go to if he was in trouble?

He was close to his younger sister, Jennifer, who was working as a waitress and a Jell-O wrestler. I made a mental note to find out what Jell-O wrestling was. I was fairly sure that it was like mud wrestling, but tasted better.

Bill McVeigh was struggling to think of good things to say about his boy, but it became apparent that he had never been a success at anything except soldiering. Was his only other accomplishment to become the most notorious mass murderer in the nation's history?

"Sir, your son is definitely involved in this bombing," Ricks said softly. "There is a likelihood that others are involved with him. Who do you think they might be?"

"You haven't proven to me that he was involved." McVeigh shook his head.

"Sir," I repeated, almost in a whisper, "who are Tim's closest friends? Who would he turn to if he really needed a friend?"

"I would say Terry Nichols and Michael Fortier. They were in his Army unit. He's closer to them than anybody."

Those were the words I had been waiting to hear. We talked for a while longer. I ushered Bill McVeigh to the door, and the agents from Buffalo whisked him to his hotel.

Michael Fortier was back in his hometown, Kingman, Arizona, on the edge of the Mojave Desert in the northern part of Arizona. We knew from several witnesses that McVeigh had been in and out of Kingman in the months before the bombing. A group of agents was already there, beating the bushes.

Around April 27, Weldon called me into his office and motioned for me to sit down. I pulled up a chair and waited. This wasn't the first time he'd sat me down in a chair before asking me to do something that was likely to get me killed.

"Danny, where's your family?"

"Back in Maryland, getting ready for the move to Texas. That won't happen until school is out."

"I thought that was the case. I have something I want you to do for me."

"Don't tell me there's a tunnel under the Murrah building and you want Blakeney and me to go clear it."

Weldon laughed. "Not that again. The focus of this case is turning to Kingman. We want you to go out there and take charge of that part of the case, with Bob Walsh from San Diego. We have to do something with Fortier. He has to be involved, and we have to get things organized and follow up the investigation out there."

"Okay, no problem. When do you want me there?"

"Today. The King Air is at the airport waiting for you. Check out of your hotel and get out there as soon as possible."

"I'm on my way."

I snagged Biff Temple, an HRT alumnus now assigned to Dallas. "Pack your gear and get ready to fly to Kingman. I don't know how long we'll be gone."

Biff grinned. "Pick you up at your hotel. Adams can drive us to the airport."

At 12:48 P.M. we were airborne and heading west. I went into my briefcase and pulled out a dog-eared paperback and started leafing through it.

Biff tapped me on the shoulder. "What you reading, boss? You look really engrossed."

"*The Turner Diaries.* Have you read it?"

"No, I've heard briefings on it. Pretty sick stuff."

"*Very* sick stuff. But you should read it. It helps to understand what we're dealing with." I tossed him the book. "Here, educate yourself. Then go wash your hands. You'll feel really dirty."

The pilot punched his intercom button. "Doc, we're about thirty minutes from Kingman."

"Thanks. I'm just glad you guys could find the place."

Bob Walsh, then the SAC in San Diego, picked us up at the airport. He had flown in the day before and would act as my number two. Walsh had already arranged for a makeshift command post in the National Guard Armory. We needed the space. In two days' time, we'd have forty-five agents and support staff in Kingman.

Walsh gave me the nickel tour, which was bleak. If you were looking for trouble, you didn't have to go far to find it in Kingman, a conglomeration of strip malls, gun stores, honky-tonks, tattoo and piercing parlors, and miles and miles of trailer parks populated by bikers, desert rats, gun nuts, and drifters.

As we arrived in front of the armory, there was a yet more depressing sight—our friends, the ever-present media, were camped across the street. Their vans, satellite trucks, and cars were lined up facing the armory parking lot. "I guess we couldn't run a case without these guys," I sighed.

Bob nodded. "Yeah. They've even tried to follow the agents when they've gone out to cover leads. We have generally been able to dissuade them from bumperlocking us, but if something big happens, they'll be all over us, as usual."

The Kingman command center looked, sounded, and smelled much the same as the one in Oklahoma City. The energy level was palpable. People were scurrying around setting things up. Computers and fax machines were going in. Radio technicians were installing a secure system so we could communicate with our agents without being monitored by our friends across the street or by anyone else for that matter.

I read everything we had on Michael J. Fortier. He had been in McVeigh's unit at Fort Riley. They had been roommates in the barracks. Everybody who had served with McVeigh said the clique was McVeigh and Nichols and Fortier. Were all three in on the bombing? Were there more? Other blood brothers from Charlie Company? The military had its share of underground hate groups.

When McVeigh had shipped out to Saudi, Fortier had stayed behind with a shoulder injury and had then mustered out. Sooner or later, his old friend McVeigh showed up. Fortier got him a temporary job at the hardware store where he worked. When Fortier married his high school sweetheart, Lori, McVeigh served as best man.

Now Michael and Lori Fortier lived in a trailer with their two small children. Agents who tried to interview him had been confronted by a next-door neighbor, Jim Rosencrans, who brandished an assault rifle and screamed. The cops said he was a user of crystal meth, short for methamphetamine, a potent stimulant that typically renders users paranoid, agitated, and dangerous.

I called Biff and Roger Browning into my office. Browning, another ex-HRT operator, was in charge of the Phoenix office's SWAT team. I told them to find out when Rosencrans was away from home. We were about to obtain a search warrant for Fortier's trailer. We would have enough problems executing it without an armed confrontation with this wacko.

The warrant came through on April 30. We didn't serve it immediately. Working with Howard Shapiro from the FBI general counsel's office and the U.S. attorney in Phoenix, Bob and I drew up a letter to Fortier, informing him that we wanted his cooperation in this case and we were asking him to make a proffer—Queen for a Day, as it's known in our business. A subject of investigation is interviewed by assistant U.S. attorneys and FBI agents, and nothing said can be used against the individual except to challenge his credibility if he testifies in the case or lies during the interview. Based upon the value of the information furnished, the Department of Justice can make a deal promising him a degree of leniency in exchange for his testimony. The Queen for a Day procedure protects the interests of the government and also of the individual. It lays the groundwork for a deal that can benefit both. We knew Fortier was loyal to McVeigh and shared his philosophy of hate, but the prospect of execution could test even the closest relationships.

Bob and I drove down to a sheriff's substation a few

blocks from the Fortiers' trailer park, phoned Michael and asked him to meet us there. Within a few minutes he and Lori pulled up in their Jeep. He had that scruffy, unkempt look I hate; scraggly goatees really get me going. We introduced ourselves and asked Michael to step inside the office. "We have a warrant to search your home," Walsh said in a matter-of-fact way. "If you'll give us the keys, we'll do the search. You can be there if you want. We thought you might like to avoid all the press that will be there."

Fortier nodded and handed Bob his keys. "I'm sick of seeing the media," he muttered.

By the time our agents arrived at the trailer park, reporters and cameramen were all over the search. They had probably learned about it from monitoring the sheriff's radio.

As they walked up to the trailer door, the agents were accosted by a more fearsome figure—Rosencrans. He came steaming out of his trailer, assault rifle in hand. But instead of pointing it at anybody, he ran off his little lot and started jogging around the neighborhood, stopping at times to wave his rifle over his head. Biff described this bizarre scene to me by radio.

"Stay with him," I radioed back. "Keep your cover and try to talk to him. We don't want a shoot-out with this guy." A media helicopter was overhead filming the entire scene. Biff and Roger followed him into a field. Roger talked him into dropping the gun and giving up. They took him into custody, and the search went on.

Meanwhile, Walsh and I jousted with Fortier. He had used crystal meth himself, but unlike his pal Rosencrans, he wasn't a screamer. He spoke softly. We sat close to each other in three small chairs on rollers. Our knees almost touched. Anyone who saw us from a distance would not know how serious the conversation was. We listened for a while and leaned in even closer. This was a time for calm words, not table banging.

"I believe in strict interpretation of the Constitution," Fortier said. "The government doesn't obey the Constitution any longer."

I dropped the friendly, understanding manner I had used with Bill McVeigh and conjured up my grandfather Bernard, who had pinned me like a bug with his stern gaze, the righteous wrath of an Old Testament patriarch smiting my feeble excuses.

"Michael, this case *will* be solved," I said somberly. "You say that you believe in the Constitution. So do we. This case will be worked every step of the way within the framework of the Constitution. We know Tim blew up the Murrah building, and we can prove it."

Fortier interrupted, "Some people believe that this is a war." These were almost exactly the words I had heard from Fred Hilton decades before, and I gave Fortier the same answer I had given Hilton. "This is not a war. You and your friends may be at war with your government. Your government is not at war with you.

"Listen, Michael," I said, pushing my face a little closer to his. "We arrested Tim under the Constitution. He was charged under the Constitution. He will be indicted under the Constitution and tried and convicted under the Constitution. And someday he will be placed on a gurney and a needle will be placed in his arm and he will be executed under the Constitution. I am certain of that. If we were at war with him, I would have thrown him out of the helicopter. We are searching your house right now with a warrant. They don't do that in war."

Fortier wilted back into his seat. Obviously, he had only practiced his bullshit rhetoric on those who agreed with him. We were giving him something to think about. It's hard to convince yourself and others that there is a war going on when the government follows the rules. If this crime had been committed in certain other countries, Fortier would likely have found his private parts wired up to a generator. What he faced was two middle-aged FBI agents whispering to him about the rule of law.

Walsh stepped in and presented him with the letter. "You need to get an attorney to explain what a proffer is."

"You explain it to me," Fortier said almost meekly. My remark about the gurney and the lethal injection had taken a little of the starch out of him.

"A proffer will give you a chance to come in and tell the whole truth about what had happened with Tim and the bombing," Walsh said. "Your statement can't be used against you unless you take the stand and change your story or lie. We are going to solve this case. The death penalty will be requested. It's in your best interest and your family's interest to get an attorney. If you can't afford one, the court will appoint one for you. We really don't want to talk to you until you have discussed this with a lawyer. You need to be sure that whoever represents you has your best interests at heart. Be very careful not to associate yourself with someone who will sell you out for a cause."

I jumped in. "Michael, the attorney general has announced to the world that the government will seek the death penalty. If we seek it, we are likely to get it, even for those who were only involved in the conspiracy. It's time for you to choose sides. You can be on the side of those that we prosecute and execute, or you can be on our side. You need to think about it."

We walked out into the parking lot and shook hands. He got into the Jeep with his wife and drove away.

He looked subdued and depressed. I guess he was thinking of his future, or lack of it. He had seemed frightened. At least we hoped that was the case.

Bob and I drove over to the Fortier trailer. One of the agents walked up to me. "Oh, Doc, some lady drove by and asked if we were from the FBI, and I told her we were."

"Do you think that she figured it out when she saw our raid jackets?" I said. "Maybe we should offer her a job."

"Probably. Anyway she said she owned the local pizzeria and she was going to bring pizzas for all of us. Isn't that nice?"

"Very nice, but we can't take them. Do you think I want Louie and Janet watching on national television as we eat pizza while we're doing a search on the most important case in the country? I don't think so. When she arrives, go over and thank her and take the pizzas. We don't want to hurt her feelings. Then you take the pizzas and give them to the media weenies. We'll get our own later, and I'm buying."

The agent nodded, but he looked a little unhappy and very hungry. "I think I see what you're talking about. I'll handle it."

"Thanks. And no cheating. Not a single slice."

It wasn't long before every cameraman and reporter was chowing down on the pizza. One camera crew that was set up right by the fence kept waving their pizza slices at me. "Hey, Danny, thanks. Want a bite?"

"Don't mention it. Anything to help you guys!"

I turned back to Bob. "I suppose there's absolutely no chance that they could get sick from those things?"

Bob laughed. "Not a chance."

"Too bad."

"Isn't it?"

Bob and I met Michael Fortier's parents over breakfast and made our pitch. Paul Fortier would hear none of it. "If he hasn't done anything, then there's nothing to talk about," he snapped.

"Michael is involved, and we'll prove it," Bob responded. "He needs to do what's best for him and his family. He needs to choose sides."

Irene Fortier stared daggers at me. I thought she wanted to stab me with a fork. "I know my son and I know he would not be involved in something like this."

I put on Grandpa Bernard's face. "Ma'am, I've arrested hundreds of men for serious crimes, and every one of them was some woman's son."

We finished eating and I picked up the check. I couldn't tell if we had done much good.

A short time later, I got a call from HQ about an international terrorism case that I had been working before the Oklahoma bombing. I was needed in Washington for a meeting with HQ and Justice people. Walsh would run the case in Kingman.

I called Debbie. "I'm coming home."

"Great," she said. "I'll tell you all about the house I'm building in Dallas." I changed the subject. I didn't even want to think about what that was costing me.

The next morning a Bureau plane picked me up at Kingman International.

A few weeks later I learned from Adams that Fortier

had decided to turn state's evidence. He had denied knowing anything for a while, but the pressure and the press got to him. He became the government's star witness against Tim McVeigh and Terry Lynn Nichols.

The plea bargain was one of the most controversial aspects of the case, but I thought the deal was appropriate. This was the crime of the century and more importantly, a death penalty case. American juries in the vast majority of cases are fair. They won't convict just because the government puts on a strong case. They really do follow the standard that guilt must be established beyond a reasonable doubt.

Under the questioning of chief prosecutor Joseph Hartzler, the U.S. attorney from Springfield, Illinois, Fortier gave a chilling recitation of McVeigh's path to Oklahoma City:

"Tim told me that him and Terry had chosen a building in Oklahoma City, a federal building in Oklahoma City. He also told me that he had figured out how to make a truck into a bomb. He explained to me how he would arrange the barrels, five-gallon drums in the back of that truck, to form something he was calling a 'shape charge.' He told me about the ratio of fuel to ammonium nitrate. That's how he would make an explosive. He told me that he would use the explosives that he had stolen from the quarry. He had drew on a piece of paper—he diagrammed the truck and the barrels, and he diagrammed how he would fuse the bomb from the front of the cab into the back area of the truck. He told me he was going to just drill a hole and run a cannon fuse through the hole."

I recognized the fusing plan. That, too, was straight out of *The Turner Diaries*. It was exactly how "Earl

Turner" and his buddies had detonated the truck bomb that took down the FBI building.

Five months before the bombing, Fortier said, he and McVeigh had driven to Oklahoma City and cased the Murrah building. Then, he said, McVeigh pointed out the glassed building face, where he would position a Ryder rental truck containing the explosive, and the spot where he would park his getaway car.

"He told me they picked that building because that was where the orders for the attack on Waco came from," Fortier testified. "He told me that he was wanting to blow up a building to cause a general uprising in America hopefully that would knock some people off the fence into—and urge them into taking action against the federal government."

That echoed "Earl Turner"'s goal of setting in motion a series of events that wound up destroying Western civilization as we know it.

Fortier said he had once asked McVeigh, "What about all the people?"

"And he explained to me . . . that he considered all those people to be as if they were the storm troopers in the movie *Star Wars*. They may be individually innocent; but because they are part of the evil empire . . . they were guilty by association."

Fortier insisted that he had told McVeigh, "I would never do anything like that until there was a U.N. tank in my front yard." But Fortier acknowledged that he had allowed McVeigh to commit mass murder by failing to blow the whistle. "There was no excuse that I could offer why I didn't," he said. "I live with that knowledge every day."

Lori Fortier, who was granted immunity, testified that

she had personally used her iron to laminate a phony driver's license with Tim McVeigh's photo and the name Robert Kling. She told how McVeigh had sat in her kitchen as her little daughter Kayla played nearby and, using soup cans, showed her how he would arrange barrels of racing fuel and ammonium nitrate in a triangle, to aim the force of the blast at the glass face of the Murrah building.

Lori said McVeigh told her he intended to set off the bomb with Tovex "sausage" explosive and blasting caps that he had stolen from a quarry. Around Christmas of 1994, she said, he asked her to wrap his boxes of blasting caps in Christmas paper, so that anyone who saw them would think they were gifts.

The story about the quarry theft checked out. On the first weekend in October 1994, someone had broken into a locked explosives magazine at a rock quarry in Marion, Kansas, and made off with a quantity of Tovex sausage explosive and hundreds of blasting caps—sixty-foot No. 8 delay Primadet caps, to be exact, the same make and type as those found in Nichols's house. James Cadigan, a lab tool-mark examiner, matched an impression made by one of Nichols's Makita drill bits to a hole that thieves had drilled in a padlock at the quarry.

Hartzler and his trial team—notably Beth Wilkinson and Sean Connelly from main Justice, Larry Mackey from the U.S. attorney's office in Indiana, and Hersley and Tongate from the Bureau—did a masterful job of organizing and showcasing the work of the OKBOMB task force. Tim McVeigh and Terry Nichols were convicted of conspiracy to bomb the Murrah building. McVeigh was sentenced to death for the murder of eight federal agents; Nichols was sentenced to life in prison.

Fortier, allowed to plead guilty to four lesser counts, drew a twelve-year term.

When I heard the McVeigh verdict, I was pleased but certainly not overjoyed. The convictions would not bring back to life one baby, one father, one mother, one brother, or one sister. I don't think there can ever be a penalty severe enough for those cowards. I wasn't in the courtroom when Joe Hartzler made his opening statement, but I heard that just about everybody's eyes misted up when he described the day-care center, with its plate-glass windows, and how "the children would run up to those windows and press their hands and faces to those windows to say good-bye to their parents. . . . But none of the parents . . . ever touched those children again while they were still alive." I kept thinking about all the times we had dropped our kids off at child care and how excited we were to pick them up. I doubt anybody in Oklahoma City, or most other places for that matter, would ever be able to know that joy again without thinking of April 19, 1995.

If I thought about those kids much longer, my feelings would probably have welled up until—I don't know what. They were still in the box where I had shoved them in the first hours after the bombing. No way am I ever going to open that box. There's too much else in there.

6

Justice has been done in the cases of Tim McVeigh and Terry Nichols. The jury was convinced they built and detonated the bomb, and so am I. Still, I can't help wondering if we really know everything about the Oklahoma City bombing plot.

I'm not talking about the John Doe Two mystery, which has become the grassy knoll of the OKBOMB case, the new obsession of the Internet conspiracy theorists. I'm satisfied there is no John Doe Two. If there is, I feel sure he would have shown up somewhere—say, among the people McVeigh had telephoned on the calling card. McVeigh was convinced no one would ever figure the card out, so he used it freely. I'm satisfied that all available evidence supports the theory that Eldon Elliott and Tom Kessinger scrambled the facts of two Ryder rental transactions. The day after Tim McVeigh picked up his rented truck, an army private named Michael Hertig came in to get a similar truck. He looks a lot like McVeigh, and he had a friend named Todd Bunting with him. Bunting resembles the sketch of John Doe Two. The conspiracy theorists can't accept the mistaken-identity explanation, but it makes sense to me. People often make small mistakes about everyday events that don't seem important at the moment.

What bothers me are some telephone calls Tim McVeigh made in the days before the bombing. The calling card records show that McVeigh made several calls to a National Alliance phone bank with a tape-recorded call to arms against the government. FBI agents interviewed National Alliance founder William Pierce, the notorious white supremacist and author of *The Turner Diaries*, but Pierce insisted he had never talked to McVeigh or heard of him before the bombing, and no evidence contradicts this.

The more troubling call was to Elohim City, the Christian Identity compound presided over by Robert Millar. The person who spoke with McVeigh isn't known, since nobody in the compound has owned up to it. Telephone company records show only some sort of brief exchange.

At the time when McVeigh placed the call, Millar was acting as "spiritual adviser" to Richard Wayne Snell, the onetime CSA associate who was on death row in Arkansas for the 1983 murder of Texarkana pawn-broker William Stumpp. Incredibly, Arkansas officials had scheduled Snell's execution for April 19, 1995, heedless of the far right's superstitious horror of the date, which they marked as the anniversary of the battle of Lexington in 1775, the Nazi destruction of Warsaw in 1943, and of course the fires at Waco. Moreover, anybody who read the far-right press in the spring of 1994 would recognize there was a real danger of contributing to the canonization of Snell. *Taking Aim*, the newsletter of the Militia of Montana, hailed Snell as "An American Patriot To Be Executed By The Beast" and published his rambling letters claiming he had been framed by President Clinton and a vast government conspiracy. The militia rallied its members to bombard Arkansas governor Jim Guy Tucker with demands for clemency.

When the news flashed that the Murrah building had been destroyed, exactly twelve hours before Snell was to

die by lethal injection, prison officials reported that he
burst out laughing.

"Governor Tucker, look over your shoulder," he told
his guards. "I wouldn't trade places with any of you or
any of your political cronies. Hell has victory. I'm at
peace."

This sounds like standard radical cant. Even so, I
can't forget about the strange yarn spun by Jim Ellison,
who became a star government witness in 1988, when
U.S. Attorney J. Michael Fitzhugh of Fort Smith tried
Snell and a dozen other extremists, including Aryan
Nations leader Richard Girnt Butler, on charges of con-
spiring at the 1983 Aryan World Congress to overthrow
the U.S. government, assassinate officials, blow up public buildings, and establish a white separatist state in the
Pacific Northwest. The Fort Smith thirteen were all
acquitted, which didn't surprise me. Fitzhugh and
Assistant U.S. Attorney Steven Snyder fashioned the
indictment around a novel theory of "seditious conspiracy." Most Americans are suspicious whenever the government tries to weave a complicated conspiracy case,
especially one that comes close to infringing on the
Constitutional right of free speech, and the Fort Smith
jury was no exception. Also, juries tend to dislike prosecutions that depend entirely on the testimony of an
unsavory co-conspirator—Jim Ellison, in this instance—
who is clearly out to shorten his own sentence.

In the wake of the Oklahoma City bombing, the FBI
and the prosecutors took another look at Ellison's testimony. He said that in October 1983, he and Snell had
visited the federal building in Oklahoma City and had
discussed blowing it up; Ellison had drawn up designs
for rocket launchers that would be placed in a trailer or

van, parked in front of the Oklahoma building, and detonated remotely. Ellison was in prison at the time of the bombing and Snell's execution. Not long afterward, he was released. Ollie had divorced him, rejected Christian Identity, and gone back to college. So he moved into Elohim City, where he courted and married Robert Millar's granddaughter.

I placed a call to an old adversary to see whether he thought there was any connection between the two plots targeting the Murrah Federal Building. Strange as it sounds, I had lately come to be pretty good friends with Kerry Noble, once Ellison's right-hand man. Shortly after I returned to Dallas, Noble called me. He was out of jail and trying to get his life together. He was living in the Dallas area with his wife and kids and had read about my arrival in the newspaper.

"I've wanted to talk to you for years and thank you for saving my life and the lives of the others in the CSA compound," he began almost bashfully. "If there ever was a time when the government could have come in and blown everyone away, this was it. You guys could have claimed that we started the shooting and everyone would have believed you."

I practically reeled in my chair to hear his voice and especially those words.

"Kerry, I guess that both sides did what was right," I said. "You guys didn't start anything either."

"I was wondering if we could get together and talk. Just to discuss what happened back then."

"Sure," I said, though I was a little wary. After all, I'd put Noble in jail, along with a number of his friends. My curiosity got the better of me, though I took the precaution of making Adams go with me. At the house, we sep-

arated, keeping about thirty yards between us as I
approached the door. Jim positioned himself by the left
corner of the house so he could see me and the left side
yard, in case I was walking into an ambush. I took a peek
on the right side and carefully scanned the windows. I
moved to the side of the front door and knocked. The
door opened slowly and there stood Noble. He extended
his right hand.

"Good to see you, Danny. Come on in."

I nodded to Adams and we entered the house. We
looked around the room and made sure that we never
stood close to each other. We'd both been FBI agents
too long to trust anybody.

Noble filled our glasses with iced tea, pulled out an
album of photos of the CSA compound, and began to
describe life in a cult of hate. Now that he was out from
under Ellison, Noble, who was working as a photographer and writer, was as gentle and cheerful as all the
other decent, ordinary people who lived in his blue-
collar suburb. We leafed through his scrapbook of his
career as a terrorist, a time he now regarded as a bad
dream. Finally, I looked up and grinned.

"Kerry, I'm real glad I didn't have to shoot you," I
said.

He set down his glass and looked back at me. "Danny,
I'm real glad I didn't shoot you too."

Now I consulted him whenever I had a question
about the hate movement. He told me he had no proof
at all, but he was convinced that somehow McVeigh had
copycatted the plot hatched by Snell and Ellison.

"When the bombing happened, I said, 'They've done
it, they've finally done it,' " Noble said. "We knew in
1983 the Oklahoma City federal building was a perfect

building to hit. It was in the middle of the country, it was easy, it was not protected, and it would have more impact than in New York or Los Angeles. Nobody expected anything in a state like Oklahoma. You wanted to have something that would have a tremendous effect. It's possible that Snell, knowing his execution date was April 19, could have initiated something with somebody on the outside."

Or perhaps there was no conspiracy at all but a common thread of inspiration and opportunity. The idea of wreaking terror in the serene American heartland is a popular theme in the writings of hate-mongers like William Pierce and many of the extremist tirades that can be found on the Internet. Feed the words *bomb*, *Aryan*, or *New World Order* into your browser and watch your screen light up like the Strip in Vegas. McVeigh could have picked up word of the Snell-Ellison plot from somebody who visited them in the slammer or from conspiracy theorists on the gun-show circuit, or it could be a huge coincidence. All I know for sure is that this chapter in our history isn't closed.

As we look beyond the year 2000, I expect—as does the FBI's current leadership—that home-grown terrorism is likely to erupt on a scale unprecedented in modern times. The Ku Klux Klan and White Citizens Council have faded, but nearly every day we read about bombings or conspiracies by new extremist factions, like the Phineas Priesthood in Spokane, the Aryan Republican Army in Philadelphia, the Viper Militia in Phoenix and the Mountaineer Militia in West Virginia.

Their ideologies differ, and the linkages among them seem to be more like a loose cobweb than a true network, but they have in common a virulent hatred of the government. It's part of our American heritage not to like or trust government. I don't have much use for most of government myself. But an increasing number of people are sliding into the subculture of the paranoid fringe that blames government—and also Jews, blacks and homosexuals—for everything that is wrong in their lives.

Time and again, we've seen the most energetic and hate-filled people within a group splinter off and go underground, planning and carrying out acts of terrorism directed against government installations, synagogues, gay nightclubs or black churches. They don't attack targets where somebody might shoot back. Like all bullies, they go after the weak—even children. In March of 1997, agents who worked for me in Dallas were tipped by a local Ku Klux Klan leader that three other Klansmen and one of their wives were plotting to bomb a natural gas refinery in Wise County, north of Fort Worth. The fireball was to be a distraction so they could rob the local bank in order to finance more acts of terror. The agents bugged the truck the group used to case the refinery and overheard Catherine Dee Adams observe to her husband, Shawn, "Oh, there's a few kids that live right over there. . . . But if it has to be. I hate to be that way, but if it has to be . . ." In July 1999, Benjamin Smith, a twenty-one-year-old Chicagoan who pledged allegiance to the skinhead-oriented World Church of the Creator, set out to spark a race war by shooting eleven Asian Americans, blacks and Jews, killing two people. He committed suicide July 4 in southern Illinois. We have cause to be particularly concerned about Identity worshippers and other radical religious groups who believe the Millennium signals the beginning of the biblical Tribulation.

On August 10, 1999, Buford O. Furrow, an Identity believer who had been married to Debra Mathews, widow of Order founder Robert Mathews, walked into the North Valley Jewish Community Center in Los Angeles and opened fire with an Uzi, wounding three small children in day camp, a sixteen-year-old camp counselor and a sixty-eight-year-old receptionist. Then he hijacked a car, drove to a residential area and murdered postman Joseph Ileto, thirty-nine, because he was wearing a uniform. A day later, he turned himself in, boasting that his acts were "a wake-up call to America to kill Jews."

When it comes to weapons and technology, there are a number of militias and other fringe groups who are better equipped and armed than any rifle company during World War II, or even the Korean war. They generally possess the same type of assault rifles used by both sides during the Vietnam War. Fully automatic M16s and AK-47s are easily available on the black market. The military's lack of control of its weapons systems is abysmal. Consequently, military ordnance, such as antitank weapons, has trickled out to a number of domestic and foreign terrorist groups. What soldier in World War II, the Korean Conflict or even Vietnam would not have given anything for an assault weapon with an infrared aiming device that would allow him to see and to fire a weapon accurately in complete darkness? Today, night vision gear and laser aiming devices are sold on the Internet, at gun shows and through catalogues, at prices just about anyone can afford.

No matter how frightening the threat, I hope that we'll never become what our critics think we are—the faceless enemy. The literature and Internet exchanges of extremist groups invest us with all sorts of mythical powers. Members of these groups are generally isolated from the rest of society. Oftentimes they stew in their own rhetoric and rumors and don't really have the chance to test their ideas against the touchstone of reality. The ability to have a dialogue with a government official who they believe will tell them the truth goes a long way toward dispelling their paranoia.

That's why, when I returned from the Oklahoma investigation, I reached out to leaders of militia groups in my territory. I wanted to know them, and more importantly, I wanted them to know me, because where there is dialogue between the government and these organizations, I believe there is less chance for violent encounters. Through the office of Sheriff Jim Bowles of Dallas County, Jim Adams and I arranged to meet with two leaders of the Texas militias.

At our first meeting, Adams and I showed up in boots and jeans, and the militia leaders showed up in suits. I commented that they looked like the FBI agents and we looked like members of the militia. We discussed the Oklahoma City bombing. They said they thought the building had been bombed by the government. They based this conspiracy theory on the fact that none of the news photographs showed the bomb crater. If there was no crater outside, then the bomb must have been placed inside the building—by the government itself. I explained to them that we had constructed a covering over the crater to protect it, and to allow us to bring bodies, debris and evidence out through the front of the building and across the hole. I assured them that there was a crater and that I'd been in it. They were obviously stunned by that revelation and seemed to believe me.

They showed us a photograph of a tall blond man with very short hair, in the company of ATF agents during the trial of the surviving Branch Davidians in Waco. This man bore a slight resemblance to Tim McVeigh. One of them pitched the picture on the table and demanded, "We want to know who this is." The implication was that Tim McVeigh was an agent of the government.

I smiled at our new friends and said, "I don't know who this is but I can tell you positively who it's not. It's not Tim McVeigh, I can tell you that, because Jim and I arrested Tim McVeigh and this is not a photograph of him."

"Of that I'm certain," Adams said. "We spent a lot of time with Tim McVeigh and took him to his arraignment."

They both seemed taken aback by this explanation. We continued to talk for over an hour. As we adjourned, we promised we'd meet again. Within a week, one of these men contacted Jim from the group's training facility north of Dallas and said his militia was mobilizing for war. They needed to talk to us pronto. We told them to stay right there. I jumped into Pop's 1975 pink Cadillac. Jim mounted his Harley. We met along the way and arrived together. Jimmy, dressed like the world's biggest badass biker, and I, in my jeans and cowboy boots, walked right through the middle of a defensive tactics class and into the leaders' office.

There we found a group of individuals in great agitation, but before they said their piece, I pointed to a bulletin board. There was a cartoon of the grim reaper with the FBI written across his chest. "This is an insult to us," I snapped. "It's bullshit. Take it down." They smiled uneasily, and the cartoon was removed.

We sat at a table and heard them out. They said that they'd heard through their network that the FBI and ATF were about to assault Robert Millar's compound at Elohim City, on grounds that some of his people had been involved in the Oklahoma City bombing. They were sure the assault would inflict great loss of life on Millar's followers. They were preparing to drive in a caravan to Oklahoma to repel the federal attack.

The whole time they were talking, I was back in my chair with one boot on the table. When they were done, without ever sitting up or looking alarmed, I said, "I know Robert Millar, and if I had an issue with Robert Millar, I'd call him on the phone and tell him I'm going to come see him."

There was silence and a look of bewilderment in their eyes.

"That's not the way the FBI does business," I went on. "We didn't assault Waco. I'm serious about Robert Millar. He helped me negotiate a standoff many years ago and I know the FBI has a dialogue with Robert Millar. Get me a phone. I'll check out your story."

I quickly dialed my office in Dallas and had them patch me through to Oklahoma City. I told the operator who I was and that I needed to talk to Bob Ricks immediately. Within a minute, I had Bob on the phone.

"What're you calling me on the weekend for," Ricks griped, half in jest.

I told him about the rumor of the Elohim City assault. Bob laughed out loud. "You must be kidding. . . . I take it you're with someone who has sympathy for him."

"You got it," I replied.

"I think I understand where you are now," Bob said.

"We talk to Millar probably once a week. If we need something from Elohim City we'll have him meet us and take us into the compound. There's no assault being planned by us or anybody else. We have an agreement about that sort of thing here in Oklahoma."

"Okay," I said. "If there is an issue, would you call me back?"

"Sure," he said.

I hung up the phone and looked across the table. "I promise you there's not going to be an assault at Elohim City," I said. "If you want to drive up there, fine, but you're going to waste your time."

I noticed that one of the leaders was carrying a Chinese-made .45-caliber pistol. It was in his holster, cocked, with the safety on. I pointed to it and said, "Why don't you buy yourself an American gun? You guys are supposed to be big patriots and you're buying a gun from the enemy."

He laughed and said, "This is a fine gun."

The other leader said, "You guys ought to come and shoot with us sometime."

"We'd love to do that," Jimmy said. "But you guys need to practice a whole lot or we'll embarrass you."

They got a big chuckle out of that. Then we got serious. "This is a great start," Jim said. "It's good you called us. We may have solved some problems here. Your entire militia group roaring up I-35 armed to the teeth would likely have caused some police attention and who knows what could have happened over a silly rumor."

"There may come a time," I added, "when someone comes to you who's not really a member of your group, who could be the next Timothy McVeigh. We want to know about him. Someone may start encouraging you to

convert your legal weapons into machine guns. That will bring you nothing but grief and a prison term. If that person does come here with these kind of ideas, then you call me, and I'll deal with him, because you do not need that kind of problem."

One of them smiled and said, "Suppose it's an ATF undercover agent trying to get us to do something illegal?"

"You call me and let me work it out," I responded. "But don't do it. It's not worth it."

We walked outside. They furnished the official drink of Texas—a Dr Pepper—to both of us. We watched their defensive tactics class. They asked if we wanted to join in.

"Maybe next time," Jimmy laughed.

We all shook hands, and we walked away. Jimmy roared off on his hog and I putted away in my macho pink Cadillac. We met down the road in a half hour or so. Jimmy jumped in my car, laughing until I thought he'd split his leather jacket. "I thought we'd had it when you told them to take down the grim reaper," he cackled. "I was counting bullets and I knew that both of us didn't have enough."

"Hell, Jim, that cartoon's bullshit, and it just pissed me off and I wanted them to know there might only be two of us but we damn sure weren't afraid of them. Anyway, we did some good here today."

7

Preventing extremist violence was only one part of my job.
Most days, I was immersed in the reality of fighting everyday crime. My agents and I torqued up the drug task force
and went hammer and tong after the crack gangs.

One of our more memorable forays occurred in late
July of 1995. We met at the Fort Worth Police Training
Academy and donned our body armor, making ready to
move out at first light. Our target was a string of crack
houses in an East Fort Worth neighborhood. Another
law enforcement agency had tried and failed to take out
one house because the crack gang had installed bars all
around it and were presumed to be defending it with a
small arsenal.

A SWAT team member crept to the front of the
house, slid a hook and chain around three or four of the
bars, and hooked the chain to the winch on our SWAT
van. The driver hit the throttle and yanked the bars off
the front porch. Then Mike Elsie was supposed to throw
a stun grenade just inside the entrance, to disorient the
dealers. That way, they would not be in firing position
when the other FBI SWAT team members rushed the
door.

But just as Mike pulled the pin, the door opened and
an elderly woman walked out. Very slowly. Mike
clutched the grenade's spoon tight and stood there, perfectly still. The other agents moved into the house and
soon had everyone on the floor and handcuffed.

I watched the action from the top of the driveway. As
I entered the house, Joe Ullman, the team leader, came

up to me and said, "Boss, we got a hot one." He explained that a pin had been pulled on a live grenade and that the only thing preventing its detonation was Mike's hand on the spoon.

"I figured. Where's Mike?"

Mike's eyes were as big as saucers. One slip and he could say good-bye to his fingers and maybe his eyes and nose.

"You got a problem, you turkey?"

Mike laughed.

"Where's the pin?"

"Boss, we can't find the pin," Ullman said. "How about we deliver it in the backyard?"

"No," I said. "We're not going to flash-bang this neighborhood. We're supposed to be here liberating these neighborhoods, not throwing grenades around outside."

I motioned for Mike to follow me to the SWAT van. I told the agents to look for a spare pin. Then I turned to Mike.

"Hold that thing tight," I said. "If you drop it, we've got a second and a half to turn around and take as many steps as we can. If we're lucky, it will just blow our pants off."

Actually, I had dealt with this problem many times before in the military explosives ordnance disposal school that I had attended, courtesy of the FBI.

I put my thumb up underneath his hand and pressed the bottom part of the spoon, my hand enveloping his fist. As I worked to get my fingers securely on the grenade, I told jokes, as I always do to relieve stress. The way I see it, in a pinch, a bad leader adds to the stress, while a good leader takes away stress.

I worked my thumb onto the spoon, held it tight, and took the device into my own hand. "Get me a piece of tape and split it," I ordered. Adams pulled out a coil of superstrength military tape, which is called hundred-mile-an-hour tape because it can be used to patch an aircraft. As I held the bottom of the spoon with my thumb, Mike and I wrapped the tape around the whole device, securing the spoon to the grenade so it couldn't spring off.

An agent came up with a pin. I inserted it in the grenade and relaxed my grasp. So did Mike. I took a step back and pitched the now harmless grenade at Elsie, who caught it and smiled, then walked away.

Later, after all the suspects were safely lodged in the local jail, we went back to the office to critique the raid. I praised Mike for not throwing the grenade. "It took a lot of guts. It showed a lot of courage and a lot of good judgment, and I'm real proud of you," I said.

Then I said solemnly, "There are two rules about stun grenades. One, throw the grenade before you throw the pin away. Two, if you forget rule one, don't hand the grenade to the SAC."

As the group broke up laughing, I presented Mike with a necklace made of a grenade pin and a piece of parachute cord. He grinned and wore the pin for days.

There were, I added, three serious lessons to be drawn from the morning's events. First, a leader needs to be on the scene with his agents, not back in the office proofreading their reports.

Second, if you slow everything down and take your time, you can fix most things that are broken, especially if you keep your cool.

Third, just because we have a problem, that doesn't

mean we can toss the grenade and upset the whole neighborhood. We screw up, we fix the problem—quietly.

Just as we were making some headway in the neighborhoods, the Ruby Ridge case came roaring out of nowhere and turned my life upside down again.

On May 2, Freeh, whose political tin ear has become famous, made the disastrous mistake of promoting Larry Potts to be his deputy director. "He's the very best the FBI has," Freeh said, adding that Potts's censure for command failure in the Ruby Ridge incident shouldn't overshadow his otherwise distinguished career.

Freeh might as well have hammered a lightning rod into Potts's forehead. The very next day, Gene Glenn fired off a letter to Justice OPR chief Mike Shaheen charging that he was being made a scapegoat in a cover-up orchestrated to protect the director's friend. Glenn insisted that Potts had cleared the *can and should shoot* rules of engagement. As proof that HQ knew all about the flawed rules, Glenn claimed I had reminded him to act in accordance with them. He also complained that the Bureau's administrative review that followed up the Berman findings was rigged to favor Potts, me, and others at HQ, since the agent who led it was Charlie Mathews, who had served as my ASAC in Portland.

Shaheen opened yet another Ruby Ridge inquiry into the actions of everybody in the chain of command at HQ. I was annoyed with Glenn but not particularly worried. I didn't expect Shaheen to come up with anything different from what had been found in the Berman investigation. I knew what I'd done, and my conscience was clear. It was true that one night Glenn had told me the Portland SWAT team had gone up on the mountain and had been confronted by an individual who they thought was Randy Weaver. The man had cursed them and told them to get off his property. As Glenn talked, I thought my biggest fear was coming true—that Weaver was demonstrating he would continue to resist lawful attempts to bring him into custody and would likely shoot any agents who attempted to do so. So I reminded Glenn to "remember the rules of engagement," referring to the rules that Potts had given Rogers in my presence. Glenn was thinking about the rules as modified by Rogers, but I had no way of knowing that.

As for my relationship with Charlie Mathews, we were professional colleagues, not social friends, but I respected him. There are only 11,500 FBI agents, most of them too junior to be entrusted with the Ruby Ridge disciplinary review. It would have been practically impossible for Freeh to have found a senior agent who hadn't worked with somebody who had somehow been involved in the crisis, either at the scene or in SIOC. I had nothing to do with the appointment and neither did Potts. From what I understand, Freeh tapped Mathews because he was an experienced agent with a law degree and a reputation for fairness and thoroughness. In fact, I think it's fair to say the Justice Department gave at least tacit approval to his selection. To do a proper job, he had to work hand in glove with the Berman task force, which means that Shaheen, Berman's boss, would have knowledge of his appointment. There's no doubt in my mind that if Shaheen, Berman, or anybody else at Justice had objected to him, the director would have replaced him before the end of the day.

I was totally unprepared for what happened next. On

July 11, Freeh suspended Mike Kahoe, the violent crime section chief, who had received a letter of censure and a fifteen-day suspension for overseeing an inadequate shooting-incident report on the Ruby Ridge affair. News reports said he had supposedly admitted to Shaheen and his assistants at Justice OPR that he had destroyed copies of an internal document bearing on the Ruby Ridge matter.

What document? I wondered when I read the story in the paper. What could he possibly have possessed that contained new information? I couldn't imagine anyone in the FBI destroying any document. Even if you wanted to, you couldn't be sure you got all the copies, which were spread all over the Bureau, where paper is forever.

The Kahoe story threw the press and the Hill into a feeding frenzy. Being somewhat politically naive, I puzzled about this for a couple of news cycles of breathless CNN and wire bulletins before it finally dawned on me that the actual content of the document Kahoe had supposedly deep-sixed was totally irrelevant. All anybody seemed to be reading were the headlines, and they insinuated that we were guilty of something very bad, though nobody knew quite what it was. In fact, the headlines fueled the impression that just about everybody in the FBI was involved in some sort of cover-up.

I thought I'd seen morale bottom out in the dark days of the Church committee, but I was wrong. In the post-Watergate feeding frenzy the FBI was accused of investigating the wrong people. That seemed almost sedate compared to charges that agents had deliberately shot a woman holding a baby at Ruby Ridge and burned children at Waco. Since the director had forbade us to comment on the charges, no matter how outlandish, the extremist movement succeeded in claiming the moral high ground without a whisper of protest from the FBI.

On July 14—Bastille Day—Freeh announced that Potts was "unable to effectively perform his duties as deputy director" and moved him to a position at the Academy. In other words, he was finished. This was a tragedy for the FBI, for Potts, and, I think, for the American people. Potts was one of our brightest executives, and now he was lost to us. Freeh appointed Weldon Kennedy to be deputy director, which would ordinarily have been good news. But he muzzled Weldon, forbidding him and everybody else in the Bureau to say anything about Ruby Ridge or Waco.

Then came the day I'll never forget—August 11, 1995. We went out at four o'clock in the morning and rounded up about thirty members of a gang that had been terrorizing the neighborhoods around Fair Park, the home of the Cotton Bowl and the Texas State Fair. Things went well; no one was hurt, a fair amount of evidence was seized, and we got some quick confessions. By 9:30 A.M., things were winding down except for processing of prisoners.

I returned to the office and began to read the morning teletypes and assorted mail. At about 10:20 A.M., my secretary buzzed and said the director was on the phone for me.

"Good morning, sir," I said, wondering if he'd found out I'd been using profanity again.

"I have some bad news for you," Freeh said. "I'm placing you on administrative leave with pay as a result of the Ruby Ridge incident. I have determined that your continued presence in the office would be disruptive."

"What charges have been made against me?" I stammered.

"I can't discuss that with you."

"Under our policy I'm entitled to know the charges against me and be given an opportunity to respond to them," I retorted.

"You cannot talk to any FBI agent. You can only talk to Jim Adams about matters of transition."

I was stunned. Freeh had been an FBI agent, a federal prosecutor, and a federal judge. The Constitution provides that you can talk to anyone to prepare a defense. He had no right to prevent me from talking to other agents, or for that matter, to anyone else. I knew he knew the law as well as I did. This told me his advisers were not giving him good advice, and neither he nor they had thought out what was going on.

In Texas, we call this a stampede.

"You are not to talk to the media about this," he went on.

"Are you going to discuss this with the media and make a press release?"

"I am not at liberty to discuss that with you. After the inquiry I might restore you to full duty or take administrative action against you if warranted."

"This is not right," I protested. "I have a right to know what the allegations are. You're ruining me and destroying my career."

He said that I could talk to Tom Kelley in the legal counsel division. "I am terminating this conversation," he snapped, and hung up on me.

I telephoned Kelley.

"Tom, what the hell is going on?" I could barely control my anger.

"Mike Shaheen has told me to tell you that the matter has been referred to Eric Holder in the District of Columbia as a criminal referral." In other words, Holder, the U.S. Attorney for the District of Columbia, had been given a criminal case on me.

"What are the charges against me?"

"I can't tell you, but you'd better get a lawyer."

"Tom, are we following our policy in this case?"

"What policy?"

"The policy that requires that I be advised of charges against me and be given a chance to respond. I called Shaheen a month ago and offered to come in and cooperate in any way after I heard about the new inquiry. I've never been interviewed."

That surprised him, which frightened me even more. The people in command didn't have the facts and were rushing to judgment. That meant only one thing: some politicians were on their backs big time and they were saving their skins at the expense of the rest of us.

"Tom, I'm in the middle of closing on my house and I will likely lose my mortgage over the publicity," I said almost resignedly.

"Well, it will probably leak out, but you won't lose your mortgage because you are being paid."

Right. I snapped a good-bye and hung up. I felt totally abandoned by the institution I'd served most of my life. I was being cast aside by the same agency that had trusted me to run a big part of the most important criminal investigation on the planet. When there were mass murderers to be found before they did it again, I had busted a gut till we got them and the evidence to nail them. Wasn't I the same person on August 11 as I was on April 19? Evidently not. I'd contracted the political equivalent of the Ebola virus, all because Mike Kahoe had supposedly admitted destroying some kind of document I'd never seen or heard tell of.

Jimmy Adams walked in and stopped short when he saw my face. I explained as best I could. Neither of us could understand what was happening. As we talked, Adams got a call from Bill Esposito, the assistant director in charge of CID, who informed him that he was now in charge of the Dallas office. Esposito didn't explain either.

I grabbed for the phone, hoping that I could get to my wife and children before they heard about it on TV or the radio. We were living in temporary quarters while the house we hoped to buy was under construction. I finally got Debbie on the cell phone in her car.

"Debbie, listen carefully," I said as calmly as I could. "Turn off the radio and go straight home. When you get there, beep me."

"Can't you tell me what's happened?"

"No. No one is dead or hurt. Just do as I say."

I don't trust cell phones. They're really just two-way radios, and anybody can tune in on them. I called her on a hard line from Pop's house. I explained to her what I knew, which wasn't much. She was as upset as I was. Then I had to drive Pop to the hospital for a postoperative procedure. He had recently had an operation for prostate cancer. The prognosis was excellent, but there were a lot of follow-up visits to ensure the operation had taken all of the tumor.

On the way, I told him I had been beached. I hated to lay this on him at this time in his life. I would never have told him about it except I knew I'd soon be hit with a media barrage.

"What have they accused you of doing?" he asked.

"I have no idea. Louie wouldn't tell me."

"Can they do that?" he sputtered.

I shook my head. "No, they can't. But they did."

Pop set his jaw. "You should leave. Those sons of bitches aren't worth it."

Since I was being stampeded, I started poring over my mental checklist of good lawyers. I was innocent, but I knew that wouldn't matter to an ambitious government lawyer who wanted my scalp. How can you indict an innocent person? Have you heard the saying "A prosecutor can indict a ham sandwich"? If you don't believe it, give me a ham sandwich and a couple of million dollars and we'll set a trial date. Prosecutors often develop a theory of their case and then look for the facts that support their theory, ignoring evidence that refutes it. When the evidence isn't there, they may try to bluff the subject with threats of indictment, hoping for capitulation. This can be effective, especially if the investigation continues for years—and remember, the federal government has virtually unlimited resources and no time limits. In politically charged cases the criminal justice system may work the way it's supposed to, so the ham sandwich will be acquitted, but in the meantime, he and his family will have gone through the humiliation of a criminal indictment and the torment of a trial, not to mention mind-boggling expense. The indictment itself is punishment enough, and—who knows?—the prosecutor knows he might just get lucky and nail somebody. The most infamous example of all this is Ken Starr's investigation of President Clinton.

The only deterrent to a hungry prosecutor is a top-notch attorney or two who can beat his brains out in court. So, after I settled Pop at the house, I called Chris Todd, who had been one of the prosecutors in the Iran-Contra investigation and was now in private practice. When we'd first met, I thought to myself this guy could win first, second, and third place in a Robin Williams look-alike contest. He was chief of the White House National Security Council team that had focused on cover-up and obstruction issues. Chris had come from the U.S. Attorney's office for the Southern District of New York, the nation's premier prosecutorial shop. His associate, Richard Mescon, was another Southern District alum. The unofficial third member of my defense team was Chris's wife, Amelia A. Gomez, who had been a federal prosecutor in Miami at the height of the cocaine-cowboy rampages and in the U.S. Attorney's office in mobbed-up Brooklyn. There were no shrinking violets in this crowd. The Todds' oldest daughter, Alexssa Cody Todd, got her middle name from William F. "Buffalo Bill" Cody, Chris's distant relative. Chris's grandmother was born in Indian Territory, now Oklahoma; one of her first memories was serving tin cups of whiskey to poker players at her father's saloon. Chris's grandfather became deputy sheriff of Kent County, Texas. Amelia's forebears included Maximo Gomez, the Dominican general who helped liberate Cuba. I knew the Todds and Mescon wouldn't be intimidated by the Justice Department's tactics, no matter how rough they played. They knew the law better than most career bureaucrats and they'd had years more trial experience.

After I briefed Chris it was time to explain our new situation to the kids. Jeff was about to start college. Jenn was about to be a sophomore and Jessie was heading for junior high. I told them what I could, that I didn't know what was going on, but that I'd done nothing I was ashamed of. They were confused but supportive. Jeff was the only one to speak. "We know you haven't done anything wrong," he said.

Then Doc called from Oregon, where he was a reserve police officer and awaiting an appointment as a full-time policeman. I hadn't been able to get to him before he heard the news on the radio.

"Everyone out here says the whole thing is just a bunch of politics," he said gallantly.

I laughed. "Whatever it is, it's not good."

I appreciated Doc's faith in me, but it was a sad state of affairs that my son had to hear innuendo about me from the media. Freeh had wasted no time putting out a press release saying that Potts, Mike Kahoe, Gale Evans, Tony Betz, and I had been suspended and were under criminal investigation for possible perjury and obstruction of justice. By the time the press and the pols got through chewing on that one, I sounded so guilty that I expected the public library to cancel my card.

For the next several days we tried to go about business as best we could, but it wasn't easy. Though Freeh had told us not to talk about the case, he was making all sorts of public statements, which I felt suggested there was strong evidence against us. For instance, in an interview with *Washington Post* reporter George Lardner, Freeh was quoted as saying the allegations were "shocking and grievous" and might be as bad as the COINTELPRO scandal. Freeh said he was sorry he had ever promoted Larry Potts. "Given the facts we now have, I would not have made that decision," he added.

When will the director start following the rules? I wondered. I could certainly appreciate the need to investigate Glenn's allegations, but damn it, we had rules. If Freeh didn't know them himself, why didn't his general counsel remind him that Justice and FBI guidelines precluded him from making these statements to the press? The answer was simple. Many were terrified of Freeh. He had enormous power and surrounded himself with a praetorian guard of people whose only job was to protect him personally and to make him look good, at any expense. We were being tried in the press, and I still didn't know what the charges were. In short, we were expendable.

Hearing terrible things about yourself day after day takes its toll. Debbie and I were in a fog, but we had a house to close on and a move to undertake. I got scores of calls from friends from all over the country. At times like this you find out who your friends are and who abandons you. You never forget either.

I was with Pop in Fort Worth when Debbie beeped me. "We've lost the mortgage," she sobbed. "Those bastards have caused us to lose the mortgage."

We had sunk our entire life's savings into the construction of this house, but we couldn't take possession without a mortgage covering the balance due. The publicity generated by the director of the FBI and his staff had spooked the underwriter. It was time for school to start, but we couldn't enroll our children in school because we had no home.

Then, out of the blue, I got a call from a stranger. "Danny, this is Sammie Petersen from Mercantile Bank. I understand you need a mortgage."

"You bet I do, but do you know the circumstances?" I said, hesitating.

"Oh, yes, I've talked to our president and he says if you otherwise qualify, we'll give you a mortgage. Can you come down to my office in the morning after church?"

"We'll be there. Thanks."

Ms. Petersen saved us. We moved into our dream house.

What else could go wrong?

A whole lot, as it turned out. On August 25, my beeper went off with a number I knew by heart. It was Tom Kelley.

"Danny, listen, an ABC news team is looking for all of you guys. They intend to go to your homes and follow you around with a TV crew. We're afraid that this will draw attention to your location and some nutcase will try to retaliate." Tom seemed to be genuinely concerned for our safety and somewhat embarrassed to make the call.

"Tom, who generated all of this publicity?" I snapped. "It certainly wasn't me."

He ignored my jab. "I'll talk to Esposito to see about some relief for you."

I had no idea what he meant. Did *relief* mean "protection"? If it did, none ever came.

"Tom, keep Louie off the fucking front page of the newspapers and stop convicting us in the media," I said. "These statements give the nuts of the world license to come after us."

"That's being addressed as we speak."

"Thanks. It's a little late for me and my family."

I hung up, then called Bob Garrity, one of my ASACs. "Bob, I've just been told by headquarters that there may be some danger to my family. Get my Car-15 out of my car and bring it home tonight. I want a fighting chance, at least." A Car-15 is a compact assault weapon that can deliver a high rate of accurate fire at fairly long ranges. I'd bought mine with my own money, and HQ had approved my carrying it in operations. I'd left it in my FBI car, which I was now forbidden to even touch.

I also asked him to bring me some extra magazines for my Browning Hi-Power. I wanted to be as ready as I could for whatever was in store for us. Garrity showed up with the arms that night.

Tom Clancy couldn't have written this one, I thought. I'd spent years developing skills known to a handful of counterterrorist operators around the world. I was proficient with virtually every small arm made. I had a black belt in karate. I'd been trained in explosives and executive protection. Now I was going to have to call upon everything I knew to keep my family and myself alive.

On September 21, I was summoned to Washington to testify alongside Potts before Senator Arlen Specter and the Senate terrorism subcommittee. The looks on the senators' faces told me we were in for a hiding, and I was right. Most of them seemed to be a lot more interested in talking than listening, especially when the cameras were on. Senator Dianne Feinstein went off on a bizarre tangent, reminiscing about the time when, as mayor of San Francisco, she had driven from City Hall to Market Street where a crook had taken a hostage at a local bank, in case the police needed her advice on what to do. Then she lambasted Potts and me for failing to commandeer a fast plane and get ourselves to the scene. "Frankly, it makes me angry," she said, "because you shouldn't duck that responsibility—it's yours."

I was absolutely outraged that she questioned my courage without even bothering to find out the facts, but my work on the Hill in the seventies had taught me that a lot of politicians angle for a sound bite on the evening news by concocting an outlandish theory before the hearing opens and spouting it over and over once the cameras begin to roll. This senator obviously didn't care about our background, experience, or the facts. Either she or a young staffer had come up with a specious charge of responsibility ducking, which had the added advantage of allowing her to hype her role in a relatively typical urban hostage situation. She wasn't going to be confused by the facts in our case.

So I responded with as much restraint as I could muster: "I think I probably can be accused of a lot of things in my career. I believe the last thing I could be accused of is ducking responsibility. I've been involved in hundreds of tactical operations and some of the biggest tactical operations in the history of the FBI. One of the most frustrating things I've ever experienced in my career is deploying the Hostage Rescue Team that I created to go to Idaho without me, or go to Waco without me. These aren't decisions that Mr. Potts and I make. This is Bureau policy. I would have loved to go to Idaho. I think I could have helped at Idaho."

"Could you pick up the phone and call and say, 'You know, this is the biggest thing the FBI has ever encountered, we think maybe headquarters ought to be on the scene'?" Feinstein persisted.

Pick up the phone? After the associate deputy director had told me not only no but hell no? I couldn't

believe she still didn't get it. I thought everybody understood the FBI was probably the most authoritarian, hierarchical institution in the government except for the military. I tried again. "Senator, it may be a good idea, and
frankly I would have liked to have gone—I concur with
that. I believe that I probably was an individual who may
have been able to help. But it is not on my authority to
go on initiative. Neither is it Mr. Potts's."

And so it went. Feinstein lectured us for a while
longer, and the other questioners weren't warm and
fuzzy either. Yet I left that cold, cavernous room feeling
better than when I'd arrived. I had a sense the senators
walked in expecting to harpoon us but that they softened
as we talked about our efforts to keep people alive. I
think they weren't so sure we were the cowboys they'd
anticipated. The exercise proved my rule that it's better
to talk to anybody, no matter how hostile, than to stay in
the dark and be a faceless monster.

Louis Freeh was called to the Specter committee on
October 19. Specter grilled him on the precise nature of
the charges that had been lodged against Potts, Evans,
Betz, and me.

Freeh's testimony, which I read soon after he delivered it, was a real shocker. He said Shaheen had showed
him some allegations against us "supported by inference,
supported by some evidence, supported by conclusions"
and told him the case was going to be referred for criminal investigation. Shaheen's inquiry wasn't wrapped up
yet, but he was sufficiently concerned to recommend
that we be suspended.

Unlike Feinstein, Specter had done his homework.
He observed that the Justice Department and FBI had
no written policy on when employees may be sus-

pended. Furthermore, a federal law covering government employees generally said they must be given a thirty-day notice unless "there is reasonable cause to believe that the employee has committed the crime for which a sentence of imprisonment may be imposed, stating the specific reasons for the proposed action."

"Unless I'm wrong, as I understand what they"—meaning Shaheen and his aides—"gave to you, they didn't meet that standard, did they?" Specter asked.

"Not in my view," Freeh replied.

When Specter asked him why he didn't wait until the evidence rose to the "reasonable cause" level, Freeh replied that "short of a probable-cause finding, if serious allegations of criminality are made against an FBI official, someone who's running an office, someone who's running a division, someone who's responsible for criminal cases, I think there is a requirement that you may not have in the Department of Agriculture or the Department of Commerce that the potential for tainting perhaps many investigations under that individual's control and purview, if the allegations turn out to be true, and having someone ask a year from now, 'How could you possibly leave that person, who's now been indicted and convicted, in charge of your most sensitive cases for nine months when you could have suspended him with pay?' So I think there may be a different standard in the Justice Department, in the FBI."

What Freeh seemed to be saying in his convoluted way was that somebody's accusing us of something was enough to justify our removal. This was simply stunning. As I saw it, Freeh was taking the position that the legal standard for suspending us hadn't been met—but that it didn't need to be met; in so many words, he seemed to be saying that he might face criticism sometime down the line if he hadn't put us on ice at the first whiff of trouble.

To follow that logic, any crooked businessman or sleazy politician—or White House aide, for that matter—could get rid of any FBI agent who was making his life uncomfortable simply by filing a claim that the agent had done something illegal or improper. I don't seriously think Freeh was signaling he would dump any and all agents based on thinly substantiated allegations of wrongdoing. But to my mind, he had established a double standard; agents involved in controversies in obscure cases might be afforded some measure of due process, but those in politically hot situations could arbitrarily be dumped to protect the reputation of the Bureau and perhaps the director himself.

It got worse. Freeh told Specter he had suspended us "because of Department of Justice policy, not FBI policy." This jibed with what Weldon Kennedy once told me—that Deputy Attorney General Jamie Gorelick had told Freeh, "If you don't do it, we'll do it." Gorelick was the department's highest-ranking political appointee, next to Janet Reno herself. She had been a high-powered Washington lawyer with impeccable Democratic Party connections and a reputation at the White House as a team player. The word around Justice was that Clinton would have replaced Reno with Gorelick in a heartbeat if he hadn't been under perpetual investigation.

Another indication that the decision had been made in Justice political ranks was something Jeff Jamar passed along after he attended a conference with Richard Scruggs, Reno's top assistant. Jamar said

Scruggs had remarked that he had felt awkward working with me in July 1995, when I was detailed to help prepare Reno to testify before a House panel investigating the Waco siege. Jamar said Scruggs had told him that at that point the decision had already been reached to place me and the others on leave. If, as Freeh said, the reasonable-cause standard wasn't met on August 11, when he suspended us, it couldn't possibly have been met a month earlier.

As the pieces started falling into place, they formed a picture even more chilling than I'd imagined. I had served under seven FBI directors and acting directors. None until the last—Freeh—had allowed the FBI to be subjected to politicization by the Justice Department. I realized that as disastrous as the suspension was for my family, it was a much graver problem for the nation. If the Justice Department can order an FBI agent placed on leave without proper cause or documentation, then the independence of the FBI is forever diminished. What FBI executive will now stand up to inappropriate orders from the department, knowing that by opposing them, he may end his career?

The FBI's tradition of independence is anchored in the belief that a completely unbiased and objective approach is the most important and critical aspect of any investigation. If that objectivity and independence is lost, the whole concept of equal justice under the law breaks down. Congress recognized that truth by legislating a ten-year statutory term for the director.

The Justice Department is a political entity, often working at the behest of the White House. Despite Reno's reputation as a feisty freethinker, her tenure is considered by many in the Bureau as the most politicized in recent years. There are vivid examples of the current political domination of the FBI by the Department of Justice. You need look no further than the campaign finance investigation. CAMCON, as it is called, has been totally controlled by departmental officials. Obviously, there needs to be cooperation between an investigative agency and a prosecutive agency, but the Department of Justice shouldn't direct the course of a politically sensitive investigation, especially one that focuses on the White House. FBI agents assigned to CAMCON have told me they've been thwarted at every turn in their efforts to pursue logical, appropriate, and meaningful lines of inquiry—in other words, to seek the truth regarding the fund-raising and spending activities of high-level White House and Democratic party officials. For this reason, Freeh himself has urged the Attorney General to appoint an independent counsel to free the investigation of the department's domination.

By contrast, under William Webster, the course of the Iran-Contra investigation was decided by the efforts and leads generated by the field agents. As the senior supervisor, I gave only initial direction to the case and then let the chips fall where they would. My only contacts with the Justice Department were periodic calls to or from William Weld, the assistant attorney general in charge of the Criminal Division, and the only thing he ever asked was whether we were getting the support we needed. Mark Richard, Weld's deputy, handled all my requests for Swiss bank records. Otherwise, no one in the department in any way impeded or attempted to give direction to that investigation.

I felt like a caged tiger. I absolutely love the FBI, and it drove me wild that I could do nothing to keep the institution from being dragged into the muck of political expediency.

Besides, I had my hands full worrying about threats generated by my unwanted fame. Sometime in early October, Adams called to warn me that a man who claimed to be a soldier in the Army of Jesus, whatever that was, had been arrested after pulling a string of bank robberies in Dallas and Garland. He was decked out in cammies and military gear and armed with an assault rifle and a nine-millimeter pistol, but what alarmed Jim was that he had my name in his pocket, along with a bunch of clippings about Waco and Ruby Ridge. He was locked up, but did he have friends? We had no way to know.

On October 27, 1995, Jim called with even more frightening news. "Danny, the Fort Worth resident agency has received a letter addressed to you that makes threats against you and your daughter. We're putting trap and traces on your phones as we speak. We'll do everything that we can."

I was so furious that I almost completely lost control. I started screaming at Jim, "This is all the fault of the goddamned FBI and their publicity campaign. I have never in my career received a threat to my life or to my family. Now through no fault of my own I have to deal with yet another threat."

Finally I stopped to catch my breath. "Sorry I acted like a prick, Jimmy. It's not your fault."

"Don't worry about it. The most important thing is to take care of the kids."

It was good to have a friend like Jim Adams. From the moment I was put on leave, he called me every day. I guess he was afraid I'd swallow my gun or take a trip to

Washington to have a come-to-Jesus meeting with HQ officials. There was no possibility of any of that happening, but I appreciated knowing that one man was there for me, no matter what.

"I'm okay now," I breathed. "Who signed the letter?"

"He calls himself Orkin. Potts and some of the others got the same letter. Yours was the only one that came to the right agency and city."

As we were talking, my cell phone began to fade and I was not able to call Debbie. Jim had not been able to contact her either. The phone company found her at work. They broke the news gently. They told her that the FBI wanted to put a listening device on our phone because of a threat to our family.

She hung up, called the children, and told them to leave the house since they might be in danger and to meet her at a shopping center. She had no idea about the letter from Orkin, just that there was a new threat and she and the children were terrified. I finally tracked her down on her cell phone and gave her the information about Orkin.

Debbie was beyond anger. We had to tell the children about the threats and what we were doing to protect them. We taught them to be vigilant and took many other precautions. Some I will discuss and some I will not, for obvious reasons. The Dallas field office installed a sophisticated alarm system in our home, with panic alarms near us at all times. There was a gun in every room of our house. My daughters are probably the only kids in Texas who went to soccer practice with an assault rifle on the seat of the family car and a father armed to the hilt with a pistol and spare magazines. Before long, there was a new addition to the family: a beautiful young

Rottweiler who would grow to be 120 pounds of muscle and speed and who wasn't afraid of anything except Katy, our yellow Lab.

Days passed. No one seemed to know who this Orkin character was. *Does he view himself as an exterminator?* I wondered. *Are we the ones he intends to exterminate?* We didn't know and neither did the FBI. Had we done enough? We would see. Was there really a threat? We certainly had to assume so. Would we prevail? I knew so. How did all of this impact upon our family? It was devastating. We were held together with love. My wife has enough grit and faith for a hundred people.

But we paid a price. I never read anyone's mail, but I snuck a peek at a letter Jessie sent to a friend in Maryland. I wanted to get an idea about how she was doing emotionally. "Can you believe that someone is actually threatening our lives?" she wrote. She couldn't comprehend why anyone would want to kill her or her family. She hadn't done anything to anyone. I guess a thirteen-year-old just doesn't understand the world we live in. I'm not so sure that her father understands. He just has to react to it and try to keep his family out of harm's way.

As April 19, 1996, approached, I got edgy. We moved out of our home, dogs and all, and went into hiding. We tried to make it a sort of vacation, but all of us lived with the knowledge that we might return to a burned-out house. Or possibly some lunatic would find us. Fortunately the date came and went without incident.

My new friends from the Texas militias found out about the death threats from Orkin and offered their services to help protect us. I guess I made some progress with them, after all.

I quit reading the newspapers. I didn't want to read, see, hear, or think about the FBI because whenever something wrong was written about Ruby Ridge, I wanted to respond with the truth, and I wasn't allowed to. Whatever bitterness I felt wasn't directed toward the institution or its people but to its leadership, which allowed us to sink into this sorry state. Every day, I got a call, letter, card, or telegram from somebody—a cop, former or present agent, prosecutor, or support staff—offering words of encouragement.

I broke my no-news rule during the eighty-one-day siege of the Montana Freemen compound outside Jordan, Montana. For one thing, Weldon Kennedy called me to consult about it from time to time. For another, I was eager to see if Roger Nisley was as good at commanding the HRT as I thought he would be. He was even better; he didn't make one false move.

The Freemen consisted of a couple of dozen people who believed in white separatism and various international-conspiracy theories and declared their 960-acre spread near Jordan, Montana, to be a sovereign nation independent of the laws of the United States. All that was legal, but they also engaged in various elaborate frauds such as writing phony checks and harassing public officials and other adversaries by filing liens against their property. The HRT was sent in after fraud warrants were sworn out.

Nisley's first move was what the ATF should have done at Waco—he took out ringleaders LeRoy Schweitzer and Daniel Petersen with an undercover ruse. On March 25, 1996, some HRT operators, posing as contractors offering to build a private communications network for the ranch, lured Schweitzer and Petersen to a hill where the "communications tower" was supposed to go, handed them some blueprints, and while they were occupied, snatched them right out of their socks.

Twenty-three adults and four children barricaded themselves inside a farmhouse with close to a hundred weapons, including some with very long ranges. Nisley convinced Freeh that this nontraditional problem required an unconventional solution. Nisley didn't array HRT snipers in a perimeter, arguing that if the Freemen took potshots at the snipers and hit somebody, the stakes would be raised enormously. As it was, the charges were nonviolent white collar frauds. Besides, the Freemen weren't fighting to get off their "nation" but to stay on it.

Then Nisley persuaded Freeh that the situation didn't warrant a full HRT deployment. Everybody was sent home, except Nisley and a couple of managers, who stayed on to direct the SWAT teams dispatched to the scene. Roger treated the negotiators and behavioral specialists as equals and integrated their views in all memos, concept papers, and option plans. There were none of the nasty surprises that had caused rifts between the tactical and negotiator teams at Waco.

At one point, the two factions reversed roles. The negotiators wanted the tactical guys to take an outbuilding in order to squeeze the Freemen when the talks stalled. Nisley balked. "Look, this is their country," he said. "It's a mistake not to buy into their silliness. You have to understand that, to them, this is an act of war, and they're going to respond with weapons." Besides, the cabin was in range of Freemen rifles; operators who occupied it would be sitting ducks. The negotiators backed off. The siege dragged on. At the recommendation of both Nisley and the behaviorists, Freeh allowed outside parties, some forty-five in all, to negotiate. It cost the FBI millions of dollars, but by June 12, seven adults and all four children had surrendered. On July 13, 1996, the remaining sixteen adults surrendered peacefully.

Because of his performance in Montana, Freeh promoted Nisley to run the Crisis Incident Management Group, in my judgment the best job in the FBI next to the Dallas Field Office. He was replaced as HRT commander by Jeff Wehmeyer.

The Texas Rangers sought the help of Nisley and CIRG in May 1997, when they laid siege to the cabin of seven extremists who called themselves the Republic of Texas. "Wait them out," the CIRG team said, and the Rangers listened. Their patience was rewarded when five of the seven walked out with their hands up. A sixth started a shoot-out and was killed; the last fled into the hills. It was about as good an outcome as anybody could have expected. I couldn't have done it better myself, though I'm not sure I'm going to tell Nisley that. I don't want to spoil him.

8

On my darkest days, when I felt as if I'd been tossed into a slime-sided well, Pop showed up with a rope. He's always had a way of seeing what's really important and kissing off the rest. I think that comes from being a country boy during the Great Depression and a foot soldier in the war in Europe. If you spend your first twenty-five years cold, hungry, scared, and stepping over bodies, the rest of your time on earth looks like a lucky accident.

One day, we picked up his pink Cadillac from the shop and headed for a joint where they make the best barbecue in the state and possibly the world. "We need to drive this son of a bitch for a while to see if they fixed it right," he said. As usual, he smoked and told me how to drive and where to go. I drove and griped.

"You know, Pop, this pink Cadillac is ruining my image. Everyone probably thinks I'm gay, or work for Mary Kay."

"I've told you this ain't a pink car. It's Bimini beige. I wouldn't drive a pink Cadillac either."

"Well, it sure as hell looks pink to me." I pulled my hat lower over my face so nobody would recognize me.

Pop's eyes twinkled. "Did I ever tell you about the bar I owned?"

"Bar, when did you own a bar?"

"Back when you were in law school. Your mother never knew about it. I used to stop in for beer at the place every now and then, and I got to know the guy that owned it. It was not doing real good. The help was stealing him blind. One day this guy that owned the jukebox and vending machines pulled up a stool beside me and said, 'Morris, you know anything about running a bar?' I told him that I sure as hell knew how to drink and dance in one, but I never worked in one before. He told me it was for sale for two thousand dollars cash and his company would help with the licenses. I asked him what he had to do with the bar. He said the bar wasn't doing business so his machines weren't doing much either."

Pop scraped up the cash from the sneak money he hid from my mother and bought the place.

"Pop, you ran a business full-time," I objected. "How did you run the bar too?"

A big smile spread across his face. "Well, I knew this old girl, Fay Latour. She was a barmaid, had worked in about a million bars, and everyone loved her. She really knew the business, so I hired her. We had this special deal. She agreed to only steal a little bit from me and I wouldn't kick her ass for the little bit she stole. Seemed fair to me at the time."

I chuckled. "Sounds like a fair deal to me too, but I think I remember Fay Latour. As I recall, she could probably kick your ass."

"Hell, she could. That's why I made the deal. Anyhow, that place made me some pretty good money, but it really screwed up my bank account. I kept putting receipts into our family account, and your mother never could understood how we kept having this extra money every month. I just told her that it was a bookkeeping error and not to worry about it. You remember the time I called you and asked if you could file a separate tax return from your family, and you told me I could? Well, that's what I did. Then I finally figured out that I had to stop putting the money into our family account. I had it all straight. I was square with the tax man and things were going pretty good, and then, blam, I had to sell it."

"What happened?" I said, really baffled by now.

"Well, one night after about a year, I went down to the bar after work and pulled up a stool at the end of the bar. Fay came over and hopped up on the stool next to mine and said, 'Honey, I have something for you.' She pulled out a roll of bills and gave it to me and said, 'This is your cut.' 'Cut of what?' I said. 'Of the take from the girls.' Can you believe it, this silly bitch was running hookers out of my bar and I didn't even know it?"

I was laughing so hard I could barely drive. "You didn't have any idea?"

"Hell no. I knew that a lot of girls from the phone company and a bunch of nurses from the hospital started hanging out there, and business sure picked up, but I didn't know that Fay was hooking them. They were a bunch of good gals, I just didn't know they were professional women."

I couldn't believe it. My own father was a once-removed pimp. "So what did you do?"

"Hell, it scared the shit out of me. Next day I offered to sell the whole damn kit and caboodle to Fay. With the money that I paid her, the money she stole, and the money from the girls, she cashed me out. Boy, was I glad to get out of that mess. I'm surprised I never told you about it. Guess I was afraid you'd have to lock me up."

"I'm sure the statute of limitations has run on that one. I'll give you a pass." We drove along for a couple of minutes in silence. Then the leprechaun smile returned to his face.

"What do you think J. Edgar Hoover would have

thought about you going to law school on whore money?"

So that was where this story was going. What Pop was trying to tell me was not to take the peaks or chasms too seriously because life was all just a great cosmic joke.

Well, God had one hell of a sense of humor. He had sure pulled a good one on me. And an even better one on Hoover.

"Hell, I don't know," I told Pop. "The Hoov probably would have liked Fay."

Almost two years to the day after I was suspended—August 15, 1997, to be exact—I was cleared. I got the news from Chris Todd, who paged me as I was out on my motorcycle, running an errand for Debbie.

"I just got the letter," he said. "It's over. They can find no reason to prosecute you."

I breathed a sigh, not of relief, but of disgust. "I could've told them that two years ago."

The investigation been handed off from Eric Holder, the U.S. attorney for D.C., because he had worked with Potts and me, and given to Michael Stiles, the U.S. attorney for Philadelphia, who promptly assembled his own special team. Stiles could teach Ken Starr a thing or two about zeal. The same thing seems to happen to just about every prosecutor who is given a single mission, little supervision, and a virtually unlimited budget. When you have one person to look at, the tendency is to focus on the person and try to find out if he violated the law in any way. That's 180 degrees from the way we at the FBI have been trained. We are told never to focus on an individual to see if he did something wrong but to follow all logical leads, and when those leads run out, to close the case.

Stiles gave us a grudging exoneration, as if we had beaten the rap by a fingernail. He put out a press release saying he had found "the available evidence does not support further criminal prosecutions of FBI officials"—meaning Potts, Evans, Betz, and me. It wasn't for lack of trying. Stiles and his team had conducted six hundred interviews of 378 witnesses, examined toll records of 226,960 telephone calls, and perused 289 computer hard drives and 351 disks. They tried everything they could think of, including insinuating that others were providing evidence about wrongdoing on my part, to squeeze me into confessing something, anything. The mind games didn't work on me because I had nothing to hide, but they made my life a living hell, not to mention that I rolled up enough legal fees to send all the kids to Harvard. I'm sure the same is true of Potts, Betz, and Evans.

Mike Kahoe was the only person prosecuted in the whole affair. He pleaded guilty to obstruction-of-justice charges relating to the document destruction flap. I still don't understand why Kahoe was charged. Chris heard that Kahoe had destroyed a rough draft of an "After Action Critique" on Ruby Ridge. I'm told this document didn't deal with any controversial issues; for starters, it didn't address the rules-of-engagement issue. Further, it was all hearsay and wouldn't have been admissible in a court of law. As far as I know, it was, essentially, a summary of an after-action meeting that I didn't attend because it was held the day Debbie was having her biopsy. So the question is, how can you be prosecuted for obstruction of justice for destroying a rough draft of an inadmissible document? I don't think you can. I can only believe that Kahoe agreed to plead guilty to get the case over with and to make sure he didn't lose his retirement.

As for the rest of us, though Stiles had no evidence to prosecute us, leaks that appeared to come from his shop suggested he still believed there was a cover-up. He saw to it that we would remain suspended and under investigation indefinitely by sending his findings to Shaheen at Justice OPR, with the recommendation that OPR conduct yet another review—the seventh, by my count—to see if any further disciplinary action should be taken against any of us. That guaranteed at least another year of legal fees and psychological warfare.

I was profoundly disillusioned. I had lived my whole life by our motto: Fidelity—Bravery—Integrity. From the day we walked into the Academy, we were taught that Vince Lombardi was dead wrong. Winning was not the only thing or even the main thing. If we lost our reputation for integrity, fairness, and compassion, we'd lose in the long run, no matter how many scalps we collected in the short run. As Louis Freeh put it in a message to the field on the occasion of the FBI's ninetieth anniversary, "Constitutional guarantees are more important than the outcome of any single interview, search for evidence, or investigation. Respect for the dignity of all whom we protect reminds us to wield law enforcement powers with restraint and to recognize the natural human tendency to be corrupted by power and to become callous in its exercise. Fairness and compassion ensure that we treat everyone with the highest regard for Constitutional, civil, and human rights. Personal and institutional integrity reinforce each other and are owed to the nation in exchange for the sacred trust and great authority conferred upon us."

On these ideals, Freeh and I are in complete agreement. I only wish that when the political heat was turned up, he had been the kind of man to apply those ideals to me and the others in the Ruby Ridge chain of command. But on their face, the core values he expresses so eloquently represent the Bureau culture at its best. All of us know, not from creeds on the wall and books of guidelines but from actual experience on the street, that the public's perception of us is our greatest asset. People cooperate with us because they think we are people of honor and we'll do the right thing. We have to be mindful not just of the investigation we're conducting today but the one we'll do ten years from today, and the cases to be conducted by generations to come. If we become brutal, arbitrary, or power-obsessed, we're lost.

For all I'd been through, I was still totally idealistic about the Bureau's values, and I just couldn't understand why rules, guidelines, the Constitution, and common decency played no part in the actions taken against us. I knew that Freeh believed what I believed. He just got stampeded by the Justice Department, where no one had any reservation about casting us onto the fires of political expediency.

"Will you get out of that organization and come on out into the real world?" Chris Todd said.

"I guess it's time," I said. "Debbie and Pop have been trying to get me to leave for months. I just wanted to get this over with. Hey, did they ever say what the charges against me were originally?"

"No, they didn't," he snorted. "And frankly I don't think there ever were any. They screwed this thing up from the start and didn't know how to unscrew it. If there were charges, they would have presented them to me."

When I got home, Debbie gave me a hug and said, "All I know is, if you'd been in that helicopter, I'd sure hope Lon would take a shot to protect you."

Horiuchi's hell wasn't over either. Six days after the Stiles report came down, Boundary County prosecutor Denise Woodbury charged him with involuntary manslaughter for reckless use of his gun. After some prodding from the Bureau, the Department of Justice filed a motion to have the case removed to federal court. Federal judge Edward Lodge, who had presided over the Weaver prosecution and had no love lost for the FBI or the Justice Department, ruled in Horiuchi's favor. After another ten months, on May 14, 1998, Lodge dismissed the charges on grounds that Horiuchi was acting within the scope of his federal authority when he fired the shot that killed Vicki Weaver. "The actions of Mr. Horiuchi had tragic results," Lodge wrote. "However, Mr. Horiuchi did no more than what was 'necessary and proper' for him to carry out his duties under the totality of the circumstances." This matter was finally resolved the way it should have been, not by some headline-grabbing politician or some Justice Department attorney trying to make a name for himself. The last line of defense that protects us even from our own government is a dispassionate, independent judiciary.

9

I put in my retirement papers in August 1997. I couldn't stand to work for the Department of Justice and the FBI another day. As I figured it, I was ahead of the game. I'd survived two bad years in the FBI, but I'd enjoyed twenty-nine good ones. I'd lived a thousand adventures and walked in harm's way with some of the bravest men and women on this earth.

Many years ago I chose a profession that is bound in violence and human conflict. I never dreamed that this conflict would finally accrue to my family and have such an impact upon them. We have all survived the terrible ordeal, and our children have flourished in spite of it. There remains, however, one last issue. Orkin. He has never been found. Will he deal with us? Will we have to deal with him? We shall see.

On the other hand, I'd never lost what was most important to me. Wonderful friends. A fantasy wife who has terrible taste in men. A fast motorcycle. Great kids. Doc was a man now, in every sense of the word. Jeff was doing well in college. Jenn, our soccer star, received no fewer than forty-two scholarship offers from top-flight universities. Jessie's grades were so high her teachers were urging her to graduate as a sixteen-year-old junior and go to college early.

Most important, I had something to believe in, something that gave my life meaning. Back in 1982, when the HRT first fifty embarked on the adventure with me, we believed that we had an important job to do for our country, a job that was predicated upon a need for safety and order and the right of citizens to live in a free country. We believed that terrorism could undermine those freedoms. We stood ready to face it. Everything we did would be within the framework of the U.S. Constitution and the rule of law. We adopted a motto, Servare Vitas—To Save Lives—because we believed that all life had value and we would take a life only as an absolute last resort. If we've done nothing else, I hope we've left that legacy to those who follow us.

When I have grandchildren, I plan to tell them this story.

A young police officer in a West Coast town was sent to arrest a man trying to break into a house. The officer found a mean-looking homeless man pounding on a door in a middle-class neighborhood. He arrested the man, who was soon released without posting bail. Later in the day, the same officer was sent back to the neighborhood, where he found the man breaking into yet another home. He arrested him again. Once more, the man was released.

A third call came from the neighborhood. As the officer pulled his cruiser up on the left-hand side of the street and started to get out, he glimpsed the man out of the corner of his eye. This time, the man wasn't so cooperative. He was running at the officer at top speed, holding a machete over his head and screaming at the top of his lungs. The officer had every justification to shoot. But he didn't. He backed behind his patrol car, drew his weapon, and yelled, "Stop or I'll blow your head off."

The man kept coming. "Stop or you're a dead man," the officer shouted, aligning the front sight of his sidearm on the man's chest and beginning to pull back on the trigger. At the last minute the man stopped and dropped the machete. The officer jumped forward, forced the man to the ground, and cuffed him behind his back.

Just at that moment, other officers arrived. "Boy, that was close," one of them said. "You probably should have capped him."

The officer just smiled. As a young boy he had listened for hours as his father talked with Christian Prouteaux, the French counterterrorist team commander, about the value of human life, even the life of a criminal. The men who had come to the boy's house to visit his father wore a sleeve patch that showed an eagle breaking a chain of bondage and bore the motto Servare Vitas. It was a philosophy the boy believed in too. When he became a man, he risked his life to be true to it.

At the end of the day some of his fellow officers came up to him in the locker room as he was changing into his civvies.

"You look like you could use a beer," one of them said. "Come on, Doc, we're buying."

AFTERWORD

Since the hardback version of this book was published, the old wounds of Waco have been reopened. The Justice Department had always insisted that only cold tear gas rounds had been deployed on April 19, 1993. But in the summer of 1999, while re-examining the physical evidence from the ruins of the Davidian compound, the Texas Rangers came across a mysterious 40-millimeter brass shell casing that had been part of a military M-651 pyrotechnic tear gas round.

This new discovery, which hit the headlines during the August doldrums, forced a thorough search of the records. The FBI and Justice then admitted that previously overlooked HRT reports did confirm that operators had launched one or two of these "hot rounds" at the "pit," the unfinished building foundation about a hundred yards away from the main compound.

Surprised and chagrined, Attorney General Janet Reno asked former Republican senator John Danforth, an Episcopal minister of great probity, to conduct a blue-ribbon investigation of the whole affair.

The Rangers concluded that the belated disclosure of the hot rounds, though embarrassing for Reno and the FBI, did not change their arson investigators' essential finding that the Davidians had torched their own compound and committed mass murder/suicide. All available evidence suggested that the hot rounds had fizzled out in a field, four hours before the fire that destroyed the compound started.

At this point, most people dismissed the flap as interesting but insignificant, and stopped reading. But there were a few individuals who stood to gain, financially or ideologically, by keeping the story alive, vilifying members of the HRT as killing machines and Reno as a perpetrator of the Big Lie. The cottage industry in Waco conspiracy theories churned out a bewildering array of allegations that may make sense to people who believe comic books are history and professional wrestling isn't fixed.

One purveyor of these scurrilous fantasies told me straight-faced that HRT operators had hopped out of a tank, raced into the fortified heart of the compound, set bombs, then made their escape through heavy gunfire from Davidian positions. I guess they must have slid sideways between bullets. They also must have known the secret of invisibility, since they weren't videotaped by the FBI Nightstalker surveillance airplane circling overhead, nor were they noticed by any of the surviving Davidians. I call this the Evil Superman theory.

The Commando Hillary scenario held that Hillary Clinton dispatched Delta Force to Waco to shoot the Davidians, man, woman and child, in order to make the President look tough. Vince Foster committed suicide, so this yarn went, because he had helped the First Lady cover up White House and Delta involvement.

Lawyers for the Davidian survivors and the victims' families who had previously filed a wrongful-death suit against the government also seized the moment, declaring that their experts had detected the signature of gunfire emanating from government positions on the videos made by the Nightstalker's Forward Looking Infrared imager. The Justice Department and FBI still denied that any government personnel fired a single shot on that fateful day.

U.S. District Judge Walter Smith Jr., presiding over the Davidian lawsuit, engaged a British firm, Vector Data Systems, to simulate a firefight scenario and to compare the resulting FLIR images with the FLIR tapes from April 19. After staging the simulation on March 19, 2000, at Fort Hood near Waco, Vector experts declared unequivocally that the fifty-seven flashes visible on the 1993 tapes were not gunfire, but heat or light bouncing off metal or glass debris or reflecting off a helicopter canopy. That conclusion was corroborated by the total absence, on the tape and in other photographs, of people at the points from which the flickers emanated. Guns don't fire themselves.

On July 14, 2000, the jury hearing the civil lawsuit soundly rejected the Davidians' arguments on all counts. The jury decided that the BATF had not used excessive force in the February 28, 1993, raid and that the FBI had not acted negligently on April 19, 1993, either by using tanks to penetrate the compound, by starting or contributing to the spread of the fires, or by not sending in firefighters to quench the blazes. A week later, Danforth declared with "100 percent certainty" that the blame for the catastrophe "rests squarely on the shoulders of David Koresh." Danforth concluded the Davidians shot and killed some of their own, including five children, and torched their own building. FBI agents, he said, had never fired a shot even as cult members rained lethal fire on their positions. "There are no doubts in my mind," stated Danforth. "This is not a close call."

As I had hoped and expected, Danforth found the

pyrotechnic rounds had "nothing to do" with the fires, and he affirmed that the HRT operators who had deployed them "had told the truth about it from the very beginning." Moreover, he said, Attorney General Reno, FBI Director Freeh, and other top-ranking officials had not engaged in a massive conspiracy to deceive the American public. But Danforth found "a few individuals" in the Justice Department and the FBI had known about the hot rounds and had failed to make that information public during the early post mortems. At this writing, Danforth is still investigating whether those people acted negligently or perpetrated a "criminal effort to cover up the truth." Either way, he said, their silence was "reprehensible" because "they undermined the public confidence with which they were entrusted."

I'm glad that Danforth has finally sorted this mess out. Over the past year or two, I've been interrogated over dozens of hours by Danforth's staff, Congressional investigators, reporters, and even conspiracy theorists. Everyone from the HRT and the headquarters chain of command has been through the same and more. To know that HRT operators who have for years lived under the shadow of baseless accusations that they caused eighty deaths have been subjected to yet more grilling has been one the saddest experiences of my life. But I am confident the team members feel, as I do, that accounting for their actions is an integral part of their responsibility. Questioning of authority is one of the key tenets of a democratic nation. The authors of the Constitution well understood that only through relentless quizzing and unfettered criticism can we keep our institutions honest and in check. Danforth put it more eloquently than I ever could: "The failure to disclose this information, more than anything else, is responsible for the loss of the public faith in the government's actions at Waco," he said. "The natural public reaction was that, if the government lied about one thing, it lied about everything. . . . Lawyers in private practice often volunteer as little information as possible. But playing it close to the line is not acceptable for people representing the United States government. Government lawyers have responsibilities beyond winning the case at hand. They are not justified in seeking victory at all costs. A government lawyer should never hide evidence or shade the truth and must always err on the side of disclosure. Government lawyers carry on their shoulders responsibility not only for the prosecution of specific cases but also for public confidence in our system of government—the 'consent of the governed' enshrined in the Declaration of Independence."

The Danforth report seems to have satisfied most reasonable people that there is no grand government conspiracy surrounding Waco, but there are still a few doubters. To them, I say this: I've seen my share of conspiracies, and some of them have been pretty clever, but none of them have lasted very long. I put my money on the seven deadly sins every time. If greed and gluttony don't bust up the tea party, wrath, vanity, and sloth will. Sooner or later there's a power struggle or a falling-out. Somebody rats somebody else out, and the whole thing falls to pieces.

These are not the reasons, however, that make me certain that the HRT operators have told the important truths about what happened at the Davidian compound on April 19. I believe them because I know them to be men of the highest character. They're not perfect. They make mistakes like everybody else. They get frustrated. They shoot their mouths off. They forget things. But when it comes to matters of life and death, they know right from wrong. They are not murderers and they are not liars.

Every day HRT operators are deployed throughout our country and around the world in the service of our nation. We ask them to handle the most dangerous assignments imaginable. They chase our worst nightmares. You won't see them on the nightly news or in the newspapers. If they do their jobs well, nobody but their supervisors and their families will know their names. They ask only the chance to honor the FBI creed—fidelity, bravery, integrity—and the HRT motto—To Save Lives.

—Danny O. Coulson
October 2000

INDEX